25th Edinburgh International Festival

August 22 to September 11 1971

Information/tickets from festival booking office
21 Market Street Edinburgh EH1 1BW and official agents

ENSEMBLE!

The Fine Arts Quartet, rehearsing on the stage in a broadcast concert studio at Radio Saarbrücken, Germany, 1962. L. to r.: Leonard Sorkin, Abram Loft, George Sopkin, Irving Ilmer.

Ensemble!

A REHEARSAL GUIDE
TO THIRTY GREAT WORKS
OF CHAMBER MUSIC

by
Abram Loft

Reinhard G. Pauly, General Editor

AMADEUS PRESS
Portland, Oregon

To Jill, David, Peter, and Mara

ISBN 0-931340-45-4
Printed in Hong Kong

AMADEUS PRESS
9999 S.W. Wilshire, Suite 124
Portland, Oregon 97225

Library of Congress Cataloging-in-Publication Data

Loft, Abram, 1922-
    Ensemble! : a rehearsal guide to thirty great works of chamber
music / by Abram Loft ; Reinhard G. Pauly, general editor.
        p.   cm.
    Includes bibliographical references.
    ISBN 0-931340-45-4
    1. Chamber music--Analysis, appreciation.   I. Pauly, Reinhard G.
II. Title.
MT140.L62 1991
    785.04'3--dc20   91-26180
                                                            CIP
                                                            MN

♫ Contents ♫

⨎ Preface ⨎

This book gives you my approach to the playing of thirty great works of chamber music, for string quartet and for mixed ensembles including strings. I have designed the book to be of help to professionally oriented groups, serious student ensembles, and amateur enthusiasts of chamber music as well.

My preparation for this writing includes twenty-five years of membership in the Fine Arts Quartet, a foursome that long enjoyed a career as one of America's foremost concert ensembles. I have performed a repertoire of some 300 chamber works, from Biagio Marini (c. 1587-1663) to Bartók and beyond, and have recorded a significant number as well—more than sixty LPs, over the years. During forty years of teaching, at first in music history and then in chamber music performance, I have coached countless ensembles, from teenagers to senior citizens, from eager novices to ensembles on the brink of their concert careers. I have talked often about chamber music, both to live audiences and through educational television.

How can a book help an ensemble that wants to play a piece of chamber music? The answer has to do with interpretation and rehearsal. Of course, there is no one way to play a great piece of music well. A fine composition lends itself to various approaches, reflecting the musical instincts of the particular performers. There are, however, many ways of playing it badly.

An especially bad way is to play the work with note-for-note accuracy, but with no point of view. Most pieces in our repertoire were written by composers who lived before the era of the phonograph. They have left us their musical designs and instructions only in written form. Unfortunately, there are not enough words or signs in our notation to cover all the shadings of tone and volume, all the fine points of inflection that enter into a performance. Players have to read between the lines, penetrate through the symbols on the printed page, to arrive at what they see as the composer's intent.

They also have to see how the successive events in the music relate to one another. The player has to remember what has happened, from the very beginning of the movement. Every note must build on earlier incidents; the piece must be reconstructed, from first to last, so that its unique logic is revealed.

In music for one player alone, the single performer controls these processes. The special fun and challenge of ensemble music is that two or more individual players join minds and perceptions to make the work come alive. Every player is not only thinking about the particular line in the music as it unfolds, but is reacting to everything that transpires in the other voices of the composition. To use an analogy from card playing, the difference is a bit like that between solitaire and bridge.

The ensemble must learn to take on and enjoy these responsibilities. In the learning process, the ear of an outside coach can be of great help to the players. I believe, however, that the ensemble should do some homework before presenting itself to the coach. For one thing, the group ought to try to work out an interpretation that the mentor will be able to appraise and adjust. Even if the coach has to suggest major changes, the players will be able to respond more intelligently if they have done some thinking about the music on their own.

Yet they may not have an able coach immediately at hand. The proper instructor will know the repertoire, have performed and taught it, know where the trouble spots are, and have a clear idea about what makes the given composition tick.

So, at last, to answer the question raised above, I maintain that this book can be of help in several ways. The ensemble can use it to prepare a work for review by a live coach. The group can also regard the book as a substitute coach until such time as a live tutor is available. Finally, the ensemble too bashful to submit itself to the gaze of a live guide will find that this written, surrogate coach has a cardinal virtue: it can encourage the players, but it cannot talk back to them!

A lifetime in the musical trenches has made me think long and hard about the techniques of playing chamber music. Even more important, I have had to ponder the interpretation of works varying widely in style. I have learned that every composition worth playing is a musical world unto itself, one that must be entered and explored and revealed in its own terms. My aim in this book is to take my readers into the individual worlds of works that I have admired and enjoyed in rehearsal and performance.

The chamber works I have included in this book are some among many, many compositions that have won my affection and respect. I chose these particular pieces because they are beloved by performers and listeners and are frequently assigned to student ensembles. Moreover, many of these pieces are likely fare for amateur musicians who want to read them during a musical evening or (I hope) study them at greater length.

In discussing each work, I move sequentially from its beginning to its end, but I do not insist on a measure-by-measure survey. My treatment and emphasis is guided by the music at hand. I want to give the ensemble my idea of what the piece is about, and point to the significant musical events that occur in the course of a movement. I deal with questions of tempo, tone color, dynamic gradation, and of balance between the several voices of the ensemble. Advice is offered about such matters as bowings and fingerings, and about choice of string for appropriate sonority. Prompting is often given as to those subtle but crucial matters of rubato and melodic inflection.

In the light of my own experience and premonition, I warn against probable pitfalls in the music and advise about ways of avoiding or surmounting them. I suggest ways of rehearsing and clarifying difficult areas in the music, sometimes areas that may not even seem problematic to the uninitiated eye.

You will find, as I have, that every chamber composition draws on the entire spectrum of skills of the individual player and of the group as a whole. The degree to which each ability is exercised (bowing agility, double stopping, management of contrapuntal textures, for example) will vary according to the particular composition and the specific passage therein. I do not presume, therefore, to label any given work as a demonstration exclusively of one aspect of performance. Études may work that way; the compositions discussed herein do not.

My musical roadmaps and signposts will be a useful supplement to the painstaking rehearsal and discussion—arguments!—of the ensemble. But I rely on the readers not to accept unquestioningly everything I say. I offer informed opinions and prejudices; these are not musical gospel but are, rather, points of departure for the ensemble in making its own musical decisions. As quickly as possible, the group must refine its musical judgment and strengthen its confidence therein. In chamber music as in solo playing, the players have to become their own best teachers.

Everything I have said applies not only to the professional and to the dedicated student, but to the amateur as well. Amateur playing is often of an impressively high level, and the musical curiosity of amateur ensembles leads them to tackle works of considerable difficulty. It is my hope, then, that the repertoire discussed in this book will prove intriguing to the lay reader. Further, even if the roster includes such extremely demanding works as Bartók's Fifth Quartet and the String Quartet of Ruth Crawford, a hands-on contact with that order of music can broaden the horizon and sharpen the perceptions of the serious amateur, both as player and listener.

The reader will note that, except for a decorative illustration at the head of one or another chapter, there are no musical examples in this book. Instead of printing hundreds of excerpts, I cite the measure numbers where each passage is to be found in a published score of the composition in question.

Consequently, the reader of this book will have to have score in hand. This is as it should be, for no instrumentalist or ensemble should study a composition, whether with my guidance or anyone else's, without consulting the score. It is in the score that the anatomy of the music, the relationship between its voices, its plan of organization, and its very logic can be clearly observed. Every ensemble should own not only its collection of performing parts, but its library of scores as well. Ideally, each member of the group should have an individual score, for personal study and notations.

At the foot of the first page of each chapter, I name the particular printed edition I used in writing the discussion of the work. Whenever possible, the source is a miniature score. In two cases (the Haydn Trio in G, Hob. XV:25, and the Shostakovich Piano Quintet), I worked from the piano score. My choice is an *Urtext* edition, when available. Further, I use current printings, readily purchased through music dealers.

Whether you use the score I name or some other edition, give preference to one that has measure numbers; these will be spaced every ten bars through the music, or else printed at the head of every brace of staves in the score. For some compositions, the only available score has rehearsal letters or numbers, usually placed at the start of important melodic or structural elements in the music. If these guide marks are not too sparsely scattered through the score, they are still useful, though not as convenient as measure numbers.

Scores that have no rehearsal signposts are very awkward for rehearsal and quick reference, unless you are willing to write in measure numbers by hand. Further, be sure that the individual parts used by the ensemble have the same measure location system as the score, unless the players are, again, willing to write in the necessary marks by hand. Consistent markings will greatly facilitate the rehearsal and discussion process.

The reference system in this book varies with the score used. Some examples follow.

If the score has measure numbers:

m. 72, mm. 23-32;

bar 17;

mm. 42 ff. for measure 42 and following.

If the score has rehearsal letters:

m. *D* – 3 means three measures before rehearsal letter D;

m. *F* + 5 means five measures after rehearsal letter F;

mm. *B* – (6 – 3) means sixth measure to third measure before rehearsal letter B;

If the score has rehearsal numbers, the system is similar to that with rehearsal letters:

m. *4* – 5 means fifth measure before rehearsal number 4...

In every chapter, measure guides appear at strategic places in the margin of the page, so you can check quickly from your score to find where I discuss a given area in the composition. For a few of the works treated here, measure numbering differs in the minuet movement. Most scores run the numbering straight on from the minuet into the trio, while others number the trio section separately (that is, starting again from 1). In such cases, my numbering follows the system in the score I have used, but I also give, in brackets, the corresponding numbers in other scores.

Documentary references in the text are arranged in a Notes section at the back of the book, under chapter headings. Full entries for these references, as well as for additional reading, appear in the Bibliography.

I welcome you to the world of chamber music, and to the wonderful discoveries you will make as you explore and rehearse the repertoire. Ensemble music has been a very demanding and very fulfilling part of my life these many years. I hope this book conveys to you some of the pleasure and stimulus the art has given me.

———

It is my privilege to acknowledge here the encouragement and advice given me during my work on this book. My special thanks to my longtime friend and Fine Arts Quartet colleague, George Sopkin, as well as to another esteemed colleague, Lois Finkel, of the Charleston Quartet. I owe warm appreciation, too, to Iva Buff, Louise Goldberg, Charles Lindahl, and Mary Rame, librarians at the Sibley

Music Library of the Eastman School of Music. I am grateful to the Sibley Library for its permission to use pages from its collection and its rare books holdings as decorative chapter headings in this book. I acknowledge also the kindness of the publishers who have granted permission to use, again as decorative chapter heads, pages from scores issued by them. Specific acknowledgment for these, as well as for the Sibley Library material, is given in the illustration descriptions at the start of the chapters in question.

It is my pleasure to thank Eve S. Goodman, of the editorial staff of Amadeus Press, for her painstaking attention to every detail in the preparation of this book; and also Reinhard G. Pauly, general editor of Amadeus Press and most valued friend, for his sage advice on many aspects of this work. I offer my renewed and affectionate appreciation to my wife, Jill, for tolerating again a book-in-progress in the home.

Finally, and in retrospect, my thanks to all the students and ensembles I have taught over the years. I trust that they learned something from me; I certainly learned much from them!

Abram Loft
Rochester, NY, 1991

❧ Introduction ❧
Rehearsal and Concert

This introduction offers some tips to help you operate effectively as an individual chamber musician and as member of an ensemble, whether for an evening or the longer haul. While the following chapters advise players on the treatment of specific works, I deal here with principles and procedures that apply generally to the rehearsal and performance of chamber music. The items discussed are grouped roughly according to type, and not necessarily in order of importance.

The more initiated performers among my readers may find some of this detail to be rather familiar stuff. In the light of my own experience, however, I feel it necessary to cover material that might otherwise escape the attention of newcomers to the chamber player's art.

REHEARSAL

Music. As I said in my Preface, each player should own a copy of the score, not just the individual part, of the composition that is being studied. Music borrowed from the library is fine for a reading session. For serious work, though, you need music you can write in—observations, bowings, fingerings, and so on. If you mark a library copy, you not only break the library's rules, but your valuable notations return to the library along with the score and are lost to you.

Use a medium hard pencil, not ink, to make your notes, and don't write too heavily. You will be changing your mind about details, and you should be able to erase earlier markings without damaging the page.

Whenever possible, and especially when dealing with older music, use scores and parts that embody the latest and most comprehensive information about the composer's intentions. Such editions will bear descriptions such as *Urtext* (the German for "original text") or equivalent terms denoting the authenticity of the version. The editors will specify the sources used in preparing the version:

composer's autograph score, first edition, and so on. In some cases, the editors provide detailed commentary showing the alternative pitch, articulation, and dynamic markings from which they made their choices for the actual print.

Music of contemporary vintage is often available in only one version, and you can assume that the publisher has worked closely with the composer in editing the printed material.

If the parts you are using are not of the same edition as your chosen, reliable score, write in any needed markings to make the parts conform to the score. As you rehearse a composition, use your judgment. For example, you may find that the composer's slurs should be regarded as phrase markings, rather than as literal bowing instructions. Again, a given edition's articulation signs (such as the wedge and the dot) may need rather broad interpretation to suit your view of the way a particular musical passage should sound. Experiment, and let your ear decide.

Finally, I urge that the scores and parts used by all members of the ensemble agree in rehearsal letters or measure numbering. This will save you a great deal of valuable rehearsal time.

Music stands. These should be adjustable, both in height and in the tilt of the music rack itself. Set your stand high enough so you can read the music comfortably, but low enough so you can see the other players easily. Elaborate stands that have a multiple head affixed to one column may be interesting items of furniture. They are not suited to serious ensemble playing, though; they force all the players to read at the same height, one that is usually too high.

Folding stands are essential for the traveling ensemble. Solid stands are convenient in the studio, for they offer more sturdy support for pencilled notations. If you use solid (so-called orchestral) stands, be sure they can be set low enough. You may want to have them cut down to size.

For technical reasons, wind players will ordinarily have their music stands higher than string players. For convenience in rehearsal and for the sake of appearance on stage, try to keep the difference in height within reason when playing a mixed ensemble work.

Chairs. The seat should be level, firm, and lightly padded. The edge of the seat must not cut into the player's thighs. Even if the individual player tends to sit still while in action, there is inevitably a certain amount of motion. The seat of the chair, then, should not be deeply scooped or otherwise confining in shape.

Especially in rehearsal, good back support is desirable. The ensemble involved in serious practice might well consider the purchase of ergonomically designed, typist chairs. This kind of seating is properly shaped and is readily adjustable in the height and tilt of the seat and the placement of the back support. Cellists may prefer to use a stool of appropriate height or a padded, adjustable piano bench.

Grouping. Sit as close together as the stands, the spread of the parts in use, and adequate bowing room permit. Make sure that all players can see each other without strain. I summarize here the customary seating arrangements for the kinds of works represented in this book.

The seating plan of the string quartet is roughly U-shaped. As seen by the audience, the 1st violin is at the left and front of the group, with the 2nd violin back, a bit to the right, and angled slightly so as to face toward the listeners. Either the viola or the cello can sit opposite the 1st violin.

With the cello in the outside position, the viola is next to the 2nd violin. Some ensembles prefer to have the viola on the outside, with the cello next to the 2nd violin and facing the audience. This gives the bass voice of the ensemble a more direct aim at the listener. In such seating, the *f*-holes of the viola face away from the audience. Even so, the instrument remains quite audible, so the player should resist the temptation to swing outward and away from the group.

In groups with piano, the violin(s) should sit on a line with the keyboard, with cello or viola—as the makeup and/or seating of the group may dictate—sitting in the curve of the instrument (presumably a grand piano). All players in the group should arrange their chairs and stands so that they can have eye contact with each other and with the pianist.

In ensembles with a 2nd viola or 2nd cello, the like instruments are, of course, seated next to each other. In a clarinet quintet, the wind player usually sits opposite the 1st violin. You can also put the clarinet at the center of the group (violins to the left, viola and cello to the right), with the wind player facing the audience.

The seating arrangement in Schubert's "Trout" Quintet is essentially that of the piano quartet. The fifth player, the double bass, stands behind and between the viola and cello.

Rehearsal room. The acoustics of the rehearsal room should not be depressingly dry. On the other hand, if the sound is too live, it will tend to dull the perceptions of the players and make it difficult to judge sonority, tone color, dynamics, and balance. Carpeting, wall hangings, and window drapes can be used to moderate too lively a sound.

Lighting. Illumination in the rehearsal studio should be sufficiently bright, diffused, and without glare. In daytime hours, shade the windows if light is shining strongly in the eyes of some ensemble members or is reflecting harshly off the music page. I would, incidentally, avoid the use of floor lamps. Such lamps usually glare in some players' eyes. And, sooner or later, there will be collision of bow or instrument with the shade or column of the lamp. The lamp usually wins in such encounters.

Temperature. If the room is too cold, players' fingers stiffen and the pitch stability of both string and wind instruments is spoiled. With too much heat, instruments are again affected, and the players get sleepy. As with the temperature, humidity should also strike a happy mean.

Fatigue. Don't rehearse too long at a stretch, or when members of the group are tired. You have to stay alert to make good use of rehearsal hours. Have refreshments near at hand, if only for therapeutic value.

Concept. Unless you are preparing for the world première of a composition, you will undoubtedly have heard performances and recordings by other ensembles of the work you are about to study. Nevertheless, develop as much of your own idea about the piece and its special world as you can. Then measure and modify that concept in the light of the viewpoints expressed by other musicians. You cannot, nor should you want to, produce a carbon copy of another group's performance.

Using the score. Very few of us have an inner ear keen enough to conjure up the sound of a work, in all its shadings and subtlety, simply by looking at the score. You will want to start playing the piece, no matter how haltingly, to get an awareness of the live sound. This also lets you hear your own part in relation to the others. Further, you can observe the connection between successive musical events, both within the movement and in the entire composition.

You should refer to the score to check musical detail and to confirm or supplement the overview you have formed. At this point, with the actual sound in your mind's ear, you are better equipped to read and interpret the printed score. As you continue this process of cross-reference between your playing and your reading of the score, you will add layers of understanding to your initial view of the work.

The tape recorder. One of the most difficult things to learn in music making is the ability to hear yourself. It is not easy to judge your own performance objectively when you are playing completely alone. The problem is much greater when the members of an ensemble have to appraise the playing of the group from within.

Having a tape recorder and playback system ready in the rehearsal room can prove invaluable. The ensemble can record a passage, section of a movement, or the movement as a whole, then listen to the recording from the vantage point of the audience. Unless the acoustics of the rehearsal room and the quality of your equipment are ideal, and the placement of the microphones just right, you won't be able to gauge matters of balance and tone color from the recording. You will find, though, that tempo, intonation, inflection and emphasis in phrasing, and rubato are clearly exposed in the playback. So also, the recording will show how convincing your performance is in revealing the connection between successive musical events in the composition. I think you will also find that hearing the tape can help you appraise that touchiest of areas: good taste.

Intelligent use of the tape recorder can save a lot of time in the rehearsal process. It can also spare the ensemble a great deal of discussion and argument—or at least focus the argument in fruitful ways.

Background reading. Everything you can learn about the composer's music and world is useful. Some helpful sources are listed in the bibliography of this book. You can get other leads by referring to the bibliographical listings of the relevant articles in *New Grove* and similar publications. Books that discuss the performance practice in force at the time the work was written are quite helpful, especially if they quote and interpret contemporary sources. Be aware, however, that there has been a fair amount of controversy among scholars in the field of performance practice. You will want to read widely enough to make an educated choice among alternative views.

Your prime source of information about a composition, however, lies within the work itself. Details about the composer's life and surroundings, no matter how close in time to the gestation of the particular composition, remain secondary to the music's own dictates.

Leading. In the course of the 19th century, many professional quartets bore the name of the 1st violinist (the Hellmesberger, Joachim, and Rosé quartets, and so on). Some of this practice endured into our own era. By and large, though, today's ensembles—string, wind, mixed, piano trio—avoid identification with any one member. One result is that an ensemble can now survive the inevitable change of membership that happens over time. But there is a deeper significance, as well.

Our audiences no longer expect, nor do ensemble members themselves accept, that the musical outlook of the group should be identified by that of the first chair. Of course, the prominent, topmost melodic voice sets an inescapable stamp on the temper of the group; the musical train cannot be driven by a locomotive in the rear. We consider the chamber ensemble, however, to be an integrated musical organism, reflecting the collective insight of all members.

In practice, this means that all members should feel not only free, but obliged, to take a hand in shaping the group's interpretation of a work. This can involve some very lively exchange of opinion. Ideally, the participants will display saintly forbearance in the process.

Solo and accompaniment. Any and every voice in the ensemble can be given the solo role. That function may pass to you suddenly and stay only briefly before moving on to another part. If your solo continues a melody that began in another part, play so that the line proceeds consistently. Your voice may be offering a sudden contrast—rhythmic and/or temperamental in nature—to the surrounding musical terrain. Be ready to assume the new character.

Two or more lines can be prominent, side by side. Here, each voice has to satisfy its own melodic requirements without stepping on the heels of the other. Also a single solo voice can be opposed by an equally prominent duet or trio of parts in the rest of the ensemble. In such case, the group solo has to be worked out separately, then balanced as a whole to leave enough elbowroom for the other, individual solo.

When your line provides accompaniment, define your function intelligently. A repeated 8th-note pattern in a Haydn quartet part may not look like much. If you play it that way, that's what it will be: not much. Hear it as part of the musical fabric; ask yourself how your rhythm contributes to the pulse and direction of the solo part. Play accordingly.

Though your line may be subordinate to action in other lines, figures of thematic significance can still appear in your part. Shape them properly, and project them so that they can be heard.

Those who play a second voice in ensembles (2nd violin in the quartet, or the added viola or cello in the string quintet and sextet) have the particular responsibility to play discerningly and with strength. Don't assume that, because your instrument is already represented in another voice in the group, you are just along for the ride. If the piece in question is worth playing, it will treat all voices as indispensable components of the ensemble. Look for the opportunities the composer gives you, and give good account of them.

A colleague who has long been a most eminent 2nd violin in America's chamber music scene maintains that that role is the most difficult to fill in the string ensemble. The 2nd has to speak for itself, yet at the same time stand ready to be the complement to every other voice in the group. Perhaps I can generalize my colleague's view by saying that, in the ideal group, no one plays second fiddle!

Balance. You have to adjust the relative prominence of the voices in the ensemble. In such a case as the middle movement of the Mozart Flute Quartet in D, K. 285, this would seem to be no problem at all: the flute is as much a soloist there as any prima donna in one of Mozart's operatic arias. Even so, the pizzicato accompaniment of the strings flares out melodically at a number of points in the movement. The notes cannot be twanged brusquely, but they should obviously be heard.

In short, adjusting the balance will be as complex as the music makes it. In which voice(s) does the action lie at any given point? You may have to shift the focus of attention as often as every quarter-beat or less (see, for example, the third movement of Beethoven's Quartet in B flat, Op. 130).

Decide the balance in the light of what you hear in rehearsal as well as by reading the score. Your choices make a big difference in the way the listener perceives the composition. A photographer adjusts the camera lens to focus the viewer's attention either on the near, the middle, or the farther distance in the picture. Balance, in effect, is the musician's lens.

Signals. If you have seen a good conductor in action, you already know something about signal giving. Conductors have to coordinate many players, and often resort to large gestures. On the other hand, some leaders (Fritz Reiner was a prime example) can evoke and synchronize even a fortissimo attack with a very small motion.

Your own group is small and seated closely together, so economical signals will do. They must be well calculated, however. The sign should come from the player with the prominent line at the moment (even at the start of a movement, it will not necessarily be the first violin, or the piano in a mixed ensemble work).

Note, by the way, that signals are given not only to start a movement, but to restart action at many points before the double bar is reached. The most obvious case is after a grand pause. Even when the music is in full swing, however, there may be entrances by two or three voices. These must be coordinated by a signal from a designated member of that subgroup, or by a concerted motion of all the players involved.

It is also necessary to signal endings. For example, a sign must be given to show when tones sustained by some or all the players should cease. Whether for starting or stopping, the mechanics of the signal are similar.

Basically, you give the signal to yourself. If you start your own part convincingly, your fellow musicians will be able to read your sign clearly and make the entrance with you.

Hold yourself ready to play, so that you can respond to your own indication. Give yourself a lead-in: the silent beat before the note you have to play. The upbeat quarter-note signal precedes an entrance on the downbeat; a downbeat signal will precede an entrance on the second beat of a measure, and so on. If the tempo is fast, you may want to take a longer lead-in: a half-measure before the downbeat entry, for example. Conversely, if the tempo is very slow, a single 8th-note upbeat might suffice to bring you in on the downbeat of a 6/8 measure. Choose the signal that is clear to your colleagues.

Your sign shows not only the tempo, but also the temper of the movement. Quiet and rather slow music needs a correspondingly gentle and expansive preparation and signal. Vigorous music needs an appropriately intense sign: small and contained to indicate hushed excitement; larger, to reflect a louder dynamic level.

The signal itself is an extension of the normal motion of breathing in and out. For the wind player, this is natural: you have to take a breath in order to blow into the instrument. It is much the same for the string and the keyboard player. An intake of breath moves your arms in the direction they normally take in preparation for drawing the bow onto the string, or in lifting the hands before the descent onto the keys. Remember, too, that your head moves up and down slightly when you breathe. A slight nod of the head is part of the signalling process.

Play the first measures of several movements, of various speeds and characters. Look in the mirror to see what you do when you start each one. Work at it until you are confident that you would be able to follow your own signal. Then try it on your colleagues; they will suggest any further improvement.

Even better than a mirror is a home video camera. If the ensemble can see itself in action on videotape, the effectiveness of individual and group signalling can readily be gauged. In general, moreover, a video playback can provide clues about the bowing styles, unity of phrasing, and overall visual impression of the ensemble. Such cameras are fast becoming almost as prevalent as tape recorders, and are of similar usefulness to the chamber group.

A video, by the way, will undoubtedly show you something interesting about signalling: the members of the ensemble not only take a signal from the leader of the moment, they also reflect it in their own motions. In short, musicians who move together, play together.

Tempo. Use your ears and your judgment. Often, the composer's own commands will throw you back on your individual resources. When you read *ma non troppo*, exactly how much is "not too much"? The translation into an actual speed will vary from one musician to the next, with the passage of the seasons, even with successive performances, or with what feels right in the acoustics of the particular concert hall.

Don't play too fast just because your fingers enable you to. On the other hand, don't let technical limitations make you accept too slow a tempo. Keep working toward the pace that moves the music at the speed that sounds appropriate. There is usually a leeway within which you can make the music seem right. Note that Bartók, who was often quite specific in his tempo indications, would sometimes offer a narrow range within which to set the speed, or would preface his metronome marking with the qualifier, "about." This reminds me of the time that Ernest Bloch came to Chicago to hear the Fine Arts prepare one of his quartets. (It was before I had joined the group.) As the run-through of one movement ended, he cried, "Wonderful! The exact, approximate tempo!"

Rhythm. The time patterns in a musical line work with, against, or around the established metric pulse. The dominant rhythm in the last movement of Schubert's "Death and the Maiden" Quartet identifies closely with the duple pulse of the 6/8 meter. On the other hand, look at the opening of the second movement of Schumann's Quartet No. 3. The theme does everything it can to challenge its 3/8 frame: the bar line is apparently shifted; moreover, through the first twelve measures, the music suggests a breathless 3/4 meter; and in the last four bars of the first section the music implies 9/8 meter before ending on an elliptic 3/8 figure. Or yet again, consider the first movement of Bartók's Fifth Quartet. On page 304, below, I describe how the composer operates within the stated meter without being strait-jacketed by it.

Just as the composer refuses to be dominated by the bar line, so should your playing of the musical line be free of such confinement. Meter and bar line offer organization and convenience, respectively, to the musical process. It is up to the player, though, to follow and realize the unique shape of the individual melodic strand; don't perforate the line with insensitive downbeat accents.

In rehearsal, be sure you are playing the rhythms of your part accurately. Differentiate between accents and other emphasis marks (line, sforzando, forte-piano, and so on). Dotted rhythms are not triplets. In dotted-8th-and-16th figures, play the short note later and shorter, not the reverse. If the short note in a dotted rhythm is at the start of the figure, emphasize the fact by stressing the note slightly, even when no specific accent mark is given.

When playing a series of syncopes, don't let accents creep into your line that reveal the metric beats against which the syncopes are reacting. Leave the definition of the metric frame to the voices that are still playing on the beat; exploit the rhythmic-versus-metric friction that the composer has written.

So also, if your line slips back and forth between duple and triple rhythms, be careful to spread the triplet evenly over its allotted space. It is very easy to fall into a distortion of the triplet unless you shift your mind-set from the double to the triple count. This is especially true when you are playing triplets in your voice against duplets in other voices (as happens so often in Brahms).

If complex rhythmic patterns are being constructed by interaction between several voices—Dvořák does much of this—rehearse the mosaic slowly. You have to get the interwoven pattern into your collective ear, so that you can keep track of it when played up to speed.

You can be accurate in your rhythms without sounding pedantic. Flexibility, however, does not mean sloppiness. Rhythmic control is vital to the clarity and impact of your performance.

Phrasing. When we talk, we group our words through inflection and punctuation—that is, by a varying mix of pitch, speed, emphasis, and silence. In playing a musical phrase, we should be just as conscious of inflection and punctuation as when we speak.

In our speech, we make subtle, improvised adjustments in our vocal pitch level and in the force of breath with which we support the voice. We also vary the speed of individual words and successions of words and the length of the silences that separate them. There are relatively few signs—such as ? , : ; . and !—to govern this. To go much farther with written instructions would clutter the page and still not keep up with the shadings we make by habit and instinct. We have learned to be able performers in our speech in order to get through life's daily round.

Musicians who already have a significant technical command of their instrument sometimes forget that they have to make their musical statements "speak." Try to shape the line you play (whether solo or accompaniment) at least as communicatively as you would your speech. The composer helps by using rests, accent marks, dynamic graduation, shades of speed, and character markings. Sometimes, in a direct borrowing from our speech punctuation, the composer even uses commas to indicate slight breaks in the line.

Read the music carefully to profit from all the printed information that is offered. Above all, listen alertly as you move through your musical line. What you are about to play is a consequence of something you, or one of your ensemble colleagues, has played just before. Your new statement will itself give rise to the next musical event, either in your own or a neighboring voice. A melodic line is abstract; it has no verbal connotations. Its shape, its rise and fall, its play of tension and release, is its meaning. The composer has built that sense into the line; it's your job to evoke it.

Singing the line can often help give you a slant on its proper shape and punctuation. This is true even when the given line does not lend itself easily to song. (Have you ever, for that matter, tried singing the voice parts of Beethoven's Ninth?) Members of the ensemble may be hesitant about favoring each other with vocal renditions during group rehearsal. In private practice, however, the individual player should feel no hesitation about trying that immediate contact with phrase or melodic detail that the voice provides.

If your playing of a melodic line or detail does not make it fit properly into the musical situation of the moment or into the larger plan of the movement, look for the reason. Ensemble collaboration in this kind of appraisal is one of the most demanding, yet essential, parts of rehearsal. This is also an area, by the way, where tact is an indispensable part of the discussion process. The players' musical intuitions are on the line here, so don't tread heavily.

Intonation. You can't hide poor intonation. It is there, to be mentioned in reviews, to be noticed by even the less-initiated listener, to darken the atmosphere in the rehearsal room. The ensemble must guard against it constantly, and with patience.

Good intonation begins with careful tuning. This is no simple matter. If all members of the ensemble tune simultaneously and loudly, they will not hear each other, let alone their own instrument. String players should tune with light, slow strokes, in the upper part of the bow. In the quartet, let the cello tune first, setting the A at the agreed level. It may help to have at hand a tuning fork that has been filed to sound an A higher than 440, to suit current taste about pitch.

The C-string of the cello should be tuned very slightly sharp, so that the interval of a fifth between the C and G is somewhat narrowed. Set the viola's C-string to form a true octave with that of the cello. The A of all three upper instruments should match the pitch of the cello's A-string.

If you don't raise the open C of the two lower voices, chords and octaves that span the broad range of the ensemble will, in practice, sound out of tune. In fact, some ensembles tune all their fifths a tiny bit narrow, to improve the aural effect of the playing.

Ideally, the instruments should tune one by one, from the cello up through the high voices. That way, you can hear yourself clearly, and your colleagues can advise if they hear that a given string is still off. Incidentally, make sure that none of your strings is false. If the open string, when plucked lightly, produces a wavering, uncertain pitch, the string should be replaced immediately. No matter how carefully tuned, a string that has gone false will not provide true, fingered intervals or harmonics.

Once you have the tuning under control, the real work begins. Even if each member of the ensemble is careful to play in tune, one musician's idea of "in tune" does not always match that of another. It is the ensemble's job to iron out the differences.

In the early stages of the ensemble's existence, and as a point of information, the players could take turns playing, quietly and in solo, a slow scale—major and minor—through two or three octaves. Hold vibrato to a minimum so that the attention can focus on the accuracy of the pitch. The group can then consult about the various step relationships in the scale they have just heard. Give special attention to the half-steps in both the major and minor scales, particularly the interval between the leading tone and the tonic.

When the ensemble is satisfied with the solo scales, try playing scales in the various duets and threesomes possible within the ensemble membership, both in unison and in octave. Then proceed to intervals and chords, always playing rather quietly, so that the focus is on the intonation.

If a chord is out of tune, try building the chord quietly, layer by layer, starting with the lowest voice. The interval relationships can be judged more effectively this way than by working from the top down.

All this is useful, but the musical lines and textures you play in actual musical compositions are complex, always new, and constantly moving through shifting harmonic contexts. Be vigilant, imaginative, and humble. Listen carefully; break down difficult passages into component voice groupings for slow practice and adjustment; and don't assume that the fault always lies in someone else's part. Watch out especially for high-register playing, where close spacing of the notes on the string increases the chance of intonation problems. Violinists, especially, should be aware that poor tone quality in the high register will aggravate any impression of flawed intonation.

In an ensemble with piano, strings and winds will have to adjust their intonation to the conditions imposed by the tempered tuning of the keyboard. Again, slow practice of problematic passages will pinpoint the trouble spots.

No matter what the instrumentation, intonation is not a sometime thing. Long togetherness is no protection. Tell each other when you hear something out of tune. If you don't, other people will.

Bowing. What the breath is to the singer and the wind player, what the touch is to the pianist—that is what the bow is to the string player. It is the bow that evokes and projects the sound of the instrument. The way the bow is used has a great deal to do with the nature of the sound that is produced and with the spirit and impetus of the melody that is being played.

There are various "schools" of bowing, differing—sometimes extremely—in such detail as bow grip, arm placement, wrist involvement, and so on. I leave it to the player to explore the various approaches, and to draw from each those aspects that help the performer use the bow most efficiently. Whatever your own approach, be sure it makes the bow an extension of your hand, not a barrier between you and the instrument. You must, in effect, be able to "feel" the contact of bow hair against string, so that you can react instantly to the slightest feedback of tactile information. That way, you can govern the color and dynamic level of the sound with great sensitivity. Also, you can foretell when a harshness or tremor is likely to surface in the tone and make whatever adjustment—whether in pressure or speed of stroke—is necessary to ward off the blemish.

Learn to use the bow economically. Don't press harder than necessary, don't draw the bow faster than need be. No matter what loudness level you need, let the bow tell you that you are rubbing the string, not rasping it. When you cross strings, orient the arm so that the crossing can be effected by hand motion, with the least possible agitation of the arm itself. Above all, try for a relaxed bowing arm; tension and rigidity will cramp every aspect of the stroke and will communicate itself immediately to the sound.

Every bow has its own traits and idiosyncracies. And the combination of a given bow and a particular player is, again, a unique situation. Find out how your bow behaves under your command. Discover the exact areas of the stick that respond best to the several kinds of bow stroke: spiccato, staccato, and so on. Find out how the bow feels when you perform a gratifying legato or *marcato*. Make the bow a part of yourself.

Every member of the ensemble is not likely to use the bow in identical fashion. But you will have to agree among yourselves about the kind of sound you want. You have to decide about such factors as: the speed and pressure of the stroke; the amount of bow to be used; the area of the stick to be used (near the tip, near the frog, and so on); and the placement of the bow on the string, whether closer to bridge or fingerboard. Within these decisions, the individual player can then work toward the desired tone quality in each musical situation.

Leopold Mozart said it in 1756: "Bowing gives life to the notes."[1] The statement still holds true.

Dynamics. Control of loud and soft is crucial not only to balance, but also to the ensemble's general style. I am reminded of the old yarn of the person who asked a quartet member, "How many are there in your group?" Upon being told that there were four, the interrogator sympathized, "Never mind, just keep at it and you'll grow into an orchestra."

Don't try to be an orchestra. The composer has cut the musical cloth to suit. Whether you are a trio or an octet, your total sound has a built-in limit. You can't play louder than that limit without crossing the line from musical resonance to a kind of intoned noise. You can, however, play softer. Every decibel you can drop the lower boundary of your sound level, while still maintaining palatable tone, makes the upper limit of your dynamic range seem louder by comparison. The listener will credit your ensemble with a vividness greater than your small number would imply. Even more: you will hold the attention of the audience.

Nothing makes a listener's eyes glaze faster than hearing a constant loud, a steady pianissimo, or an endless in-between. Even more important than the hearer's attention span: if your dynamics settle into one narrow groove, you are unfair to the composer. The play of loud and soft is an essential device in the composer's arsenal. Think of the first movement of the Beethoven Quartet in E minor, Op. 59, No. 2. Recall how often you are asked to play a pair of chords, set all the way from pianissimo to fortissimo, each time contrasting the sound against an ensuing silence. Beethoven is listening to this contrast with an intensity made all the greater (I believe) by his own encroaching deafness, and he makes us all listen with him. There is perhaps no better illustration of the critical part that dynamic gradation plays in music.

Tone color. Every instrument has not only its own distinctive kind of resonance, but also a range of tone qualities within that sonority. Play a note that lies high or low on the instrument; play it with expansive or confined stroke; near the tip or at the frog of the bow. Produce the sound with a staccato or legato inset. Bow over the fingerboard or near the bridge. Use or avoid the sustaining pedal in playing the piano. Play softly or loudly, whether on string, keyboard, or wind instrument. All these factors and more will affect the sound that is produced.

The string player often has to choose the string on which to play a given pitch. In many passages, technical realities dictate the choice. When there are alternative possibilities, the decision will be influenced by tone color. An open string does not sound like its stopped equivalent. The lowest B♭ on the violin A-string does not sound like the same pitch played high on the G-string. Choice of string must be matched with the kind of bow stroke, the amount of vibrato, and the dynamic level in force, and evaluated in terms of the musical circumstance of the moment.

Experimentation with these coloristic possibilities is one of the exciting aspects of all music making. It is especially important in the small ensemble. Skillful use of the tonal spectrum helps realize the composer's intention. Words and markings point you in the direction of that intent. Then it's up to you.

Vibrato. The music historian, Robert Donington, once wrote,"Sensitive vibrato not only can but should be a normal ingredient in performing such music: while leaving the tone transparent, it is quite indispensable in bringing it to life."[2] Donington was discussing the use of vibrato in playing music of the 16th to 18th centuries. But his observation—especially the word, "sensitive"—is relevant also to the performance of music of more recent vintage.

String sound can be produced completely without vibrato, as well as with very intense oscillation. These are extremes and have their place. Don't, however, attach yourself dogmatically to either limit. Vibrato should be used with discernment, as an attribute of tone color and dynamic shading. Quiet sound can vary from a totally nonvibrated, "cool" tone, to one whose warmth reflects hushed excitement. Loud playing tends to sound slablike and uninvolved if it is entirely devoid of vibrato.

The key elements are: variety, discretion, and agreement. Vibrato must not be ever-present and unyielding in the group sound. You are playing music, not lacquering an automobile. Vary the frequency and amplitude of the vibrato (that is, the number of shakes per second and the length of the shake on either side of the pitch center) to suit the musical context. You can't measure this with stopwatch and ruler. You judge it by ear and with that elusive factor, taste. In general, a more relaxed vibrato will suit the slow, lyric passage; and an intense vibrato, the vigor of a massed fortissimo. There is neither cause nor opportunity to use a great deal of vibrato in rapid passage work, though you can apply it, within reason, to help highlight selected notes en route.

It is often necessary to make one or more voices in the ensemble stand out from the rest, either in detail or in general, in a given passage. Here, vibrato can again be used effectively, along with sensitive loudness contrast between voices. Once more, experiment to determine the best effect.

Fingering. The string player often has to choose whether to stay in position and cross back and forth between strings, or else to minimize string crossing by shifting from one position to another. Assuming that your technique makes you comfortable with either alternative, your decision will be based on taste and sound. Will the string crossings introduce a strong contrast of tone colors into the melodic line? Do you want that contrast? If shifting is preferable, can you carry out the shift so that it is either concealed entirely or else revealed to just the right expressive degree?

In an ensemble, such questions may have to be decided by group appraisal. The choice can, perhaps desirably, make the individual voice stand out in contrast to the others. If, however, the part writing demands that a given treatment be echoed in other voices, be careful that the effect does not pall through repetition.

Experiment first with fingerings that are clean—those that require the least amount of shifting consistent with the desired tone color. Shifts as small as a half-step will inevitably be necessary, especially in chromatic passages; they should, however, be made as unobtrusively as possible. Larger shifts can be added, as the expressive needs of the line dictate. Edit such shifts, however, by adjusting the speed and lightness both of the shifting finger and the bow stroke. Avoid anything that smacks of a glissando effect unless it is specifically called for by the composer or, in your estimation, is demanded by the musical context. Nothing emits the aroma of sentimentality more quickly than a syrupy slide.

Instruments. In a string ensemble, it's almost as difficult to match instruments as to match players. Even if all the instruments come from one gifted maker, that does not assure that the tone qualities of all will be suitable. Of course, each instrument should be clear and open in sound on all four of its strings, with no harsh contrast in projection or color of sound among them. Beyond that, there are special requirements for the several voices in the ensemble.

The 1st violin should maintain its clarity and warmth of tone right up into the high reaches of the E-string. In many a chamber work from the 18th century to our own time, parts written for the 1st violin rival violin concertos in technical and musical demands. The instrument used for such music should ideally be of the quality that could serve in a solo performance.

The instrument of the 2nd violin should generally match the sonority of its companion, though perhaps shading a bit more into a mellow coloration, as befits the alto of the group. It must be able fully to hold its own within the ensemble, for it is often called upon to duet with one of the other voices, to lead the accompaniment, or to perform in solo role. I reject out of hand Karl Geiringer's suggestion that "Haydn apparently took into consideration the fact that the player [the 2nd violin] who usually performed a part of minor importance assumed in the long run a quality of tone different from that of the leader of the ensemble."[3] The Haydn quartets themselves, to say nothing of the rest of the repertoire, give the lie to this statement.

From personal experience, I sympathize with the search for the ideal viola, one that is easy to play, has great tonal beauty, and above all, can project. By way of a cautionary note, let me quote here the sage observation of Thurston Dart:

> The large, and large-toned, viola is an admirable instrument for concertos and sonatas; but it is very much open to question whether instruments of this kind have a proper place in classical and romantic chamber music, for they profoundly modify the balance of tone between the instruments of the violin family that the composers had in mind.[4]

The viola is a very individual voice in the string ensemble. It makes its presence felt both by its unique resonance and by the kind of parts written for it in our best chamber repertoire. The ensemble that has a strong violist in its roster is fortunate indeed; the group balance should adjust to exploit that resource, but always with respect for the constraints imposed by the music. Most fortunate is the ensemble comprised of players of solo caliber who are able to subordinate the ego of the soloist to the needs of the chamber composition.

Except in the limited chamber repertoire that includes double bass, the cello is the foundation upon which the string chamber ensemble rests. I believe that, after the 1st violin, it is the cello that listeners hear most in the ensemble. The instrument must be warm in resonance, though not fuzzy. It should speak clearly and quickly and be free of any nasal quality in its A-string registers. The parts written for the cello—and by no means only in Mozart's "King of Prussia" quartets—are often worthy of the concerto soloist. Accordingly, the ideal ensemble instrument must be of excellent quality, and of bold sound.

String ensemble members aiming at a professional career will probably have to do some switching of instruments to find those that are tonally compatible. Concern about instrument compatibility also affects woodwind and brass ensembles, but I leave discussion thereof to wind experts. I understand, though, that—for winds as well as strings—the instruments themselves are only half the battle. Equally important for the ensemble is to choose members whose styles of playing, whose concepts of sound and of musicality, are allied closely enough to become even closer in the course of rehearsal and performance. You want to be able to persuade, not hammer on, one another.

IN CONCERT

Stage presence. In concert, the playing is the critical part of the job. Nonetheless, everything that surrounds the performance contributes to the effect. Getting on and off stage, bowing, tuning, between-movement deportment—everything counts. Stage presence, like the music itself, takes rehearsal.

With the concert about to start, the ensemble should be lined up in the wings, in order of seating. The player whose chair is farthest from the stage entry should be first in line, and so on. Be ready to enter the stage as soon as the auditorium lights have been dimmed and the stage lighting turned up. If you wait too long, the audience fidgets, and the expectant hush gives way to a buzz of talk, coughs, and the rustling of programs.

Walk on as though you are about to enjoy the performance. If the audience sees mournful or scowling faces, they will fear the worst. On the other hand, hilarity or conversation in transit will create a sense of amateur night. Serious, but not lugubrious, is the watchword.

Tuning is essentially a backstage procedure. Once on stage and seated, tune only if absolutely necessary, and very quietly and briefly. Get started with the concert as soon as you can.

Between movements, again hold tuning to a minimum. The break should be only long enough to allow for the change of mood from one movement to the next. Be especially careful with the break between the first two movements on the program. This is when latecomers are seated, and your readiness to proceed will let everyone know that the interruption should be as short as possible.

The taking of bows sometimes looks as though it should have been rehearsed. I don't say that the ensemble members should move as though synchronized by some kind of bowing machine. If, on the other hand, the players bob up and down completely at random, the effect can be disconcertingly comic. Take turns looking at the rest of the group doing their bows (or, even better, have a video taken of all of you) to see what procedure makes for the best effect. You'll probably get some good laughs in the process.

Enjoy the applause, but with an air of dignified congeniality. If the audience calls you out for three bows at the concert's end, it may be appropriate to present an encore. One well-chosen movement should suffice after a full-length program.

Exits, by the way, should be roughly the reverse of the entry: last in, first out. If there are both men and women in the ensemble, I leave it to the group to decide how—or whether—to adhere to the traditional ladies-first sequence.

Preconcert warm-up. I assume the ensemble has had opportunity to hold a dress rehearsal on the concert stage. This is particularly important if the group is playing in the given auditorium for the first time or after some extended interval. Familiarity with the hall's acoustics is essential, so that you are not surprised at the sound when you start the actual concert. Of course, the acoustics are never quite the same with the audience in place. Don't assume, though, that the audience will change the sound greatly; it rarely does.

You may instinctively adjust tempo in response to the acoustic feedback you get from the hall. I urge you, however, not to alter your accustomed dynamic range. The audience has to do its part by listening alertly.

Because of travel schedule or hall availability, you may have time only for a short, preconcert warm-up on stage. If so, don't let the occasion turn into a last-minute revamping of the interpretation of the music. That way lies madness; a few such unsettling experiences can shatter the togetherness of any ensemble.

Even the dress rehearsal itself should be for touch-up of detail, not a time for major overhaul. If the dress rehearsal has taken place on stage, in fact, it is best to skip the ensemble warm-up and allow the individual players to prep themselves backstage before the concert, as they see fit.

If you do hold a warm-up, don't occupy the stage longer than is proper. The audience should be admitted at the hall's accustomed opening time.

Body English. Some musicians move more than others when they play. String players generally move more than wind players; they have no embouchure to worry about, and drawing the bow often involves rather large motions. If you swing and sway too much, it can be disturbing both to your colleagues and your audience. I should know, for many years ago a review of a concert of ours in New Zealand complained that "the second violinist positively grovelled on the floor." The comment was exaggerated, I am sure, but I did become more sedate in my habits in later years.

Motion in playing remains an individual matter, but please keep it within bounds. The ensemble members should, nevertheless, learn to read each other's body language. It is part of the signalling and communication process within the group.

One aspect of body English really should be ruled out: foot tapping. If the tapping is your way of keeping your place in the passing measures, you are in trouble. The complexities of rhythm in the music demand mental, not physical, calculation. It could be, on the other hand, that the tapping shows you are being carried away by the music. In that case, Robert Benchley's old quip about the emoting concert goer is apropos: you have not been carried away far enough. In a word, when it comes to tapping your foot—don't.

Program building. Try to hold the total length of the program to about one-and-three-quarter hours, including intermission. Chamber music is fairly intricate stuff. If the audience is to listen carefully, they should not be asked to concentrate for an excessively long time. In arranging the sequence of the program, put the most complex music on the first half of the program, the most brilliant at the end of the concert.

Ordinarily, you will be choosing works that contrast in style, and usually from different periods of time. In the case of certain masters, one-composer programs are feasible: Beethoven, Mozart, Bartók, a few others come to mind. Again, however, you will have to choose the works and their sequence with an eye to program length and balance.

Be imaginative in your programming. Your audience can absorb only so many Beethoven or Mozart performances, especially when every other ensemble is presenting the same works. Seek out interesting and seldom-heard compositions by composers both old and new. Search through library holdings and publishers' catalogues. If you have the means, commission new works from our composers or present interesting new music that is already available.

In general, contemporary works should be programmed together with standard repertoire. This does not imply that the modern piece requires bolstering with more conventional fare. Rather, it is to avoid any sense that contemporary music needs to be segregated, as though in some kind of musical freak show. What we call classical music was, after all, contemporary music in its own day.

Talking to the audience. Ever since Leonard Bernstein showed how well it could be done, musicians have felt that they must talk to the audience. Unless you turn the performance into a lecture-concert, with a reduced amount of music to allow for the talk, it is preferable to reserve the speaking for a preconcert gathering. Also, unless you are very good at off-the-cuff speaking, write out your talk in advance, at least in detailed outline. Then, try to deliver it with the same informality that the extempore talk would display.

Have something pertinent to say about the music, and check your terms and your historical data beforehand. Be straightforward and don't condescend to your audience. Above all, don't condescend to the composers. In the rush to tell all about music, some familiar names in the mass media have made a career of hogwash.

Orchestral musicians in chamber music. Whether they are principals or section players, orchestral musicians are expected not only to play well, but to deliver robustly. When transplanted into chamber music ensembles, as in such-and-such symphony orchestra quartet, the orchestral player must recognize that there is no longer the need to contest against the sound of a larger group of players. With only one player per part, the whole scale of dynamics has to be adjusted accordingly.

The challenge is greatest for the orchestral string player. Even the section principal hears sound, day in and out, in the context of ten or more people playing the same line. It is all too easy for one's tone to become bulky in the course of years of such experience. A distinct shift to a smoother, more contained tone and a refined attention to detail is needed immediately upon stepping into the chamber context. Every performance of a chamber work is, in effect, a solo audition for every member of the ensemble.

Togetherness. The dividing line between fatigue and annoyance is a fine one. In a fixed group that is working toward—or has already begun—a professional career, you see each other constantly. Differences in musical outlook, even jaundiced views of personal mannerisms, take on aggravated importance. Be sure you have enough time away from each other during the year so that such pressures can be relieved.

On the other hand, be patient. It is upheaval enough when a player leaves a group after some years of membership. But I have been grieved to see an occasional student ensemble break up within the space of a semester. That's especially unfortunate; there is plenty of time for artistic temperament to rear its head later on, when you're old enough to know better!

Business. There is more to the concert career of a musical ensemble than rehearsal and performance. You will have to: maintain cordial and imaginative relations with arts support groups in your community; deal with concert management (domestic and foreign), travel agent, and tax adviser; write or oversee program notes and publicity releases; cultivate opportunities for performing on radio, television, and in recording. The list goes on. If you are fortunate enough to obtain a campus residency for your ensemble, you will have to balance your teaching and concert activities, and act effectively in both.

As your group rises in prominence, you may be able to delegate much of the detail work to others. You can never ignore those details entirely, however. Divide the various areas of concern among the members of the ensemble, according to the individuals' interests and competence. Each of you will find that you have to draw on everything you have learned, in schooling and experience, to deal with the business concerns of the group. The excitement of the concert performance is your ultimate reward.

An important point: try to keep the business side of the ensemble's work from encroaching on your rehearsal time. It will help, for example, if phones in the practice room are disconnected during rehearsal hours.

Postscript. Whether your ensemble meets only for a musical evening, has formed for a semester, or looks toward years of concert giving, remember why you are playing chamber music in the first place. The music is the best there is. You and your fellow musicians are working together because you like each other's way of playing. Your rehearsals are opportunities for the meeting of musical minds. You are all trying to construct a valid and individual way of interpreting the composition. Most important: you want to enjoy what you are doing. Make it happen.

———

REHEARSAL COMMANDMENTS

I
Don't shoot from the hip. Let the music soak in, especially at the first rehearsal of a work.

II
Do your homework. Be ready to explain your view clearly and concisely.

III
Listen openmindedly to your colleagues' playing. It may well be convincing. If it is, say so!

IV
Don't get hung up on words. Play the musical alternatives, tape them, listen, then decide.

V
Be consistent. Follow the built-in logic of the work. The composer put it there; reveal it.

VI
Talk music, not personalities. Your target is the musical problem, not each other's psyches.

VII
Be punctual for rehearsals. And don't stomp out in a huff—that wastes time and strains patience.

VIII
Avoid "free lessons." You're in a collegial group, not a teacher-student situation.

IX
Play interestingly. Nothing is as boring as a rehearsal that lacks musical spark.

X
Rehearse efficiently and imaginatively. Avoid meaningless repetition. As with solo practice, *think.*

FINALE.

CHAPTER ONE

❦ Haydn ❦
Quartet in E flat, Op. 33, No. 2
("The Joke")

Humor is serious business: timing, nuance, gesture—everything must be controlled, seemingly effortless, natural. This is true of spoken or visual humor (the stand-up comic, the cartoonist); it is equally true of music, and especially in instrumental music, where the humor must be conveyed by sound alone, without the benefit of words. It takes imagination by the composer to invent the humorous situation; it takes intelligence and alertness by the performer to translate the composer's drollery into sound. Above all, you have to get the joke in order to retell it. The work we explore in this chapter will test your wit as well as your playing ability. You are dealing with a man whose keen and sophisticated intellect has been honed by years of practice in the art of composition.

Beginning in 1761, and for the next three decades, Haydn was musical overseer at the court of the princely Esterhazy family. In addition to supervision of the musical retinue and paraphernalia, he was charged with the preparation of a wide variety of performances at the court, both of works by others and of music he was required to compose. In his first years at the court, Haydn wrote, among other works, twenty-eight string quartets. In these, culminating with the six quartets of Op. 20 (1772), he moved from short, relatively simple compositions to music that crystallized the medium, setting standards for the writers to come—most immediately the young genius, Mozart.

After Op. 20, nine years passed before Haydn returned to the medium.

SCORE: Joseph Haydn. 1988. *Streichquartette. Urtext-Ausgabe. Quartetto Es-Dur, Op. 33, No. 2, Hob. III:38*. Ed. R. Barrett-Ayres and H. C. Robbins Landon. Vienna: Doblinger. Miniature score No. 449.

Left: Joseph Haydn: Quartet in E flat, Op. 33, No. 2, first page of the score of the finale. Berlin: Trautwein, 1840. Reproduced with permission from the collection of the Sibley Music Library, the Eastman School of Music, University of Rochester.

Apparently as early as mid-October of 1781, Haydn was arranging with the publishing firm of Artaria, in Vienna, to issue a new set of six quartets that he was then completing.[1] By early December, in a letter to a music lover in Zurich, Haydn offered manuscript copies of the quartets by private subscription, in advance of publication. The letter contains the oft-quoted statement that the quartets are "WRITTEN IN A NEW AND SPECIAL WAY (FOR I HAVEN'T COMPOSED ANY FOR 10 YEARS)."[2]

I have often played the quartets of Op. 20, and especially enjoyed the fine points of the fourth work in that set (in D major). It always puzzled me that Haydn's own statement would imply that those earlier quartets—the last in a series of eighteen innovative works composed in 1771-72—were somehow less estimable than his new opus. I am relieved to note, then, that Jens Peter Larsen, a leading Haydn scholar of our time, suggests not taking the phrase too literally, for "more likely it was primarily intended as a selling point."[3]

That Haydn was carrying on a small sales campaign for the new quartets is evident from another letter, of the same date, to a Bavarian prince, with the "special way" message again included, though now in discreet lowercase.[4] Indeed, as indicated by the concentration of musical idea and material as well as the deft part writing in "The Joke" quartet, the works of Op. 33 certainly merit the esteem given them by the composer.

It is also possible that he was promoting a different tone in these pieces, one more suited to the tastes of a lay, even though initiated, audience. This is by no means frivolous music, but it is, in Larsen's words, "lighter, more easy-going"[5] than the preceding set. We can compare to Op. 33, for example, the pensive slow movement of Op. 20, No. 4, the far-from-capricious Capriccio of No. 2, or the turbulent Allegro di molto of No. 3, and the various fugal finales of the set.

The break in quartet output between Opp. 20 and 33 did not, however, necessarily constitute a period of wonderment on Haydn's part about the direction his quartet writing should take. What with producing eleven symphonies and a dozen operas and dramatic works in the years 1773-80, among his assorted creative and performing duties, Haydn simply had other things to think about. He had not lost interest in the quartet medium, but would continue into old age writing fruitfully in that vein. Op. 33 stands at midpoint in his productive career; the freshness of his viewpoint is vividly evident.

I   *Allegro moderato.* The nickname of this quartet comes from the way the finale ends. I think, though, that it should also apply to some earlier aspects of the work, and certainly to the quartet's beginning. Note that the 1st violin is asked to play the opening theme in *cantabile* fashion. Everything is sweetness, light, and elegance. The inner voices might well play their 8th-notes in the first three measures at the tip of the bow in order to reinforce this sense. The same holds true for the cello in its bass quarter-notes, and especially when it joins the inner parts for the cadence in

4   bar 4.

Fine, but where's the joke? Just look at the 1st violin part. Why does it break its easy, legato stride with the tripping, compressed jumps in bars 2 and 4? Why does it

5   let these leaps lead it astray into the agitations of bars 5 and 6 (answered by the eager chirps of the inner voices)? From here to the mock military stampings of m. 7

8   is the next step in an apparent change of character. In bar 8, however, the melody seems to smooth itself, as though slyly commenting on its own inconstancy. Then

9   again, in mm. 9-12, we find the melody is its old, *cantabile* self. We are obviously dealing with a musical coquette.

Haydn is not through flirting with us. The bridge passage, starting at the upbeat to m. 13, begins as though it is a development based on two elements of the 13
opening theme. Here, the several voices have to adopt either the singing or the vivacious tone, as the individual part and moment dictate. Well and good, so long as our maneuvers will get us to the second theme. But there proves to be none; we arrive at the dominant, B♭, in m. 21, to be sure, and that key is trumpeted in forte 21
chords a bar later. Much promised, little delivered: over the next two bars, we tiptoe forward, gradually aware that we are passing beyond any possibility of a theme. Bar 25 throws the 1st violin into a flurry of activity—the dotted notes here should 25
be more on the string than off, for proper sonority and brilliance. Drumrolls for all hands, trumpetlike flourishes for the violin, and the quartet finds itself (mm. 28-32) 28
playing the close of the exposition. The stuff of these measures, appropriately enough, is again the chuckling figure first heard in m. 5, and is best played, I think, with light, pointed strokes near the tip of the bow.

The joke is on us, as players and listeners. We have been fed an ambiguous theme, an abridged, seemingly incomplete (and consequently, very short) section. Carrying out the repetition of these opening lines simply reinforces our sense of having been conned by a master of musical sleight of hand. Maybe we'll fare better in the rest of the movement. Maybe.

But don't count on it. Note the teasing, tentative forays, led successively by the cello and 1st violin, in the first two bars of the development. Safety looms over us, for the very next measure offers the haven of the opening theme—in the wrong key. Over the next five measures, the cello and violin vie with each other to possess the theme. The harmonic motion disorients us, so that when the violin offers the theme in the tonic, E♭, with the sense of a return to home base (mm. 41-42), we can no 41
longer trust the feeling. Sure enough, we are now led into an extended game of tag, which all hands must play with suitably *misterioso* tone. The two violins should begin their long notes (mm. 44-49) with little pulses of vibrato and bow speed (so 44
also the lower voices in bar 45). Viola and cello should imbue their comments with an air of breathless excitement in mm. 46-49. 46

All this energy culminates in the 1st violin's long, sustained tones of mm. 51- 51
53. Underneath, the chain of short, thematic gasps in the lower voices finally impels the violin to its own, responding chain (mm. 54-56) and to the sextuplet that 54
follows. Here, both in shape and placement in the section, the sextuplets mirror the earlier flurry of mm. 25 ff. We are home at last: in C minor! This is a last joke before the actual return at the upbeat to m. 63. Note, however, that this development 63
section has been no trifle; it is fully as long as the exposition that preceded it.

The recapitulation is some measures shorter, because it gives up a repetition of the theme statement, moving instead directly into the bridge passage. Moreover, it manages without any coda whatsoever. It ends just as did the exposition—with a tag based on the rhythm of the theme's opening. In fact, the 1st violin's last three notes are exactly those with which it started the movement. Even if the ensemble chooses not to repeat the development and recapitulation, everyone will clearly feel the implication of an endless round of repetitions.

With or without the repeat, the 1st violin would do well to make a very slight comma between the A♭ and B♭ of its last measure, then play the thematic sign-off with some flavor of the movement's opening. Don't overdo; use just enough of a melodic wink to include the audience in the fun.

Scherzo. Allegro. The 1st violin is alone on each of the first three upbeats of II this movement. In each case, all four instruments join for the low chords that follow. I think it is a mistake to pummel the daylights out of the chords. They are orchestrated fully enough to make themselves felt. There will be more fun if the violin's couplet 8th-notes shine out above a relatively restrained, low-register

4   chorus. By the same token, the 2nd violin should be aware that its A♭s, in mm. 4-6, are the top voice of the moment. They should be played on the E-string, to glow through the piano dynamic, rather than be colored with the subdued sonority of the A-string. Then, the impetus of the 1st violin's trapeze-like swing through the 8th-

6   notes of mm. 6-8 should not be crushed by oafish stomping on the quarter-notes of bar 9; rather, the line should carry through to the cadence's resolution in m. 10.

11   The alternation of violins in 11-15 is just that, not a contest for prominence. Each line should shade the end of its statement so the partner's entrance can be heard without forcing. When viola and 1st violin join for the tripping, 8th-note

16   descent of mm. 16-18, they must construct a line that moves easily to, and through, the completion of the motion in the ascending run of the 2nd violin and cello in

19   mm. 19-20. The downbeat of m. 19 is the center of emphasis in the whole complex. After all the bouncing that has been going on, it is doubly important that you play the quiet music of mm. 20-23 not only truly quietly, but very smoothly, linking the 8th-note couplets in legato fashion.

34   Now, for the trio: there's simply no way around it; Haydn apparently did, very deliberately, call for one-finger slides and glissandi in the 1st violin part. All I can say is, "Easy does it!" Use light finger pressure during the slides, and also slow the bow stroke during the actual voyage from one note to the other. Any overemphasis on the slide will turn the composer's good-humored sound effect into a ghastly buffoonery. The smeary slides that marked even the serious performance of some soloists and ensembles in the 1920s have long passed from favor. All the more reason to treat Haydn's inspiration here with the respect and moderation it deserves. The 2nd violin will need special sensitivity if it mirrors the 1st's slide in

58   their duet in mm. 58-60. Two players on banana peels?

51   The violins' duet actually runs, of course, throughout the trio. In bars 51-56, the 2nd violin is clearly as important as the 1st, and must play the 8th-note line with soloistic innuendo and rubato. In the rest of the trio, however, the performer cannot retreat into the mentality of a simple Alberti bass player. There must still be a bit of melodic illumination to the line, responding to the motion of the 1st violin, not just offering a static background to it. Both instruments, incidentally, can step up the dynamic level somewhat for the first portion of the second section (up to the

60   fermata in m. 60). The single indication of piano at the start of the trio really cannot remain unchanged for the entire episode. For that matter, the piano should be restored and even reduced to pianissimo, especially for the closing measures before the da capo.

    As for the lower voices in the trio: they, too, will necessarily be influenced by the events in the violin solo. There can be no stolid and inflexible timekeeping. In

46   measures 46 and 50 (with attendant up- and downbeats) the low voices serve as important, melodic connective tissue and must act accordingly. The cello's

56   monotone line in mm. 56-60 (with the viola as an ally) needs flexible treatment to reflect the innuendos of the violin lines.

III, 4   *Largo e sostenuto.* Don't misinterpret the *tenuto* indication in bar 4. The resolving stress of the opening phrase belongs on the first beat of m. 3, with the succeeding notes treated as accessories to, and runoffs from, that emphasis. The decrescendo in m. 4 should actually begin during the preceding measure to produce the desired effect. On the other hand, in the second set of four measures, rounding out the opening phrase, the closing stress does belong at the end, on the B♭ at the start of m. 8. Haydn verifies this approach by his handling of the second [8] statement of the phrase. The cello tremolo (actually an ornamented pedal point on the dominant) begins in bar 11, highlighting the initial resolution; in the second half [11] of the statement, the corresponding tremolo in the 2nd violin occurs precisely on the full resolution in bar 16. [16]

As you look ahead through the movement, you will note that the 16th-note oscillation is a consistent feature of the writing. After its first appearance as cadential decoration, it becomes an essential element in the ornamental foils that set off the theme. This rhythmic figuration appears also in the closing bars of the contrasting theme (mm. 25 ff.), again with a characteristic decrescendo marking. [25] Use some opposing crescendo in the course of bar 29, even though the entry of the [29] two lower voices, forte, at the end of that bar helps provide dynamic thickening through the orchestration itself.

In the ornamented setting of the first theme that now follows, the 1st violin would do well to reflect the indicated decrescendo of the inner voices in bar 35, [35] returning to a stronger level through the fourth quarter of that measure. Haydn is astute enough not to overdo the 16th-note figures as he progresses through the movement. The four-measure beginning of the contrasting theme, as well as the brief offshoot thereof (mm. 60-61), are left in the clear. Around these islands, [60] however, the rhythmic foliage prevails. Whichever instrument carries the rhythm— for the most part the 1st violin and viola, with a few measures for the 2nd violin at the end of the movement—the motion must be treated as a freely improvised garland around the underlying melodic line. A rigidly counted performance of the 16ths will coat the melody with cement, absolutely defeating the musical inventiveness of the composer.

Finale: Presto. Now, the joke we've all been waiting for. In all things [IV] humorous, the element of surprise is central to the effect. The unexpected must be imposed on the senses of the person surprised. This implies that the "victim" will first have been conditioned to expect something that is eventually either denied or replaced by something incongruous.

Considering the way this finale ends, it's clear that Haydn was acting with (good-natured) malice aforethought when he contrived the theme. A squarer subject would be difficult to construct. There are three statements of an identical rhythmic pattern within the space of eight measures. Indeed, there would be four such two-measure segments, except that the third adds a diverting tag before moving on to the short cadential run, enlivened with a grace note, in the 1st violin part. The repetition of the opening segment inoculates the listener with the shape of the theme.

The second segment, too, reinforces the message. Although the third and fourth statements here (mm. 13-16) have modified endings, they bear the trademark [13] rhythm of the theme. A four-bar flurry (mm. 17-20) offers contrast and relief. The [17] next measures, however, already contain a hint of the eventual surprise, without actually giving the trick away: note the interruptions in the violin parts in mm. 22, [22] 23, and 24, and the sighing cadence in mm. 27-28. Here, incidentally, the piano [27] dynamic that is given "in some Mss." (see footnote, p. 15 of the score used here) is an advisable bit of musical business, pointing up the element of momentary surprise that results from the sudden frustrating of the running-triplet 8th-notes. Just in case you have forgotten the oft-heard rhythmic pattern, you get a further dose of it in the remaining bars of the section; and yet again, for good measure, in the repeat of the section as a whole.

In view of all this musical lecturing, I would take the opening indication of forte with an interpretative grain of salt. A light approach will keep matters from turning tedious and will help convince the audience that they are party to the fun making. Similarly, the bagpipe chorus played by the three lower parts in mm. 41 ff., under the 1st violin's merry dance, should not be pressed too hard. Give the forzandi a shot of vibrato, a slight spurt of bow, and then continue easily to the next emphasis point.

41

It's all part of the gag that, after sprinting along for some thirty measures, the violin should suddenly and without warning run into the roadblock of the three downbeats, mm. 68-70. (Avoid suicidal impact!) The last of the downbeats is followed by an extra measure of pause. The ensemble may conspire by stretching this silence very slightly, then resuming the opening music at full tilt. Thus all can enjoy the sense of non sequitur here.

68

Things resume in carefree manner, with a note of fresh hilarity introduced by the imitative repartée of the three lower voices (see mm. 108 ff.). Note that the 1st violin switches to a spectator role for part of this passage, tootling away on a string of B♭s. In effect, the violin is taking over the role of bass in this inversion of part writing, since the cello had played its own B♭s in a supporting role in mm. 22-28 and 87-99. The exposure of this monotone tattoo in the brilliant register of the violin's E-string gives it a special and exuberant flavor. Emphasize this state of affairs by playing the line with some melodic insistence, rather than try to tame it into a semblance of modest support.

108

22
87

The cat is all but out of the bag now: three beginnings (mm. 132 ff.) run into a silence; another two starts run into the familiar, sighing resolution. This time, though, the sigh is spelled out by Haydn's fermate over both notes thereof (mm. 139-40). Notice the third hold, on the quarter-rest immediately following. Don't prolong this unduly, for it is meant only to suggest what is to come.

132

139

Yet another beginning, seemingly successful this time, founders on the ultimate interruption: silence. The hold on the rest in m. 148 should be fully savored, not only for its dramatic effect, but also to allow for an adjustment of the mental time frame to the quasi-recitative Adagio that lies just ahead. In the Adagio itself, the stentorian, forte chords are followed by the demure murmurs of the 1st violin, raising the gag to a clownish level. The violin needs to play the hushed couplets in these bars with a certain palpitating flutter; otherwise, the slightly ridiculous alternation of the pompous louds and the modest, quiet notes is minimized, if not entirely lost.

148

The Adagio, in turn, has set us up for—at long last—the joke. We have been thoroughly prepared and thoroughly confused by Haydn's shenanigans. We have been conditioned not only to expect a complete rendition of the theme of the movement, but have also been programmed to recognize that the theme can be broken along its rhythmic fragmentation lines. Finally, we have been taught that breaks between the fragments can be extended. Now, however, the composer goes that one last step: the tune is played in full, consecutive order, but a two-measure rest follows each melodic unit. Very strange, we admit; even so, we absorb this latest musical manipulation or mistreatment and are all set for a repetition of this crippled version—and are made to wait through fully four measures of silence before the replay starts. (Don't shortchange this rest by one iota!) Now comes the first fragment of the expected repetition, loaded with the emotional freight suggested by the composer's call for pianissimo. There is no more, however; this is the end and, as we have seen, it is an ending suggested by the very beginning of the movement.

By now, it must be clear that this joke is really meant for the sophisticated, initiated ear. The more we listen to the movement, the more we appreciate the skill with which we are prepared for the trick ending. Haydn actually compels us to educate ourselves for this last surprise.

FINALE
Rondo, *in the Gypsies' stile*
Presto

III

CHAPTER TWO

❧ Haydn ❧
Piano Trio in G, Hob. XV:25
("Gypsy Rondo")

My very first chamber music experience was in a piano trio at music school in New York City. I must have been about nine years old. I'm sorry to say I don't remember what our ensemble played, but I'm relieved that I also can't remember how we played it! My next chamber effort was in a family ensemble, some years later. I can recall how I acquitted myself then, but I'll try to steer you in a better direction. As it happens, the piece we played *en famille* was the one here at hand, the "Gypsy Rondo" trio of Haydn. I'm sure the reason we worked on that particular trio was for the fun we had with the gypsy finale. We didn't know it then, but Haydn was giving us more than a whimsical title—he was feeding us some authentic Hungarian folk music in that third movement. Something else that I did not recognize then is now clear to me: there is great musical profit and pleasure to be won from the first two movements as well.

This trio was one of a number of such works composed by Haydn during his second stay in London (February 1794 to August 1795). It appeared as the second of a set of three trios, which are now catalogued as Hob. XV:24-26. The set was written in the summer of 1795 and published by the London firm of Longman and Broderip in October of that year. The trios were dedicated to Rebecca Schroeter, a London widow to whom Haydn developed a warm attachment during his visits to England.[1]

Andante. This is a set of variations[2], so we cannot assume that our opening

I

SCORE: Joseph Haydn. 1970. *Trio No. 39, in G. (Hob. XV:25)*. Urtext. Ed. H. C. Robbins Landon. Vienna: Doblinger. Score and parts. Diletto Musicale No. 489.

Left: Joseph Haydn: Piano Trio in G, Hob. XV:25. Urtext. Ed. H. C. Robbins Landon. Vienna: Doblinger, 1970 (Diletto Musicale No. 489). Page 12 of piano score. Used by permission of Music Associates of America, agent for Ludwig Doblinger (Bernard Herzmansky) K. G.

tempo will hold true for each of the sections of the movement. Find an andante swing that will allow the theme itself to move at convincing pace, without laborious prominence of the 8th-notes in the measure. The signature is 2/4; but beyond that, we should look toward the relationship of larger gatherings of measures and try to reveal those groupings in our playing.

4
10
Our first resting point is the downbeat of m. 4; our next is six measures later, at the downbeat of bar 10. There is a lesser punctuation after the third 8th-note of the second bar; this is implied by the wedge mark on that note in the violin and the piano treble. Today we tend to think of the wedge as denoting a short, sharp attack on the note in question; I ask you to regard it here, instead, as a call for lightness and lift, a breath taken before proceeding with the melody.

1, 11
2, 12
I hesitate to quarrel with the authenticity of the markings in an *Urtext* edition, but I fail to see the point of dividing the violin line into two 8th-note couplets in bars 1 and 11, while the piano part proceeds with one slur over the whole measure. I would rather have the violin pursue the same continuous motion toward the downbeat of bars 2 and 12.

5
4
6
The ensemble ought to give some thought to the articulation of the cello and piano-bass lines in mm. 5 ff. The slurring is again inconsistent, both within the line and in relation to the activity in other voices. Why are the notes in the low lines slurred in bar 4, but not in m. 5 (certainly the first three 8th-notes should be tied there)? And again, why slur the cello part at the end of m. 6 and throughout bar 7, while the corresponding notes in the piano-bass are shown as detached? You should appraise such differences throughout the piece, and settle matters on a case-by-case basis.

8
9
The turn on the second 8th of the violin part in bar 8, as well as the fact that both violin and piano will be joining in such embellishment in the next measure, justifies the difference in articulation between violin and piano-treble in m. 8. Note, however, that the piano figure on the second 8th of m. 9 should be slurred.

12, 17
I am puzzled once again, however, by the difference in slurring between piano and violin in bars 12 and 17. I hope this does not mean the editor condones a strong contrast in texture between the playing of the lines in the two instruments. There seems no compelling reason to have the keyboard play in detached fashion at the same time that the violin treats the figure in legato. Even so, the string performer knows that the two dotted figures can be played with snap and incisiveness within a single stroke, when desired.

19
In mm. 19-20 of the theme, the cello and piano-bass should play as though the downbeat of bar 19 is the true close, the rest of the phrase falling away, though with a supplementary emphasis on the final downbeat. At that spot, by the way, the wedge mark should again be treated circumspectly.

Var. I/22
In Variation I (mm. 22 ff.), my own impulse is to take a slightly faster tempo, in keeping with its darker and aggressive tone. The 16th-notes in the piano-bass that enlivened the cadence of the theme now become a prominent thread in the action of this variation. The pulse is revealed continuously from the fifth measure on, in middle- and high-register placement. This area, cast in B♭ (the relative major of the section's tonic), is lit by the high solo of the violin. As in the theme, the cello reinforces the bass line.

This raises the question of the nature of the keyboard in music of this vintage. In Haydn's time, the ensemble would still have had its choice between using harpsichord or piano in performing the trio, the decision depending not only on preference but on availability of instrument. The sound of the harpsichord is not without sustaining power. The tone, however, is rather delicate and seems to die away quickly. It was, therefore, the habit of composers in the 17th and 18th centuries to reinforce the bass line of the keyboard part with the sound of a sustaining instrument such as the cello.

For that matter, the piano in the later 18th century, the fortepiano, was a softer-toned instrument than the one we play today. Our grand piano is engineered to produce significantly louder sound than the instrument Haydn and Mozart knew. When it comes to the full-size, concert grand, there is absolutely no contest: even with the lid of the instrument fully closed, a determined pianist now can blanket the efforts of his string colleagues.

The answer is clear. You may be playing this trio in a concert hall of some size. Nonetheless, this is intimate music. The ensemble must work for the balance inherent in the writing. You can play the modern piano so deftly that some semblance of the older, lighter, drier sound emerges, one that indeed allows for the collaboration of the cello's complementary tones.[3] If this happens, you and your listeners will enjoy some of that delicate mixture of tonal flavors that our ancestors relished and exploited.

In the second section of the theme statement, there was a quickening effect produced by the succession of various ascending, dotted figures (see mm. 13, 15- 17). In Variation I, similar figures appear in mm. 31 and 33, supported by the tremolo 16th-note line in the piano-bass. Indeed, that support is a middle-register thread of turbulence, one that already appears in the later bars of the variation's first section. The cello line, also in middle register, provides a broader version of the piano's sustaining bass.

13

31

The tremolo rhythm becomes a prominent part of the closing lines of the variation. There the 16th-note motion in the piano eddies around the broader melodic lines of the two strings. A pivotal measure in this activity is bar 35, where the violin's triplets create a strong crosscurrent against the 16th- and 8th-note pulse in the other two parts. This bar must be played with suitable agitation and a hint of acceleration. You want to get to the peak of the high D in m. 36, from which the tension will recede all the way down to the double bar.

35

36

Before discussing Variation II, let's look back and ahead in the score. In the statement of the theme, 8th-notes dominate the rhythmic flow. As already seen, 16th-note motion is prominent in Variation I. In the second variation, the 16th-note pulse quickens to triplets. This remains the governing rhythmic unit in Variation III, intensified now by more vigorous and compressed intervallic leaps. Variation IV, the closing part of the movement, goes one notch farther: 16th triplets are replaced by quadruplets of 32nds.

Fairly obvious? If you think that, so will your listeners. They will only hear a theme, followed in rather pallid fashion by four echo sections. The ensemble has to play as though the composed speedup of note values is exciting to them. Please don't treat this Andante and the slow movement as inconsequential preludes to a familiar and more exciting finale. One scholar, indeed, seems to suggest that Haydn might have calculated just such a relationship between the three movements, inasmuch as the first two "hardly prepare one for [the finale's] burst of energy."[4] Though Haydn learned how to attract and hold the attention of his London audiences, I don't think he would have gone so far as to have his listeners sleep through the opening movements of this trio in order to sharpen their relish for the third.

In any event, Variation II in this Andante belongs to the piano. The violin plays the theme throughout and joins the keyboard in some of the triplet activity in the second half of the section. Overall, though, it is the piano that provides the distinctive rhythmic ornamentation of this variation. The bass line, shared by cello and piano, does some leaping to suggest incorporation of two voices, and also takes some part in the triplet rhythms (see mm. 47-49).

A few particulars about the part writing in the piano voice: at the beginning and also at a later point in the variation, the triplets are presented in antiphonal response between the keyboard bass and treble. In bars 47-48, at least three lines are at work in the one instrument: triplet repartée between "soprano" and "alto" parts in the right hand, and supporting bass (two-voiced in its own right) in the left. Try to lend a distinct sonority to each of the participant voices in these patches of conversation.

There are, to be sure, limits to the tonal shadings that even the skilled pianist can evoke. But you can also use phrasing, articulation, and rubato to good effect in illuminating the part writing. The bass triplets in mm. 43-44 might be played a bit on the hale and forthright side; the "soprano" reply in bars 44-46 can be both more demure and expansive. This attitude can, in turn, affect the bass line's continuation of the triplets in its descent in m. 46. The contrast between the spreading and more forward-moving attitudes can then be carried forward by the high and middle parts in bars 47-48, where the responses seem to take place in each half measure. Both characters can intermingle in the extended sweep of triplets in bars 49-51. The string instruments and especially the violin—since it carries the tune—are naturally involved in all this. Experiment together to see what can be worked out.

All hands will be cooperating closely in the interlocking doubling of parts in mm. 57-58. And m. 55 gives the piano a great opportunity to trip the light fantastic in the upward scale of 32nds, as though to the amazement of the onlookers, who are represented by the three lines of sustained tones. A moment of poise on the high C♯ in m. 56 should precede the resolution on D and the resumption of motion in the second half of the bar.

The 8ths in mm. 61-62 should not be phlegmatic; move with the triplets in the piano-treble. Once again, the strings should translate the wedge marks in these lines into light and pointed strokes.

As in Haydn's "Joke" Quartet, the nickname of this trio comes from its finale, with the added point that Haydn himself, this time around, gave the gypsy title to that movement. I think, however, that the composer is foreshadowing the finale in his treatment of the third variation of the first movement. Some of the gypsy flair seems already in evidence in the violin part here. Don't minimize the diving and swooping of the line in the first measure and in similar bars later on. Take the string crossings smoothly, of course; but bring attention to the up-and-down topography of the line through the use of rubato. The temper of this solo is best served by on-the-string playing, in the upper half of the bow.

Wedge marks are printed in the piano part in the first half of the variation. In view of the vigor and angularity of the violin line above, a correspondingly sharp interpretation of the piano's marks seems appropriate here. It is also fitting that such marks are absent in the opening measures of the second section, where the violin line itself is smoother both in shape and temperament. On the other hand, you should think of the wedges again when playing the accompaniment in bars 75-76, unless the violinist has chosen to end the scene with an emphasis on the pathetic side.

Var. II/42

47

47

43
44

46

47
49

55, 57

56

61

Var. III/63

75

Variation IV, as already mentioned, gives the movement a lively close, owing to the constant patter of 32nds in the piano part. You have to be careful not to make the music sound as though it just runs off the edge of the page. The solution is not simply a matter of stepping on the musical brakes over the last couple of measures. Throughout, make the shape of the theme emerge clearly from within the barrage of notes. Var. IV/78

Haydn does everything he can to help the players: his slower-moving lines serve as the frame on which the rapid-fire tracery is draped. The piano should listen to the violin and cello—and to its own bass line—and try to coordinate the 32nds with those voices. Conversely, try also to direct the course of the string lines by the way you bend your virtuoso display.

As an example: in mm. 83-84, the slower-moving lines go through the two 8ths on the first beat of the bar to get to the second quarter-beat, then rest on that note. In these two measures, the piano treble is held within the frame of the motion in the other voices. Mm. 85-88 progress toward the A in the violin (the start of bar 86), then steadily onward and downward to the D of bar 88: that is, through the fifth of the dominant, then on to the dominant proper, D. In all four of these bars, the piano leads the way. 83
85
88

In the last measures of the movement, the piano obviously leads in bars 93-96. From the true end of the movement—the downbeat of m. 97—all three instruments float down to the lower G major chord. Before resolving to that chord, linger a bit on the dissonance created by the suspension on the downbeat of the last measure. Haydn has used the device at the end of Variations II and III. Now, at the final double bar, you have time to enjoy the tart flavor of the sound. 93
97

Poco Adagio. There are no great technical problems in this movement, but there is that unending sea, that quicksand of triplets. Except for the downbeats of the section endings, mm. 8 and 16, and the sustained chord of the last two bars, triplets occur on every beat of each of the pianist's 64 measures. Resist the rhythmic siren song and keep your wits about you. II

8, 16

In the first movement, the ever-quickening line of the variations was a vehicle for the decoration of the theme. In this Adagio, the triplets start as an ornamentation of the bass line. The motion flows into the treble register of the piano part at certain points, sometimes filling in while the bass rests at a cadence. With these exceptions, though, the triplets are the floor upon which the musical structure rests.

On a floor of battleship-grey linoleum, you might move about with smooth efficiency. A richly detailed floor of fine woods or mosaic tile, however, would become to some degree an inspiration to your feet. So it is in this movement. There is melody and accompaniment, but it is not easy to tell which has the greater appeal to the ear. The melody has the interest that comes from the succession of contrasting note values; the accompaniment has only one rhythmic element, but uses it to trace constantly around imaginative shapes and through ever-shifting harmonic colors.

In bar 10, the triplets in the piano-treble have become the solo voice. In the following measure, the bass line, now so high that its figures are written in treble clef, merges at very close interval with the melody in the upper staff of the piano part. By bar 12, there is the suggestion that the accompanying triplets have risen to coloratura heights, to move in parallel thirds with the topmost, melodic line. 10

12

In the middle episode of the movement (mm. 17 ff.), the bass role is assigned to a sustained line, set quite low. Now restored to its original register, the triplet 17 melody (for so it has become) can duet with the violin melody at some distance. The space between the high, middle, and low strata in these measures creates a sonority rich beyond what one might expect from the simplicity of the writing.

The violin melody in this section of the movement is ineffably beautiful, deserving comparison with the best of those contrived even by Mozart. Follow the *cantabile* instruction, but don't overheat the tune. In fact, the tone should be a touch on the cool side, with moderate vibrato, reserving increased warmth for measures such as 22-28. Even there, the greater intensity should begin only with measure 25. Another moderate wave of intensity will make itself felt in bars 41-44, before the movement settles back into the first theme.

In the recall of the opening, the violin plays in octaves with the piano. Especially in view of this doubling, the players must make a choice. Either assume that the octave statement of the theme implies that it now should be played as a louder apotheosis of its original self. Or decide that the total sound should be no stronger than before, but endowed with a new color. Experiment to see which effect is more convincing to your ensemble.

The group can scarcely ignore a point that Haydn makes at the end of the movement. Two measures before the double bar, the composer prepares for the resolution on the tonic by sounding the chord of the dominant seventh. At the same time, the piano is given a low E, which clashes with the preparatory chord but announces the tonic to come. To make sure there is no doubt about his meaning, Haydn also assigns the E to the cello, but has that instrument play it in triplets; this gently drums the note into the attention of the listener. The ensemble should not overstress this insistence. Still, let the cellist play the triplets with a bit of rubato flair—it is, after all, a solo.

For that matter, the cello is generally a partner in the activity of this movement. The instrument gets bits of legato melody from time to time, either directly doubling the piano-bass or defining a progression that is concealed in the piano's triplets. In these places, the cello is clearly part of a duet with the violin. Even when rests interrupt the cello's progress from one tone to the next in the supporting line, a sense of broad melodic continuity can be achieved.

In short, this is a challenging movement for all three players. The tempo lets you float easily from solo to accompaniment role, with constant enjoyment of the changing perspective. Try to adjust yourself to this kind of thinking in rehearsal and maintain it also in your concert performance.

Finale. Rondo in the Gypsies' stile. Presto. Haydn presents us with a rather dandified gypsy, one who—like the minstrel of old—has been admitted at least to the fringe of the courtly circle. A contemporary drawing, indeed, shows a gypsy band in action at the Esterhazy palace.[5]

Our protagonist seems willing to dance sedately, though quickly, in two-, four-, and eight-bar phrases. Even more: he is ready to go through a literal repeat of the steps, though an octave higher, in order to let the violin double the piano—clearly, a gypsy well schooled in the ways of classic composition.

By attaching the specific title to this finale, Haydn appeals to his English hearers' taste for the exotic. But the Hungarian folk-dance influence was far from new in Haydn's music. Bence Szabolczi lists sixteen Haydn works, dating from 1766 through 1802, in which such influence may be discerned.[6] Included in that roster, of course, is the *Allegretto alla zingarese* ("in the gypsy manner"), the minuet movement of the D major quartet, Op. 20, No. 4.

22
25
41

63

III

In the present finale, the G major tune that serves as the refrain, and at least two of the contrast tunes in the movement (those in G minor—see mm. 67 and 121—with the B♭ sequel to the second of these as well) have all come from the popular repertoire of the time. The minor tunes, in fact, are both drawn from one of the dance melodies that were "used for the recruiting of soldiers by Austrian officials, who employed Gypsy bands to entice the [Hungarian] peasants to the [tavern to enlist], seduced by the strains of the most interesting 'folk music' in Europe and plied with the local *Tokay* wine."[7]

The composer apparently wants to assure that we recognize the gypsy in our midst, for the upbeat forzandi in bars 16 and 17 seem to have been added by Haydn himself. These are quickly gone, so make the most of them. The next whiff of exoticism comes in m. 35. The violin's long G, and its fellows in later measures, is a rather theatrical touch. I am surprised that Haydn did not put an accent or forzando on the note, but perhaps he felt that such signs would gild the lily. Nonetheless, the note needs a bit of pressure, something like a mezzo forte or even louder inset, with a decrescendo through the length of the dotted quarter, and a rebuilding of level leading to the downbeat of bar 37.

Underneath, the cello and piano should be drumming away, with bluff emphasis on each downbeat 8th. The piano can reinforce the violin's trill on the second beat of bar 37 with suitable pressure on the treble chord at that point, and then proceed to play the 16ths of the next downbeat as a rather snappy flourish of notes. In the violin part, by the way, every one of the four onbeat 16ths in m. 36 should be played with a bit of bow thrust, so that each 8th-note step is brusquely accented. (The same for similar measures to come.)

All three instruments need a short catch of breath before the last 8th of bar 38, so that the repeat of the phrase can be properly introduced. The violin's short trill at the end of that restatement (m. 42) should have an accented start and be played with very athletic finger.

In each four-bar unit from m. 51 through 66, the first pair of measures needs a slightly—but noticeably—slower tempo than the fortissimo second pair. In mm. 59-62, the cello should strongly project the grace notes attached to each beat. This involves not only a firm bowing attack on the grace note, but also a finger (ready to vibrate) thrown briskly onto the string to play the 8th-note that follows.

Unleash the liveliest presto yet attained in the movement when you get to the change of key at bar 67. Play the forzandi in the piano and violin with some reinforcement from accompanying instruments, even though the supporting voices are not so instructed.

The pizzicati in the violin in bars 83-86 should be played with the left hand, in order not to pull the tempo back. In the second and fourth measures of the group, use the third finger to pluck the open D, both for best resonance on the note and also because that finger is not involved in playing the preceding 8th. For extra flavor in the performance, I suggest a slight acceleration over the four bars from m. 89 to 92, with a sudden pullback to basic tempo in bar 93.

Mm. 121, 122, 125 and 126: each needs to be followed by a short comma, to identify the bar as an individual unit. On the other hand, the two measures that complete each four-bar phrase (123-24, 127-28) should be played in a continuous sweep, with proper thrust on the offbeat sforzando.

In the next section, mm. 129-30 and 131-32 must be clearly defined as two-bar units; then, move without hesitation through the eight measures from bar 133 to

135
141

140, with enough thrust of bow and vibrato on the second 8th of mm. 135 and 139 to spice the activity. The repetition of all this in fortissimo (mm. 141 ff.) calls for more of the same, but now at a fiery level of intensity.

152

I don't see how you can run, loudly and at full tilt, into the double bar at the end of m. 152 and then drop abruptly into the demure quietness of the refrain in bar 153. Permit yourself some relaxation of tension and a decrescendo in the one-measure scale run that leads into the return.

Now for the coda. Does Haydn choose to end on the more courtly note of the refrain, rather than make an exit in gypsy vein? I suggest that you play as though the gypsy in you can no longer be suppressed. At the very least, indulge in a quick acceleration to something like a prestissimo. As the old stage instructions have it, "Exit laughing."

My advice about this finale may perhaps smack too much of present-day, stereotypical assumptions about gypsy music. On the other hand, Haydn himself was using his borrowed melodies to appeal to his audience, as Robbins Landon has surmised: "Probably the English public had had very little opportunity to hear this 'exotic' music, and [Haydn] found that it was very popular with the 'nobility and gentry'."[8] He had also had experience with English interest in folk music generally; for, starting early in his first visit to England, he lent his hand and name to arrangements of Scottish, Irish, and Welsh folk songs that would eventually amount to a list of almost 400 titles.[9]

I encourage you to take sensitive and educated liberties in realizing the composer's intent in this movement. If you are hesitant about this, be aware that Eva Badura-Skoda has suggested that the Gypsy Rondo was meant to be played on a fortepiano that "has a percussion stop—a drum attached underneath."[10] By the time you decide where the drum stop might appropriately have been used in this movement, I think your inhibitions will be somewhat relaxed. It seems clear that Haydn indicated only in the most sparing terms the shadings and contrasts that he wanted the players to make. The rest is up to you.

MENUETTO.

Allegro ma non troppo.

CHAPTER THREE

❧ Haydn ❧
Quartet in D minor, Op. 76, No. 2 ("Quinten")

In the first chapter, we saw Haydn intently cultivating high humor in a quartet written when he was approaching the age of fifty. We turn now to a work from his middle 60s. This quartet is a different cup of tea, but Haydn is again very serious about his musical concerns. And once more, the basic premise of the composition has given rise to its nickname: the "Quinten," or "Fifths" Quartet. Haydn puts the interval of the fifth, and himself as well, through all possible paces. The challenge to the player is almost as great.

Prince Nikolaus Esterhazy, Haydn's master for three decades, died in the autumn of 1790. Under the regime of his son, Prince Anton, the court music was greatly curtailed; now on pension, Haydn moved to the city of his youth, Vienna. Before the year was out, he was on his way to London for the first of two triumphal visits to England. Back in Vienna from mid-June of 1792 until leaving for England again in January of 1794, he wrote the six quartets of Opp. 71 and 74, intended for presentation during his next London stay. The first visit to London, its auditoriums, and its audiences had made a lasting impression on Haydn and affected the 71 and 74 quartets.[1] It was after his second return home, in late August of 1795, that—in 1797—he composed the set of six quartets, Op. 76.

On hearing these pieces, the English musicographer, Charles Burney, wrote these oft-cited words of praise:

SCORE: Joseph Haydn. 1982. *Streichquartette. Urtext-Ausgabe. Quartetto D-moll, Op. 76, No. 2, Hob. III:76.* Ed. Reginald Barrett-Ayres and H. C. Robbins Landon. Vienna: Doblinger. Miniature score No. 480.

Left: Joseph Haydn: Quartet in D minor, Op. 76, No. 2, first page of the score of the Menuetto. Berlin: Trautwein, 1843. Reproduced with permission from the collection of the Sibley Music Library, the Eastman School of Music, University of Rochester.

They are full of invention, fire, good taste, and new effects, and seem the production, not of a sublime genius who has written so much and so well already, but of one of highly-cultivated talents, who had expended none of his fire before.[2]

If you have had the pleasure of studying and performing, for example, the variations movement of the "Emperor" Quartet (Op. 76, No. 3), the first movement of the "Sunrise" Quartet (Op. 76, No. 4), or the slow movement—in F♯ major!—of the extremely innovative quartet in D (Op. 76, No. 5), you will agree that Burney did not exaggerate. Let us turn now, however, to the quartet at hand, Op. 76, No. 2.

I   *Allegro*. When Haydn invented a concept for a composition, he pursued it ingeniously and with great persistence. Now we find these qualities displayed with particular intensity in the "Quinten" Quartet. So sharp is the focus on the central motive in this opening movement, in fact, that I was relieved not to have to play the work too often in the later years of my quartet career. In part, this was because I found more excitement and stimulus in other works of the Op. 76 set (especially Nos. 4 and 5); more important, I secretly resented being lectured so sternly by Haydn about the inescapable theme. Yet I have had a change of heart.

In fact, on fresh and considered reinspection of the work, I now recognize it as one of Haydn's most convincing quartets. Further, the piece warrants study because concert audiences demand it, though perhaps not as often as they should, amateur groups love to play it, and, last but not least, student ensembles have to learn it. I credit an imaginative article for acquainting me with niceties in the work that had previously, I must confess, escaped my jaundiced eye.[3]

First, however, a cautionary word from my own experience with the work: please do not attack the opening as though you are about to deliver a lecture on the power of the interval of the fifth! I myself was a willing partner in such a performance of the piece in one of our Chicago concerts, long ago. I was irate about the review, though I now realize that I should not have been surprised that it took us to task for the brusqueness of the interpretation.

The crux of the melody will be quite evident without a heavy-handed leaning on the half-notes that spell out the motive. A rather *cantabile*, elastic approach to this forte statement will prove effective and will carry you into the quicker rhythm of the third and fourth measures, and so to the resolution on the final A. The lower

1   voices should treat the 8th-note rhythms in mm. 1-2 as though they are spelling out the resonance of the parent half-notes, reflecting also the top line's impulse toward the second half of the phrase.

This impulse is exploited in the piano restatement of the theme, accounting for

7   the additional measures (7-10) that extend the phrase; be sure to follow the arch of those bars lightly and swiftly, with the slightest hint of a pause before the decisive

11   resolution in mm. 11-12. In the passage that follows, there is a wonderfully exuberant and frolicsome air about the 1st violin line; it would be remiss to make it starchy and sober. It demands a light touch; the overlapping statements of the fifths in the lower voices should be clearly heard, without submerging the top line.

20   The forzandi in mm. 20-21 are deliberately placed; Haydn subordinates the sound of the falling fifth to the scalewise ascent of the downbeat tones. Play each bar as though it presents the resonance of a whole-note, only parenthetically

22   subdivided into halves. The ten measures that follow (22-31) are all fun and games, a kind of follow-the-leader episode—except that there is no leader. Of course, you

follow the 1st violin; but if all four players are not "leader" minded, such tricks as the rush to the downbeat of m. 25 and the sudden change to the half-note motion,   **25** or the equally sudden shift to the syncopes of bar 27, will never come off   **27** successfully. Incidentally, the *Urtext* score in use here shows no dots on the 8th-notes in m. 22, a fact I interpret as meaning that the on- and offbeat tones should be   **22** allowed to resonate freely, with some overlapping of the sounds. In short, the effect should be free, not crabbed and ascetic.

This certainly applies to the bold release of mm. 32 ff. The bowing of the 16th-notes in the 1st violin should be an energetic legato in the upper part of the bow,   **32** evoking a freely breathing resonance from the instrument. The thematic reference in the violin duet in mm. 34-35, with the trilled exchanges between the two players,   **34** should be generous and expansive, and so also the continuation of the idea in the inner voices in the ensuing four bars. There ought to be a hint of the juggler's art in the cellist's tossing of the 8th-notes in bars 34-35, with the transfer of the rhythm to   **34** the 1st violin in m. 36 figuratively resembling the catching of an exceptionally wide   **36** throw.

The octaves and assorted other intervals in the 1st violin in mm. 41-43 are   **41** easier than they look. Haydn is doing two things here: playing on the 8th-note rhythm that has figured so prominently in earlier measures; and amplifying the resonance of the drone and moving lines. The bowing should hug both strings and be legato in stroke, as though you are playing double stops that are only very slightly separated into the component tones. The effect is that of lightly drummed 8th-notes (the middle Cs), with the upper melody emerging through the sonority. In the lower voices, the broader sonority of the interweaving 8th-note lines emerges. All told, this is a marvelous exploitation of quartet sound.

Note that in m. 48, as in m. 18, the forzando is carefully placed on the middle   **48, 18** of the bar; in both cases, avoid any stress on the first note of the measure. The line must find its goal as shown, on the third beat, not before. Then, as the 1st violin makes its climb into the upper reaches of the E-string, let the lower voices go easy; this is no time for a shouting contest. As matters turn out, Haydn is en route to a tease: the violin suddenly becomes fascinated with its 16th-note turns, inspecting them during the four bars, 51-55. Play for the effect.   **51**

The cello threatens to continue this game; you will note that our score places the crescendo in bar 56 only on the last two beats of the measure. In the first two   **56** beats, the cello seems about to carry on the monologue it has inherited from the 1st violin. Only with the third beat and its crescendo is the chain broken; we are moved ahead, whether to the repeat or the development.

This development is a theme writer's holiday. Beginning with an inversion of the part writing and a mirror image of the theme in the cello part, Haydn contrives to have some manifestation of the figure's outline and rhythm, including versions in diminution and syncopation, in every measure of the section. The four last bars, 95-98, are an exception, though I suspect the theme may be present even there, in   **95** the guise of the whole-note double stops in the viola part. In such writing, the idea of four equal players is again of the essence; the musical ball passes from hand to hand so quickly that each member of the team must be ready to shift from accompanist to soloist role at a moment's notice.

Sometimes the two functions are combined, as in the 2nd violin's 8th-notes in bars 69-70. In one sense, these notes accompany the flashier gyration of the 1st   **69** violin line; at the same time, they are important as a duetting voice against that

85   part. Or again, what about the 1st violin's musings in mm. 85-88: are they more important than the cello's contemplation of the theme, some two octaves lower? In the same measures, the inner voices obviously have an accompanying function; yet

91   their 8th-notes, translated into the responses of the disguised syncopation in bar 91,

92   will then become the philosophical, all-but-solo quarter-notes of m. 92. It is clear, too, that in the last four measures of the development, the 2nd violin must consider itself an additional 1st.

99   The reversed dynamics in the theme statements that open the recapitulation (piano followed by forte, instead of the sequence at the beginning of the movement) must be religiously observed, since they are a calculated part of Haydn's layout of

115   the movement. Also deliberate is the succession of swells in mm. 115-17 and 123-25 (as well as in the coda), an expanded version of the compressed swells found earlier in mm. 26-27, 29-31. If overdone, however, the effect will sound like a chorus of barking seals.

130   As for taking the first ending, I'm against it. The transition (mm. 130 ff.) to the coda is so carefully worked out, and the dramatic impact of the voyage from the development into the recapitulation also so finely tuned, that I find the repeat of the latter two thirds of the movement to be anticlimactic.

The coda is a final, little development section in its own right, calling again for the democratic involvement of all members of the team. In the *Urtext* score, there

143   are no slurs over most of the quadruplet groupings of 16ths in mm. 143-48. The ensemble will have to decide whether the effect of the detached notes is gratifying. In any event, avoid a quarter-beat stress; play for the half bar. Harmonically, the

152   movement could be thought to end on the downbeat of bar 152. It is clear from Haydn's writing, however, that the peak of the fortissimo must be reserved for the very last chord; even there, the sound should be warm, not slashed.

II   *Andante o più tosto allegretto.* 1st violins of the world, hear my plea! I make it as a longtime inner voice in a quartet, and veteran of many a Haydn performance. In this Andante, you have a wonderful opportunity to inspire that captive stage audience of three—your fellow ensemble members. Your colleagues can invest their accompaniment with the nuance and artistry it well deserves, but they are hearing you play the solo line in what is probably far from the first concert presentation by your group. Please don't bore them to tears; play beautifully, and with that same, fresh enjoyment you had when experiencing the music for the first time. If you can surprise your friends with a new shading of inflection here and there, or with an unexpected (though logical) rubato, they will appreciate it and respond. They should not feel that they are part of a cut-and-dried exercise in musical bookkeeping.

In your approach to the solo, be aware that Haydn has done everything he can to avoid a humdrum treatment of the 6/8 meter. Note the placement of the many forzandi. They are always cast within the frame of a *mezza voce*; regard them as warmings, not poundings, of the tones in question. Along with a *tenuto*, an accent mark, dotted figures, and ornamental turns, these occur on any beat except the first in the measure. In fact, the first two or three 8th-notes in the bar are subordinated, set in the middle distance of the musical perspective, serving as points of rest rather than centers of activity in the melody. The offbeat, off-center targets of emphasis and motion, along with the constant shift between rest and propulsion, give this music a whimsicality and charm that should evoke the kind of freshness in performance that I called for above.

In the second strain of the opening (mm. 5 ff.), as well as in the section with   5
change of key signature (D minor, B♭ major?), there are many upbeats with dotted-
rhythm figure. See to it that these are not rubber-stamped, but are varied in
inflection to suit the dictates of the moment. When they occur in the close
succession of mm. 26-28, they can vary according to their place in the melodic arch.   26
As in bars 10-12, the absolute repetition of the 8th-note figure in mm. 28-31 demand   10, 28
very imaginative timing and shading—note Haydn's strong hint in the pianissimo
in m. 29—to underscore the changing play of musical light on the passing array of   29
rhythms. The lower voices can help here, by assuring that, in placement and timbre,
their chords fit exactly to the corresponding 8th-notes in the violin line.

This kind of coordination is important, of course, from the very start of the
movement and is especially tricky when the accompanying voices are playing
pizzicato. Since the plucked sound is very narrowly pointed, the three voices must
be precisely aligned for each chord, and the succession of chords should bend
gracefully to the outline of the violin solo as it emerges in performance. The 2nd
violin needs to lead the playing of the chords while gauging, through eye and ear,
the requirements of the musical events in the top line. Stay vigilant in the bowed
measures, too, for the transparent texture there won't forgive any sloppiness.

Most demanding on the ensemble in this movement is the ornamented
statement, or figural variation, of the theme that begins in bar 36. Here the 1st violin   36
embarks on fifteen florid measures of 32nd-notes. Within the bounds of taste and
musical logic, the player must be free to trip the light fantastic, with the
accompaniment meeting the line unerringly at every point. Again, the 2nd violin
must take the responsibility of leading. In this section, I think the touchiest
measures are 40-41, 43-44, and 49-50. Here the lower voices must attend to melodic   40
business of their own, while still heeding the give-and-take with the 1st violin.

To some extent, the shoe is on the other foot in mm. 51-53, where the chirping   51
of the 2nd violin requires some allegiance from the top part. Control passes to the
cello in bars 54-59 (with due allowance for the violin cadenza in m. 57), then briefly   54
back to the 1st violin before transferring to the viola for the last measures of the
movement. Even the ascending flights of the violin in bars 64-65 must respect the   64
continuing pulse of the viola line.

Menuetto: Allegro ma non troppo. I think the title of this movement is   III
important. The music is far too dark and serious to suggest either a courtly dance or
a Scherzo. That, however, is just the point; the ensemble can all-too-easily divide
into the two teams that make up the canon and whale away at the lines with stolid
and rather surly independence from each other. As I hear it, the movement benefits
greatly from a hint of lightness, with the forte regarded more as a sign of verve and
spirit than as a call for rough-hewn vigor. In this respect, the *Urtext* division of the
8th-notes in bars 1-3 into slurred couplets rather than groups of four helps leaven   1
the sound. Similarly, the dots over the quarter-notes throughout suggest lift and
animation rather than sternly *martelé* bowing.

Above all, play the lines with great sensitivity to their shape, their rise and fall.
They ought to twine around each other, stepping in and out of the spotlight and
directing the ear to the highs and lows of the register as the canonic voices echo
back and forth. In short, let the music sound like a somewhat humorous
contrapuntal essay rather than a grimly academic exercise.

If we need any clue to the temper of the piece, we can find it in the sly way
that Haydn converts the viola/cello resolution—the low D that follows the second

ending—into the upbeat of the Trio. Further, the opening of that section is ambiguous; it sounds as though it might be the static runoff from the Menuetto.

40 The addition of the viola's F♮ in mm. 40 ff. reinforces this idea by suggesting that D minor continues in force. The forte trumpeting of the D major then shows the listener the error of such assumptions, with the prim twitterings of the 1st violin, a

49 few measures later (49 ff.), seeming to add further comment on the hearer's gullibility.

The second half of the Trio extends the byplay; the lower voices are static, the 1st violin debates aimlessly with itself, the entire foursome considers again whether it should recede into D minor, and the blare of D major is once more triumphant. This time around, both violins join in the mock delicacy of the hushed epilogue.

To reinforce the jocular spirit of the Trio, I suggest short, repeated upstrokes for the *sempre staccato* quarter-notes in the measures marked piano. The slurred 8th-

57 note couplets in the 2nd violin in mm. 57 ff. will require due accommodation, of course. Overall, though, the dry, crisp, and airy sound of the upstrokes seems effective. Even in the forte quarter-note measures, some air and light should be allowed to color the back-and-forth bowing.

In the second section of the Trio, by the way, you will hear a certain metric

62 ambiguity in the passage of mm. 62-69. The quarter-note exchanges between violins and low voices (the 2nd violin serving alternately in both groups) allows the ear to think that the bar line may have shifted back one beat. It is not until the forte

70 upbeat into m. 70 that all doubt is dispelled. Of course, the ensemble could insist on accenting the true downbeats in the preceding measures. There is always the possibility, though, that Haydn intended to keep the listener in some suspense in this passage. Try it both ways, and see what your ensemble thinks.

IV   *Finale: Vivace assai.* About tempo: the vivace swing will work best if we think of the theme in two-measure units. The odd measures take the major stress, with the syncopated figure serving as "downbeat" to the complementary, broader rhythm of the even measures.

As to the theme overall: after the indoctrination of the fifths theme in the first movement, I can't help seeing it here as well, in the initial fourth (an inverted fifth) and ascending fifth (mirror of the descending E-A) that frame the first eight measures of the 1st violin part. I'll say no more about this, for it is too easy to find the interval of the fifth embedded in any melody constructed in tonal harmony.

In the *Urtext* version, there is no dynamic mark for the start of this movement. I lean, nonetheless, toward the quiet level to which I am accustomed from the editions of decades past. There is a somewhat breathless eagerness about the writing that is well served by a hushed beginning. This sets the stage for the

21 contrast of the loud outburst of mm. 21 ff., when the 2nd violin takes over the theme at the lower octave. That instrument should have been leading the lower voices since the outset; it resumes that function after yielding the melody back to

28 the 1st violin at bar 28.

41 In fact, the 1st violin becomes leader, as distinct from soloist, only at bar 41;

62 from there until the fermata at m. 62, one or more of the lower voices is playing in

46 direct rhythmic unison with the top part. In mm. 46-51, the viola should consider itself not so much as complementing the violin duet, but rather as carrying on a vigorous dialogue with the cello. From the listener's perspective, this dialogue is

51 the focus of interest in these bars. Mm. 51-56 should be played one bow to the bar in the two top lines, to help the 1st violin avoid false accents on the detached fourth

8th-note of the rhythm. In mm. 58 and 60, the 1st violin's bow pressure should favor the G-string, so that the low-register tremolo can be heard through the drone B♭. A similar approach applies in mm. 128, 218, and 220. The multivoice chords in bar 57 and other such spots later in the course of the movement should not be brusquely played; try for an open sonority and when (as here) there is some individual motion in the viola line, don't submerge it.

58

128

57

The double stops in mm. 62-66 (and again in mm. 232-36) should take advantage of the open strings, as marked in the *Urtext* edition, in order to gain resonance. For the same reason, the stroke should not be so heavy as to repress the sound. In the succeeding measures, as well as in the corresponding bars later in the movement, the dotted quarter-notes need circumspect attack, to avoid roughness. If overdriven, the line may suggest a musical rendition of a donkey's bray; perish the thought—you're not playing incidental music for *Midsummer Night's Dream*! The effect should properly be that of a connected line of the longer notes, sparked by the brilliance of the 8th-notes. You may find that a one-to-the-bar bowing will prove helpful, even in the measures containing the large intervallic leaps. The lower-voice chords need a light touch, for these are subordinate to the long notes of the top line.

62, 232

67

A bar-to-the-bow stroke will again produce the desired effect in mm. 93-114. The cello responses that start in bars 95 and 99 should be incisive, while the three upper parts play their sustained chord with suitable restraint. See to it also that the viola's very short solo in bar 108 can be heard. In the passage from bars 114 to 125, there is an important dialogue between 1st violin and cello. The second and third 8ths of each cello measure must be prominent enough to link into a continuous chain of notes with the violin fragments, a chain that takes on special appeal because of the constant shift in tone color.

93

95

108, 114

You will probably want to drop the dynamic level enough at bar 144 to allow for a rise into the piano level of the theme restatement at m. 148. The accompanying chords in these measures should not be dry, but should offer enough resonance to support the violin line. As for the body of the restatement, I need scarcely say that the cellist has the predominant role from bar 169 to the change of key, except for the two measures where the 1st violin assumes the line.

144

148

169

With the change to D major at bar 180, Haydn is confirming something we should long have recognized: this quartet may be serious, but it is not grim. The bagpipes are brought in (the inner voices, mm. 182 ff.), the theme is modified into a striding march, the stage is set for the final innovation. Just when it is leaving, and for the first time in the entire movement, the 1st violin breaks into triplet rhythm at m. 249, eventually prevailing on the lower voices to join in the arpeggio flourishes that mark the closing cadence.

180

182

249

VIOLINO SECONDO

Molto Allegro

CHAPTER FOUR

❦ Mozart ❦
Quartet in G, K. 387

Mozart was sixteen years of age when Haydn wrote his six quartets, Op. 20, in 1772. Young Mozart turned out a spate of quartets of his own in the years 1772-73, responding to the stimulus of the older master's path-breaking work in the genre.

Mozart was freshly inspired by Haydn's Op. 33 quartets, published by Artaria in Vienna in 1782, a year after Mozart moved to that city. In the very year of that publication, Mozart again took up the writing of string quartets. That December, he wrote the first of six such works that he would compose in the space of little more than two years: the "Haydn" quartets, so-called because of the warm dedication of the set to the older master.

The six, originally published by Artaria as Op. X, are now known by their Köchel, or K., catalogue numbers: 387, 421, 428, 458, 464, and 465. Together with K. 499, 575, 589, and 590, they make up the mature—the ten so-called "celebrated"— quartets of Mozart. These are works of major importance, not only in the string quartet literature, but in our musical heritage generally.

The experience of hearing the first six of these quartets moved Haydn to make his famous comment to Mozart's father, that "your son is the greatest composer known to me..."[1] Aware as Haydn was of the difficulties of writing quartets, he saw that Mozart had mastered those problems in his own way. In particular, he had matched or even excelled Haydn's ability to treat all four participants in the quartet as equally important members of a team. Furthermore, and to a striking degree, Mozart had given each of the six quartets a musical personality, a dramatic premise all its own.

As with the quartets Haydn had produced up to that time (certainly the

---

SCORE: Wolfgang Amadeus Mozart. 1964. *String Quartet in G, K. 387*. Urtext. Ed. Ludwig Finscher. Kassel: Bärenreiter. Miniature score No. 141.

Left: Wolfgang Amadeus Mozart: Quartet in G, K. 387, first page of 2nd violin part, finale. Vienna: Artaria, 1785. Reproduced with permission from the collection of the Sibley Music Library, the Eastman School of Music, University of Rochester.

quartets of Opp. 20 and 33), these compositions of Mozart are worlds away from mere entertainment music. Even in their most effervescent movements, they demand intent listening. Moreover, again like Haydn, Mozart is not writing music for casual performance. Whether the ensemble be amateur or professional, it will need technical ability, serious rehearsal, and musical intelligence. A reading can be fun, but it will only challenge the group to return to the music again and again in an effort to command its detail, its surprising nuances, and especially its deep perception of the human spirit.

I   *Allegro vivace assai.* If you have played much of Mozart's music, you know that as a rule he uses few dynamic marks, relying on the performer's sensibility to provide appropriate loudness gradations. The G major quartet clearly departs from this norm. Looking at the 1st violin part alone in the fifty-five measures of the exposition of this first movement, we find a total of thirty-two fortes and pianos, five forte-pianos, one pianissimo, and six crescendos. Add to these the comparable markings in the three lower parts, and it is evident that the play of loud and soft is of vital concern to the composer in this piece. The need to control and synchronize the dynamic shading helps make this quartet a supreme test of the ensemble's technical skill.

1   We feel this challenge immediately in the first four bars of the piece. The theme would be quite acceptable if played at just one dynamic level. Mozart, however, deliberately casts the melody in two planes: first and third measures, loud and in the foreground; second and fourth bars, quiet and heard from a distance. Simply varying the amount of bow or pressure of stroke is not enough; the tone color must also shift, from warm and vibrant in the loud measures, to cool in the background bars. Control of the left hand is vital here.

       Each lower voice is vigorous and melodically interesting in its own right, even though subordinate to the top line, and must be played as though the performer enjoys it. The action of the 1st violin part is actually answered and rounded off by the viola and 2nd violin, respectively, in the second half of mm. 2 and 4. The lower

2
1   parts should be careful about the detached quarters in the first half of m. 1; these notes counter a slurred pair in the top voice, and must be played so that there is no false accent on the second beat.

       The writing is consistently democratic, and all members of the team should stand ready to function as solo or accompaniment, as the moment demands. Notice

5   how the melody is built by the three upper lines in succession in mm. 5-7. The piano mark for the 1st violin in bar 7 implies that a louder level has been built over

8   the two preceding bars. Note, further, that the crescendo in m. 8 highlights the deceptive cadence on the third beat; the parallel marking in bar 10 offers a compensating thrust toward the full cadence.

10   With its forte on the last 8th-note of m. 10, the 2nd violin assumes the lead; its melody should be played on the G-string to provide resonance and to keep the line

12   audible even when the instrument yields prominence to the 1st violin in bar 12. Both violins must play with projection, though quietly, in building the short chain

13   of trilled figures in mm. 13-14. You may prefer to play a simple turn, rather than a trill, in these figures. Certainly there is no time here for any dogmatic starting of the ornament on the upper note; you will be doing well to make the printed note of the trill heard clearly in the quickly moving line.

15   Both in the layering of voices in m. 15 and in the pyramid sequence of the next three bars, each player needs a sense of soloistic importance. And always, every

part must be ready to lead. The successive rhythmic impacts in mm. 20-21 can work 20
only if the cello, the inner voices, and the 1st violin act as self-motivated units in the
ensemble. Even in the simultaneous forte-pianos of bars 22-23, the impulse must
come from each of the four players, not just from the 1st violin. Certainly the
synchronization of the 16ths in the three top parts on the second beat of bar 24 24
comes off only if each player takes a "push-off," discreetly marking the downbeat
ending of the suspension from the preceding measure.

So also, the 2nd violin will have to give a slight but definite signal to itself to
mark the fourth beat of m. 24, not only to gauge the actual length of the 8th-rest, but 24
to be able to launch from that into the upbeat 8th that starts the second theme. The
player must be sure to take this theme well down in the lower part of the bow, so
that the spiccato 16ths can be placed where the springiness of the bow and the wrist
action of the right hand can quickly generate a bouncing stroke. Both here and in
the restatement of the theme by the 1st violin and viola, the accompanying voices
should play their leaping figures with appropriate energy, because they fill in the
measures of (relative) relaxation in the solo line.

The alternation of loud and soft is distilled to its most concentrated form in
bars 37-38. You could even suppose that Mozart planned the entire movement just 37
to set up this particular spot, as well as its recurrence later in the movement. The 1st
violin has played a quiet, chromatic line in bar 34. Here, on the other hand, Mozart 34
casts the scalewise line of that instrument into extremely disjunct form, spreading
out the successive notes over a two-octave span. He further jolts the leaping
progression by marking piano and forte, alternately, on the sequence of quarter-
notes. Draw the bow slowly on the quiet notes, suddenly faster on the loud ones,
and alternate a calm and a vibrating left hand further to underline the contrast
between the several notes.

The effect is angular; the listener is jarred into attention, only to be soothed by
the flowing streamers of 16ths in the measures that follow. When the violins join in
the octaves of mm. 40-42, the 2nd violin should predominate slightly in the balance. 40
The two upper voices seamlessly hand over the running line to the cello in bar 41,
and must be equally smooth in rejoining the ascending 16ths several measures later.

Play the piano tones of mm. 48-49, starting with the preceding upbeat, at the 48
tip of the bow, for hushed, pointed effect. All four players must take the lead in the
alternation of loud and soft, from the fourth beat of m. 49; only such unified
impulse can properly convey the energy of the writing. On the other hand, only the
2nd violin can effectively lead the tiny stretching of time that makes its pianissimo
echo (m. 53) of the 1st violin suitably wistful. 53

All four parts again control the sly, two-bar exit from the exposition. Play this 54
leave-taking in reversed bowing, at the tip of the stick. Both because of its moderate
length and the intricate texture of its events, this first section of the movement
invites the repeat called for at the double bar; I heartily recommend it.

Mozart should have been a movie director. Judging from this quartet, he knew
about cinematic technique even before the invention of photography. In fact,
Hitchcock himself could have found some pointers in the opening of Mozart's
development section here. I do not exaggerate. The scene about to be played out
must have come directly from Mozart's long experience in writing for the stage. But
the closeup view of character here suggests nothing so much as the use of a camera,
panning from one face to another, intimately inspecting the people involved in a
dramatic situation.

55   The 1st violin leads off with the opening fragment of the theme, but veers into a brief, florid, emotional outburst. Again, dynamics are a critical part of the musical action: the solo starts in forte, fades into a decrescendo, and ends with the alternating forte and piano of an indecisive cadence. The lower voices exclaim their sympathy; note that the detached quarters of the first measure are retained here, their impact now heightened with detachment marks, an emphasis we should observe in the playing. Then suddenly these voices shift from forte to piano, fall silent under the solo's lament, and return with bated notes to witness the end of the

60   statement. It is then the 2nd violin's turn to emote, up a notch in pitch, and at greater length. To establish the individuality of the plaint, the player must exploit the extended declamation, especially in the timing and inflection of mm. 64-65. Don't rush things; have a good cry.

67   The viola, for its part, avoids grieving, choosing instead to launch into an extended run of the 16th-note element that has formed part of each statement in this dramatic trio. That, of course, is a fascinating aspect of this opening scene of the development: each voice has imitated the one before, but only as a point of departure for its own, personal musings. The cello alone has persisted in the role of

72   concerned onlooker. Now, as the 16th-notes move from one upper voice to the next, the cello's 8ths pace the rhythmic accompaniment; and, as ever, the shading of loud and soft, near and far, continues. From bar 78 until almost the end of the

78   development, however, everything recedes into a piano context; this now becomes the norm around which the ensemble will have to scale forte-piano, sforzando, and pianissimo, all in proportion.

86ff.   Within this frame are short, contrasting episodes—two, three, or four measures in length—recalling the various rhythmic and melodic elements that have appeared earlier in the movement. This kaleidoscopic review is important to the development process; don't plow indiscriminately forward. Whether an intervening rest of an 8th or quarter length is provided, or only a dynamic contrast, set the episodes off somehow from one another, even if only by the slightest catch of breath.

100   The quarter-rest at the end of m. 100 takes some special thought. The bar as a whole is the end of a two-measure musical unit; the melodic figure of this second measure, however, returns as the subject of the high-and-low dialogue of the next three bars. Yet that conversation begins as rather a fresh thought in m. 101, not simply as an extension of the preceding measure. When this dialogue, in turn, runs without interruption into the release, at last, of the forte measures (104 ff.), the playing should breathe expansively in response to the event. It is obvious, finally,

106   that the *calando* return to the recapitulation, mm. 106-07, has to be led by the 2nd violin, since the top line's syncopes can move only in reflection of the onbeat pulse.

108   Don't overlook the changes in ornamental detail and in part writing in the four measures that open the recapitulation. Play as though you recognize these changes; rely on the audience to remember the opening clearly enough to enjoy these changes with you. The octave duet of the violins in the 16th-note runs is more extensive this time around. Both players need fingerings that involve minimal shifts, in the interests of clarity, intonation, and synchronization.

169   If you make the indicated repeat of development and recapitulation (I don't urge it), the last two measures should move in tempo, though some breath on the final 8th-rest will help define the sectional return. If, on the other hand, the closing measures actually serve to end the movement, a touch of *calando* in the last bar is desirable. In either case, the rest between mm. 168 and 169 should be long enough

to set off the closing bars. Recall, by the way, that the close in the exposition was piano. Here it is marked pianissimo: the movement ends way off in the distance.

Menuetto: Allegro. The first movement's play of dynamics is continued in the Menuetto, in the alternate piano and forte on the successive quarters in the tune (mm. 3-6 and elsewhere). Here, though, the resulting suggestion of duple meter within triple might possibly be a caricature comment on some of the intricacies of the step patterns in the danced minuet of the 18th century. For the player, the dynamic alternation will certainly require a corresponding contrast of relaxation and intensity in the left hand. II
3

The first edition marks this movement as Allegretto, which might indicate a somewhat slower tempo than the autograph's Allegro.[2] Whichever word you choose to read, play in a speed and manner that produces an easy, one-to-the-bar feeling. A pace that is too slow will give the music in general, and especially the piano and forte alternation, a labored stiffness.

Be graceful with the 8th-note figures that move through the voices. Leaps or string crossings, as in the violin parts in m. 10, must be smoothly made. Where the figures combine static and moving lines, as in the 2nd violin and viola, mm. 21-25, let the active melody emerge with appropriate prominence and inflection. Thus, the 2nd violin figure carries forward slightly to the next downbeat, while the viola response eases back a bit, without fragmenting the overall swing of the phrase. The descending chromatics in the three upper parts (mm. 30-38) need lively fingers, moderate pressure against the fingerboard, and very clean shifting. No smearing allowed! The effect should be as clear as though played on a keyboard instrument. 10
21

30

In the second section, the opening events prepare for a surprise that will arrive at m. 54. The quarter-note measures in the pyramid of the four voices in mm. 43-46 should join as one line, with slight prominence of the first beat of each bar. The sustained note in each part must immediately subordinate itself to the current entry of quarter-note rhythm. As the voices pile up, the dynamic stays at piano level, with crescendo reserved until indicated in measure 47. I believe that the reason for the piano in bar 49 is to direct the attention of the ear to the later, corresponding measure, 53. That bar remains in forte, clearly in contrast to the unexpected quietness of the resolution in bar 54. **54, 43**

47

53

This drop, in turn, prepares us for a further surprise at bar 63. The trilled figures in the three lower voices in mm. 55-58 have to be played as suspenseful comments on the deepening hush of this passage. Mozart seems ready to release us from this suspense as he calls for crescendo and forte in the move to the return of theme at bar 63. That return, though, drops us suddenly, and again unexpectedly, back into the piano dynamic with which the movement began. 63

The 1st violin will have to use some physical response (akin to swallowing one's breath) to carry off the effect. There is no change of register from bar 62 into 63; the listener, therefore, will feel the shock of the change from forte to piano only if the player emphasizes the loudness contrast. A very slight hesitation before playing bar 63 will help by suggesting that the player, too, is surprised by the dynamics. This kind of contrast, though not always so abrupt, prevails until the end of the section. 63

In the Trio, the dynamic alternation is raised to an aggressive level: the massed ensemble is overwhelming, accusing in tone. (The trills in the upper voices add menacing intensity to the simpler version of the line in the cello.) The 1st violin's response seems timid, pleading. That instrument, by the way, will want to take its Trio

5[98] E♭s in bar 5 [98] on the D-string, approaching the notes with a clean and unsmeared shift. (Press lightly with the shifting finger, extend the finger that will play the higher note, and draw the bow lightly and slowly during the slide.) Under the second response, the sustained lines in the lower parts should be pianissimo, to leave room for the breathless utterances of the violin. Conversely, the violins'

22[115] chords in bars 22-23 [115-16] must be balanced so that the viola can project its figure without having to force the sound.

26[119] The ensemble ought to tape and hear the polyphonic web of mm. 26-31 [119-24] to be sure that the interweaving strands are clearly discernible. The simpler

39[132] texture of mm. 39-47 [132-40] needs intelligent playing: from the 1st violin, to translate its interrupted line into a convincing intensification of a sustained C; from the 2nd, to offer sympathetic reinforcement in the quiet emphases of mm. 45-47

45[138] [138-40]; and from the low voices, to provide resonant, but not growling, support in their rising harmonies.

III *Andante cantabile.* Let's look at the lower voices first. The pattern of cello 8ths and inner-voice syncopes recurs at a number of points in the movement. Where, as at the beginning, the cello has forte on the first 8th, piano on the second, translate the marks as a forte-piano, proportioning the emphasis to suit the piano context. I would suggest taking the four detached 8ths on one gently articulated upstroke, to assure proper ease of effect. So also, the inner voices should bow the second half of their measure on one upstroke and should treat their entire bar as a very tranquil reinforcement of the cello rhythm.

As for the solo, its ornamental turns in the first three utterances should be treated as integral parts of the melody, starting broadly and growing more intense and contracted as the crescendo moves toward the G in the third bar. Recognize that this note, prominent though it is, is only a way station; the melody continues

4 on to the C in m. 4 before sinking to its ultimate goal, the low Cs in bar 7. The three lower voices have to assist in outlining this melodic journey.

7 The close interweaving of all four parts is manifest in the next phrase: the melodic strand moves from cello to 1st violin in mm. 7-8, descends through the inner voices in bar 9, returns to the 2nd violin in the second half of bar 10, then rises from the wave of 16ths in that line to move once more to the 1st violin in the course

12 of m. 11. The rising 8ths in the 2nd violin in bar 12 must carry the ascent of the solo violin; and in m. 13, the 2nd violin leads the lower voices as they accompany the free flight of the 1st violin in its florid cadence. Take care to link the triplet figures of the three lower voices in m. 14: use easy landings on the 8th-notes, with enough sustaining of those tones to forge the connection to the next-entering line of notes.

15 The melodic chain leads back to the cello in bar 15. In dynamic level and melodic activity, that line is clearly the solo for four measures. Nevertheless, the movement in the various pairings of upper voices forms a very interesting background to the cello; they are countermelodies, not mere accompaniments.

The cellist's way with the line is important: it gratifies the player; and it sets the stage for the even freer virtuosity of the 1st violin's 32nd-note melody that follows. You will note that Mozart restricts the lower parts there to intermittent chordal commentary, the better to free the solo violin's flight of melodic fancy. Note

22 also that, when the violin finally returns to sobriety in mm. 22-23, the lower voices become an important solo factor in their response to the sustained tones of the upper part; the dynamic level and inflection in bar 23 must change in response to the shift from B to B♭ in the top line.

The 2nd violin's three upbeat 8th-notes in bar 25 should grow in warmth as 25
they move toward the flowering triplets of the following measures. Those garlands
contain harmonic shifts that must affect the pacing and inflection of the line. The
more so, when all four parts take up the triplet figures in unison in m. 29. No 29
metronomic counting here! The line has to move subtly toward the B♮ of the third
beat, and through that to the trilled emphasis of the leading tone, C♯, on the
downbeat of m. 30. Even youthful players will sound aged unless they respond to 30
the challenges of this kind of fluid writing.

The next episode of the movement opens in tones of religious solemnity. Since
the violin solo is set quite low in the instrument's register, the accompanying voices
must play very quietly to keep from hiding the melody. Yet the accompaniment
itself is an essential part of the solo; the 8ths and syncopes need flexibility to fulfill
the implications of the leading line. At the end of bar 34, the lower voices thrust 34
toward the downbeat, only to meet with the silence of the 8th-rest; the sudden
interruption lends special poignancy to the solo above.

We could view the offbeat 8ths in bar 35 as supplying the missing 16th-note in 35
each quadruplet of the 1st violin part. That would be misguided, however; starting
with the upbeat 16th of bar 34, the solo violin is making three separate, little 34
statements that finally lead to the complete melodic sweep of m. 36. The lower
voices in bar 34 are certainly responding to the top voice; at the same time,
however, they constitute a melodic chorus in their own right, and must play in that
conviction. Two bars later, under the syncopes of the 1st violin, the solid motion of
the accompaniment gives stability to the musical fabric. And again, it is the lower
chorus that restores calm after the lyric outburst of m. 38; only after this, and by 38
virtue of dividing into individual voices, are all instruments drawn into the
interplay of mm. 46-47, where triplet figures and dotted rhythms wind around each 46
other.

Mozart remains in control; the four-octave span of bar 46 contracts to one 46
octave by the end of the next measure, in preparation for the end of the outburst.
And what an end! The ensemble is reduced to a stammer, as though in a more
placid version of the "Mors stupebit" setting in the Verdi *Requiem*, still a century off.
The pacing of the utterances in mm. 48-51 must suggest that calm breathing is 48
gradually being restored after the turbulence just experienced.

As in many such ensemble situations, there can be no one leader here. The 1st
violin may give the signals, but the several entrances must be made by a common
impulse, achieved in rehearsal, but freshly realized at the moment of each
performance. Sensitive musicians will learn to read each other's intent.

Ahead lies a passage that is more difficult than it looks: the long, emotional,
and harmonic detour that begins in bar 58. First there are the three self-denials by 58
the cello, again making those crescendos that lead to a contradicting piano. Then,
however, there are the measures in which all players have to hold their breaths:
bars 63-68, with the inner voices drawing their bows extremely slowly, the cello 63
playing octaves made of spiderweb strands, and the 1st violin tracing an 8th-note
reverie that progresses as though in slow motion. The episode is one of the most
suspenseful in the literature; not ominous—simply suspended in time. Great
control is needed here, not only of the instrument, but of the self.

The release that follows is easier precisely because the music can flow freely.
Although the cello and 1st violin solos correspond to those heard earlier from mm. 70
15 to 21, their impact is different here: first, because they come out of the eerie

74 passage just described; second, because the cello, not entirely shaking off that eeriness, is now cast in minor; and finally, because the violin flight, formerly accompanied only by intermittent chords in the lower voices, is here countered by more of the thematic strand that has backed the cello triplets. Now, though, this backing is assigned to the 2nd violin alone (mm. 74-76), with the two lower voices providing subordinate accompaniment; the 2nd needs to play its line with soloistic conviction, for it is the framework against which the other, florid violin line is draped.

81 Both inner voices should be forthcoming, also, in playing their material in bars 81-83, since the lines are now cast a fifth lower than in the first part of the movement, and consequently in a weaker register of the instruments. On the other

85 hand, let all four instruments avoid gruffness in the forte unisons of mm. 85-86.

104 The brief codetta of the movement is difficult for the two inner parts. Coming out of the ensemble interplay of mm. 102-03, they suddenly find themselves quite alone in their duet of triplets. The first 16th-note of bar 104 is both the resolution of what has come before and the springboard for the duet to follow. In playing that note, the 2nd violin and viola must look to each other to coordinate their progress to the second note of the triplet. They have to synchronize that voyage in order to move beyond it into a unified shaping of the entire duet. The fact that a piano marking is placed precisely on that second 16th is hard on the nerves; it will help if the players contrive not to be too near the frog of the bow when starting the measure. This is so that the weight of the stick does not overwhelm the delicacy of the line, especially in the descent to the final pianissimo. It will help even more if the two players have a pretty clear idea of how they want to shape the duet, so that no remedial adjustments are needed in the actual performance.

IV *Molto Allegro.* Like Haydn before him, Mozart—in this first of his mature quartets—faces the problem of writing a suitable finale to the work. The closing chapter has to measure up to the stature of the first three movements, and at the same time provide a bright and stimulating ending. Mozart solves the problem by composing a musical puzzle for the listener. In effect, he is asking his hearers to decide whether the movement is fast or slow.

The puzzle works because the listener is not looking at the score and, although possibly aware that the composer has marked the movement as "very lively," does

1 not know that the time signature is *alla breve* (to make things very lively indeed). Nor does the listener realize that the opening measures consist exclusively of whole-notes. One more, very important, fact: the 2nd violin plays the first four bars completely alone, leading the defenseless listener to hear four whole-notes as though they are the component quarter-note beats in a rather slow 4/4 measure.

5 The audience may begin to suspect that it has been had when it hears the 2nd violin's syncopated countermelody under the 1st violin's statement of the theme. The ruse should be fairly clear when both violins interweave in a fast four-quarter pattern behind the cello and viola statements. And the cat is completely out of the bag when the 1st violin unleashes the 8th-note torrent that runs through the several

17 voices starting in bar 17.

The trick is all the more effective because the time values speed up very quietly. Calm, innocent playing of the opening solo by the 2nd violin is essential to the success of the riddle. None of the players should get excited, either, in playing the syncopes that follow. Even the 8th-notes should be played with some

31 nonchalance. It isn't really until the forte of m. 31 that Mozart permits you to come

clean about the musical swindle you have played on the audience. *Now* you can be excited.

The forte passage, mm. 31-38, focuses on the cello, with the viola a close second in importance, and the two violins lending very interesting background motion. Starting in bar 39, the viola launches into twelve measures of 8th-notes that hardly budge from the note, A. At this tempo, this kind of line is far from dull. It drives the whole musical mechanism and also drives home the puzzle aspect of the movement by insisting on its smallest, quickest rhythmic element. The violins help, of course, by loping through the syncopated chromatic descents above the viola line. And—shades of the first two movements—let all four players exploit the stark contrasts of loud and soft that close this first part of the Allegro.   39

We can also interpret the imitative entries, beginning in m. 52, as deriving from the syncopated countermelody of the movement's opening. Each voice should step back to allow the opening measures of the next part to be heard. The detached quarter-note in the second and third measures of each voice should be bowed in the same stroke as the preceding long note, thus avoiding a false accent; use the lower half of the stick, so that you can play the detached quarters of the fourth and succeeding bars comfortably and in sprightly fashion. When the whole-note theme returns, starting in the cello at bar 69, the stroke should be pointed and militant, with a short vibrato impulse for each note, to match the temper now in force.   52   69

With bar 92, the second surprise of the movement is upon us. The opening episode may have been a riddle, but it was an erudite one, with each voice unwrapping and revealing the layers of time in a contrapuntal web. Now Mozart goes plebeian on us, giving the 1st violin a tune that a teacher of mine once described as a *Gassenhauer,* or "street song." Under it, the lower voices should trot along like a small and active German band.   92

The 2nd violin has interesting finger exercises in the rapid Alberti figures of mm. 100-06. Be sure not to fall back—there is little danger of rushing ahead! Rather, stay with the quarter-notes on either side of you and be ready to lead the lower voices in the sudden, forte ascent of bar 107. The most difficult measure of the violin part comes just before that ascent, when the player suddenly has to dart over to the G-string to play the two C♯s. See it coming, and don't be taken by surprise. Also, since you will play that bar on a downbow, plan to tie in the first 8th of m. 107 on the same stroke, so that you won't have to play the ascending run in reverse bowing. Similar advice applies to the viola at that spot. The cello will be taking the downbeat quarter of bar 107 on an upstroke, so its run will fall into place naturally.   100   107

I recently learned, by the way, that an esteemed 2nd violin colleague plays this entire passage (as well as its counterpart at mm. 243 ff.) with separate strokes, rather than in the printed slurs. I feel that the sound of the detached bowing is so different in effect, though, that I would vote against it.

The entire ensemble has to cool down from all this exuberance, pulling back into the piano murmurs of mm. 115 ff. The exposition is so much fun that the quartet will certainly want to take the repeat. Whether for the return or for going into the development, it is up to the 2nd violin to create a stealthy, catlike mood in its brief chromatic ascent in mm. 123-24. This approach is especially important at the end of the repeat, for now the chromatic figure, and its mood, will dominate in the first part of the development.   115   123

The viola and cello predominate in the chromatic conversation; moreover, their exchanges climb, step by step. Their duet, by inflection and timing, should reflect   129 the color changes that these harmonic shifts create, not just repeat the figure in treadmill fashion. The same is true for the dialogue between cello and 1st violin on the minor version of the riddle subject (mm. 143-58), and for the short, ensuing discussion based on the quarter-note background rhythm (mm. 157 ff.).

After the pregnant silence of mm. 173-74, it is up to the 2nd violin to signal a very determined downbeat chord, the trigger for the return, not of the original key, nor of the riddle theme, but of what? By now, with the repetition of the first section, we have heard the riddle twice, so there is no need to puzzle it out yet a third time. Instead, Mozart throws us right into the rapid-fire 8th-note run that originally resolved the puzzle. Also, instead of the tonality of G, we are given its subdominant, C. Only when the second subject appears in a shortened passage, in mm. 208 ff., are we allowed to hear G major.

The *Gassenhauer* is also heard, properly in G major; for the 2nd violin, this key makes for some very interesting fiddling. The Alberti figures now involve rapid-fire string crossing in six of the seven measures in which they appear. Playing these bars is hilarious fun, but you will survive only if you use a moderate amount of bow, with minimal crossing motion. To the onlooker, the bow should seem to be playing sustained double stops. Fingering and bowing must be absolutely coordinated; there is no room for doubt or hesitation as you spin out this pattern.

I would advise against any slackening of pace as the ensemble plays the decrescendo of mm. 260-61. The spread-out phrasing in mm. 262-66 will suggest an easing of time. There is no need to stretch the tempo there, either; the music does it all.

In the coda, the chromatic echoing among the four voices will probably make for some spreading until the 2nd violin and cello, in their statement beginning at the end of bar 276, carry the ensemble into the forte and forward to the triumphal phrase that extends from bar 282 to 291. Note, incidentally, the ingenious *stretto*—a last inspiration—that presents the whole-note theme at one-measure intervals in three of the voices. The exception is the 2nd violin, who compounds the stunt by starting on the half bar and playing once again in the syncopes that have added so much life to the movement.

The leave-taking in the last seven measures of the finale should be played quietly but with enough motion to suggest that the movement may yet have more thematic business to conduct. The sense of ending crystallizes only with the three lower voices' entrance in bar 294, and with their enigmatic harmonization of the melody. Some broadening of tempo in the last three measures is in order, but everything, including the trill and the last chord, should merge into the silence of the last measure.

I recall a performance of K. 387 that our quartet gave in Berkeley, years ago. Some in the audience started their applause after the triumphant downbeat in bar 291, forgetting that the quiet tag of the last seven measures was still to come. The eminent music historian, David Boyden, was in attendance and insisted to me that the listeners' confusion arose from the excitement caused by our too-rapid tempo in the finale. I remain unconvinced by this argument. The movement works only within a very narrow range of "lively" tempos. At speed, the sense of ending at bar 291 is very convincing indeed. It might even be that Mozart was playing a sly game of musical entrapment by adding the hushed ending. Anyway, the close adds a last touch of fun to a very engaging movement.

When you have finished the cadence, hold still for a couple of seconds. After

143

173

208

235
243

260

276
282

292

294

291

all the hubbub of this movement, the audience deserves a moment of calm before returning to the real world.

76.

Quartetto.

Allegro

Claucembalo.

op: 24.

CHAPTER FIVE

❧ Mozart ❧
Piano Quartet in G minor, K. 478

In June of 1788, a complaint about a piano quartet of Mozart appeared in a Weimar newspaper devoted to "style and luxury." The grievance was not aimed at the work, but at what was being done to it. The quartet was being played at social gatherings by dilettantes trying to make a splash with the piece and failing miserably because of lack of expertise.

> What a difference when this much-advertised work of art is performed with the highest degree of accuracy by four skilled musicians who have studied it carefully, in a quiet room where the suspension of every note cannot escape the listening ear, and in the presence of only two or three attentive persons![1]

The item does not say whether it is referring to the G minor quartet, K. 478, or to the second quartet, in E flat, K. 493, both of which had appeared within the preceding two years. I would think the subject is the relatively lighthearted E flat; its brilliance and humor would have appealed to players seeking effect, while its virtuoso demands would readily have confounded their fingers and their sense of ensemble.

The G minor quartet, on the other hand, would not have been a likely choice for salon performers. In fact, Franz Anton Hoffmeister, the Viennese publisher who had brought out the work (it was composed in October of 1785) lamented to Mozart that it was selling slowly because of its difficulty.[2] On the basis of my own experience, I would guess that the problem lay not only in the technical challenges of the music, but even more in its temperament. The quartet truly has what Alfred

---

SCORE: Wolfgang Amadeus Mozart. n.d. *Quartet in G minor, for Pianoforte, Violin, Viola and Violoncello, K. 478*. London: Eulenburg. Miniature score No. 158.

Left: Wolfgang Amadeus Mozart: Piano Quartet in G minor, K. 478, first page of the piano part. Vienna: Artaria, 1794. Reproduced with permission from the collection of the Sibley Music Library, the Eastman School of Music, University of Rochester.

Einstein terms "unwonted earnestness, passion, and depth. For this is no longer in any sense music of mere sociability, which can be listened to superficially and with a smile."[3]

Even today, when we all know how many-sided was the nature of Mozart and his music, the G minor quartet—and specifically its first movement—comes as a surprise and something of a shock. The performer must not gloss over the special intensity of the work. At the same time, to overreact to that fervor is to risk crushing the music. The ensemble has to feel its way very carefully in this quartet.

I *Allegro.* I first played this work in chamber class in my freshman year at college. It was a disheartening experience. There is a grimness about the opening Allegro of this piece that lies very near the surface. This invited a correspondingly grim approach on my part. The result was not only serious, but deadly. As in the case of Haydn's "Quinten" Quartet, it took time for me to recognize that a deft touch is very beneficial to the performance.

In my discussion of the Haydn work, I noted how often the theme of the fifths and its derivatives occurred in the course of the opening movement. The thematic motive of this Mozart piano quartet seems to recur just as frequently. If you are too beetle-browed in your treatment of the theme, it will soon sound obstinate and pugnacious, rather than intense and focused. Keep in mind, above all, that Mozart himself will unleash a fortissimo barrage of the theme in the last thirteen measures of the movement. If you don't save some of your vehemence for this last salvo, you will be tempted to mangle the sound of the closing measures in an attempt to top everything that has gone before.

2 In fact, I feel that it is a good strategy to view this movement from its less intense moments, moving out from them to the more assertive passages that frame the whole. At the start of the Allegro, the piano's response (mm. 2–4), though certainly not dispirited, has a fleetness and spaciousness, with its upward leap of an octave and its flashing descent, that bespeaks a free kind of energy. Note that here, as well as in all such statements later in the movement, the resolution of the descending, scalewise run is not forte, but piano. This suggests to me that the piano's solo measures, already thinner in texture than the massed orchestration of the first measure-and-a-half, carries out a composed decrescendo over the thematic phrase as a whole. Further, the massed statement of the opening has the theme doubled at the octaves by the viola and cello, with each string line further doubled by the piano. This demands that each player listen to the sonority produced by the ensemble, rather than attack the individual part as though the effect of the passage depends solely on the force of that line alone.

That the initial forte carries over into the piano solo of m. 2 should not blind you to the essential and dramatic opposition between the "tutti" of the opening and the piano's answer. I think of the former as accusing, the latter as imploring. After

5 the second, heightened interchange (mm. 5–8), the chorus assumes a more sympathetic role, the piano maintaining its original defensive posture, though now stating its case more briefly. When all join forces for the expanded accusation (mm.

13 13–16) that rounds out the first theme complex, it is again important to play with intelligent restraint. Here, the piano bass doubles the viola line, but the treble provides the sonority of the octave above the violin part. Make sure to balance the lines so that this new tone color can be heard.

17 The austere doubling of the tutti figure changes to a chordal setting at m. 17. While observing the sense of the piano dynamic indicated there, see to it that the

motion of the closely spaced strands is evident. Treat the conversation between strings and piano (mm. 17–22) as one episode, balancing so that the piano's statement does not stick out.

Matters go even farther in the next portion of the movement (mm. 23–44). More than before, we are dealing here with music lifted bodily from the world of the piano concerto, with the three strings constituting a miniature orchestra to back the keyboard virtuoso. Don't take this analogy too literally, however; the viola line in mm. 23–27, the thematic dialogue between upper-voice duet and cello in mm. 32 ff., are important commentaries on the piano solo. For its part, the solo—though played with all due clarity and brilliance—would do well to think of itself not only as protagonist, but as a counterfoil to the essential musical business taking place in the string corps.

23

32

When, at bar 45, things take a more chamberly turn, be aware that you are dealing with a quintet, or even a septet, since the three strings are weaving around each other in trio, with the piano providing a duet that is doubled at the octave in both staves. Take care to maintain transparency of texture in these measures, so that the individual strands of melody remain clear.

45

The cello's 8th-note bass in mm. 50–51 is transformed into the 16th-note texture of the upper strings and piano treble in m. 52. Try to make this relationship clear by playing the 16th figures so that their important tones predominate. The repeated octaves of the piano treble, and even more the quarter-note progression in the cello and piano-bass in bar 52, will help in this. A slight drop in loudness at the start of this measure will encourage a sense of progress toward the downbeat of m. 53.

50

This, however, is not a stopping point. The piano immediately continues the rhythmic texture (now once again openly in 8th-notes) for a measure, then invites the upper strings to join in a conversational presentation. Lightly does it, not only here but also in the lyric descent of 16ths in the upper strings in bar 55 and the silvery arc of piano notes in bar 56. (Be sure that the string trills in this measure are nonchalant enough to leave the piano's flourish unobscured.)

55

You may already have noticed that there has not been a single moment of silence since m. 23. There will be one such at the second beat of m. 60, and that only a quarter-beat in duration, effectively bridged by the sustaining sonority of the preceding chord. I think you will agree, though, that there has been no oppressive sense of endless sound. Contrasting musical events, textures, and sonorities have unfolded effortlessly, one after the other.

60

One such transition is here at hand, for in m. 57 the piano alone takes over from the strings. The octave alternation in the piano-bass should not be too staccato, but ought rather reflect the sonority of the cello's repeated 8ths in the preceding bar. The duet in thirds in the piano-treble needs as much *cantabile* as the player can bestow, to suggest the kinship of the keyboard with the sound of the upper strings.

57

When the three strings join the piano in bar 61, the effect is surprisingly rich, once again suggesting the sound of at least a septet. In view of the full orchestration in these measures, you should not overemphasize the sforzandi in bars 61–63.

61

Note how the four-part setting for piano alone, in the second half of m. 63, prepares the ear for the still slighter sound of the string trio in the next two bars. The three-voice passage must be very light, especially in the broidery of the viola part. Through subtle emphasis, that player should reveal the fact that the first 16th-

63

66 note of each half measure is in duet with the half-notes of the cello part. Further, the second half bar in mm. 66 and 68 in that voice must be projected with suitably soloistic verve and resonance.

69 The forte of the violin and viola duet in mm. 69–70 should be lighthearted in tone. Pay attention to the dot over the final quarter at the start of m. 70. There can be no suggestion of finality on that chord. The cello has insisted, by virtue of the sustained F in the second half of m. 70, that matters must continue. The duet carries forth, at least for a time: past the E♭ chord at the start of bar 72; through the pointed footwork of the 8th-notes that follow; and on to the resolution on B♭ at the

74 downbeat of bar 74.

The piano, however, insists with dolce primness on redoing the whole passage before allowing it to settle. This repetition can only too easily sound like a dull retread of something that was already clear to begin with. Take advantage of the sound of the new orchestration (piano and strings), and especially of the piano's

76 interrupting response in m. 76. Make the most of the chuckling 8th-notes in the second half of that bar; also, see if the violin's takeover of that same rejoinder in the next measure can be, yet again, a bit different in inflection. Use your ears and your imagination to interpret what is set before you on the page.

69 Earlier in the movement, there was a direct transition from the descent of m. 69 to the ascending line of bar 70. In the present revisiting of the passage, there is an

78 exuberant elaboration of the original proceedings. The descent of bar 78 leads to an extended, more gradual rise than before. Drop the dynamic level a bit at the start of bar 79 to leave room to emphasize the process by an increase in sound. Don't overdrive m. 81; leave it to the sudden addition of the strings to provide some of the forte. The viola will be forgiven if there is a touch of jazzy inflection to its

82 oscillating line of 16ths in bars 82–83, especially if the half-note support in the other two string parts is played with some slight, impelling sting on the start of the successive tones.

I am sure that the violin will find there is time only for a crisply played turn on

84 each of the trilled notes in the ascending scale of bar 84. The line certainly cannot endure any slow-up in favor of an attempt to take the trills at face value.

This violin passage is only the first of a marvelous succession of solos that moves on through the piano-treble and viola before resolving in the figurated bass

87 line of bar 87. In that measure, there are three voices giving tongue to the sustained trill. Please go easy here again, or the ensemble—instead of sounding exuberant— will resemble the legendary flock of geese sounding the invasion alarm.

88 In the codetta that rounds out the exposition, heed the indicated quietness of dynamic level. This is a nostalgic bit of reminiscing among the five melodic strands. The characteristic, upward leap of the octave (in the original response to the aggressive theme motive) is transformed here into altered, more tranquil rhythmic forms in the piano-treble and violin lines.

98 The end of the codetta (downbeat of m. 98) transits directly into two final measures of brooding half-notes. The piano's offbeat responses in these bars should be quiet enough not to break the hovering mood of the sustained tones. This is, of course, a curtain raiser for the repeat of the exposition. The tone of the music, though, is so wonderfully involved with the opening of the development that I feel some resentment at having to return to the opening.

98 When—with or without the repeated exposition—you move into the development, there are apparently only six measures (98–103) in which to effect the

transition. The crescendo and forte that occupy the last four of these measures call for some moderation, lest the sound grow too thick. It seems to me that, with this increased density of texture, Mozart implies an immediate return to the opening, but now in C minor, only to surprise us with the sudden reversion to the quiet music that actually follows.

The transition in half-notes has in fact set the stage for a longish episode based on a whole-note figure of the descending fourth—obviously an augmented reflection of the trademark interval of the opening theme. For as long as possible, maintain a quiet, *cantabile* mode of playing. The fortes in mm. 111, 115, and 119 can be moderate, treated more as forte-pianos than as heavy outbursts.

104

111

A current of 8th-note figures forms the floor for the activity through almost the entire development. These should be played with flexibility, so that they participate on equal footing with the other voices, rather than merely offering a rigid and detached background.

The forte figure in the 1st violin in m. 124 (and in the viola and cello soon after) needs emphasis on the trilled note. This works to advantage against the ascending scale-run in a neighboring voice (as in bar 126), supplying the sting needed to lift that run from its suspended first note. The pyramid of such runs in the strings in mm. 130–32 will produce an automatic crescendo. Don't let this loudness get out of hand; the successive downbeat chords, including the bass octaves in the piano, should be the center of interest. Sting each downbeat, then recede a bit so that the ascending run can be heard; and save the musketry for the piano's runs in bars 133, 135, and 137.

124

130

135

Here again, the analogy of the piano concerto should figure in your thinking, with the string tutti responding to each of the piano statements. In these responses, the emphasis should be on the downbeat of the second measure of the figure (that is, bars 135, 137, 139), for two reasons: first, the shape of the downbeat 8th-note figure is not like that in the original theme, and some indication of that fact should be offered the listener; and second, the confluence of the string chord and the piano's sustained note at each of these points creates pungent clusters of sound, which the ear should be able to enjoy.

Please note the cello's ascending run in bar 140; it is that line which actually carries us into the recapitulation. With this in view, the piano should temper the loudness of its doubled runs in the preceding measures, leaving a bit of the thunder for the string group. By the same token, the violin and viola should go easy in the second half of bar 140, so that the cello run need not be forced.

140

The crescendo and forte in bars 148–51 should be moderate, I feel; there is a poignant, *misterioso* quality about these measures, and especially in m. 151, that is damaged by excessive force. Also, these four bars are a shortened, pathos-filled replacement for the material that earlier occupied fully twenty-four measures (bars 8–31). It is angst, not force, that is needed to carry this compressed message.

148

What I have called the concerto passage now returns in the tonic minor, rather than in the relative major of the corresponding spot in the exposition. So also, the ensemble-style episode that follows is now heard in a lower register than before. I hope the players will be sufficiently affected by these changes in perspective so that they seek out their own ways of exploiting these shifts in mode and tone color. This especially sober movement demands thoughtful treatment.

152

The temper of the key of G minor has colored the entire recapitulation section. Nowhere do I find its impact more telling, however, than in the closing measures.

Music that had a pastoral, even dancelike effect when in B♭ (see mm. 88 ff.) now—
212 from bar 212—takes on a rather dejected tone. Try to underscore this change. Where, earlier, you might have leaned toward mobile pacing and sprightly bowing, you ought now to pull back on speed, play for smoothness of line and muted **222** dynamics. Bars 222–23, in particular, should have a very hushed sound, to heighten the shock of the return of the theme in forte. There might even be some retard over the second of these bars, though you will have to be subtle about it.

Keep in mind that the movement's opening has already been heard at least three times (assuming you took the first section repeat and skipped that of the recapitulation). It seems to me that Mozart is being both insistent and surprising in **224** bringing the initial phrase back yet again at the start of the coda. He challenges the listener to join with him in his obsession with the *idée* fixe.

Instead of reviewing the entire theme-complex, however, he makes a crucial **229** change in the piano's response in bar 229: for the first time, he gives us the sound of the minor ninth rather than the expected upward leap of an octave. This stretching to the E♭ should be well tasted by the pianist, with a suitable rubato elongation on the dotted-8th/16th figure as well as on the downbeat E♭ before making the scalewise descent. I would even suggest that the descent itself be stretched a bit, as though the reaching for the higher note has produced a certain lassitude. The 8th **231** note debate that now ensues between the piano and violin (mm. 231 ff.) can start— very quietly—from this relaxed tempo, picking up both loudness and speed as it makes its way to the final passage.

239 That fortissimo should be taken at full allegro, as the excitement of the moment will dictate. The torrent of 16ths in the piano part should not be relentless, but should breathe with the phrase, so that there is a sting on the start of the half-notes and emphasis on the first note of the slurred 8th-note couplets. Arrange your dynamics and phrasing in these measures so that a special, dramatic stress can be **247** given the last appearance of the theme, mm. 247–48. Take your time on the rests in mm. 248 and 249, then finish the movement with a stentorian flourish.

II *Andante.* The preface to the Eulenburg score of this quartet describes this Andante and the concluding Rondo as being "rooted in their time" (the later 18th century) as compared to the first movement of the work. I think the commentator is looking for a graceful way of saying something many of us may feel—namely, that the truly unique chapter of this quartet is its Allegro, and that the second and third movements can easily seem pale or even routine by comparison.

I am embarrassed to write such a thought. Yet, having heard performances of the work (my own included!), I know that the task of meeting the musical and emotional challenges of the first movement is exceeded only by that of putting the other two movements somewhere in the same frame. This applies especially to the Andante. Its melody is handsome enough: is there any unacceptable Mozart tune? However, hearing it after the baleful measures of the Allegro, and especially after the intense onslaught of that movement's coda, I have the sense of coming out of the heat of the forge into the gentility of a tea party. Could Mozart, in a way, have been apologizing for the rugged temper of the first movement?

There's no help for it. You obviously can't get away with playing just the Allegro. And there's no denying that audiences have long enjoyed listening to all three chapters in sequence. Let's take a deep breath, switch mental gears, and see how to deal successfully with the Andante.

To begin with, watch the tempo. You can't afford to count your 8th-notes laboriously or trudge heavy footed through the measure. Mozart himself writes this cautionary comment into the music: the three 16ths at the end of bar 4 carry you through the phrase punctuation, forward into the remainder of the eight-bar melodic unit. At the end of m. 8, you have the decorative line of 32nd-notes to sweep you into the reorchestrated repeat of the opening.

4

8

Take care with the dynamics. At m. 9, the strings make their entry, and all four instruments are instructed to play forte. Perhaps to reinforce the seriousness of this movement, performers sometimes take the forte instruction too literally. With the close spacing of the part writing in this passage, such procedure results in a logy effect. Throughout the movement, try to let the orchestration of the writing build the loud spots; don't force.

9

There are a lot of 32nd-notes in this movement, arranged in garlands of quadruplets. Avoid a dogmatic *one*-two-three count of the 3/8 meter. Even at an appropriate tempo, the resulting effect is dull. You might, with some justice, say that these streamers of small notes are decorated counterfoils to the broader 8th- and quarter-note rhythms that are being played in other voices. It is certainly true that those broader rhythms must themselves be organized within the frame of the still larger phrase units they comprise. Even so, the lines of 32nds, in whatever voice they may appear, should be played with sufficient rubato and with dynamic coloration. The player must discriminate between the tones in the series, and show that some are more important than others.

19

In part, this involves the way you look at the construction of the phrase. Let me suggest, for example, that—starting in bar 19—you think of the piano-treble line as made up, first, of four 8th-beats; then three; two more to bring you to the start of m. 22; and five more to bring you to the second beat of bar 23 in the piano-treble. This view of the melody seems to go against the grain of the quarter- and 8th-note rhythms in the other voices. Those rhythms, however, threaten to impose that inexorable, triple pulse I spoke of before. Experiment for the freshest possible treatment of the music.

19

Be sensitive to what your colleagues are playing. Notice, for example, that in measures 20, 21, and 23, the tones heard on the downbeat in the string parts are in a state of harmonic unrest, finding their resolution only when they move to the chord on the second beat of the bar. In the piano-treble in these same measures, the 32nd that falls on the downbeat is even more foreign to its context and is again impelled to find resolution at midbar. Try playing the entire passage from m. 19 to m. 33 slowly, sensing the frictions within and between the several voices and observing the flow of musical tensions and resolutions. See what effect rubato within the individual lines has on simultaneous events in other parts. This will be especially interesting in such measures as 26 and 28, where there is rhythmic friction between the piano-treble and the viola, as well as with the contrasting rhythmic flow of the violin line.

20

26

In your slow practice, try to find the inflections within the individual lines that work best with those given to parallel strands of the music. Then, see whether the same approach works as well when playing up to tempo, or whether the faster speed suggests yet other approaches. Let your ears be the judge, and don't be stingy with your experimentation. Trial and appraisal in the rehearsal will contribute greatly to the flexibility of the eventual performance and will spare your audience the ordeal of a cut-and-dried, uninformed presentation. If I point out that more than half of the 149 measures in the movement have some amount of the

32nd-note motion, to say nothing of the reappearance of more sedate rhythms, you will realize the importance of the kind of experimentation I have suggested.

35 Some other things to watch for: the forte-pianos in mm. 35–37 are scarcely more than warmings of the tone through a combination of vibrato and bow speed.
40 The forte in bar 40 and the sforzando in m. 41, though obviously of somewhat larger scale, should still be adjusted to the quiet context of the music. Whether in a rhythmic support function, as in the cello in bars 35–38, or in more melodic context,
47 as in all three strings in bar 47, repeated 16ths should display some forward impulse. Don't let the rhythmic texture turn into graph paper.

58 A passage such as that in mm. 58–65 is particular fun for the players. Piano-bass and cello collaborate in a moving support line; the piano-treble lyricizes, with the encouragement of the viola; and the violin, in true coloratura fashion, holds forth in a sustained note over all.

66 Be careful about mm. 66–70. The literal repetition of the two-measure groups can sound fairly tiresome. Throw some shade of difference over the second pair by a change in inflection and a shift in dynamics, even at the risk of producing a cliché echo. Further, recognize that the line continues on (after the slightest of breaths)
74 through the end of bar 74, poising there on the E♭ before embarking on the return of the theme. In the course of that return, note the change (bar 82) in the piano solo from the relatively staid 32nd to the more propulsive triplets. These last will fire
83 you into the reorchestrated version of the opening's forte passage. Here (at bar 83), my earlier caution against too pressed a forte applies even more emphatically. The active bass, doubled at the octave between the cello and the lower piano line, should be played for transparency rather than thickness: consommé, not porridge.

Again, as in the first movement, be on the lookout for the sonority changes that result from the recasting of the secondary material of the closing section, here in the tonic major. You won't be dealing with mood (or mode!) changes, except to the extent that the lower register affects your perception of the temper of the music. Still, the change in the sonority itself, slight though it may be, should be evaluated as you adjust dynamic balances in your review of familiar material.

139 If played melodically, not merely as a stereotyped spray of notes, a little detail like the arpeggiated ornament of the downbeats of mm. 139–40 in the piano part can add to the richness of the sound texture. The string players should allow room for these figures, and also for freedom in the pacing of the 32nd-note lines with which the strings lead on from the piano's flourishes.

144 If you compare mm. 144–47 of the piano-bass line with the corresponding place in mm. 66–69, you will see that Mozart has given the closing passage a shift in register for the repeated pair of measures. The change to the lower octave is by way of reinforcing the sense of finality and departure of the movement. Take full advantage of the new sonority and of its implications. Above all, endow the two
148 pianissimo 8ths of the final bars with the most ethereal and suspended effect you can contrive.

III ***Rondo. Allegro.*** It is easier, I think, to move from the Andante to the Rondo than from the first to the second movement. The last two movements seem more closely akin in spirit, though they obviously differ from each other in temper.

I can't recall a more exuberant theme in the Mozart literature than the one he produced for this finale. Nor do I know of any movement of his that maintains such animation more constantly throughout. I don't know whether Mozart would have considered using the qualifier, "moderato," in designating the character of the movement. According to the NMA edition, this movement had no title in the autograph; was called Rondeau in Hoffmeister's first edition; bore the name of Rondo in the reissue of the first edition in Mannheim, c. 1787; and acquired the added instruction, Allegro moderato, only with the edition of André, in Offenbach am Main, about 1823.[4]

Even the *alla breve* time signature by itself is not enough to assure the intense, propulsive force that this music demands. Nothing less than a one-to-the-bar feeling will do.

Beyond this, proper grouping of the measures of the theme is essential to its successful performance. The thrust of the upbeat couplet into the first half of bar 1 is, of course, inescapable. But the principal emphasis in the first four measures must be given to the downbeat of m. 2. Just as clearly, the target of the second four measures has to be the downbeat of m. 7. This produces a rakish, off-center shape for the first half of the theme, throwing its momentum downward in the vigorous leaps of mm. 2 and 3. From there, the progress is flatter, the line racing upward toward the peak in the second part of the melody—again off center—from which the cadence unrolls. The bass line has a shape and thrust of its own; the pull between the high and low strands of the writing lends further impetus to the theme. All in all, this theme is a finely tuned, musical mechanism, seemingly capable of perpetual motion.

As the strings join in for the rerun of the theme, extra motive force is provided by the line of 8th-notes in the piano-treble. That strand is marked legato, but I would suggest a somewhat drier touch, both for the sense of mobility of the phrase itself and to preserve enough contrast of texture against that of the music that follows.

The threefold repetition of paired measures that starts in bar 16 benefits, I think, from setting the second of these units down somewhat in dynamic level. This had best show some new inflection, coming as it does after the piano's own statement. At the end of the string repetition of this unit, the cadential repartée between strings, piano, and tutti (mm. 33–36) deserves some jocular treatment by the ensemble. Play around with the length of the rests between the responses. Also, if the fortissimo outburst of the third statement (in sign of mock impatience) is robust enough, you may want to delay the slightest bit to let the dust settle before the close of the cadence in mm. 36–38. On the other hand, the entrance of the piano on the second 8th-note of bar 38 should be quick enough to evoke the sense of the riotous windup of the next six measures.

A lot of the fun in this movement comes from the give and take between the piano and the string corps. The composer gives you ammunition for this dialogue. In the string response that starts in bar 52, note the 8th-note turn in the second half of the measure; the oscillation in the viola part, two bars later; and the motion in that instrument in m. 56 that leads to the extended upward leap of the violin in the following measure. All these details differ from corresponding points in the piano statement that precedes. The playing should take these differences into account, so that the listener is aware that no simple repetition is under way.

Now we head into one of the white-water rapids of the movement: a lively tune in D major, framed at each end by a measure of flourishes, throws the pianist into a blazing streamer of triplets. These, in turn, fling open the curtain for the strings' D major theme (mm. 70 ff.), yet another gem from Mozart's endless store. That this melody is written in syncopated quarter-note figures automatically makes

1

7

16

33

36
38

52

56

59

70

it seem like a rest-and-recuperation point in the movement. It should, nonetheless, be played with jaunty energy. Besides, you get only four bars of the unadulterated rhythmic flavor before the pace starts picking up again in the strings' Alberti figures.

The title of the movement means, of course, that a refrain alternates with contrasting melodies as the music unfolds. I think that Mozart may also have had some dance idea in mind, for there is constant handing off of the action between the strings and the piano. Thus, at bar 84 the piano plays several measures of solo transition, paving the way for the strings to turn up their motors as they head for their own solo. This is a flashing 8th-note dance, which the cello at first supports as an onlooker, then joins in full force. The piano watches from the sidelines, then goes the strings' performance one better by unleashing a flurry of triplets.

Part of Mozart's alternation plan in writing this finale rests on the kind of speed change we have just witnessed. After topping its own sally with a still-faster flight of 16ths, the piano immediately yields place to some of the slowest-sounding music in the movement. In so sophisticated a work, you have to be discreet in the barnyard tune that now follows (mm. 111 ff.). Certainly the violin has to display some courtly grace in its line; but a slight touch of bumpkin in the cello quarter-notes and the viola's bagpiping will be appreciated by the audience. The flavor has already changed by the time the piano takes its turn with the tune, for the string background is now exclusively in sustained tones, calling for a more delicate treatment than was available to the village band that has just quit the stage.

The trumpetlike fanfare of the strings in mm. 134–35 merits a bit of retard in preparation for the portentous fermata that awaits. From now on, however, a forward drive is essential. There is a full-scale review of tunes to come. More important, you have to traverse a rather stormy section in E minor, complete with musical thunderbolts (see mm. 179 ff.)—the closest temperamental link, if in fact it was so intended, to the first movement.

I would like to suggest one last bit of time play: the mock indecisiveness of the discussion between piano and strings in mm. 342–48 really requires some coquettish rubati. After that, though, the progress to the double bar should be an Olympic sprint for four.

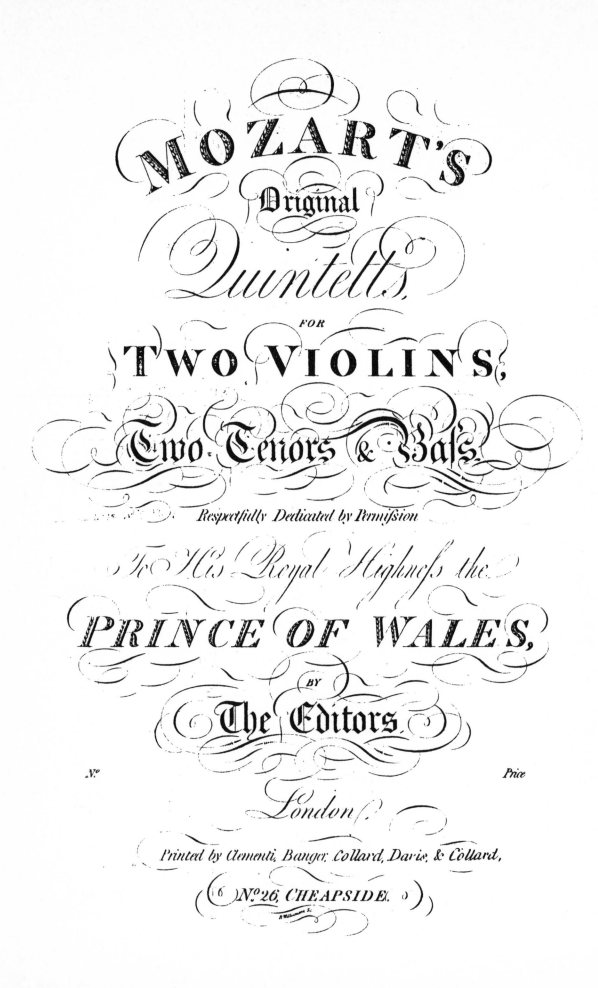

MOZART'S
Original
Quintetts,
FOR
TWO VIOLINS,
Two Tenors & Bass.

Respectfully Dedicated by Permission

To His Royal Highness the

PRINCE OF WALES,

BY

The Editors

Nº   Price

London

Printed by Clementi, Banger, Collard, Davis, & Collard,

Nº 26, CHEAPSIDE.

CHAPTER SIX

❧ Mozart ❧
Viola Quintet in G minor, K. 516

Among my warmest memories is that of a musical evening in Chicago, years ago, when the great David Oistrakh sat in as second viola with our ensemble for a reading of a Mozart viola quintet. In so doing, he demonstrated not only his own collegiality, but also the point that in fine chamber music, there are no subordinate parts. Each voice is participant in a profound musical experience.

Any list of the great and the profound in the chamber repertoire would have to include at least four of the Mozart viola quintets. Technically, the catalogue includes six such works. Mozart originally composed five of these for strings. He arranged the sixth, in C minor, from the Serenade for wind octet, in the same key, K. 388 (384a).[1] The music of the C minor is sober and dramatic, and a gratifying experience for the string ensemble. To my ear, however, the sound of the wind version of the work has more bite and pungency, as befits the prevailingly dark color of the music; Mozart's original choice of instrumentation was correct.

The first of the string quintets, K. 174, in B flat, written in Salzburg in 1733, is engaging in its own right, but is slighter than the remainder of the group, which were all products of his final decade. The last two, in D major, K. 593, and E flat, K. 614, were written in 1790 and 1791, respectively. They are superb examples of his imagination and skill as composer, particularly in their finales, which are dazzling in their intricacy. These two quintets are not heard often enough, yielding place in the concert repertoire to the monumental pair, the C major, K. 515, and G minor, K. 516, both dating from the spring of 1787.

Although the G minor quintet is one of the most favored works in today's

---

SCORE: Wolfgang Amadeus Mozart. 1986. *String Quintet in G minor for two Violins, two Violas, and Cello, KV 516*. Urtext. Ed. Ernst Hess. Kassel: Bärenreiter. Miniature score No. 154.

Left: Mozart: Viola Quintets. London: Clementi (c. 1815). Title page. Reproduced with permission from the collection of the Sibley Music Library, the Eastman School of Music, University of Rochester.

programs, it—like the G minor Piano Quartet—might well have been regarded with some suspicion by the average, entertainment-minded Viennese listener in Mozart's day. Robbins Landon suggests, first, that "it must have been obvious to Mozart that, at least as far as the Viennese were concerned, his popular appeal had in some way begun to fail"; and second, that, despite this, the composer's emotional mind-set at this time made it impossible for him to avoid the somber character of this and other late works.[2] Mozart, in fact, achieves in the G minor quintet a brooding intensity so keen that it is difficult to match in any other work in the repertoire.[3]

I
1

Allegro. If the 1st violin chooses to play the opening theme with the printed bowing (that is, with the fourth 8th-note detached), it would normally be with the lower part of the bow. With the modern bow, even in skilled hands, this results in a light texture, not well suited to the mood of this opening. Worse still, it can produce a false accent on the detached note. My own preference is to tie the fourth 8th to the preceding, slurred group, but with enough gentle articulation to preserve its identity as a separate note.

1

In accord with this rather legato and horizontal approach, the 8ths in the accompanying voices should be played in what I call a legato spiccato, with only moderate lift from the string, and with due sensitivity to the rubato inflections in the solo line. Carry through the measure, marking the half bar with a slight emphasis on the fifth 8th-note. Changes of pitch in these voices are important. They impel the harmony and also provide points that react with the motion of the solo line. The lower lines also contain details that make up part of the solo: the last three

4, 6

8ths in the viola in m. 4; in the 2nd violin, the last three 8ths of m. 6, the second half of m. 7; and so on.

Any exhibitionistic treatment of the solos is out of place in this music. Virtuosity here must be subordinated to the sober message of the work. By the

18

same token, the forte peak of this first-theme complex (mm. 18 ff.) does not call for fiery emotionalism. It is simply a stronger counterpart of the restrained contemplation suggested by the opening measures. If any reminder be needed, it is to be found in the piano echo that comes on the heels of the melodic flourish of

24

m. 24.

In the bridge passage, Mozart (who seems to have supplied dynamic marks only when he felt them to be of special import) offers mezzo forte or piano

32

instruction six times within the space of the twelve measures, 32–43. He not only indicates stress points, but calls for moderation in those emphases. In fact, the first place in the movement where the players can feel justified in letting go is in the

64

forte passage, mm. 64–83. Even here, two short piano interludes temper the flame.

While allowing for the generally subdued tone of this movement, we should still project important elements, wherever they occur. Thus, the brief cello transition

8

in m. 8; the 1st viola's assumption of the theme in mm. 8 ff.; the violin duo in mm.

18, 89

18 ff.; the 2nd violin exhalation in m. 89—these are some of the places in the exposition where the instruments involved must be clearly heard.

A moment of special impact in this section, and again in the corresponding

43

spot in the recapitulation, occurs in mm. 43–48. The 1st violin, building to this point

32

since the E♭ in m. 32, then moves through the G and B♭ in later bars, finally

43

sweeping to the high D. Its florid descent from that point needs freedom to emote. Here the other instruments are silent, as though frozen in their attention to the solo line; this silence also leaves room for judicious rubato in the 1st violin part. The

46

cello is roused from its contemplation to respond to the high voice; the effect, however, should not be simply one of a low-register echo, but of extending and realizing the implications of what the violin has stated. Bar 48 is a crucial part of the process: between them, the cello, 2nd violin and viola, and 1st violin have to lead the way back from the reverie of the preceding bars to the regenerated tempo of mm. 49 ff.   49

Bars 49 to 56 seem about to repeat themselves in the next measures. The rivalry here between 1st viola and 1st violin, as well as the change in the cello line, should immediately help dispel that notion. The viola apparently takes over the solo with the upbeat to m. 56. But the 1st violin, which now seems to be the imitating—and 56 hence secondary—voice, pulls into the predominant spot by being the first to introduce the B♮ (downbeat of m. 57). The answer, of course, is that the two parts make up a duo; violin and viola must speak equally.

The ensemble must play the first passage (mm. 49 ff.) so that it prepares for the   49
fulfillment offered by the second (mm. 56 ff.). Some slight moderation of the   56
crescendo and forte of mm. 53–55 is in order. A *very* slight urging of the pace,   53
starting in bar 56, is also desirable. The 2nd violin should add its own impulse by
sufficiently reinforcing its ascending thirds, at the end of mm. 57 and 59. 1st violin   57
and 1st viola need to rejoice a bit in the active and cross-grained writing in their
duo of m. 62, not rush inflexibly toward the trill in the following bar. Play so that   62
the audience can enjoy the detail of the writing with you.

Once the trill in bar 63 starts, the 2nd viola has a solo of its own: a measure of   63
8th-note Fs. Not much? Actually, this solo is quite important, not just because it is
the one moving element in the measure (the trill is timeless), but even more because
it connects the extreme activity of the duo in the preceding measure to the resumed
thematics of cello and 2nd violin in bar 64.   64

I referred earlier to the letting-go at m. 64. The passage has all the excitement
of a staged music-drama. There is an organized hubbub of contrasting and
opposing characters in mm. 64–67 and 72–75. Following each comes a passage of   72
hushed surprise, with the second one unfolding into the fluttering, swooning
triplets of the 1st violin (mm. 79 ff.). The robust assurances of the lower voices   79
support the broad cadence of bars 82–85. An operatic scene is all but visible here,   82
even though no libretto is offered. The brilliance of this passage is intensified by
contrast with the simpler part writing of the measures that follow, and by the sense
of darkening and doubt that creeps back with the G♭ of m. 91.   91

There is a fermata on the 8th-rest just before the double bar. I think the pause
should be somewhat longer when it precedes the repeat than when it leads into the
development. Returning to the opening represents a real break, a wrenching of
direction. The connection from the end of the exposition to the transition measures,
95–96, is much more immediate, and so requires less hesitation.   95

There is no fermata over bar 96; but a grand pause is very explicitly written   96
out in the form of the rests that fill the bar. This break must be not only precisely
measured out, but even extended a bit. There is a surprising shift in harmony just
ahead, and again a brief switch from dark to light. Let the dust settle before
proceeding.

Always exercise judgment. At the opening of the development, for example,
the cello exclamations, in piano, are answered by the descending lines in the violin
duo. Though marked at the same dynamic level, these descents are subordinate to
the cello and should be more quietly played, especially since they start out in a
high, more brilliant register.

The development is rather short, but very clearly and effectively laid out. Except for the momentary E♭ in the 1st violin part at its opening, the section reserves its high point for the D♭ in m. 119, in the course of a passage of tightly knit responses among the voices of the ensemble. This compression gives way to a seemingly long descent to the recapitulation. The voyage lasts only nine bars, but is dangerous. Unless the players deal with the rhythmic sequences imaginatively, these measures can be a dead spot in the movement. The descent is step-by-step, but the ensemble—through subtle rubato, change of tone color, dynamic shading—must make the audience sense the fading of the light, the lowering into an almost palpable gloom.

149   The most vigorous episode in the movement is that of mm. 149–62. Here the close interweaving of sinewy melodic strands deserves assertive playing from all hands. A late reflection of this temper comes in the five-measure outburst after the
234   grand pause in m. 234 (itself a culmination of two fermatas in the measures just before); the chromatics in these bars demand agitation—a giants' causeway of half-steps.

251   Toward the very end, there is a trap for the 1st violin: mm. 251–52 exactly repeat the two preceding bars. To play them as carbon copies, however, is to confess to boredom or lack of inspiration. Try a more distant tone color and a change in inflection in m. 251 and a very slight retard as you approach the sighing, falling, minor seventh on the last beat of bar 252. This will convey the truth that the end of the movement occurs on the downbeat of measure 253.

     Allow for a brief instant of meditation on the quarter-rest. Then play the two chords of the cadence with unforced tone and full resonance.

II   ***Menuetto.*** Any last vestige of courtly grace still attached to the dance title is consumed by the intensity of this music—especially when the fabric of the dance is torn by huge chords, twice in the first section, three times in the second. Instinctively the players may feel they should rip these chords out of the
4   instruments. For truly effective impact, however, the heat of the sound should come as much from the left hand as the right. The bow should be drawn rather slowly, clinging to the strings but not rasping, and as close to the bridge as the sound of the instrument and the skill of the player will allow. If the surrounding, piano tones are played at proper, contrasting level, the aural impact of the chords will be overwhelming.

     Contrast management is the touchstone from the very start of the movement. The first few notes are orchestrated for the entire ensemble, at forte. Immediately after, there is solo voicing, in piano, with very light accompaniment added. Then comes the first of the famous chords. You will observe that the melodic line continues on an even course, sailing on through the changing currents of instrumentation and past the chordal cliffs. Follow Mozart's lead, move alertly in the sudden shifts between loud and soft, and the music will be well served.

     In the closing phase of the second section, the chordal exclamations are arranged on three upward steps that feel much larger than they actually are. Then
35   you have to go one step farther, to the forte in bar 35. In the preceding, loud chords, you only had to use the bow judiciously, then let the resonance dissipate in the ensuing quarter-rest. In m. 35, the forte must be sustained in a continuing melodic line. Don't try to top the loudness of effect that you established in the chords. Settle for a realistic and grateful level in the sustaining line that is now to be played. There are five of you at work, and the effect will be full enough.

The four lower voices play the downbeat of the second ending. From this, there should be no break to the 1st violin's B♮ that starts the Trio. Only thus can you fully exploit the very dramatic shift out of the minor version of the melody, and the magical transition from the B♭ and A♭ of the 2nd violin in m. 40. In both sections of the Trio, the viola duet—so moving in its own right—is made the more intense by the slow tremolo of the pedal point in the cello and the two violins. These oscillations must be played warmly, and with gentle emphasis on the passing downbeats.

In the second section of the Trio, the lyric interweavings of all five parts, but especially of the 1st violin and cello, produce an intensity that is all the greater for the understated dynamics that prevail. Here, in mm. 65–74, is one of those rare moments in the chamber literature when the sensations of pain and pleasure crowd close upon one another.

Such minglings come often in this quintet. Restraint with eventual outburst in the first movement; the framing of the Trio by the dark Minuetto; and now, the contrast between two slow movements. For, immediately following the *Adagio ma non troppo*, the "official" slow movement of the work, comes the Adagio prelude to the final Allegro. Though the second Adagio is only thirty-eight measures long, its gravity gives it the stature of an independent movement. Its unrelievedly deep lamentation, moreover, sets it off from the supernal musings of the first Adagio.

The air of philosophical detachment about this first slow movement is remarkable in so sober a work, nearly as remarkable as the effervescent spirit of the concluding Allegro. Mozart unerringly adds to the otherworldly tone of this *Adagio ma non troppo* by asking that the instruments be muted. This veiling of the already quiet lines creates a dreamlike, visionary air that is wonderful to experience. I have always felt that the two danger spots in this movement come at mm. 18 ff. and mm. 55 ff. The attempt to lend dramatic weight to the pulsating 16ths can easily lead to a slowing of pace, thus overriding Mozart's *ma non troppo* admonition at the very moment when mobility is needed.

The 1st violin line has to move forward through the successive sforzando points in mm. 18, 20, and 21. This impetus depends on the cooperation of the lower voices. They have to mark the passage from one half bar to the next, never rushing, never dragging.

The commentaries of the 2nd viola in mm. 19 and 21, though offering rare moments in the spotlight for that instrument, do not justify a pullback in tempo. They are a response to the violin solo, and cannot assume control of the passage. (The same applies to the corresponding area, mm. 56 and 58.)

A word of caution, too, about the passages at mm. 27–32 and 66–71: here the 1st violin and cello govern the music, which must flow smoothly and with some spirit. The inner voices cannot labor over the offbeat 16ths or slurred 32nds. If the players ride along with the motion of the framing lines, the rhythmic responses will fall neatly into place.

For me, the points of greatest intensity in this movement occur in mm. 8, 45, 49, and 77, where the convoluted melodic lines contend in forte against the restraint of the mute. Under the player's ear, this pent-up force takes on almost tangible shape, and is certainly physically felt; I think this same sense transmits to the audience.

It is worth noting that the pulsating 16th-note accompaniment, already encountered twice before in the movement, returns in the closing measures of this

43

40

65

III

18
55

18

19

56
27, 66

8, 45
77

Adagio. The same kind of rhythmic background, changed in meter and augmented to 8th-notes, runs throughout the finale's Adagio.

IV

Adagio—Allegro. In the preceding movement, the 16th-note figures needed separate strokes, in a very gentle, low-profile spiccato. In the present Adagio, however, the 8th-note rhythm in the inner voices requires broader, more legato bowing. To avoid the risk of the pedestrian effect that might emerge from one stroke per note, as given by the printed bowing, you should link the detached notes

1

(as in m. 1) in an easy *portato* stroke, three to the bow. Forgive me for mentioning that, within this bowing, the notes must still sound as though grouped in the three couplets dictated by the 3/4 meter. Most important, the inner voices should once again recognize that they are not merely accompaniment; they provide a

4, 9

sympathetic, choral response to the elegy of the 1st violin. The cello's pizzicato bass joins in this; in two places, that voice changes to bowed figures that participate even more directly in the solo process.

I will not presume, verbally and at long distance, to guide the 1st violin in the playing of the solo line. Here, direct example is the best instruction. Moreover, if too much illustration is needed from the live coach, the player at hand is clearly in need of broader musical experience. Listen to sensitive performers as much as possible, especially in their interpretation of slow, lyric music, and learn their use of inflection, tone color, and rubato for expressive purpose. Much of a performer's impact on the listener is psychological. The musical devices that effect this can and should be taught by live demonstration; even more, however, the student learns such devices through alert observation.[4]

The grace notes in the last two measures of the 1st violin part should be played as onbeat, stressed 16th-notes, taking precedence over the printed 8th-notes to which they are attached. The final grace note, then, lines up with the chord presented by the lower voices. A slight broadening of time in the last measure prepares us for the fermata that precedes the double bar.

Can there be any justification for the gaiety of the final Allegro after all the sober movements that precede it in this quintet? Even more to the point, how can we tolerate its mirth after the experience of so grieving a prelude as the Adagio?

Let me say that this is by no means the only such play on opposites in Mozart's writing. Think, for example, of the contrast between the eerie mood of the slow introduction to the C major quartet, K. 465, and the energetic force of the ensuing Allegro. Recall the alternation of the ominous tolling and the feverish scurrying in the overture to *Don Giovanni.* Then too, there is the exceedingly touching music of love and farewell in the vocal quintet in *Così fan tutte,* framed by the brusque march that sends the two heros off to the wars. Mozart's exploitation of the pull between contrary emotions is characteristic, and undoubtedly reflects something basic in his own nature.

In any event, the relation between the Adagio and Allegro in the G minor quintet was clearly a matter of deliberate decision on Mozart's part. He originally began to write an Allegro in minor, but opted instead for the present solution.[5] The problem, and Mozart's answer to it, remind me of that somewhat similar case, Beethoven's F minor quartet, Op. 95. There, again, is a work that remains dark and troubled in temper right up to the brink of the end. Beethoven waits until the very coda before flinging his way out in an electrically brilliant leave-taking.

Mozart's insistence on the high spirits of this Allegro can be seen in the sforzando he places on the third, highest figure at the opening of the movement (m.

39); it's as though the rising rhythmic sequences are being tossed in a blanket. 39
Again, in mm. 46 ff., note how the rising arpeggio in the low voices pushes the 1st 46
violin up and over into the downward rush of 16th-notes.

Speaking of 16ths, the ensemble should collectively help decide how the 1st
violin is to handle the figures in mm. 50–51. The sextuplets must be played either 50
very clearly as sets of duplets or, just as definitely, as a series of triplets (a rhythmic
grouping that is readily forthcoming, because of the shape of the line). I prefer to
hear them as duplets. Something betwixt and between is bound to be
uncomfortable to both listener and accompanying instrumentalists.

You may already have felt some discomfort, or at least puzzlement, because
the opening theme of the movement starts on the half-bar, even though its sound
suggests that it begins on a downbeat. The theme does seem to have more lift if you
are aware of its metric placement; this intensification may be lost on the audience,
however, unless they have the score committed to memory!

As for the performers, all is well until m. 53. After the preceding *calando*, and 53
before the grand pause of the first part of m. 54, this bar stands momentarily in 54
limbo. It might understandably produce a slight disorientation in the players, even
as they read their parts and count measures. The 1st violin can help by giving a
discreet downbeat signal in m. 54. This will probably not be necessary when the 54
ensemble is familiar with the passage, for the lower voices will simply watch for the
solo's entrance on the second beat of the measure.

There is again a slight shift of metric gears in mm. 58 ff. The lone entry of the 58
1st violin will inevitably sound like a stressed downbeat, even in piano; but the
quiet, massed entry of the four lower voices in m. 59 favors recognition of the true 59
downbeat. I think Mozart must have greatly enjoyed the deliberate ambiguity that
he creates here and at many other points in the movement. In any event, the players
dare not relax their vigilance, for they can sometimes be surprised by the measure
count in this movement.

A repeated-note motive appears in the 1st violin in m. 64; in various degrees of 64
prominence, it will remain in evidence for the rest of the movement. Violins, go
easy on the octave Ds in bar 68. Combining with the cello line, two octaves lower, 68
they should not be so loud that the accompaniment outweighs the viola duet. On
the other hand, the same motive of repeated notes assumes greater prominence in
bars 76–82. You will have to gauge the appropriate projection for the figure as the 76
movement unfolds.

Some of the fun and exuberance in this finale comes from the 16th-note scales
that race down, or up, in the several voices. This element appears initially in the 1st
violin in mm. 89 ff. Whoever gets a turn at the scales, please take my word, "race," 89
with two grains of salt. It is very possible to dash madly after your bow as it
decides, with a mind of its own, that an accelerando is just the thing. Control! Play
cleanly and steadily, think of the half measure, and pace yourself. I speak with
some feeling about this; I often felt—with my one shot at the figure in m. 224—like 224
a genie released from a bottle. Happily, my cellist colleague never seemed
distressed at the tempo I handed over to him.

Another spot where a calm approach to 16th-notes is very much in order is
found in mm. 261 ff. (a bit of the same also occurs back at mm. 134–36). The slurred 261
sextuplet in the 2nd violin part, in every second measure, must be very aware of the
underlying 8th-note pulse. Only thus can the link between the successive 8th-note
figures of the 1st violin be effective. So also, the continuous chain of sextuplets—

267   from 1st violin to 1st viola to cello—in mm. 267–70 needs unhurried graciousness.

The 1st violin will strongly feel Mozart's technical demands in this Allegro. I
50   have already mentioned the rhythm of mm. 50–51. More challenging are the 16th-
112   note figures in mm. 112, 114, and 116; very precise fingering and clean shifting are
needed to carry off these chromatic runs. The same goes for the melodic turns in
127, 131   mm. 127 and 131. So also for the broader, convoluted figures like, for example,
133, 260   those in mm. 133–142 and mm. 260 ff. Whether slow or fast, these melodic
260   flourishes require not only clarity but flexibility, so that the solo line's conversation
with itself as well as with the responses of the lower voices makes sense to the ear.
266   At bar 266 in the second of these passages, it will be the cellist's job to initiate the
extended wind-up of the conversation.

189   Later in the movement come such nuggets as the roulade in m. 189 or the
especially difficult (because of its placement on the violin fingerboard) figure in
258   m. 258. In every case, experimentation will be needed to find the cleanest fingering,
the most favorable string crossing. For the figure in m. 258, I would suggest starting
in fifth position; for clarity, play both the D♯ and the D♮ with the third finger. Move
260   to sixth position for the 8th-notes in mm. 260–61. In all this, your string crossing
will have to be exceptionally smooth and economical.

197, 310   At two points in the Allegro (mm. 197 ff., 310 ff.) the part writing presents all
five instruments in an ascending pyramid, with the repeated-note element
prominent. Nothing is better calculated to reveal the strength of the links in the
ensemble chain. The players should see to it, then, that there is collective agreement
as to temperament, smooth rhythmic connection of the several entrances, and the
greatest possible continuity of tone color in the shift from low to high register. For
serious performance, the instruments used in the ensemble should be tonally
compatible; otherwise, the players will be hard put to it to mask wide differences in
character of sound. Within even the closely matched ensemble of instruments, the
inevitably varied resonance of the voices, from low to high, will still make for a
wonderful play of sonority in the passages under discussion here.

322   All hands should be on the alert for m. 322. In effect, this figure, touching on
high G in the 1st violin, resolves the ending of the arpeggio (on the same G) in
319   m. 319. Musically speaking, the intervening arpeggio run to the G in mm. 320–21 is
320   an accessory motion, a melodic detour. Accordingly, there has to be a bit of special
emphasis on m. 322 to distinguish it from bar 321, and especially to underline the
difference in function between the identical triplets, D–B–G, in these two measures.

I have given some technical and musical advice about this quintet. To play the
work with the depth and subtlety it deserves is another matter, however, and will
require much study and experimentation by the ensemble. This composition is a
towering landmark in our musical heritage. Moreover, it is one of those most often
heard. For both reasons, the ensemble that seeks to add its own interpretation to the
existing roster has its work cut out for it.

Larghetto

CHAPTER SEVEN

ꙮ Mozart ꙮ
Clarinet Quintet in A, K. 581

Especially from the 16th century on, European instrument makers set out to create entire families of instruments. Within each family, members of varying size were constructed, so that the several registers of a composition, from high to low, might be heard in homogeneous tone color. This concept is evident, for example, in the string quartet, which came into being in the 18th century and has remained a dominant medium in small-ensemble writing ever since.

A taste for contrasting tone colors has been equally strong in Western music, from long before the Renaissance and on into the present. The large symphony orchestra of the past two centuries combines various families of instruments into one large, multicolored ensemble.

Instruments that differ in sonority have also been brought together in small groups. A significant portion of the chamber music repertoire is written for such mixed ensembles. A favorite example of this in our concert programs is Mozart's Clarinet Quintet. Here, the composer focuses on the individual flavors of clarinet and string quartet sound. At times he integrates the wind instrument into the part writing of the five-voiced texture, the clarinet strand shining through the weave. Far more often, though, he presents the clarinet in a solo role, set off against the voices in the string group, particularly the 1st violin.

The clarinet is an instrument of impressive dynamic range, from the most subtle pianissimo to a fortissimo that can cut through fairly massive orchestral sound. Also, it commands a wonderfully broad spectrum of tonal nuance and color, from a warm and open low register to a brilliant and penetrating top gamut.

SCORE: Wolfgang Amadeus Mozart. 1956. *Quintet in A major, for Clarinet, two Violins, Viola and Violoncello, KV 581*. Urtext. Ed. Ernst Fritz Schmid. Kassel: Bärenreiter. Miniature score No. 14.

Left: Mozart: Clarinet Quintet in A, K. 581. Urtext. Ed. Ernst Fritz Schmid. Kassel: Bärenreiter, 1956. Miniature score No. 14. Page 18 of score. Used by permission of Music Associates of America, agent for Bärenreiter.

Over the years, seasoned players have debated whether vibrato can appropriately be used in the production of clarinet tone, especially when performing late 18th-century music. I leave it to the individual clarinetist, then, to decide if—and where—vibrato can figure as an expressive device in that voice in the Mozart quintet. The string participants will, of course, adjust their tone colors accordingly.

Whatever the group decision, sensitivity is paramount. Whether in string, wind or vocal music, vibrato must always be proportioned—both in frequency and amplitude of the oscillation—to the musical situation at hand. Nothing is more distressing to hear than music slathered over with fevered shaking, without any adjustment to tempo, spirit, or compositional style. Vibrato should be an adornment to accurate pitch, and applied discerningly, with an eye to the demands both of melody and mood.

Mozart wrote his Clarinet Quintet in 1789. He had admired the instrument at least since 1778, when he wrote his father, lamenting the fact that the court orchestra in their home town of Salzburg did not have clarinets: "You cannot imagine the glorious effect of a symphony with flutes, oboes, and clarinets."[1] It was especially the playing of Anton Stadler that drew Mozart to the clarinet (a relatively new and still developing instrument in his day). In 1784, when already a member of the imperial wind band in Vienna, Stadler took part in the première of Mozart's Quintet in E flat, K. 452, for piano and winds. It was for Stadler that Mozart wrote (in 1786, 1789, and 1791, respectively): the Trio, K. 498, for piano, clarinet and viola; the Clarinet Quintet; and the Clarinet Concerto, K. 622. The latter two were actually composed for Stadler's "basset clarinet," an instrument with an added major third in its low register. Instead, the normal clarinet was the instrument specified in the published versions of these works.[2] Stadler was also a virtuoso on the basset-horn (in effect a tenor clarinet), which he played in one of the two obbligati that Mozart wrote for him in the opera, *La clemenza di Tito.*

Stadler's liking for the bottom register of the instrument is reflected by the frequency with which the clarinet part visits the lower portion of the range. The resulting tonal horizon is quite broad, and gives room for virtuoso sweeps of scalewise and arpeggiated passage work. There are also large intervallic leaps, as in Variation I of the finale. The performances I recall with particular pleasure, however, are those in which the clarinetist captured the subtle shadings of the slow movement. Here, as in the slow movement of Mozart's Oboe Quartet and of the Flute Quartet in D, the wind player can truly shine.

I
7
4, 2
6

Allegro. There should be a mental slur over the opening bars, ending at the downbeat of m. 7. Only the slightest of punctuations should be used at the end of m. 4, even less at the close of bar 2. The 8th-notes that enter the lower string parts in m. 6 carry into the next measure and to the flight of the clarinet. On paper, that flight is segmented by six slurs. Any technical considerations aside, musical considerations dictate that there be only one slur, extending from the beginning of

7
8

m. 7 to the downbeat of m. 9. The first note of each 16th-note group can, and probably will, project a bit. The melodic line in bar 8, though, actually moves through the tones of the dominant seventh chord—outlined by the first and last notes of each quadruplet—to resolve on the final, quarter-note A. Use enough artful rubato and emphasis to show the listener the distinction between essential and accessory tones.

9

What promises to be a repeat of the opening, in mm. 9 ff., is not a literal copy.

Only the first two measures are the same as before. From measure 11 on, there are   11
changes in assignment, shape, and direction of line in the individual parts. The 2nd
violin gets what might be called a "blue" note (the A♯ in m. 11). There is also the
introduction of a sustained note and syncope. These details must register in the
playing, since they help impel the changed flight in the clarinet part (mm. 15–16),   15
the violins' responding arc immediately after, and eventually the clarinet's seamless
introduction of the bridge passage at m. 19.   19

The half-bar slurs of the two violins in m. 17–18 are desirable as bowing   17
marks, to keep the sound from getting cramped. As in the comparable clarinet
phrases, however, you want to ascend the 8th-notes as though they are one
continuous side of the melodic arch, and descend through the 16ths just as
smoothly. There can be very slight punctuations at the half bar, but your primary
aim is to follow the trajectory of the line.

The players need to read the printed signs with musical intelligence. Why, for
example, should the violins' line in mm. 20–23 be interrupted at the start of m. 22?   20, 22
The half-notes flow as continuously as the clarinet line in these measures. Yet that
melody is in fact slurred by the half bar. In both cases, there can be no reason why
an accomplished player would feel compelled to break the melodic thread in literal
obedience to the slurring. If adhering to the half-bar slurring out of musical
conviction (a decision that is certainly possible), the clarinetist will have to vary
both the spacing between the successive groups and the stress and inflection of the
units themselves. Otherwise there is risk of a *left*-right, marching sound that would
be deadly in this context.

The downbeat quadruplet of 16ths in mm. 23 and 24 is answered by a similar   23
group on the second beat of the measure, but from another voice. There is no reason
to try for an *enchaîné* effect here; neither, though, should there be any more than the
slightest emphasis to mark the entry of the answering group. As for the long
melodic arches in the cello and 1st violin in mm. 26–32, I need not add to what I   26
have suggested about earlier and similar passages. However, about the three lower
voices in mm. 30–32: regard the quarter and 8th rhythms as an energized version of   30
the half-note rhythm of the inner voices in the preceding phrase. The quarter
should have easy, sustained resonance; the 8ths should emerge from the quarter-
note, as though filling the sound of an imagined half-note.

In measures such as 36, the clarinet whole-note is properly without forte-   36
piano. That emphasis—a quiet one—is to be supplied only by the low strings,
leaving the clarinet free to alight gently on its sustaining tone.

The rhythms of the strings in bars 40–41 can certainly move by the half bar, to
reflect the landing points in the clarinet line. At the same time, the accompaniment
should head with some continuity to the third beat of m. 41, to meet the clarinet at   41
its note of resolution. The ensemble chord there should be played with lift, and
without excessive impact. Merge the resonance of the chord with the quarter-rest
that follows, and allow for a suitable pause before moving in to the second theme.

Within the indicated piano, give dynamic shading to the long line of the 1st
violin in mm. 42–49. The melody is already cast in twilight, despite its major   42
coloration. Let it relax a bit as it approaches its low point in m. 46, then brighten   46
slightly through the second half of bar 47. The shaping of the clarinet in its response
(mm. 49 ff.) must inevitably differ, owing to the arrival of the minor in m. 50 and to   49
the changes and extensions of the line in succeeding measures.

The accompaniment should be sensitive to the events in each of the solo lines.

This is especially important in the syncopes under the clarinet; play them with as subtle a wash of tone color and flexibility as though in some piece by Debussy. When you emerge into the 8th-note rhythms of mm. 57–60, don't turn suddenly staccato and peremptory. The stroke should become crisper only step by step, reaching full brightness with the lively writing of bars 61–64.

The piano dolce marking for the close of the exposition (mm. 65 ff.) can only hint at the spirit of the playing. The tempo may be allegro; the vision should be of Elysian fields. You need all the tenderness you can evoke from these measures in order to highlight the contrast (typical Mozart, I think) of the brilliant flash of the clarinet line at the double bar. The temper of the dolce, moreover, pervades the shadowed descent into C major that opens the development.

One of the pleasures in this movement is the élan with which an exhilarating line passes back and forth between several voices or is joined by an added part in midflight. Mm. 130–32 and 189–90 are cases in point. The most difficult of these passages occurs in the development section; here Mozart pursues the device at extraordinary length. Each of the strings has to deal in turn with the two-measure flourish (originally announced by the clarinet at m. 7), and the 16th-note figures therein are not particularly grateful on the fingerboard. Perhaps precisely because he knew this, Mozart insists on having the strings hand them back and forth to one another for fully twenty-six measures (mm. 89 ff.). Arranging fingerings and string crossings to make this sound graceful will take some cogitation.

The twelve-measure passage starting in bar 99 is dangerous musically, as well: the clarinet's up-and-down succession of 8th-note arpeggios and the constant streaming of 16ths in the strings can all too easily make the passage sound as though the ensemble has started practicing études on stage. Try to play the sequence in two six-measure units; within each of these, the clarinet's second and third arpeggio arches will sound as responses to the first. To aid in this effect, the strings have to scale their forte-pianos so that those in odd measures are stronger than in the evens, with progressive reduction in force over the three pairs of measures that make up the group of six. The 1st violin's B at the start of the second six measures (m. 105), makes a solid kickoff point, both in register and underlying harmony, for the new phrase group.

It is very likely that the tempo will have picked up in the course of these maneuvers. If so, the ensemble can restore calm by relaxing the pace gradually from m. 115 into the return at m. 118. In the measures of 8th-note rhythm that form part of the lead-in, bar 115 has dots over the notes, while none appear in mm. 116–17 (though the cello quarters continue to be dotted there). I would choose to regard the omission as a deliberate indication that the spiccato bowing should become extremely gentle on its way into the legato half-notes of bars 118–19.

It is characteristic of Mozart that he steps up the flourish with which the clarinet ends the bridge passage in the recapitulation (see mm. 146–47). I think the player is entitled to luxuriate a bit by lingering very briefly on the first 16th of bar 147. The treatment of the resolving chord and the fourth-beat rest is similar to that suggested for m. 41.

There are noticeable changes in the clarinet's second theme solo (mm. 155 ff.), as compared with the corresponding passage in the exposition. Play for the increased pathos. For me, the heart stopper is m. 162; I would want to hear a velvety pianissimo in the last three 8ths of that measure and the two quarter-notes that follow. Avoid any suggestion of shrillness.

57

61

65

130, 189

7

89

99

105

115

118

146

41

155

162

The coda section expands and, in a way, develops the idea of the corresponding area of the exposition. Here (mm. 175 ff.) the voices have to float over and under each other. A reminiscence of the development's arpeggios, along with a bit of ensemble fun, awaits at bar 185. Starting here, the strings have to waft the clarinet's 8th-note and triplet arabesques on neatly placed sustaining chords. These chords are pointed, but should still be smooth in stroke and lively in left hand, so that there is enough resonance to fulfill the support role with appeal. If this underpinning is suitably delicate, the clarinet can disport itself without forced tone. 175

185

A word about the last measure: as in the earlier, corresponding bar (m. 79), the violins in particular must not crush the second beat. The emphasis of the cadence is on the downbeat, with the next two quarters serving as follow-ups. The bowing of the violin chords should be on an upstroke, avoiding undue pressure. 197, 79

Larghetto. This is one of the most ineffably peaceful slow movements in all the chamber repertoire. Peaceful, not sleepy; as an innocent bystander, I have participated in some performances in which the clarinetist opted for so slow a tempo that—had I a coverlet—I could have slumbered on my chin rest. By all means, keep the Larghetto moving. II

Mozart instructs that the strings be muted. This lends the sound of the music extra sheen and atmosphere. At the same time, there is danger of the 1st violin sounding nasal in its higher-register solos, as for example in mm. 24–26. In part, this will depend on the quality and adjustment of the instrument the player is using. But the style of playing has much to do with this, as well. Apply vibrato judiciously, and never at too rapid a frequency. Further, don't squeeze the string with the bow. Use as light a stroke as is consistent with good sound and with the dynamic level required. Draw the sound out of the instrument, without forcing. 24

I hope the strings will instinctively play their 8ths with very gentle finger impact in the left hand. The notes that continue from the clarinet resolution into the second half of m. 4 should be projected enough to support the solo line. In general, the accompaniment should be neither overbearing nor spineless. Chord changes are important, and the voices involved in the linear motions that effect such changes must make themselves heard. The accompaniment also reflects punctuations in the solo line; at the end of m. 9, for example, bend the pace of the last three 8ths. Not to do so would clearly be pedestrian. 4

9

Similarly, there should be alert flexibility in the lower voices in such measures as 17–18, where the clarinet dives from soprano to baritone register and back. Quite aside from any technical difficulty involved, this action in the clarinet amounts to a conversation with self. The responses need time. 17

The extended and marvelous dialogue between clarinet and 1st violin, and clarinet and quartet as a whole, mm. 20–50, calls for great musical sensibility from the participants. By all means, tape this passage and hear it from the listener's point of view. You have to determine whether the musical conversation—especially between the sustained-tone and 32nd-note scales in bars 34–37—comes off convincingly and with a sense of interaction between parts. 20

34

Give special attention to the melodic line in bars 21, 38, 41, and 71. Practice the turns so that they are heard as integral parts of the melody, not pasted-on ornaments. 21

Looking ahead to the end of the movement, we find one of those musical gifts that Mozart bestows. Earlier ideas are modified in deceptively simple, highly

imaginative ways, to create an unexpected exit scene. The 1st violin's 16th-note line
17   that was heard in mm. 17 ff. is transformed here into a closely related triplet
77   version, mm. 77–79, and then moves into the even more sensitive stream of
continuous triplets of the coda.

74   The clarinet, for its part, transmutes its quarter-note line of mm. 74–75 into the
80   chromatic descent of mm. 80 ff. This evokes a beautifully shaded response from the
1st violin and, for one measure each, from the viola and cello. Let me add that,
though I have concentrated on the clarinet and 1st violin, the other three voices
have treasures of their own. Among them: the lovely quarter-note duet of the 2nd
24   violin and clarinet, then of violin and viola, mm. 24 ff.; and the suspensions and
33   resolutions in the lower trio in mm. 33 ff. The simplest aspect of the
accompaniment, the undulating 8th-note figures in the middle voices (see the
opening), can be magical to play.

       I hope that the ensemble gets Mozart's message and reacts to it with an
appropriately subtle and free reading. This Larghetto is again one of those
movements that will separate the doves from the donkeys.

III   *Menuetto.* Watch out for the start of the movement. It invites a distressing
tendency to gulp the initial upbeat, perhaps because of the visual impact of the
forte written on this detached quarter-note. In the opening section and its return,
there are enjoyable nuggets of motion in the individual parts: for example, the
3   crossing of parts in 2nd violin and viola in bar 3; and the 8th-note details in the
4   viola in mm. 4–6.

       The phrasing opens out luxuriously in the second section. There is hardly a
20   seam in the writing until you get to m. 20. And there, the long E of the clarinet
bridges the gap, pulling everyone forward until the music rolls into the return at
25   bar 25. This is sunlit music; make it glow.

Trio I   By and large, this refrain section of the movement goes smoothly. The Trios, on
1[33]   the other hand, are problematic. In Trio I, there are several things to watch for. First
violin, sing your line with enough pathos, but without crossing over into maudlin
7[39]   musical posturing. In such measures as 7 and 8, approach and leave the low, forte
8th-note adroitly, and without an explosive impact. Note that the lower voices are
marked forte-piano. Though the *f* and *p* are printed with some separation in the
violin solo line, the relationship is still that of forte-piano in a dynamic context that
is piano overall.

       Another item: in much of this trio, the overlapped placement of the quarter-
note rhythms in the several voices means that all four strings constitute the solo. Of
course, the 1st violin leads in this, as the dynamic balance must reveal. Even so, the
inflections in the lower voices, and especially in the 2nd violin, must reflect and
25[57]   impel those of the companion line. In mm. 25 ff., the viola takes up a duo role with
28[60]   the 1st violin, and should be especially forthcoming in the excited measures (28–31)
where it engages in the agitated 8th-note repartée.

Trio II   Trio II can be dangerous. The clarinet solo starts out as though playing a beer-
garden tune, and the oom-pah string accompaniment reinforces that perception.
There is no middle ground, it seems to me. Either go for the bumptious
interpretation and try to keep it from sounding too buffoonish; or treat both solo
and accompaniment gracefully, as though playing a sophisticated waltz. Events in
the middle section of the trio make me lean toward the waltz concept: especially the
28[101]   elegant, and typically Mozartian, descending pyramid of sound in mm. 28 ff.; and
the brief passage of interweaving between clarinet and violin in the return section.

The more plebeian approach should not, in any case, be an accidental result of awkward playing. It should happen only by design, and with polished technique.

Allegretto con variazioni. Eyes on the *alla breve* sign! Don't rush, but step into the theme with spirit. Move resiliently to the first and third beats of each bar as you march through the four-measure phrase unit. In keeping with this bounce, the 2nd violin figure at the start of the second section will move most happily if the two detached 8ths are linked in one sprightly upstroke. In the theme as well as throughout the movement, play the dotted-8th-and-16th figure with proper snap. — IV

The canonic imitation between 1st violin and viola in mm. 9–11 has an easy lilt to it. Still, the viola should make its reply with quiet gusto. Under it all, there's a bass line fit for a cellist with a sense of humor. — 9

In Variation I's first section and ending, the theme in the strings, both high and low, must not be too subordinate to the clarinet line. Do allow enough elbowroom for the valiant leaps in the clarinet part in the second section of the variation. Whether this should mean that the entire variation should be taken at a broader tempo than the theme is something you'll have to decide. I know from my own experience, with various clarinetists, that the slower tempo seems usual. Discuss it. — Var. I

In Variation II, the motor drive is in the hands of the three lower string parts— in the striding cello line, of course, but also in the bubbling triplets of the 2nd violin and viola. The slurred triplet groups must project, as well as the duet's descending scales in m. 36 and the triplet turn in the last measure. — Var. II / 36

Violin and viola should lead each other, so that the triplets stay synchronized. Don't take too much bow on the slurred triplet, or you'll be struggling to keep the stick in the proper spot for the spiccato of the detached triplet.

The tempo will be on the bright side. Hold it fairly steady, to make life easier for the triplet players. The clarinet adds its voice to the festivities twice, but the variation belongs to the 1st violin. Play that line with animation, but not (I hope) with such virtuoso panache as to take the ascending chromatic triplets of m. 44 in one, staccato upstroke! — 44

The viola and 1st violin might well prepare for Variation III by listening to Pedrillo's Romanze, *In Mohrenland gefangen war* ("In Moorish land enslaved was"), from Act III of *Die Entführung aus dem Serail*. The same kind of exotic tone heard in that song is carried to even greater lengths in the present variation, and the solo lines must be colored accordingly. — Var. III

For the viola, this means in particular that the grace note figures should be played with sobbing effect, especially where Mozart insists on the detail, mm. 51–52, 55–56, and 63–64. The 1st violin should exploit the chromatic progressions in its line, in mm. 58 and 60. At the end of the repeat playing of the second section, the ensemble must decide whether to move right into the clarinet pyrotechnics of Variation IV, or instead to raise the curtain with a slight pullback in the final measure. — 51 / 58

As for Variation IV itself, the ensemble, in consultation with its clarinetist and 1st violinist, may well decide to hold the tempo back slightly in deference to the acrobatics of those two very active lines. The pace probably has slowed a bit anyway for Variation III, to allow for the hand-wringing of that episode. Even with moderation of speed, the brilliant lines will sound fast enough. More of a problem will be to play the perpetual-motion melodies with musical, not just technical, virtuosity. — Var. IV

Through the half-bar phrasing of mm. 81–82, Mozart has in effect written a — 81

deceleration into the music. To complete this broadening, the players will have to
83   impose a *calando* on mm. 83–84. This carries through the fermata and delivers us to
the Adagio, which is a variation even though not so labeled. Listen to the arias and
ensembles of Mozart's *Così fan tutte* for the ideal guide to the interpretation of this
section. The vocal lines would certainly not include such an instrumental flourish
93   as the 32nd-note ascents in the clarinet's mm. 93 and 95, but in other respects the
parallels will be manifest.

     The return of the theme in the Allegro needs joyful briskness. Even with the
forward motion, though, the clarinetist will want to play the chromatic line of mm.
118   118–21 with a touch of sultry innuendo. There will be no second such opportunity;
the next passage only promises to duplicate its predecessor, but veers back instead
into brighter light.

     In yet another example of his musical generosity, Mozart seems to weave an
imitation of barrel-organ sound into the clarinet, 2nd violin, and viola parts in mm.
134   134–37. Play the vignette in such fashion that the audience can enjoy the idea with
you. And, in the forte bars of the last three measures, let the dotted figures prevail
over the chords.

PREAMBULO: discusión de las obras del programa por el
Fine Arts Quartet a las 20:30 horas

HAYDN, (1732-1809)   Cuarteto Op. 76, Núm. 3 "The Kaiser"
                                                    1. Allegro
                                          2. Poco adagio, cantabile
                                            3. Menuetto, allegro
                                                4. Finale, presto

BARTOK, (1881-1945)   Cuarteto núm. 3
                                                1. Prima parte
                                            2. Seconda parte
                    3. Recapitulazione della prima parte
                                                        4. Coda

                            i n t e r m e d i o

MOZART, (1756-1791)   Cuarteto K. 590
                                          1. Allegro moderato
                                                2. Allegreto
                                      3. Menuetto, allegretto
                                                    4. Allegro

CHAPTER EIGHT

❧ Mozart ❧
Quartet in F, K. 590

On July 12 of 1789, Mozart wrote to Michael Puchberg, wealthy Viennese merchant and musical amateur, that he was at work on six quartets to be dedicated to King Friedrich Wilhelm II of Prussia. From June of 1788 through June 1791 (the year of Mozart's death), Puchberg was to receive 20 letters from Mozart, all containing requests—sometimes desperately worded—for financial assistance. In June of 1790, Mozart wrote to say that straitened circumstances had forced him to sell off the quartets in question very cheaply.[1] He had written only three of the projected six; the quartet in F was the last of the three, and the last quartet he was to produce.

In number of works, 1790 was a slack period for Mozart. True enough, *Così fan tutte* was finished in January. After that, though, the only works of importance were K. 589 and 590, (second and third of the "King of Prussia" quartets) in May and June, the D major Viola Quintet, K. 593, in December, and—also late in the year—an Adagio and Allegro, K. 594, for a clockwork organ. I am no doubt arbitrary in grouping this last with the other works mentioned, celebrated as they are. Note, however, that even though Mozart said it was only for the money that he was writing for so ineffectual-sounding a contrivance,[2] he couldn't help himself: the Adagio is a composition of highly charged emotion. His concept of the work went far beyond the limitations he found in the intended medium.

By the same token, the anxiety he expressed to Puchberg—there were nine begging letters in 1790—is not the pervading tone either in the quartets or in the D major quintet. As is so often evident in music, the genius of the composer seems insulated from the cold facts of his physical life. Though Mozart is ever ready to mix the dark with the bright in his mature work, it is remarkable that the tone of

---

SCORE: Wolfgang Amadeus Mozart. 1964. *String Quartet in F, K. 590*. Urtext. Ed. Ludwig Finscher. Kassel: Bärenreiter. Miniature score No. 89.

Left: Page from the program for the concert series by The Fine Arts Quartet (Abram Loft's last appearances with the ensemble), San Miguel de Allende, Mexico, June 1979.

these major instrumental works of 1790 is predominantly optimistic.

Mozart himself describes the three completed quartets as "very difficult."[3] He was referring to the effort that went into their writing. Players would certainly agree, however, that the description attaches also to the demands on the performers. These quartets are known for the unusually bright spotlight they turn on the cellist; as Mozart well knew, King Friedrich Wilhelm played the cello. To my thinking, for that matter, the cellist is already well tested in many a passage of Mozart's earlier quartets of the 1780s. In these three late quartets, in any case, there is challenge enough for all hands, and certainly for the 1st violin. Like any of the mature quartets, these are pieces meant for the well-equipped professional or amateur ensemble.

The difficulties are partly technical, of course. Other composers have written higher, faster, more intricate lines; have called for double stops of greater density and tougher reach, or have imposed sterner bowing and string-crossing demands. With Mozart, however, there is a special clarity both of melody and of the interweaving of the component voices of the quartet. To convey this clarity in performance forces the players to make discerning use of all their skills as instrumentalists. The musical demands are higher still. Mozart's flaws as a man (and they are not the clownish ones so broadly drawn in *Amadeus*) could not dull his amazing insight into the human character. This perceptiveness shows in his operas, of course, but also in his instrumental music. Quartet players must match their own sensibility, flexibility, and quickness of observation to that of Mozart himself.

Moreover, you have to meet these demands at every turn. To a degree approached at the time only in the quartets of Haydn, the several movements of a Mozart quartet hold to a uniformly high level. There is no relaxing in slow movement or minuet, no fluffing off of the finale as an easy exit piece. Nowhere is this more apparent than in the work considered here, Mozart's last quartet. There is an air of incisive sobriety in the first three movements, countered by a highly compressed exhilaration in the devilishly acute finale. Only intelligent musicians need apply.

I   *Allegro moderato.* To begin, Mozart offers a lesson in intonation and in the spatial exploration of quartet sound. The four voices are massed in unison and octave, first soft, then loud; listeners are called to attention.

In addition to matching intonations carefully, the players must remember to blend the sound toward the cello line; this kind of balance helps the sonority of massed doublings. Further, all four instrumentalists should gently signal the third

2   beat of m. 2, the better to synchronize the ensuing run of 16ths. In the process, though, be careful not to thump the end of the sustained C that opens the measure.

Immediately after assembling the four instruments in one forte group, Mozart

4   goes to the other extreme, presenting the 1st violin in a solo measure at piano level. By the harmonically shifted coloring and reshaped ending of the theme's repetition, this solo strikes a pensive note, in contrast to the positive aspect of the opening measures. In dynamics (hushed!), tone color (pale vibrato), and inflection (a bit of easing in the resolving turn), the reaction of this phrase to the opening must be made clear. Yet another solo measure, and the theme material is now used in motoric repetition, aided by propulsive 8ths and quarters from the lower parts.

Do not be misled by the static appearance of the inner voice lines; in dynamic

8   gradation and rubato, the linear 8ths must bend slightly in response to the

inflections of the solo melody. Bend too much, and get a shapeless mess; too little, and the accompaniment sounds as though remote and disinterested. Experiment for the best effect. In the solo line itself, the downbeat couplets of mm. 9–11 must be inflected so that their relation to one another is manifest. Simple repetition of the three measures of rhythmic sequence is not enough. Part of the rehearsal process here is the appraisal, by the 1st violin and by the group as a whole, of the success of this monologue. 9

Both inner parts must be ready to take the spotlight in mm. 12–13, where their fanfares solicit the response of the 1st violin and incite the cello's impetuous descents. In mm. 16 ff., they are back in an accompanying role, having now to shape their lines to the demands of both the cello and the 1st violin as those two instruments carry on their dialogue. The cello starts this conversation, and thus will influence it, but will also be open to the suggestion of the violin's responses. There is only a single mark of piano (m. 16) to govern the passage, but the ensemble may well permit some dynamic shading en route to the crescendo in m. 28. In that measure, the viola joins the 2nd violin's flight, already in progress; only with the third beat should the viola move closer to the spotlight. 12 16 28

In mm. 21 ff., the melodic turn first heard in m. 6 becomes the subject of this little dialogue, first between the outer voices, then briefly the inner, moving finally through a composed retard to the cello's grand entrance in m. 30. That instrument brings us to the second theme, itself an offshoot of the starting subject. Here is a case in which your interpretation must subtly aid the composer's clear intent. A slight stretching of the third and fourth beats in m. 30 helps introduce the cello's upbeat entry with proper grace. The cello, in turn, must play the solo arpeggio of m. 31 with a bit of cadenza-like freedom, to carry the line up to the theme proper in m. 32 in appropriately exuberant manner. The inner voices should respond actively to this new solo via the slurred and detached series of 8ths. 21 30 32

In m. 33, the 2nd violin's 8ths embody both a static and a moving line. The latter parallels the 1st violin in opposing the contrary motion of the cello at this point. It is up to the 2nd violin to distinguish dynamically between the moving line of the onbeat 8ths and the subordinate, intervening notes. A similar situation is found in mm. 41–42, where the 2nd violin duets first with the viola, then turns to partner the 1st violin. Both in mm. 33 and 41, it is imperative that there be a slight forward lean toward the resolution at the start of the following bar. 33 41 33

A very brief solo awaits the viola at the end of m. 34; the part fills a gap in the cello line, then immediately steps back to an accompaniment role. In the next measure, the 2nd violin provides an active "bass" (almost a solo in its own right) under the cello's high-register solo, and must play with suitable projection. The 2nd violin line seems restrained in mm. 43–45, but in reality presents an important countermelody to the 1st violin. Again, the part needs to be played with some soloistic sense. 34 43

All four parts in m. 49 must collaborate in giving the violins' half-measure figures a forward thrust. The previous bar has tensioned the spring; now the release must be allowed to move subtly toward the first target (m. 50) and on to, and through, the florid and impulsive violin figures of the measures that follow. 49

The viola passage, mm. 54–56, belongs in every player's excerpt book. I leave it to the performer to find the best fingering for mm. 55–56; just be sure that the chromatic steps are distinct, not smeared in the shifting. A light touch in handling the bow, along with rubato to taste, will prevent the passage from sounding like a finger étude. 54 55

57   As for the 2nd violin, its meteoric ascent at the start of m. 57 must rise precisely and without frenzy out of the end of the viola run: a test of alertness, nerve, and bow control. The same goes for the 1st violin and cello, who have to follow after the 2nd violin as though flying in formation. The chords of m. 60 need suitable nobility, and the duets of high and low voices, as well as the grouped ensemble, over the next measures, should offer proper sweetness and relaxation after all this brouhaha. I might point out to the 1st violin, incidentally, that the 16th-

70 note swirls in mm. 70 and 72 are *not* verbatim duplicates of each other.

    The treatment of the last bar of the exposition will vary slightly, either leading to the repetition or going forward to the development. To return to the quiet opening calls for some gentleness and ease of timing; moving into the sudden forte

74 of the next section, however, implies that the 16th-notes of m. 74 should run directly (though without any hint of crescendo) into the double bar, to intensify the surprise of the loud downbeat of m. 75.

77   Mm. 77–93 test the ensemble's musicality and dramatic insight. Here is an extended conversation between the two outer voices, with interesting exchanges

83 and shifts of roles in mm. 83 and 90; the viola joins in this discussion in the last few measures, but otherwise the inner parts must carry out their function of vitally concerned onlookers. Let the attention of the accompaniment players slacken for an instant, and the passage will sound intolerably long and lackluster: four dispirited

94 performers on a treadmill. The stormy passage that follows (mm. 94 ff.) is almost simpler to carry off, since accompaniment and solo roles move so quickly from voice to voice; everyone is instantly important, and thus fully on the alert.

105   Among the many pleasures in this movement is the elegant close (mm. 105 ff.) of the development. The 1st violin declares, then questions, at length and in brief, heeding the response of the lower voices, as it makes its way at last to the recapitulation. To effect this return stylishly calls for the instinct of an actor as much as musician, especially for the lower voices, who must answer the violin as with one voice, yet with constant flexibility in the dialogue.

    Another challenge: the five measures of unison and octave for all four (mm.

184 184–88). Here the ensemble has to synchronize not only the thematic rhythms, but also the dynamic stings and the jagged harmonic descents in each measure. The

187 forte in m. 187 must, like that at the start of the development, be brazen without being raspy. Finally, the need for delicacy and fancy footwork in the closing measures will be apparent. Players will inevitably relish this arch leave-taking, right up to the 1st violin's wistful octave at the double bar.

II   ***Andante.*** This is Mozart's marking in his own manuscript of the quartet. In the first edition, the marking was changed to Allegretto. Whichever you choose, keep in mind the literal meaning of Andante: "Going." If the quartet thinks statically at the start of the movement, they will get stuck in the 8th-rest, lurch into the next 8th, and probably bump along on the remaining notes in the measure as well. Remember that the 6/8 meter is essentially duple: two groups of 3/8 each. Count two pulses, not six, to the measure, and play accordingly.

    The dots on the notes should not translate into a staccato stroke, nor yet into anything approaching a spiccato. If the four players can imagine humming the measure, with just enough articulation to render the rhythm clearly, and with a sense of leaning toward the long note of the second measure, all will be well—providing that the ensemble gathers the next six measures into the same long line:

4, 7 build to a first goal at m. 4 and a second at m. 7. Experiment for the most desirable bowing; one effective possibility is to take one bow per half measure. Whatever your choice, be sure to treat the rests as though they are notes—part of the stream of sound, not dead interruptions.

At m. 8, the 2nd violin takes over the theme, now actually incorporating both | 8
violin parts in one, via double stops. The 1st violin remains free to cadenzify above the 2nd. This relationship may well encourage fervent discussion at rehearsals: should the cadenza prevail, or should it rather be heard as an ornamental filigree to the 2nd violin? Both egos should finally recognize that the two parts are a duet. Throughout the movement, remember that lines showing a lot of ink tend to look predominant on the printed page; in actual sound, they are not necessarily more important than the slower-moving lines they parallel.

In the 16th-note line that passes from voice to voice, starting in m. 16, take the | 16
dotted notes that follow three slurred notes (as in m. 17 in the cello) in one | 17
upstroke, both in order to minimize "creep" of the bow and to subordinate those notes to the slurred group. The *stretto* presentation of the thematic motive by the high and low duets (mm. 33 ff.) should move lightly forward to the mini- | 33
explosions—vibrant, not crushed in sound—on the fortes in m. 37, with an immediate restoration of piano thereafter.

To the 1st violin, concerning the elegant line in mm. 40 ff., I can only say: play | 40
beautifully. To the ensemble as a whole: respond almost physically to the eerie change in harmonic color after the second ending, so that the cello line can be heard to emerge therefrom toward the light. And to the cellist: don't sound "skinny" in m. 52, which is the first, high portion of your descent through the gamut of the | 52
instrument.

In its own way, this movement represents the essence of quartet writing as much as does the third movement of Beethoven's Op. 130. True, the four-way dialogue is very much less compressed and intertwined than in the Beethoven example, but episodes such as mm. 47–61 and 63–78 show the evenhandedness | 47, 63
with which Mozart treats all four instruments in the group. The thread of iambic rhythms woven around the theme from mm. 64 to 77 makes every participant a | 64
soloist. Play the figures with live fingers. Try to string the melodic fragments into comments and lines that enjoy fresh and shifting sidelights.

The brief passage of overlapping duets centered on the theme (mm. 97 ff.) | 97
needs attention: each pair of instruments must consciously play the arched shape of its melody, leading toward a highlighted topmost note. The upper and lower melodic threads need to be heard as distinct and individual, horizontal lines. Don't let them get lost in the weaving of the musical fabric.

A fine example of democratic ensemble writing appears in the final measures of the movement, where the 16th-note figure ascends and oscillates through all four | 118
voices. The 1st violin is left to fade the figure delicately away in the stratosphere of the E-string. That's a tough assignment, since the alternating, high Bs and Cs are so close together up there. Get the left arm well around, so that the hand is under the least possible strain. Put the smallest possible areas of the playing fingers on the string, and concentrate on keeping the C close enough to the B. In addition to playing in tune, try at least to think about the possibility of vibrato; a tiny glow on the sound won't hurt.

Menuetto: Allegretto. This movement is an outstanding demonstration of the | III
importance Mozart gives the minuet in his chamber music. For him the minuet is no mere diversion, but an impressive structure, always with some freshness of

approach that sets it apart from its fellows. Whenever I play this one, I feel that I am in a musical observatory, with the several lines describing distinct and contrasting planetary orbits around one another. I sense this especially in the second section of the minuet, which seems to arch boldly in two great sweeps from one double bar to the next. (By the way, can it be entirely accidental that the 1st violin's line, five measures before the end of the minuet, so strongly reflects that instrument's voice at the end of the slow movement?)

2

6

The grace notes should be played on the beat in the Menuetto, and before the beat in the Trio, as the editor has indicated in the score. To do otherwise would run counter to the more serious and the lighter temperaments, respectively, of the two sections. In our ensemble, I played mm. 2–3 of the 2nd violin part in first position, crossing strings in order to give the freest possible resonance to the sound. You might even try this for m. 6 if you can control the sound of the open E enough to avoid brashness. Free is also the word for the impulse of the 2nd violin line, which should move in compliance with the direction of the 1st violin part.

8

The viola part in mm. 8 ff. is obviously one of two simultaneously important solo lines (the other is embedded in the slurred 8th-note parts). It must be played not for mere loudness, but so that the successive fragments, with their harmonic nuances, add up to a meaningful melodic line. This is again the kind of passage the ensemble should appraise by hearing a taped playback.

15

16

24

At the start of the second section, m. 15 is a trap: the inner voices will sound like clodhoppers if they are too rough in sound and if they don't move through the quarter-notes to the next measure. It will help to use downbow on the slurred upbeat group, and a lighter, articulated upstroke on beats 2 and 3. The 1st violin in mm. 16–25 has to make clear the distinction between the drone C in the upper edge of the part and the rising-and-falling chromatic scale in the lower notes of the line. Use subtle variation in pressure on the two strings, along with selective stress on significant notes in the lower-note path. The inner voices in mm. 24–25, by the way, should produce the sforzando with left-hand intensity, not too much with bow pressure.

30

The theme carried by the viola solo line in the first section becomes more prominent when the violin duo takes it up in mm. 30–35. All possible grace and melodic perspective should prevail, and the forte should not be overdriven. At the end of the Menuetto, ease the time after the downbeat, then move through the upbeat into the swing of the Trio.

Trio

5[47]

3[45]
11[53]

The Trio, distinct though it is, seems to me to adapt its ideas and its spatial treatments from the minuet proper. Play both sections of the Trio for the longest possible phrase units: the breathing-points lie in mm. 5, 10, 18, 23, and 33 [47, 52, 60, 65, and 75]. Any shorter punctuations should not be allowed to break the flow between these major resting spots. Further, with so many little dots of sound in this Trio, the expansive, slurred touches (see mm. 3, 8, 21, 26, 29–30 [45, 50, 63, 68, 71–72], and especially 11–16 [53–58]) must be played with enough projection to offer the needed contrast.

For the "chirping" figures themselves, as in the 1st violin at m. 46, warm the 8th-note with enough vibrato to make it resonate beyond the brevity of the bow stroke. The same applies to the two 8th-notes with which the cello ends the Trio, and particularly at the close of the repeat.

IV

Allegro. This is Mozart at his most astounding level. In complexity, verve, and sheer audacity, this movement is matched only by the finales of the D major and

E flat viola quintets. I think that all three reflect Mozart's known love of dancing. In fact, some of this particular finale shows also that he would have been very much at home in a night club of recent vintage.

The theme may very well be related to the 16th-note run at the start of the first movement. Here, though, it sounds suspiciously like a jazz player's "hot lick." And in true jazz fashion, it is handed—either whole or in part—to each of the four instruments in the course of the movement. The opening should be truly piano; the movement overall, for that matter, will benefit from exploiting the quiet side, both for clarity of texture and for the excitement that understatement can produce. The 8th-note accompaniment to the theme should be neatly in place, supporting but not inflaming the pace of the 16th-note line.

Some fine touches: the 1st violin's trilled riffs in mm. 33–37; the 2nd violin's determined, whirling line that leads the brassy (but not too much so!) descent onto the fermata in m. 42; and the 1st violin's two coy and hesitant echoes of this descent. The hesitation is justified, for Mozart now unleashes an infernal storm. 33 42

Here the 2nd violin whips along obsessively on a version of the 16th-note theme line: try tying each of the detached downbeat 16ths of mm. 53 ff. to the preceding slur; the inertia of the bow change will give the note the snap and emphasis it needs and will make it louder than with the printed bowing. Viola and cello provide rousing support with 8ths and syncopes. And above all this, like a Queen of the Night emoting on the bandstand, the 1st violin swoops dramatically from one edge of the fingerboard to the other. These grand leaps in register need bite and vibrancy to project the rugged geography of the musical terrain. 53

Soon after (mm. 77 ff.), Mozart uses his thematic motive to wind silken descents through the several voices; each player will have to find fingerings and string crossings that preserve clarity and crispness in the figures. At the same time, Mozart weaves a counter-subject, derived from his original accompaniment figure, into the two violin parts. The repeated 8ths in these measures are best taken in a single upbow, to lend enough edge to the line. 77

At the end of the exposition (a section that has contained a fair amount of development as well), there is a special bit of musical devilment. The 1st violin, and later the viola, plays just a scrap of the theme, converting it into a series of triplets contained within quadruplets. I don't dare ask you to play this as though you are actually thinking of triplets; that way lies madness. Anyway, the intricacy will be apparent to the listener even if you think fours; just don't belabor the metric beats. 121

To prove again that there are no subordinate voices in a good quartet and that Mozart is never stuck for a melodic idea, the 2nd violin gets to play a figure heard only here (see mm. 122–23, 126–27), one that almost demands a "wa-wa" mute. Exploit the jazzy effect, don't stifle it. 122, 1

There's more: after the flip ending at the double bar, led by the viola, the lower voices hit into a sustained chord, a surprising (I would bet that Mozart's contemporaries would have found it shocking) minor second up from the close of the exposition, over which the 1st violin launches into more of the three-within-four figure. Immediately following the start of the chord, let up on it so that the violin solo can be heard without strain. 134

Various reminiscences of the earlier section of the movement take us for an active ride through a 50-measure development. Again, in passages such as that in the 1st violin's mm. 136–39, and for all instruments in the bars that follow, the player must find fingerings and shifts that make for the clearest and cleanest 136

155   projection of the quadruplet groups. The repartée in mm. 155–64 needs very delicate balance between the running-16th figure, on the one hand, and the sparkling 8th-note commentary, on the other, since both elements are vital to the intended effect. This whole process is thrown into a much bolder scale in the

165   passage immediately following (mm. 165 ff.), where agile string crossing is at a premium. The lead-in to the recapitulation just slips out of the three-in-four figure; this maneuver has been suggested often in the development, but is especially elegant at this point.

    The pacing and shading of the three upper parts as they pass teasingly

210   through the three fermatas of mm. 210–19 are objects of happy experiment for the ensemble. Experiment not only in rehearsal, mind you, but in the performance as well, for there will always be an improvisatory sense about this passage, truly an operatic vignette embedded in a string quartet.

    Urged on by the ensemble, the 1st violin runs the gauntlet of a last virtuoso

287   flourish in mm. 287–97. Immediately after, the 2nd violin will have to decide how to

298   play the jazzy figure (mm. 298 ff.). Mozart can't bear to write it exactly like the corresponding tune in the first part of the movement. This time around, the "wa-wa" effect is replaced by a grace-note treatment. If you play this too crisply, it will have a rather prim air about it. I suppose that's all right, but I prefer a slightly broader spread to the rhythm, implying (without actually performing) a glissando from the grace note to the principal tone. This gives the line a certain insinuating quality, which I think Mozart would enjoy.

    The entire foursome will have to experiment with the ending; it seems to run off the end of the page, but some slight bending of tempo will avoid too great a feeling of abruptness. The sound of this exit should have a nonchalance matching the composer's own. Grace, clarity, strength, and judgment must all be in evidence in the performance of this finale. When properly played, the movement leaves everyone within earshot feeling improved and uplifted.

RONDO
con
Espressione.

CHAPTER NINE

❧ Beethoven ❧
String Trio in C minor, Op. 9, No. 3

The string trio is a test for both the composer and the performers. Like the string quartet, the trio has the advantage and the limitation that come from the homogeneous sound of its setting. All the instruments are from one tonal family. But the composer must be all the more inventive in treating the musical material, for the tone colors of the mixed ensemble are not available to lend their contrast to the sound.

In omitting a 2nd violin, the string trio still retains the distinctively individual voices of the remaining violin, the viola, and the cello. Now, though, the composer has an even smaller field of operation. Unless using intolerable force, three instruments will find it difficult—even when playing in massed chordal grouping— to sound as loud as four. Dynamic contrasts, then, have to be achieved within a restricted frame. Also, the web of part writing that is woven with three lines is inevitably more transparent than that in a quartet. The composer's skill and intellect lie fully exposed.

The same transparency also reveals any technical flaw or lack of inspiration on the part of the players. In a string trio, perhaps even more than in a quartet, each performer is called upon to display the same command and flair that would be needed in a solo work. The passage work will possibly be less difficult than that in a concerto. On the other hand, each player has to perform the individual part adroitly and sensitively, while at the same time fitting to—and making room for— similar subtleties in the lines of the other participants.

For the amateur and student group, there is a very practical side to the string trio: you won't need a fourth to play the repertoire. And with one fewer player, you

SCORE: Ludwig van Beethoven. n.d. *Trio in C minor, Op. 9, No. 3, for Violin, Viola and Violoncello*. Ed. Wilhelm Altmann. London: Eulenburg. Miniature score No. 44.

Left: Beethoven: String Trio in C minor, Op. 9, No. 3. Leipzig: Hoffmeister (1808). Violin part, first page of third movement. Reproduced with permission from the collection of the Sibley Music Library, the Eastman School of Music, University of Rochester.

may just possibly have less to argue about!

Beethoven wrote a number of string chamber works en route to the string quartets, Op. 18, his first published set of works in the quartet medium. Prominent among these earlier compositions is the String Trio in C minor, Op. 9, No. 3. It cannot rank with that landmark in the string trio literature, the Divertimento in E flat, K. 563, of Mozart. That is a major work, dating from 1788, when Mozart was at the height of his powers (his last three symphonies—the E flat, the G minor, and the "Jupiter"—were written in the three months preceding). Beethoven's trio, however, is lean and incisive, a powerful composition in its own right, and a fitting preview of his chamber music to come.

The three trios of Op. 9 were composed in 1797–98. Beethoven had written two string trios before then: the E flat, Op. 3 (before 1794) and the Serenade in D, Op. 8 (1796–97). Op. 3 casts its six movements in the same keys as those of Mozart's Divertimento, though not in the same sequence; Op. 8 is also in six movements, but so devoted to D major that only the fifth movement shifts to F, while the fourth movement oscillates between D minor and major.

Mozart's Divertimento, despite its title, rises far above the level of diversion. The Beethoven pieces, on the other hand, are seriously constructed, appealing—and pretend to nothing more. The untroubled spirit persists in the first two trios, in G and D, of Op. 9. With No. 3, Beethoven turns to sterner stuff. In this, he reflects the sequence of his Op. 1 piano trios (1794–95), where a third work in C minor also closes the set on the dark side. However, Beethoven's temper is much more convincing in the Op. 9 example.

I   *Allegro con spirito.* It has been said before, but I must point out that the pattern of the first four notes in the theme of this movement reappears, shifted to C♯ minor, as a central theme in the final Allegro of Beethoven's quartet Op. 131 (1826). There, indeed, they stand as a reordering of the opening fugal subject of the entire quartet.

To the matter at hand, however. The theme of the C minor trio places successive dynamic stings within a frame of a tensely quiet sound. Coupled with the surging of the melodic line and its surprising extensions, this must have been heady stuff for Beethoven's hearers in the 1790s. It still is, provided the players fly forward as the music demands and use their bows with proper bite and release.

The theme makes the group seem larger than life. Low register in the first
4   measures; higher in bars 4–6, a peak on the sforzando A♭; then the two-octave descent in violin and viola in mm. 6–10: the line races us through the tonal space of
10   the ensemble. Putting the theme in the cello for the restatement (mm. 10 ff.) gives us another way of looking at this space. In this inversion of the part writing, the violin gets the accompaniment line, but whips it into a bravura solo in its own right. We
17   run with it, only to be jolted by the closely spaced sforzando chords in mm. 17–19, and brought to a jarring halt by a fortissimo thrust in bar 20.

I know I am overdramatizing the state of affairs, but not by much. This is not sedate stuff. It is music for determined players, who combine precision with a flair
10   for the dramatic. It would not be amiss, for example, to stretch the 8th rest in m. 10 ever so slightly, to set off the forte recurrence of the motive. By the same token, an
20   even greater stretch is appropriate in the grand pause in m. 20. Beethoven allots a full half measure of rest there to allow the dust of the fortissimo to settle.

Take advantage of the break. The length of the rest and the entry on the ensuing downbeat will be indicated by subtle yet definite signalling by the violinist (or even better, by all three players in agreement). In a sense, you are starting the movement afresh, though now with the second theme.

That this is a piece for three equal soloists is clear from the way the melodic thread passes from violin to viola to cello in this episode of the movement. The violin disguises its turn at the accompaniment role by dressing up its arpeggiated line; each principal (onbeat) tone in mm. 27, 29, 31, and 33 carries with it a lower neighboring tone as decoration. The chirping couplets of 16ths, however, must be balanced so that they are subordinate to the viola and cello presentations of the theme. 27

In this second-theme area, any voice that is ostensibly accompaniment must be ready to seize advantage and responsibility. From mm. 21 through 35, viola and cello alternately have passages in sextuplets of 16ths. In most of these sextuplets, the first note of the group needs extra bow pressure. The remaining five tones can be subordinated, though they—along with the first note—contribute to the harmonic fabric of the moment. 21

In bars 21 and 23, the five repeated tones in each viola sextuplet fill spaces left by the rests in the violin line, and should consequently be held in the background. In mm. 22, and 24–26, the situation is different. There the violin melody sounds throughout the measure, and the viola line is melodically active throughout the sextuplet group. Accordingly, make the viola figures project. 21 22

The cello line in mm. 21–26 is not an accompaniment. It is scarcely less important than the violin solo and, indeed, carries on a musical conversation with it. This is especially apparent in mm. 22 and 24; even in the rest of the passage, its offbeat responses to the violin make it part of the solo activity. 21 22

The active outline of the two lower voices in mm. 36–39 is more than equalled by that of the violin part. In actuality, the violin is playing the same kind of line as its partners, except that the added, decorative notes convert the part into a florid melody of 16ths. The more reason, then, for the violinist to warm the melody with vibrato and rubato; otherwise the part becomes ornamental background to, rather than full collaborator with, the other voices. 36

Don't rush the violin part in these measures. You must be able to make a gracious transition from the flurry of notes into the held rhythms of mm. 40 ff. I assume that the violin will have started the 16ths in bar 36 on an upstroke. This means you will begin m. 40 also on an upstroke, one that includes all three of the detached 8th-notes. And that will present you, very properly, to the sforzando on the downstroke. This up-and-down sequence will apply to all three instruments throughout mm. 40–45. Again for reasons of proper accentuation, you should arrange your bowing so that m. 48 starts on an upstroke. 40

The viola's offbeat responses to the other two instruments in m. 52 and the first half of 53 should start with enough accent to emphasize the cross-rhythm effect of the writing. For all three instruments, avoid excessive force on the sforzandi in mm. 48–49 and 54–55. In fact, the sforzandi throughout the movement should be treated with some restraint. They make their point as much by their placement in the rhythmic figures as by any vigorous attack. And always, the left hand can supply the warmth of tone needed to supplement whatever impact you give the bow stroke. 52 48

The effectiveness of any sforzando is determined partly by a quick retreat from the initial emphasis as you sustain the rest of the note. In much the same way, the serenity of smoothly flowing and quiet measures such as bars 56–60 intensifies, by 56 contrast, the strongly marked rhythms in adjacent passages.

63   In mm. 63–64, be sure that the viola response matches the violin in intensity. The violin's ascending line of trilled figures in mm. 65–68 benefits from some modest acceleration. This is impelled by the 8th-note motion in the lower voices. Don't let the dot on the last quarter of each violin group mislead you. The note should have full value, during which the sound is drained away by slowing the bow stroke. A slight comma after each quarter-note provides the lift called for by the dot and also sets off the trill that follows.

68   A very slight stretching of the grand pause is in order in the middle of bar 68.
73   Then, full speed to the last goal in the exposition, the downbeat of m. 73. Be alert to each other for the pacing of the two pianissimo chords that end the section. These must be deliberate, very quiet, and played with a quickly decelerating stroke, so that the sound of each note has a suspenseful air.

        Four chords open the development; make them strong and intense, not gruff.
78   The 1st violin leaps upward to the high D♭ in bar 78. The fall-off from that note should be histrionically rapid, as though an operatic diva is fainting her way down the cascade of 16ths.

84   A very definite impulse must come from the cello on the downbeats of mm. 84, 88, and 94, to set the chain of 16ths among the three voices neatly under way. You will better control the linking of the 16ths if you keep the bow close to the string during the brief rests (as though the rest itself is being "played"). That way, you return to the string for the ensuing notes without any lost motion.

90   When the cello gets its turn at the solo, in mm. 90–91, give special care and incisive fingering to the grace notes, so they speak clearly in the low register. It will help if the finger is thrown onto the sforzando note with an intense, vibrato impulse. Somehow this vitalizes the fingers that play the preceding, decorative notes. The same instruction applies to the corresponding violin figures, though the high register will facilitate projection there.

99   Experiment with the pacing of the successive explosions in mm. 99–102. I think you will find that a literal counting of the grand pauses in this passage makes pretty tame listening. Try a very slight, but progressively greater, stretching of the silences as you go from one measure to the next; then, return to tempo immediately
102   in m. 102. The quiet flow of mm. 103–09 will give the impression of a slower speed, even though (as is proper) you maintain full tempo there.

        Keep up the pace relentlessly until you reach the violin's virtuoso plunge
122   (m. 122) into the recapitulation. Beethoven neatly overlaps the flight and the return.
120   The first theme makes its reentry in the low voices in m. 120, but it is not until the
124   first cadence in the melody (m. 124) that the violin alights. Even then, it is only to take off immediately again as the three voices spin out the rest of the theme.

116   The entire passage from m. 116 through 131 is a virtuoso run for the violin.
122   Making a clean scalewise descent from fifth position in m. 122 is tricky. I would suggest shifting down to third position on the fourth 16th of the bar, with a shift to first on the last C in the measure. If you shift to second position on the downbeat of
130   bar 130, you will be set for the remainder of the run. The lower voices have half-bar
128   triplets in mm. 128–31 (and again in mm. 192–95). Try to avoid ungainly emphasis
130   on these short units; play so that the phrase extends to the midpoint of m. 130, then carries straight on to the downbeat of bar 133.

149   The descending arpeggiated figures in mm. 149–52 are tricky for the viola and violin. Practice these carefully and, in performance, see them coming. If they fall on

you unawares, your attempt to render them in fortissimo will sound frenzied. I suggest that you play on the string, just above the middle of the bow. Spiccato in this context is likely to sound like musical popcorn. In bar 150, the violin might try starting in second position, shifting to first with the third couplet of the measure. The viola, in m. 151, will of course start in first position; I suggest half position from the third couplet through the remainder of the bar, in order to avoid a couple of blurry shifts. | 150

In intensity, the violin's outcry in m. 163 outranks the corresponding spot (m. 50) in the exposition. You can indulge yourself with a bit of a dramatic stretch before diving into the next measure. | 163

Check the intonation carefully in the octaves in mm. 188–90. It is a natural temptation for the violin to play the B♭ in bar 189 as an open A. Please be sure that the sound, as well as the tuning, of such a solution fits well with the notes in the lower voices. | 188

The on- and offbeat pairs of 8ths in mm. 196–206 provide a double stop at each juncture. I think, though, that Beethoven wrote this pattern in order to exploit the rivalry between the participating voices. Accordingly, try varying the relative emphasis on the successive couplets, so that the on- does not always take precedence over the offbeat unit. This is especially important, for you want to establish contrast with the clear-cut stress on the metric pulse that occurs in mm. 207 ff. | 196 ... 207

Beethoven plays on this kind of opposition right up to the end of the movement. Not only does he keep hitting second beats, but even makes the last upbeat a fortissimo, eleven-note chord. The final downbeat is low, a simple octave doubling of the C. We all know where the bar line is, but the composer has enjoyed fighting it.

Adagio con espressione. In the opening measures, the detached, simultaneous 16ths in the three voices are all part of a melodic line, not isolated clumps of sound. The silences at the ends of the bars are dangerous, for they can split the phrase into units that are too small. Two complementary pairs of measures make up the first segment; next there are two interlude bars; and finally, four measures that move to the peak on the second beat of bar 10 before making a rapid descent and close. | II ... 10

The violin's 32nd-note streamers in the next few bars are played against pedal points in the lower voices. Take advantage of this fact to play with a certain amount of Romanze-like freedom. I don't advise taking this to gypsy-fiddler lengths; just enough to enjoy the freedom. Such flutterings will appear often in the rest of the movement, but never with such open accompaniment.

The cellist should not be misled by the dots and the staccato marking in mm. 14 ff. At least two lines are being woven here, to say nothing of color shifts that result from changes in register and in size of interval. The part is as soloistic, in its way, as the two upper voices; don't treat it as a clocklike accompaniment. As for the viola, the composer is obviously enjoying the instrument, presenting it as a completely equal partner to its fellows. In fact, the handling of all three instruments in bars 14–18 produces a very luxuriant texture. And there is more to come. | 14

The sudden shift to E♭ major at the end of m. 21 demands a suitable stretching of the rest just preceding. Because the ensemble will have cadenced in pianissimo, they must decide whether the new episode should be brought in even more quietly, or on a higher and more determined level. In either case, grade the dynamics carefully from this low point to the fortissimo outbursts of mm. 29–32. | 21 ... 29

22
This entire passage weaves the three in highly imaginative ways. In mm. 22–23, viola and cello combine to weave a complex rhythmic pattern: a figure of one 16th-two 32nds emerges as a result. The dotted 16ths themselves construct a melodic line that winds around the violin statement of the theme. The cello is left to
24
continue its offbeat 16ths in mm. 24–26, while the viola part becomes so florid that for one-and-a-half measures it outranks the violin in prominence.

The ornate line returns to the violin for a time, then winds its way back through the viola and on into the cello, growing louder as it goes. Each player has to keep the melodic flame going while in possession of the line. At the same time, the thematic motive is present in other voices, swelling dynamically so that, by
28
m. 28, the demure 16ths have become engorged 8th-notes. There is great temptation here to stamp heavily on the thematic rhythm. I think the antidote is to rehearse the entire passage in a steady pianissimo, devoid of any crescendo. Make the music sound appealing in this quiet setting, then add the dynamic gradations without blotting out the sensitivity.

30
Your severest test, I think, lies in mm. 30–32. Beethoven willfully plants a sforzando on each 8th-note, inviting a ham-fisted approach from the unwary. Be aware, though, that there are niceties of detail in this storm. Bar 30 has the sforzando on the start of each 8th beat. In the first half of m. 31, the emphasis is spread over the first two 32nds (note that the sforzando is on the dotted 16th, not on the initial 32nd, of each viola figure).

31
In the teeth of the gale, the viola suddenly has a few notes in piano at the midpoint of bar 31. This is a deliberate, dramatic ploy, for the timid appeal is immediately crushed by the massed response of all three instruments. In that reply, the sforzando has moved to the offbeat 16th. All these are among the subtleties that you need to rehearse in this muscular passage.

32
Even the final, fortissimo G for all hands in m. 32 requires care. If you clip the note, it will sound as though you are coughing out your relief at being finished with a rough and nasty passage. Give the 8th-note enough length and resonance to endow it with some grace.

The return of the opening section assumes that each will want to improvise wonderful ornamentations. But Beethoven, already a renowned improviser in his
41
own right at the time he wrote this work, has done the job for you. By mm. 41–44, the lyricism is positively exuberant. The three of you must be suitably operatic in
44
your approach here. Viola, watch out for your rhythms in bar 44. After the melodic plumage you enjoyed in the preceding measures, you might feel that you have now been asked to play in Morse code. Actually, your line here provides an essential rhythmic bond between the cello 16ths and the coloratura of the violin line. Play the repeated double stops with all suitable bend and mobility. Use only as much bow as necessary, and cling to the strings.

48
The instruction in bar 48, *Con espressione*, applies to all three parts. In this coda, dramatic verve is replaced by equally thespian exhaustion. The two lower voices should make a carefully gauged, but very apparent, crescendo and warming of the
51
sound in the first half of m. 51. This marks the viola's rise to catch the swooning violin line. As for the composed expiration scene in the last four bars, I'll leave that to your own best devices. You've all been to the theater. Let me ask only that you be sure to keep some sense of motion in the last measure. The 8th-notes must seem to carry forward to the fermata chord, even as you retard.

III
Scherzo: Allegro molto e vivace. I don't know whether Mendelssohn could

have known this movement and drawn inspiration for his own scherzi from it. Players would do well, though, to think of the Mendelssohnian spirit as they deal with this movement. The ethereal way the sound makes its escape at the close of the movement offers a clue to the interpretation of the entire chapter. The music must wing its way lightly, pointedly, and with delicate handling of the dynamic stings that are indicated.

The melodic line is constructed of half-bar figures, quarter- to 8th-note. Within the rhythmic units, the emphasis naturally falls on the quarter-note. Be careful to grade the stress on the successive bow strokes. After the initial forte-piano, the melody must leap up, glide downward into bar 3, then arch smoothly through bar 4   **3** to alight on the next downbeat. From that forte-piano, the line immediately arcs higher still, and seems to land in m. 9. At that point, though, the viola fires a   **9** compressed series of rhythms. The melody falls forward at double speed, rights itself for one last flight, and cadences in m. 13.   **13**

Everything must be played in the lower half of the bow, so that quick transitions between legato and lifted strokes can be managed. Use the least amount of bow that will support the required resonance, and support the sound with the intensity of the left hand.

There is an eerie quality about this music that is destroyed by too forceful playing. The fortes serve only to mark the peaks in a world of piano. So also, the many sforzandi in the second section of the Scherzo must sting, not hammer.

In mm. 28–30, and in similar places, right on into the coda of the movement, an   **28** onbeat couplet of 16ths in the viola part is followed by a couplet in the violin. The placement of the rhythm in the violin is already familiar, because it is a characteristic feature of the theme itself. It is important, then, that the viola couplet have enough bite to mark the new treatment of the figure.

The tightly squeezed series of sforzandi in mm. 35–37 is a musical tongue   **35** twister. With these accented couplets, it is certainly possible to think of a hemiola. But it seems to me that, by having all three instruments line up in these rhythms, Beethoven wants to break us loose from any metric frame in mm. 35–36. The couplets thrash to and fro, and the 6/8 pulse just manages to restore itself in the course of bar 37. If you choose this approach to the measures in question, there is some danger of rhythmic vertigo. Hold on to the sense of downbeat in mm. 36 and 37 surreptitiously, without revealing it in your sound, then snap yourself back into the triplet frame with the fortissimo in bar 37.

For the C major trio section, I would suggest a slow, light bow stroke, perhaps a bit over the fingerboard, to give the swaying musical figures a far-off, muted atmosphere. This will lend a three dimensional sense of depth to the movement, especially when contrasted with the forte downbeat that marks the return of the Scherzo proper.

The pianissimo that starts the second section of the trio should really be triple piano, and should extend through the downbeat of bar 58. In the trio's return, the   **58** viola part (m. 59) initiates a harmonic detour and extension and should be played with enough soloistic projection to mark the fact.

In this extension of the melody, there are punctuations at the midpoint of every second measure, starting in bar 60. These breaths should be minimized, for the line   **60** has to continue as though in one sweep, right on to the cadence in bar 72.   **72**

At the coda's end, see how softly you can play the decrescendo and pianissimo and still make a credible sound. The more of a disappearing act you can manage, the better.

IV   ***Finale. Presto.*** This is another difficult movement to carry off. It rushes headlong through a succession of musical scenes, each one having to be grasped and presented vividly enough for the listener to absorb before being hurried on to the next. The players should, in effect, deal only with the music up to the downbeat

4
8   of m. 4 before shifting their attention to the next unit. Then they focus on the material up to the downbeat of m. 8; and so on.

     Play the opening swirl of triplets downbow, in the upper half of the stick, with the quarter-notes taken in short, gently detached strokes at the tip of the bow. It must sound as though you have been blown onto stage by some passing breeze.

2   The second statement of the theme (mm. 2–4) is played more quietly. Don't let the phrase settle until the cadence on the downbeat of bar 8.

10   The fortissimo doubling of the theme in bars 10–12 has three of you at work; concentrate on resonance, not loudness. The same for the sforzandi in m. 13 and the like.

13
21   Bar 13 has abruptly thrust aside the repetition of the theme to start the bridge. Its own repetition (mm. 21 ff.) is in turn interrupted by the composed deceleration (m. 28) into the contrasting theme, in E♭ minor. This melody is in just as much of a hurry as the opening. Any tendency toward mooning around is broken off by the

37   peremptory thrusts of the low voices in mm. 37 ff.

     I suggest that the violin take the triplet of the fourth quarter of mm. 37–40 on a downstroke. (The same bowing is advised for all voices when such figures appear

41   elsewhere in the movement.) The sforzando, suspended half-notes in bars 41, 43, and 45 work well as upbows, for they deliver you to the lower half of the bow for properly incisive playing of the detached 8th-notes.

     The sforzandi in these measures must be relieved immediately after the initial sting, to allow the lower-voice rhythms to be heard without forcing. Viola and cello, in m. 41, introduce a tremolo that will eventually involve all three parts. The tempo is rapid enough to make the triplets sound like a tremolo. But the rhythms are indeed triplets, and they must be cleanly played and in perfect synchronization. Some slow practice and the imposition of a slight accent on each half measure will help matters.

47   The music in mm. 47–49 is as close as this movement gets to any suggestion of ease. Be prepared, then, to give the impression that you are out for a brisk, but unconcerned walk. Then return immediately to the fray with the sforzando of m. 49.

     Work for clarity and precision in the repartée between the violin and the lower

57, 61   voices in mm. 57–59. In bar 61, the accompanying chords can stretch a bit; this will allow the violin an exultant lingering on the high C before taking the triplet plunge

63   of the following measure. From bar 63 through 74, the viola is the leader. The pacing of the four-measure components of that line sets the frame within which the violin melody is performed.

     The development opens with two outcries. Put a very short fermata over the

80   grand pause in bar 80. This helps make the transition into the second oasis of relative calm in the movement. Besides, the sudden shift to F major is abrupt

84   enough, even with the breather. When the viola takes over the theme in m. 84, the harmony has again shifted, this time to D♭. Hold your own against the violin's countering line so that the migration of the theme is apparent.

     It is important, too, that the viola project the little swirls of 8th-notes in

91   mm. 91, 95, 99, and 103. They serve as connecting links in the chain of phrase units

and (m. 99) in the line of modulation.

The line of descending triplets that fires down through the three voices in mm. 107–12 is a climactic point in the development. Work for accurate connection of the segments, but don't neglect the accent on each set. If a sforzando is missing in the cello part on the downbeat of m. 110, write it in. Also, the forte in the violin part in bar 107 should be raised to a fortissimo, to match the marks in the lower parts. For that matter, the fortissimo marking in all voices in this segment should also be interpreted as a sforzando, to be consistent with other markings in the passage overall.

Certainly, you should practice the three-part conversation of mm. 115–26 for accuracy. Even more important, you should rehearse for the hushed excitement that Beethoven intends. Some of the tension comes from the muted cries of the violin mm. 118, 122, 124, and 126. Play this passage dramatically, and you'll have the audience popping out of their seats.

There are two approaches to the bowing of the repeated quarter-notes in the viola and cello in mm. 127–33. You can follow the printed slurs, with gently articulated strokes near the tip of the bow, gradually broadening the stroke as the crescendo proceeds. Or else, you can take all the notes in repeated upstrokes, in the lower part of the bow, changing to separate and broader strokes in bar 132.

Violin: watch the A♮ on the downbeat of m. 140. That note unveils the surprise of the A major setting of the theme, and needs a slight stretch and a shot of vibrato to give it the spotlight it deserves. The 8th-notes in the viola in mm. 143–48 celebrate the sunshine that has now fallen on the music. So, without kicking over the traces, swing your way exuberantly through the line. This goes also for the slurred 8ths in mm. 149–51.

The rest of the recapitulation corresponds to events already discussed in the exposition. In the last ten bars of the movement, play just as quietly as you can, and hold still for a bit after the final note. You want to draw the lines of perspective so that the audience hears its way to infinity as you finish.

110
107

115

118

127

132
140

143

149

QUARTETTO II.

CHAPTER TEN

❧ Beethoven ❧
Quartet in G, Op. 18, No. 2 ("Compliment")

It is now some 70 years since Walter Cobbett, chamber music enthusiast *par excellence*, wrote that "the quartets of Beethoven have constituted for a century past the favourite musical pabulum of innumerable chamber music lovers, the bulk of them amateurs." He goes on to single out the Quartet in C minor, Op. 18, No. 4, as a specially tasty dish for amateur ensembles, "for whom it provides many glorious opportunities without too much technical strain."[1]

My readers—whether student, avocational, or professional—will join with me in taking some amusement from Cobbett's observation. As veteran of many a Beethoven quartet-cycle performance, I can testify to the fact that there are no easy Beethoven quartets. Precisely in the C minor quartet, for example, I have often felt some apprehension about starting, in lonely splendor, the eggshell-delicate Scherzo movement, right after the rough-and-tumble close of the opening Allegro.

I recall one concert in Boston when I had my bow poised to start this daunting Scherzo. Our cellist (we sat next to each other in our quartet) sought to reassure me by tapping out, so quietly that none but I could hear, the opening rhythm of the even more difficult Allegretto of Beethoven's Op. 59, No. 2. I noted this moral support, but was too preoccupied to laugh. Besides, I still had to begin the Scherzo by myself.

The musical public in Beethoven's own day recognized the distance that Beethoven traveled as he moved from the Op. 18 quartets at the start of the century, through the so-called middle-period quartets and on into the late quartets of the

SCORE: Ludwig van Beethoven. 1962. *String Quartet in G major, Op. 18, No. 2*. Urtext. Ed. Paul Mies. Kassel: Bärenreiter. Miniature score No. 202.

Left: Beethoven: Quartet in G, Op. 18, No. 2. Mannheim: Heckel (c. 1840). First page of score. Reproduced with permission from the collection of the Sibley Music Library, the Eastman School of Music, University of Rochester.

1820s. The works become more complex and, in most cases, much larger than the early quartets. The differences, however, have led to some misconceptions among players of chamber music. If the late quartets are thought to be mountainous, mysterious, and rather inaccessible, then the early must be of human proportions and easy to comprehend.

Don't be too sure about this. Certainly when it comes to performing any of the Op. 18 quartets, you will find none of them to be free of "too much technical strain." They have a transparency, a crystalline edge and geometry, a crispness of detail, an intensity of gesture that makes each of the six an individual musical world to conquer.

In short, your work is cut out for you in the Op. 18 quartets, and not least in the composition here at hand, the deceptively gracious Quartet in G. You will enjoy the quartet immensely. But I think you may find that the familiar nickname that has been attached to the piece, "The Compliment Quartet," belies both the temperament of the composition and the demands the piece makes on the performers.

I   *Allegro.* This movement begins with a sustained chord for all four players. For the 1st violin, however, there is a complication: the sustained D is decorated with a 32nd-note flourish. In playing, remember that this decoration, though it must be clean and elegant, is secondary in importance to the relationship between the initial note and its ending on the downbeat of the second bar. The major portion of the bow stroke in the first bar is given to the quarter-note; the flourish occupies perhaps

2   the upper third of the bow, and the downbeat of m. 2 is gently drawn on the upstroke, using just enough bow to join unobtrusively with the end of the chord in the three lower voices.

The first four measures spell out a tonic-to-dominant progression; in effect, however, the 1st violin's opening D bridges the melodic and harmonic excursion of

3   bar 3, en route to the downbeat of m. 4. It is as though the opening tone has sustained itself until it resolves, at least temporarily, on its lower octave. Thus, if the flourish of m. 1 is subordinate to the initial D, then the extension of the line to m. 4 must be at least as quiet, played neatly at the tip of the bow (the 32nd-note upbeat taken on a downstroke). with a motion focused in the wrist and fingers, and with warm left hand to keep the resonance alive.

The note G dominates the second four bars. Although the dynamic level may

5   rise very slightly in mm. 5–6, the overall effect should be that of spinning out the
8   initial piano up to the ensemble resolution at the start of bar 8. In short, play as though there is one musical exhalation extending over an eight-measure phrase.

Beethoven's strategy is calculated: a long musical stroke is built of short units

9   fitted into a continuum. This is followed (mm. 9 ff.) by a set of short strokes deliberately contrasted with each other: an alternation of loud and soft statements (mm. 9–16), then a genteel forte roar that falls away again into a soft ending (mm.

17   17–20). In the process, the composer sets this twelve-bar complex against his opening eight-measure unit, a good way to keep the listener off balance—and intrigued.

It is certainly clear by now that this is music filled with nervous tension. Sharp

21   dynamic contrasts split the first eight bars of the bridge passage (mm. 21 ff.), and the march from piano to forte over the next measures explodes at last into a rocket of triplets. At all points, loud as well as soft, the bowing must be contained and focused; too broad a stroke will dissipate both the sound and the energy of the writing.

This is true also for the second theme. The sforzando of m. 37 needs a stroke drawn slowly enough to end at a spot that will allow the ensuing 8th-notes to work back gracefully to a location that permits the 16th-note spiccato run to be played comfortably. Though this affects only the two violins, the lower voices will want to match their bow speed to that of their partners. | 37

For the extension of the second-theme area (mm. 51 ff.), the bowing of all hands should take place in the middle third of the stick. This contributes not only to the clarity of the playing, but also suits the understated intensity of the passage. This sense continues on through the codetta, where excited 16th-notes dominate the texture of the writing. In the three lower voices, the 8th-notes that accompany the flight of the 1st violin (mm. 68–77) should not simply follow the solo line; the momentum of that part depends on the melodic sense and drive of the more broadly moving lines. The last four bars of the section call for an appropriate relaxation of tension by the ensemble to provide a graceful exit and transition to the development. | 51 ... 68

Relaxation is especially important here because the respite is very brief. The forte in bar 84 breaks the mood. From here right on through m. 104, the characteristic intensity of the movement prevails. Note the thematic interruption in mm. 101–02. The rest on the third 8th of bar 100 should be full enough to let the dust settle before the impending E♭ reference to the opening melody. | 84 ... 101

Starting in m. 105, the quartet sets out on one of those characteristic Beethoven assault marches, extending over at least 25 measures, and even beyond, right up to the triumphal entry of the recapitulation and its vindication of the theme at bar 145. The *sempre pianissimo* for the first 19 measures of this march to the recapitulation should be heeded, or the requisite stealth and *misterioso* quality of the writing will be lost. Part of the success of this passage rests on the management of bow distribution for the long notes in the several voices; either through well-concealed change of direction or through speed of stroke, or both, the long note must always end at a point where the spiccato of the 16th-notes can be comfortably initiated and maintained. | 105 ... 145

Both the 2nd violin and the viola, when they are assigned the figure with 32nd-note moving to 8th-note (mm. 117 ff.) must see to it that the 32nd is always properly late and fast. There should be no possibility of the listener confusing the 32nd with the 16th-note rhythm that is being played in other parts. | 117

The successive fanfares that herald and accompany the return to the opening theme require a rather quick release of sound after the sforzando in order to clear the way for the next voice in the pyramid. This will also assure that the theme itself (and especially its 32nd-note flourish) is not buried under the musical paving. Pay special attention to the balance in m. 150, where the low-register statement of the 2nd violin can too easily be blotted out. | 150

The pianissimo chain of theme incipits in the two violins in mm. 161–67— actually a brief patch of development—needs very incisive playing to escape garbling. It will help to start each 32nd-note group with a slight impulse in the bow, just enough to get the flourish off to a clear start, but not so much as to sound like a real accent. This is again more important in the 2nd violin part, since it is cast in the middle register. That player should use especially active fingers in mm. 166–67, where the flourish starts from a suspension and can thus be all the more easily lost to the ear. The crescendo helps here, and the player should not be too bashful about raising the level. | 161 ... 166

176   The same holds true for the viola in mm. 176–82. That part is set against the two violins, and most of all against the E-string sound of the 1st; the violin duet should balance the level of their downbeat quarters in these measures so that the viola 16ths can be heard. It is just as important that the viola play with enough soloistic sense and direction to deserve the favor.

187 ff.   Under the second theme, Beethoven introduces fresh interest by having both inner voices join with the 1st violin in spinning out a chain of 16th-notes. Though this activity is cast in piano, it should be played incisively enough to make itself felt in the texture of the part writing.

214   In bars 214–18, as in the corresponding measures in the exposition, the three upper parts will need sensitive bow control when moving from the detached-and-slurred figures, into the spiccato sextuplets or quadruplets. The first of the spiccato groups always comes as a bit of a surprise to the bowing arm, and any clumsiness in the playing of the new texture will have to be worked through.

233 ff.   In the coda, mm. 233 ff., Beethoven uses much the same kind of teasing that is found at the end of the sixth quartet in this opus, the B flat. Play along with the gag.

235   On the downbeat of bar 235, the 2nd violin joins the pyramiding, tonic chord, making it veer harmonically by adding the seventh, F. The three lower voices are justified in spreading the tempo somewhat in the four 16ths on the second beat of the measure. In so doing, they set the stage for the further harmonic diversion in the next measure, where the 1st violin leers its way into the A♭. Note that Beethoven pushes the effect by calling for holds and swells. Don't overdo things on this first hold, for two more follow immediately, as though Beethoven wants to make sure the whole world gets the point. Save something for the third pullback, the one that delivers us to the tonic and to the last statement of the theme.

245   The composer has one last trick up his sleeve: he throws the 1st violin up an octave in mm. 245–46. This is a very deliberate move, since it stretches the sound range in preparation for the low-register response by the viola in the last two measures of the movement. I leave it to the ensemble to "milk" this little bit of dramatics with inspired play of tempo and dynamics.

II   *Adagio cantabile.* It seems to me that Beethoven may have been trying to match Haydn at his own game when he wrote this movement. In corresponding chapters in his quartets, Haydn often displayed a wonderful ability to ornament his themes, especially in their recurrence in later episodes in the movement. Beethoven doesn't wait that long. In this Adagio, the 1st violin decorates the melody as though it has already been made familiar in simpler state to the listener, who can thus be expected to discern the frame of the tune through the overlay of decorative notes. Beyond Haydn, Beethoven might also be emulating Mozart's operatic writing for such a character as the philosopher priest, Sarastro, in *The Magic Flute*. Whatever the source of inspiration, our 1st violin will have to think noble thoughts in performing this melody.

    The writing is a combination of aria and *recitativo accompagnato*. In much of the first half of the theme, the violin is left alone, either actually or in effect; the low-

2   voice chords on the third beat of mm. 2 and 4 might be described as composed silences. Left to its own devices in this way, the violin can freely work its ornamental wiles.

    The ornaments are carefully calculated in length, speed, and shape: a four-note turn in bar 2; a six-note run in m. 4; a flourish of sixteen 32nds in m. 7; and a more elaborate and convoluted swirl of the same length in bar 9. In the second half of the theme, dotted figures serve both to relax, vary, and impel the line. The pace is constantly and inventively altered: a very rapid roulade leads to the last 8th-note of m. 13. The line then resumes a more tranquil vein, eventually giving up even the impulse of the dotted figure. By mm. 19–20, the melody has returned to the broad rhythm of the opening measures, only to end with another elaborate roulade.

13
19

Though the flexibility of the writing is clear from the appearance of the print, it will be lost to the ear if the tempo is too slow. Even if the bar moves fast enough to avoid sticking on the 8th-notes, the music founders if counted rigidly. As ever, the written ornamentation must imply improvisational freedom. No matter how supple the decorative line, moreover, it cannot run into a dead stop. The three 8th-notes in the lower voices in m. 8, for example, must sound as though they gradually release the energy received from the 32nd-notes in the preceding bar; that is, they carry out a slight deceleration to the middle of the measure.

8

It should be obvious that the short, choral epilogue (mm. 23–26) is also a curtain-raiser for the Allegro midsection of the movement. The 16th-note groups in bars 23–24 preview the rhythmic motive of the fast episode. In that function, they should move with some forward impulse, the more so since the Allegro motive will be played so quickly that it will inevitably sound "straighter," its internal flexibility replaced by that of the larger line in which it becomes a rhythmic constituent. In a way, the identity of the motive can best be established in the slower, parent version.

23

A word about the tempo of the Allegro: the preface of the Bärenreiter score provides (p. VI) metronome marks—ostensibly the composer's own—that the Beethoven scholar, Gustav Nottebohm, reprinted in the 1880s. Also given are marks from an early edition of the quartets, published by Haslinger in Vienna, which was overseen by people who knew Beethoven: among them, the violinist and quartet leader, Ignaz Schuppanzigh. In the case of every fast movement or section, Beethoven's marking is significantly faster than that offered by his friends. (Be advised that the friends' mark of 88 to the half-note for the first movement is a typographical error in the Bärenreiter score. On p. III, in the German-language preface, the mark is correctly given as 88 to the *quarter-note*.)

You can try Beethoven's setting of 69 to the half-note for the Allegro section of the second movement. You may well decide, however, both on musical and technical grounds, to settle for a speed closer to 132 to the quarter-note, as suggested in the Haslinger source. It should be noted that the metronome was not in production until 1816, so that Beethoven was providing his markings years after the composition of the quartet, and at a time when he was already quite deaf. The marks reflect how he heard his music mentally, and might have been different if he could have heard their application in actual performance. Still, his settings give insight into his idea about the character of the music.

The larger line in the Allegro demands a specific approach in bowing. The first two statements, in detached strokes, are no problem. It is the combination of one detached note and three slurred that makes trouble. The single note must have enough of a stroke to provide room for the three notes to be taken on the return; but it must be light enough to avoid a catatonic accent. The slurred group, on the other hand, needs a slow stroke, so that the bow does not creep to an awkward spot in the stick as the chain of figures unfolds.

The task of both violins, especially the 1st, is complicated by the fact that they have to play some of the figures in reverse bowing, with an upstroke on the first 16th of the quadruplet (see, for example, the 1st violin part, mm. 29–32). At speed,

29

this can be confusing. The answer: play near the tip of the bow, focusing the motion as much as possible in the fingers and wrist of the right hand, involving the arm only to the smallest extent possible. The lower voices, whether joining the violin for short responses or in longer sequences, must be very aware of that line's momentum, so that they can swing into and out of action without breaking the stride of the solo.

The effect for the listener should be that of a well-oiled musical mechanism, with the purring sound of gears meshing smoothly. Smoothness counts, also, in the running-out of the section. From m. 52, the downward pyramid inverts the whole ensemble, transferring the melodic line from the 1st violin to the cello. To that instrument falls the job of making the transition back to the Adagio; and it happens in the space of one downbeat, in m. 58. I don't think you can rely only on the fermata over the final 16th to do the trick; there must be some deceleration over the four notes of the figure, reflecting the fact that the hold in the three upper voices covers the entire quarter-beat.

Though the opening Adagio is fairly well loaded with ornamentation, Beethoven moves almost to the saturation point in decorating the return section. For one, there is the delirious sweep of 64th-notes in the 1st violin in m. 67. Beethoven's further tactic is to move the 32nd-note flourishes to the cello line in mm. 68 ff., thus not only inverting the ensemble, but setting the stage for responsive ornaments from the inner parts and the particularly ecstatic warbling of the 1st violin in bars 70–71.

For the 2nd violin, there is the challenge of mm. 79–80. There have just been two bars in which the rich sound of pyramids of 32nd-note figures in the three lower voices has sustained the broad violin melody. Now the 2nd violin is suddenly left to provide this rhythmic undercurrent by itself. The figures need enough rubato to prepare logically for the eventual duet with the 1st violin (beats 2 and 3 of m. 80) that closes the movement. There remains, of course, the coda that actually brings us to the double bar. The ensemble will follow the 1st violin in these closing measures, with proper deference to the individual comments by the viola and cello.

Scherzo: Allegro. If you include the Allegro of the second movement (and discount the fact that it is in duple, rather than triple, meter), this quartet has two scherzo movements—which goes to prove that the young Beethoven was as determined to do things his own way as when he was older. As in the second movement's Allegro, the Scherzo proper requires a particular way of using the bow: for the 1st violin, the stroke should be a contained one, placed in the middle part of the stick, with the rhythmic figure started on the upstroke. The quarter-note that ends the figure should be drawn with a slow stroke and (with some decrescendo) sustained for the full value of the note. In their brief responses in the same rhythm, the lower voices should again play in the middle of the bow, but with a short upstroke; this assures that the 8th-note that ends the figure will sound with suitably airy effect.

In whatever voice, the accompanying quarter-notes should follow by leading, so that synchronization with the rapid-fire solo violin part is encouraged. Each scalewise run of 8th-notes should move toward the resolving quarter-notes (as in m. 11), and through them to the ultimate resolution on the downbeat of the bar beyond. In the second section of the Scherzo, the compressed chain of thematic rhythmic units (mm. 22–24) needs especially adroit bowing so that the entire set is played in midbow, without noticeable "creep." Anti-creep bowing is also used in

the 2nd violin part in mm. 30–32; draw the bow slowly on the long notes and hook   30
the ensuing 8th-note (mm. 31 and 32) onto the end of the stroke to avoid any
awkward, gulping effect on the short note.

In the Trio, the forte-piano, dotted half-notes should start near the midpoint of   Trio
the bow so that a slow stroke will suffice to end the note near the tip, ready for the
détaché strokes of the quarter-notes that follow. In m. 13 [56], the three quarter-note   13[56]
strokes will spread out from a midbow starting point as a natural outcome of the
crescendo, arriving at the tip of the bow for the start of the sforzando half-note.

The chain of triplets between 2nd violin and cello (mm. 20–27 [63–70]) calls for   20[63]
the usual approach in such situations: the receiving quarter-note in each voice
should be unaccented and sustained full-length with some decrescendo, so that the
triplets in the partner voice can be clearly heard. The 1st violin solo and the
oscillating figure in the viola will have to be balanced so that the solo and triplet
lines are properly exposed and set off against each other.

A slight accent and "bite" of the bow will help give the 2nd violin's trilled
interjection sufficient point in mm. 31–34 [74–77]. In the last couple of measures   31[74]
leading to the da capo, the 1st violin will probably find it appropriate to make some
slight retard, to indicate some teasing indecision before at last falling into the return
of the opening.

Beethoven gave this movement, by the way, a metronome mark of 52 to the
dotted half-note. The Haslinger edition again opts for a slower tempo, with 132 to
the quarter-note. Once more, you will have to use your own judgment in selecting a
performing speed.

Allegro molto, quasi Presto. I wish Beethoven had not been so hesitant about   IV
his tempo characterizations. "Quasi Presto"? To be sure, he did not know at the
time of this quartet that he would be writing Presto as the title for the so-marked
section in his Op. 131; there the quarter-notes fly past like 16th-notes, which would
certainly not do in the present instance. Here, let the 1st violin play through mm.
34–37, or the three lower voices through mm. 112–19, before choosing a realistic   34
speed. In effect, Beethoven uses Presto as a spicier, alternative title to focus the   112
character of this movement.

Your own view of the nature of the movement will again help you choose its
tempo. Beethoven once more gave a faster tempo (92 to the half-note) than did his
friends (152 to the quarter-note). If you try Beethoven's marking, you will be
playing some very fast 16th-notes, with absolutely no "quasi" about it!

I said earlier that this is a quartet with two scherzi. I misspoke: the finale is yet
a third, extended, and frenetic scherzo in its own right (I use the term here in its
literal sense, "joke," rather than as label for a particular musical structure). How
else can we regard the temper and teasings of this writing? Only a mind set on
jocularity could preface the development section with a slyly introduced dominant
seventh, highlighted by a fermata, only to side-slip into a thoroughly foreign E♭
major to launch the new section. Much later, and after many harmonic acrobatics, E♭
figures again, this time with its own seventh and fermata (m. 234), as quiet herald   234
for an A♭ return of theme. And that, in turn, undergoes fast, chameleon
transformations into a D major dominant (again with seventh and fermata!),
depositing us at last in the desired G major.

The very manner of the movement's opening threatens mischief. I would love
to suggest here a German version of "Old Macdonald had a Farm" (though the
words would not fit), for that is called to mind by the cello's quiet outcry and the

equally quiet, massed, choral response. Statement and answer must be played, obviously, in the lower part of the bow, to produce a sprightly, dryly humorous sound. When you get to the loud version of the tune (mm. 21 ff.), the two lower voices have to provide a light-handed simulation of tympani-cum-bass-drum support. The same, of course, applies to the inner voices when they sustain the dialogue of the two outer parts in bars 38 ff.

21

Starting in bar 28, incidentally, the 1st violin will want to take the first 8th on an upstroke since, from here until bar 38, the figures and dotted-note articulations will work best with reverse bowing.

28
38

In a passage such as that in mm. 55 ff., the sound of the detached 8th-notes should suggest the quality of crisply tongued woodwind notes. The sforzandi in bars 72 ff. need gentle emphasis, both on and especially off the beat. As for the inverted, legato version of the theme, both in literal and diminished time (mm. 76–83, 90–95), the stroke must be as smooth and velvety as possible. So also, the pianissimo in mm. 94–103 should take us to Schubertian, otherworldly realms, by way of respite from the generally hard-driven temper of the movement. The sense of these measures is that of a spreading, of rhythmic augmentation, even though in reality no such change has taken place.

55

72

76
94

Back to the raucous, real world: the 16th-note runs in the lower voices in bars 112–19 should be neatly engraved by the fingers, but at the same time need to sound as though they are careening intoxicatedly around the melodic race course. The syncopations in the three upper parts (in the 1st violin line they are disguised, spelled out melodically) in bars 120–21 help apply the brakes. These take hold full force in the next measures, through the broader rhythms and the ponderous tread of the sforzando half-notes. There is an abortive speedup in mm. 128–34, countered by the retard that is built into the last five measures of the section.

112

120

128

At this point, there is a fermata, calling particular attention to a chord (the dominant seventh) that in effect serves as a first ending; that is, both players and listeners are led to expect that a return to the opening and a repeat of the exposition is at hand. This is a snare and delusion, a trick which Beethoven seems to highlight by using a double bar with*out* repeat marks. The ensemble should react to this situation in two ways: first, by a slight pullback in mm. 138–39, coupled with particular attention to the pianissimo marking of those bars; and second, by not rushing through the first eight measures of the development section. It is at this point that you are suddenly in that strange world of E♭, as we noted earlier. The abruptness of this turn must not be taken for granted; you're going to have to work your way out of this.

138

A dilemma is precisely what Beethoven seems to indicate as he resumes a quicker rhythmic flow in mm. 147 ff. You observe that he still has not left E♭; it is not until the end of bar 154 that he begins the escape. To my thinking, the energy of the tempo should be restored gradually after that point, with full force reserved for the arrival at the forte of bar 163. Understand that I am not asking for blatant distortion of tempo in all this, only for something other than a heedless racing through this interesting musical scenery.

154

163

The quarter-notes in the inner voices in m. 163 should not be clipped too short, despite the dots indicated, and certainly the offbeat quarters in the succeeding bars need enough length to match the resonance of the quicker-moving, outer parts. The texture of these quarter-beats should be a loud version of the piano responses that are spaced out, immediately afterward, under the 1st violin's flight of transition to

163

the return section.

The stroke in the detached 16ths of mm. 163–70 should be on the string as much as possible, both for resonance and to prepare the way for the legato texture of the slurred quadruplets to come. Moreover, in those same measures the soloist ought to suggest a dialogue-with-self in the two-measure alternations of high and low segments of the line. I might also prompt a very slight bend in tempo in m. 175   175 and again at the start of bar 177 to help point up the final descent into the theme.

The descent is not so final, after all, since the theme here is in C major, again a delusion. The true state of affairs is hinted at by the *stretto* interweaving of parts that sets in with m. 186. I did not mention this at the start of my comments on this   186 movement, but it should by now be apparent that the stress point in the theme is the dotted-quarter at the start of its second measure. Beethoven underscores this by the sforzando emphasis he provides in the *stretto* passage, but it is true throughout. The stress on the first 8th-note of the theme's third measure is a subordinate one, and the final 8th of the theme should always be treated with airy lift.

The debate between participants in the *stretto* should be intense without raising the ensemble's dynamic level above a piano; the sforzando stings will be the more electric if heard within that frame, and the fortissimo to come will stand out all the better. Another strong contrast should be forthcoming at mm. 215 ff. The   215 bowing has to be utterly legato here, with the gentlest of articulations to separate the successive slurred groups from one another.

This time around, the fermata at bar 234 should be held enough to portend another one of those harmonic surprises; now, however, there is no surprise: we remain in E♭. This is quite civil treatment—except that E♭ is the wrong key. It will take another twelve measures to arrive at the brink of G major. In view of the fool's errands we have been through, the ensemble should express some doubt by stepping gingerly, and extremely quietly, through the A major of mm. 241–42.   241

The 1st violin shows off shamelessly with its gyrating counterpoint to the cello theme in mm. 248–66. Think of a strut, a cakewalk, a baton twirler—or even a ham   248 violinist, anything that will help you realize the fun built into this display.

For the low voices, the swirl in bar 270 must be absolutely together, and not   270 too loud. The mini-solo comes off only if the sound is clear and unforced. Note that Beethoven marks the passage starting in m. 284 as fortissimo. The assignment of the lead to the cello, the casting in minor, the heated commentary by the 1st violin, all this justifies the step-up in loudness. Even more important is an increase in intensity; like the corresponding passage near the start of the movement, this one must be played with blazing energy.

At the end of the recapitulation, there is again one of those fateful fermatas. We are then dropped into C major, so we might expect that the coda will start with   388 another harmonic detour. In fact, the succession of phrases is like that which precedes the development, implying that we are in for extended maneuvers. The side trip proves to be quite brief, however, for we move through a broad IV–V progression to arrive quickly at G major. In order to play along with the composer's teasing, though, we should exaggerate the pianissimo dynamic and follow the tempo rather freely. The pauses at bars 391 and 399 can be stretched a bit in order to   391 point up the questioning inflection of the phrases, and a slight extension of the sustained chords in mm. 393 and 395 is also appropriate, for the same reason. You can use a last, sly hint of retard in mm. 400–01. After that, lean forward into the   400 composed acceleration of the closing bars of the movement.

CHAPTER ELEVEN

❧ Beethoven ❧
Quartet in E flat, Op. 74 ("Harp")

The impetuous fury of his strength, which he could quite easily contain and control, but often would not, and the uproariousness of his fun, go beyond anything of the kind to be found in the works of other composers... The thing that marks him out from all the others is his disturbing quality, his power of unsettling us and imposing his giant moods on us.[1]

This comment was written by George Bernard Shaw in 1927, the centenary of Beethoven's death. I am sure that the ensemble face to face with the quartet Op. 74 will agree with the Shavian view. Certainly, the 1st violin, swimming through the apparently endless storm of 16th-notes (only twenty-five measures, actually) in the coda of the first movement will perceive the "impetuous fury." Only the most self-assured of composers would have unleashed this tempest just as the double bar is within sight.

And who but Beethoven would write a scherzo that opens with a furiously driven Presto, only to follow it with an even more unbridled trio? He enjoys the rise in pressure so much that he insists on running you through the entire process twice. So concerned is he about the exact layout of the movement that he writes about it to the publishers, Breitkopf & Härtel, on three separate occasions in 1810, the year of publication of the quartet.[2] (Players will be gratified to note that, in the first of these letters, Beethoven also cautions the engraver to see to it that the page turns are feasible!)

SCORE: Ludwig van Beethoven. 1970. *String Quartet in E flat major, Op. 74*. Urtext. Ed. Paul Mies. Kassel: Bärenreiter. Miniature score No. 233.

Left: Beethoven: Quartet in E flat, Op. 74. Mannheim: Heckel (c. 1840). Page from the score of the second movement. Reproduced with permission from the collection of the Sibley Music Library, the Eastman School of Music, University of Rochester.

Op. 74, however, also plumbs the other side of our emotions, through the tremulous wonderment of the quartet's introduction and the beauty and sensibility of the slow movement. This is a work that will stretch the minds and fingers of the ensemble.

Poco Adagio. The start of this quartet has no dynamic marking. Instead, it offers something akin to a stage direction: *sotto voce.* Literally, this means, "in an undertone." In dramatic terms, we might interpret it as signifying an aside, something not to be overheard. And, in fact, much of this Adagio introduction sounds as though it might be a private musing of the ensemble. The group is deciding whether to play at all, let alone launch into the activity of the approaching Allegro.

Begin noncommittally, with cool, quiet sound. The addition of a D♭ to the E♭ chord at the downbeat of m. 2 is a surprise; it is received calmly, however, and the chord simply fades into the silence that fills the remainder of the bar. I suggest that you stretch this silence a bit, for in effect you have been stopped dead, and have to agree whether to begin again. Bar 3 should be an exact duplicate of the first measure; save any sense of change until you hear the E♮ of the 2nd violin at the start of bar 4. The impulse of that note cannot be ignored; the several voices begin to move more actively now, though still in trancelike state, and with only moderate warming of the sound.

In bar 8, the violins—with their two rests—seem to resist the forward push of the low voices. The 1st violin suddenly yields, however, breaks into the ornamental flourish of m. 9, and leads the ensemble in the expansive gestures of bar 10. Just as matters seem to be warming up, there is the abrupt pullback to the hushed chord of the next downbeat. The *espressivo* of mm. 11–13 truly promises a more positive view of things, but the ringing forte chord (it should be sudden, and free in resonance) in m. 13 throws up an even more effective roadblock than its quiet forebear, of bar 11. Harmonically, in fact, it feels as though we have been set back to the original point of hesitation, the chord in bar 2.

Undaunted, however, the lines pick themselves up and make their way forward—only to run up against the same chordal wall in m. 17, with the D♭ at the top of the barrier now set an octave higher than before. This shock throws the harmony into minor. It is only by dint of some chromatic burrowing that the players now tunnel their way up toward the B♭ platform of bar 24 and from there make their escape into the daylight of E♭ and the—

Allegro. The downbeat chord is already orchestrated for fullness, so you can work for resonant, unforced sound. Regard the dots on the next three quarter-beats as an instruction for nonlegato playing, but don't make the notes hard or clipped in effect.

A somewhat sustained quality is needed on the downbeat of m. 26, for that resonance spawns the winding, 8th-note line of the 2nd violin. In that part, the inflection should play on the relationship between the first and fourth 8th in each quadruplet. Think of those notes as points in two melodic voices that respond to one another; that will keep the part from settling into a dogtrot. The melodic integrity of this 2nd violin passage is important for two reasons: it enables the voice to speak melodically to the broader lines in the other instruments; and it demonstrates a link to the similar, though slower, motions in the Adagio, as in bars 11–12, 15–16.

This, in fact, is only one of several aspects that bind the Allegro to its prelude.

I

2

3

4

8

9, 10

11

17

24

26

The 1st violin figure at the start of the Allegro reflects the outline of the melody of that instrument in the first two bars of the Adagio. The dotted rhythms in the 1st violin in mm. 29–30 and the viola in mm. 33–34 suggest a recall of the process in all four parts in the closing phase of the introduction. And the deliberate alternation and contrasting of patches of slow, faster, and still faster rhythms in this Allegro seem to have been forecast in miniature by the events of the quartet's opening.

29, 33

Concerning faster rhythm, it is pertinent to note that Beethoven chose a metronome mark of 84 to the half-note for the Allegro (as given in the Bärenreiter score, p. IV). This will certainly set a blazing trail through the violin solo to come in mm. 221 ff. As I suggested in my discussion of the tempo markings in Op. 18, No. 2, you may want to take Beethoven's speed indication under advisement. You should, however, try to approach it, and certainly regard it as a clue to his concept of the music.

221

In mm. 35 ff., the 8th-notes should be played with gentle spiccato. If the stroke becomes choppy, you will obscure the broad chordal succession that underlies the rhythmic pattern. Also, the hubbub will make it difficult for the pizzicato, quarter-note arpeggiations to be heard.

35

I urge the 2nd violin to play the second quarter of mm. 43 and 45 robustly, but not stridently. You can't hope to match the massed impact of the downbeat chord; besides, your double stop is only the aftershock of that chord, serving to transmit the line to the sustained voice of the viola in the second half of the measure.

43

The ensemble will probably be taking the sforzando of m. 48 on a downbow. Slow the stroke immediately after the impact, so that you are not too high in the stick when you have to play the detached 8ths that follow. And please be circumspect in the cross-string 8ths in m. 51. With three of you involved in this pattern, there is danger of sounding like a convention of carpet-beaters. Keep the crossings snug and the spiccato on the gentle side. The crescendo is moderate, and you have to drop quickly back to piano.

48

51

An easy touch is needed, too, in the 16th-note runs of mm. 52 ff. The figures have to be synchronized between pairs of instruments, or else linked in succession. Emphasizing the quarter-beat in these swirling lines may seem to help togetherness, but it kills the gracefulness of the melodic swirl. Practice the passage slowly, work for a half-bar flow of the music, and rely on the ensemble's sense of tempo and motion to merge the lines neatly together. Except for bar 55, there is always a more broadly moving rhythm in one or more parts that can help pace the running voices.

52

In larger perspective, think of mm. 52–57 as one phrase unit; then try to keep things moving from m. 58 to m. 69. Perhaps I ought to indicate the forte chord of bar 70 as the goal. That chord, however, seems to break abruptly into the preceding activity. It should be thought of as the start of the eight-bar codetta that closes the exposition.

52

70

Try to avoid a gap after the fifth 8th of m. 70. Draw the bow slowly enough on the sustained note so that you are still in the lower half of the stick when it is time to play the detached 8th-notes. The sforzando offbeats should be compact and vigorous, not rough in sound. Also, be sure to carry the diminuendo of the last six measures down to a true pianissimo. The fading of sound creates a sense of depth and dimension in the music. Also, it sets up the contrast against the sudden forte, both when you make the repeat and when you go ahead into the development.

70

The slurred 8th-note figures in mm. 79–85 are set at a lower dynamic level than

79

the broader lines. Even so, the passage floats on these wavelets of 8ths, so play them cleanly and with a sense of carrying through the slur and beyond. So also, the figure made up of two 8ths resolving into a quarter-note (mm. 86–88) must show the drive toward the quarter. In this brief space of three measures, note the brief conversation between high and low duets, and then the chain of the rhythmic figures in the violins. That sequence ignites the explosion of motion that runs through the rest of the development.

86

You want energetic but not overbearing playing on the 16-note lines, especially when both inner voices are at work simultaneously, as in mm. 93–108. Give the sforzando notes a good shot. Also mark significant changes of pitch. In bars 96 and 97, for example, the first 16th of each half-measure should get extra pressure; in m. 98, emphasize only the first 16th; and in bar 99, mark the first 16th, then all 16ths from the fourth 8th on. That is, you should bring out the broader melodic motion that underlies the 16th-note rhythm. In this way, the inner voices complement the dialogue that is taking place between the two outer parts of the ensemble.

93
96
98

The 1st violin and cello are blazing merrily away at each other, loping along in dotted rhythms and recharging the energy of the passage by their two triplet dives (mm. 97 and 101). The four players realign for the long chain of statements and responses in bars 109–24. Second violin and cello should not be relegated to an echo function here; nevertheless, the phrase should move in whole-bar units. The large arpeggio, C–E–G–C, binds mm. 109–12 together. From there, the diminuendo, the detached 16th-note texture, and the harmony move us through six measures. A further group of six measures is denoted by a drop in level and a change to slurred 16ths that murmur in intervals of a second. The conversation between duos should be full of suspense, with the effect intensified by the reduction to a very dramatic pianissimo.

97
109

The sustained chords of the 1st violin in mm. 125–37 are the lid on a pressure cooker. These long double stops can't just lie there inertly; keep them alive with a moderate but active vibrato, and draw the bow slowly enough that the sound does not become diffuse. Underneath, the pizzicati must be resonant and full-bodied, even though hushed. Practice the chains of plucked notes so that there is a consistent level of sound as the figures mount through the ladder of voices. Also, try to match the style of pizzicato, so that the arpeggiations have no hard or skinny areas.

125

The change to bowed notes in m. 134 should not make too startling a contrast to the pizzicato that has come before. I'm sure that Beethoven would have continued the pizzicati (hence the nickname, "Harp") if he thought it possible to play them in the rapid triplets, and if he did not have to prepare for the return of the Allegro's opening. In any case, the cello—first in line with the bowed notes—should make the transition in sound as smooth as possible.

134

A remarkable fact about this movement is that the coda (mm. 204–62) is just a few bars shorter than the recapitulation. The dramatic significance of the closing section shows in the dynamic level from which Beethoven has it begin: triple piano. He holds to this for eleven measures before starting his climb out of the gloaming. Use exceedingly small bowing here; the quartet should sound as though it is coming from another world.

204

On the other hand, you have only six measures to move from pianississimo to forte, and from measures of whole-notes to bars filled with tumbling 16ths. This is a radical shift of scene, so you will have to practice the building of excitement.

Talk about exciting! The 1st violin solo, starting in m. 221, is pure musical adrenalin. It also threatens temporary paralysis of the right arm to the unwary player. This is not a passage to be attempted in an evening's chamber-music reading session. You will want to work out appropriate fingerings and program the string-crossing patterns into your bowing arm. On the basis of the crossings, the passage divides at measures 226 and 240. There are changes within these segments, of course, and these must be accounted for.

Despite the effort that goes into the top line, be aware that it is only part—though a dazzling one—of the action here. The strands of pizzicato and the *cantabile* melodies (mm. 232 ff.) are equally important. Actually, I think that the final test of the 1st violin is to be able to rejoin the relatively sedate pace of the rest of the group after the triumphant arrival at the downbeat of bar 246. Unobtrusive rest and recuperation has to be postponed until the short interval between first and second movements.

Adagio ma non troppo. In rehearsal, try starting this movement on the second measure. If this feels convincing to you (and I think it can), add the two upbeat 8ths as though they are a gently hummed lead-in to the melody. Don't let the bow get hung up on the dots of the introductory 8ths. You can, as a matter of fact, try playing those notes on a downstroke in the upper half of the bow, if that contributes to smoothness.

The 1st violin—the other instruments as well—should feel free to change bow as best fits the sound and shape that the phrases require. At the slow tempo called for, even if *non troppo*, the printed slurs will inevitably lead to a feeling of cramped confinement in the bowing. The slurs indicate melodic contour and direction; you can preserve the intent of the markings without following them slavishly. If you need convincing on this point, look at bars 6–8. The slurs of the four parts do not agree, even though the thrust of the phrase is the same for all.

There are few breaks in the opening of this movement. The first breath comes after the second 8th of m. 9; the punctuation in bar 5 is bridged by the 1st violin's quarter-note and the viola's slurred figure. In bar 8, the 1st violin E♭ again covers over a rest in the lower voices. The phrase that follows does not end until m. 24, this time with the cello sounding through the cadential rest. In bars 13–14, the sforzandi (lean on them gently, please) serve to urge the music forward. The piano, A♭ chord in m. 18 is the resolution of the preceding phrase; it should receive the decrescendo of the measure before without break. Yet at the same time this chord is the beginning of the seven- measure close.

I find that the *cantabile* instruction for the 1st violin, and the *mezza voce* for the lower voices, makes an ill-advised distinction between the parts. All four should be playing singingly; and the hushed atmosphere of the opening applies to the solo line as much as to the other strands. Even the ornamental figure and forte of mm. 16–17 are colored and restrained by the contemplative tone of the writing. The 32nd-note dialogue of viola and 2nd violin at the phrase end (bars 22–23) is more pensive still.

The short slurs in mm. 25–28 should not mislead the 1st violin; the only real punctuations in the line come after the second 8th in mm. 26 and 28. In bar 31, the second and third beat of each voice is made up of a 16th-note couplet. Both notes in the couplet are of identical pitch, and are bridged by a slur. Since no further marking is given, you have to apply common sense: play the couplet with a very gentle *portato* stroke, as though each 16th has a line printed above it.

221

226

232

246

II

6

5, 9
8
24
13

18

16
22

25
26, 3

37   The C♭ in m. 37 of the 1st violin part finds its continuation in the same note in bar 39. Accordingly, the three upper voices should be careful to treat the active writing of mm. 37–38 as a low-register echo of the preceding solo.

49   Looking ahead: note that, after the resolution in A♭ minor in bar 49, the action continues from the third beat of m. 51—now in A♭ major. The intervening conversation between the cello and the inner voices is an interlude and should not be rushed. Take enough breath after the second 8th in mm. 50 and 51 to let each of the short statements make its point.

58   A bit later, you are asked to play four isolated chords expressively (mm. 58–61). Try these bars a number of times, experimenting with a different succession of spacings, dynamic levels, and tone colors in each round. You might also rotate the leadership in these repetitions, to make sure that a full range of approaches is tested. When you find the concept you all agree is best, be aware that yet other inflections will turn up in the course of many performances of the work. Let them happen.

62   From the fourth of these chords emerges the 1st violin's flight of 32nds. Make this a lyric, improvisatory outpouring, suitably free but not gushing. The 2nd violin will lead the lower voices in fitting the chord in bar 62 precisely to solo line.

64   The restatement of the opening melodic complex in mm. 64–86 is brimful of inspired ornamentation. Don't let this carry you away. The piano dynamic still sets the frame for performance. Temper your enjoyment of the writing with sobriety. As far as I know, Beethoven never wore a plumed hat.

86   In the D♭ section of this movement (mm. 86–102), the inner voices have 32nd-note ribbons that incorporate drone and melodic lines. Inflect them so that the moving lines are heard as full partners to the melodies in neighboring voices. The trio of 1st violin, viola, and cello will have to rehearse for freedom and

93 synchronization in the expansive cadence of bars 93–94. So also for the commentary

95 the 1st violin offers to the trio of lower voices in bars 95–102.

115   In the next restatement of the principal melody (mm. 115 ff.), the 2nd violin has eight bars of detached 32nd-note filigree. Here the word, *staccato*, is simply a reminder that the notes should not be slurred. The player still has to decide whether the dots on the notes mean spiccato or on-the-string playing. If spiccato, then the stroke has to be low enough in the bow to preserve the tempo (too high in the stick will make you strain to hold the speed back, with harmful impact on both the sound and the inflection). Even then, you may feel some awkwardness in controlling string crossings and the spacing of the succession of notes. I would suggest, rather, that you play the passage on the string, with notes cleanly detached, near the tip of the bow. Use reverse bowing in much of the line, since

117 upper-string notes (as in m. 117) will be taken more gratefully on the upstroke as you cross strings. Above all, play flexibly.

      The same goes for the viola pizzicati and the cello's offbeat pulses throughout, up to bar 130. Resonate the plucked notes so that they are long enough, and keep the cello notes on the short side, so that the two parts can sound compatible with one another. At the same time, make the low duet fit the shape of the upper voices. Every player must watch and listen intently.

128   The 32nd-note couplets that appear in the three upper voices in mm. 128–34 should be played so that the metric pulse of three-to-the-bar is preserved. In other words, the second couplet of each 8th-note unit will be subordinate to the first, although with appropriate emphasis on important melodic notes, as in the second

130 half of bar 130.

In mm. 147–51, the pyramid of 16th-note couplets in each bar matches the 147
violin solo in importance. The pacing of top and lower lines is interlocked, of
course, especially as you approach the sudden catch of breath at the end of bar 149. 149
Fitting this rhythmic mosaic together convincingly will take some patient trial and
repetition.

Plan to spend some thought on the "expressive, dying away" measures that
close the movement. It may help your synchronization if you try counting mm.
165–66 as one broad and decelerating 3/4 bar. Revert, of course, to 3/8 thinking for 165
the final three measures.

I am impressed anew at the force of Beethoven's imagination when I read
(Bärenreiter score, p. IV) that his speed for this movement is 100 to the dotted half-
note. This is a tempo you can regard as a goal, but I think reality will call for a
slightly more sedate pace—which will still be quite fast.

Presto. There seems to be some contradiction between the forte, aggressive III
rhythms and the marking, "lightly," at the start of this movement. The massed
orchestration of the writing, however, justifies the instruction. Certainly the low
tones of the 1st violin in bars 1 and 2 will never be heard if the inner voices grind 1
too forcefully on their running figures. Also, the passage in the second half of this
section will simply sound like static if not very quietly and neatly synchronized.

Mm. 8–16 will go more comfortably at this high speed if you hook the long 8
note to the three 8ths that follow in each bar. That is, m. 9 will start downbow;
m. 10, upbow; and so on. Here again, and especially since all four voices are in
unison and octave, be both strong and easy. I think, by the way, that the 1st violin
might also find hooked bowing a workable way of playing the opening of the
Presto, as well as similar passages later on.

The rapid flight across the fingerboard in bars 17–18 and 25–26 is not easy for 17
either violin. It is a bit tougher for the 2nd, who has to reverse course suddenly to
dart onto the A-string for the fortissimo notes of bars 19 and 27. Try playing your
8ths in second position, so that you need only jump down to the long note when
you finish the pattern, without a change of string. Second position is an equally
good choice for the 1st violin at these spots.

In the lower voices in mm. 34–36 and 40–42, synchronization between the 1st 34
violin and the downward pyramid, and the linkage of the pyramid itself, are
automatic, provided that everyone holds strictly to the metric pulse. So also for the
lineup of parts in passages such as mm. 43–49 and 57 ff. The pianissimo measures 43
that end the section are completely under the control of the drumming 8ths of the
cello.

Più presto quasi prestissimo. Beethoven must be kidding. There's no "quasi"
about it: this is prestissimo, or a very good imitation thereof. The composer pulls
the same psychological trick in the Presto section (No. 5) of the C sharp minor
quartet, Op. 131. There too, you watch a stream of quarter-notes rush past. The
sensation of speed is great, especially because you don't normally associate such
swiftness with so innocent a note sign. If you can imagine a bobsled run, with the
snow and ice zipping out from under you at seat-of-the-pants level, you get the
idea. I don't deny that it's a thrill, but you have to like it and survive.

To give you a mental handle on the situation in our *quasi prestissimo*, Beethoven
tells you to "imagine a 6/8 meter." To put it more plainly, think of each two of these
bars of three quarter-notes as being translated into one measure of six 8th-notes. As
for gauging the speed of this compound measure, Beethoven himself (see

Bärenreiter score, p. IV) instructs that you relate it directly to the tempo of the original Presto. There you have been counting one to the bar. When you hit the forte downbeat of the *Più presto*, immediately start counting the same "one" to each of the imagined 6/8 measures (that is, to every pair of measures in the printed line). The connection works, and you will be playing quite fast enough.

You will also find that the melodies in dotted half-notes breeze merrily along. Just remember that your pals will be playing three notes to your one, so have mercy and don't push! My guess, though, is that everyone will be having such a good time that you may have to hold each other back.

I don't think you need much guidance on the temperamental approach to this section. If you've heard a good wind band play very lively stuff, you'll know exactly how to proceed. Let me just ask that the staggered entrances of the sustained-note lines (as in mm. 96 ff.) start with an accent in each part, and with an accent also on each pitch change. If you inspect bars 96 to 103, you will see that, between them, the two voices provide a new pitch for every measure. Make sure the musical leapfrog comes across to the listener.

The accent pattern is different in the chordal passages. In mm. 104–13, for example, the three lower voices should put emphasis on bars 107 and 111. The 1st violin, on the other hand, needs greatest stress on the downbeats of mm. 109 and 113. These contrasting focal points of energy add to the excitement of the entire section.

When you approach the fermata at the double bar, there should be no pullback; or, if any, just a tiny bit the bar before. This musical car has great brakes.

You get a chance to test those brakes again, for both the Presto and the *Più presto* get another full run-through. Then, yet another return of the Presto, but this time with a couple of differences. First, instead of running at full steam, the dynamic level is reduced to piano at bar 353. And there it stays, so that figures already difficult when loud are now made even tougher to play in the utter transparency of the enforced quietness. You will rise to the challenge, nonetheless.

Another change is the addition of a coda. With the exception of a couple of slight rises, this section makes its way to the double bar in a constant pianissimo. The cello has the most exacting task here, having to keep a steady line of 8th-notes crisply clear without forcing any rise in the overall dynamics. All four instruments join in hushed conversation in this rhythm as the harmony veers toward a long held and very inconclusive dominant seventh chord. The coda has become a transition. Straight ahead, into the—

Allegretto con Variazioni. The theme is ambiguous: does it start with an up- or downbeat? It is difficult for the listener to tell, especially since the theme's recurrent rhythmic figure has a short last note, with a dot to indicate lightness. If you take this instruction literally, you will really keep the audience guessing.

Beethoven might well have intended this uncertainty. In mm. 17–18, he places a sforzando on the upbeat, to assure that you stress the start, not the end, of the rhythm. Yet elsewhere in the movement, he goes out of his way to focus on the downbeat part of the figure. In mm. 68–70 of the third variation, for example, he writes sforzando on the second half of the rhythmic figure in the 2nd violin part. Unfortunately, the cello part, starting a beat later, also has sforzando on the second half of *its* figure. Thus, between the two parts, you end up with a stress on each beat of the measure. Checkmate!

I suppose we'll have to play the game according to Beethoven's rules. Let the theme start in its own, ambivalent way. The last 8th-note in the first section bears no dot, so you can let that note have enough emphasis to indicate the true state of affairs. You might also help by putting some stress on the downbeat of m. 7. The offbeat sforzandi at the end of the theme (mm. 16–18), however, will prevent you from making an improvised accent on any but the very last 8th-note. | Theme

7
16

There is no problem in the first variation. The staggered entrances of the four parts make the ear listen to the music in quarter-note bites. Within the individual voice, as well as in the relation between successive entries, there is still room for the equivocal shape of the rhythmic figure. Beethoven's instruction, *sempre forte e staccato*, moreover, favors a certain flattening of the musical terrain; this again keeps the ear guessing. Notice the lone sforzando on the last 8th-note in bar 31. This is the first time an accent has been placed so late in the measure, and is another dig at the listener's powers of perception.

For this variation, use bold détaché in the upper half of the bow. I suppose that a bluff spiccato near the frog would also work, but there would be a hint of lightness that doesn't quite fit the temper of this part of the movement.

There's no doubt about the metric frame in the second variation. The steady change of chord at the bar line, as well as the predominantly measure-by-measure slurring of the solo part shows the true anatomy of the theme. The clear lineup of the several parts carries with it, however, the danger of sounding not only straightforward but dull. It's up to the violist to play the solo with enough shape—both of dynamics and rubato—to reveal the outline of the theme within the ornamentation. This approach will also let the solo mitigate its own regular bowing and the march of the accompanying chords.

A survey of the movement shows that Beethoven exploits the contrast between quiet and brash, flowing and angular, as he moves from one structural division to the next. Accordingly, give full heed to his instruction, *sempre dolce e piano*, in this variation. For your own sake, as well as the listener's, you want to relax while you can. To help in this regard, you can set the tempo of this variation somewhat slower than you have been following thus far.

Variation III, on the other hand, is the energy peak of this Allegretto. Return at least to your opening tempo, and perhaps even a bit beyond. In musical terms, this episode is the equivalent of the soldier's double time march. There is no call for such niceties as rubato. You may allow yourselves just a hint of dalliance in the quiet moment of dialogue between the interlocked duets (mm. 72–76). Except for that, however, the brisk play of 16ths against the offbeat 8ths should proceed with metronomic strictness. Some dynamic shading is certainly permissible, however. For example, the second half of bar 64 and the first half of 65 is an almost verbatim repeat of the preceding two quarter-beats. Try parenthesizing the repetition by cutting down on the loudness. Don't overdo the effect; just a hint will suffice.

Give special vigor to the forte in mm. 76–80. You are, in a way, making up for the coquettishness of the piano measures that precede.

The fourth variation is the counterbalance to the third. Push and aggressiveness give way now to expansive good will. Here your tempo can swing back to the slower edge of allegretto. Although there is no doubt that the rhythms are aligning with the downbeat impulse at this point, it is curious that the 1st violin line consistently steps from upbeat to down. Only at one point, m. 85, is there a slight jar as the melody switches to a downbeat start in midphrase.

The whispering tone of the last four bars of this variation can be underlined

Margin notes (right column):
Var. I
Var. II
Var. III
72
64
76
Var. IV
85

with a slight retard at the end of the repeat. This helps set up the surprise of the militant entry of the next variant. Take a short breath before calling in the cavalry.

Var. V   Once again, step up the tempo for the fifth variation. Let pomp and circumstance prevail. The bow strokes and vibrato of the three lower voices should absolutely pop with exuberance and pride. Riding on this support and encouragement, the 1st violin charges up each ramp of 16th-notes. Each sforzando landing tips the line into the next trajectory. Beethoven must have seen some Viennese quartet performing on a trampoline.

112   You might try relieving some of the athletics by making a slight drop in dynamic level at the second half of bar 112, right after the high-rising flight of the 1st violin. From there, the sound can resume full force as it moves toward the end of bar 116.

Throughout, take care that the sound does not become choked and brutal. The bow strokes should not slash. Relieve the pressure and speed of the stroke immediately after each emphasis or sforzando. The 16th- note lines will sound right if they have the ring and clarity of good trumpet playing.

The instruction, *un poco più vivace*, signifies to me that the pace of the final section should be a peppy one-to-the-bar. A slight pulse on each downbeat in the cello part will move things along. The triplet rhythms are marked with dots only

177   from m. 177 on. Spiccato bowing is in order, however, from the very beginning of the episode; its lift and sprightliness can be shaded according to the musical needs of the moment. Even at the forte peaks, the stroke should never be entirely on the string.

In general, the loud points should be moderate. Much of the excitement in this section comes from a sense of hushed understatement. The energy is always there, but under wraps, lest it burst uncontrollably forth. All swells, even the longer ones

142   that start in bars 142 and 146, are abruptly quenched.

152   The trills in the 1st part in mm 152–55 turn each 16th-note quadruplet into an ornamental swirl. Don't try to preserve a strict series of 16ths. Let the rhythmic group swing forward and up.

163   The lower voices should take advantage of the short swells in mm. 163 and 167. Especially with the harmonic coloration of the chord involved, these measures shiver with an excitement that is reflected in the 1st violin immediately afterward.

169   I think you will have worked up a good head of steam by the time you reach bar 169. Hold the speed and the pianissimo steady as you head into the firefly dialogue of the following measures. Use very short strokes, on the string. Lighten and slow the stroke at the end of each group; that way, you can give the relief (indicated by the dot) without having to lift the bow from the string.

177   Before you rehearse the accelerando of mm. 177–84, practice the final Allegro. Beethoven asks (see Bärenreiter score, p. IV) for a speed of 84 to the half-note. Find out exactly how fast the four of you can play the 16ths cleanly, together, and with time to snap the sforzandi on offbeats. In particular, make sure you can play the

191   short burst of chromatics in mm. 191–92 neatly. After you know your realistic Allegro pace, you can arrange the acceleration to deliver you to the tempo you need.

Rehearse the staging of the last measures of the piece. With the control of acrobats and jugglers, you want to rush to your final landing point, the downbeat

193   of bar 193. Then, with utter nonchalance—hair unruffled, breath calm—you make

your exit. The last two, quiet 8th-notes must wink at the audience. Hold still, so that you can hear them chuckle.

CHAPTER TWELVE

❧ Schubert ❧
Quintet in A, for piano, violin, viola, cello, and double bass, D. 667 ("Die Forelle," "The Trout.").

The "Trout" Quintet was finished in the later part of 1819. Since that time, it has become a favorite among music lovers and continues in prominence to this day, both in concert and recording. The reason for its popularity is perhaps best captured in the words of the Austrian musicologist, Bernhard Paumgartner (namesake of Sylvester Paumgartner, the work's original patron):

> This is wonderful music-makers' music, filled with gracious fantasy, wandering blissfully through field and flower. Here speaks high seriousness, but only in tones of cheer. What mastery, to achieve so complete a blend of naturalness and easily understood expression![1]

Paumgartner has put his finger on both the charm and the difficulty of this work. The "Trout" has become so popular, so pervasive, that some among us have grown too jaded and blasé to acknowledge the solidity of the composition. Consider, for example, the comment of the English musicologist, Jack Westrup, writing in the 1940s:

> The Quintet is not a great work. The double bass is not a happy member of an intimate team... [Schubert] had already wrestled with formal problems in his earlier quartets, and could have solved them again here

SCORE: Franz Schubert. 1988. *Quintet for Piano, Violin, Viola, Violoncello and Double-bass, A major, D. 667. "The Trout," "Die Forelle."* Ed. Anke Butzer and Jürgen Neubacher. London: Eulenburg. Miniature score No. 118.

Left: Schubert: Piano Quintet in A, D. 667. Braunschweig: Henry Litolff (c. 1895). Piano score, first page of the fourth movement. Reproduced with permission from the collection of the Sibley Music Library, the Eastman School of Music, University of Rochester.

if he had wanted to. Clearly he did not want to. This was holiday music for amateurs, and he was not prepared to display science on such an occasion... [The Quintet] is entertainment music from first to last, and should be listened to with simple, unsophisticated enjoyment. To drink—even to talk—during a performance would not be blasphemy.[2]

Clearly, Westrup likes the piece, but will permit himself to accept it only within severe limits. If the performer, too, feels this kind of ambivalence, there is trouble afoot. Heaven knows that there are enough technical difficulties in this quintet without the added burden of wondering about your commitment to the composition.

Let us turn, then, to the rather more sympathetic view of the "Trout" offered by the critic William Mann (again English). For him, the bass gives the string group "a fuller contrast to the resources of the piano, and is particularly suited to antiphony between piano and strings." Further, he admits to enjoying the slow movement's "naïve rambling... [that] hides a harmonic scheme worthy of a crossword expert." As for the unabashed, transposed repeat in the layout of the finale—more on this in our discussion to follow—Mann is slightly more forgiving than Westrup:

> If Schubert takes the lazy way out, we may remember that he was on holiday, and that the holiday relaxation of the "Trout" Quintet has always been its most engaging feature, the inspiration of some of Schubert's most generously captivating melodies.[3]

Again, that troubling reference to the holiday! The vacation in question took place in the summer of 1819. During a sojourn in the town of Steyr, just south of Linz, Austria, Schubert was asked to write a quintet with precisely the instrumentation we now find in the "Trout." The request came from Sylvester Paumgartner, an administrator of the regional iron mines, leading local music enthusiast, and amateur cellist.

Paumgartner got the idea from the quintet, Op. 74, published a few years earlier by the Austrian virtuoso pianist and composer, Johann Nepomuk Hummel. (That work also existed in a septet version for the even more exotic setting of piano, flute, oboe, horn, viola, cello, and bass.) Hummel himself may have found the precedent for the five-part grouping in the quintet, Op. 41, published in 1803 by the Bohemian pianist/composer, Jan Ladislav Dussek. Moreover, despite Westrup's misgivings about such instrumentation, it has enough appeal to have surfaced again in recent decades in works by the Swedish composer, Hilding Hallnäs, and the Dutch composer, Henk Bijvanck.

To sum up: in playing the "Trout," you certainly have to evoke the cheer of the music, but in so doing must approach the task soberly. If you regard the piece as mere entertainment, you will turn it into out-and-out kitsch, and your audience will indeed have to console itself with a beer. Your course is clear.

I *Allegro vivace.* The opening chord of this piece is the trigger for an ascending arpeggio. Together, chord and arpeggio serve as the introductory flourish, the attention-getter, for the movement about to begin. At the same time, they make a thematic statement: both elements will serve as musical ingredients in the Allegro. I would like to think, also, that the flashing arpeggio is a musical metaphor for the liquid currents that will run through the variations of the fourth movement.

This fanfare needs a light touch. A brilliant, ringing resonance is more inviting to the listener than a brusque attack. Be advised by the double-bass note: it starts forte, but continues without interruption into a piano, then pianissimo, level in the second and third measures and beyond.

If you look ahead to the start of the recapitulation, at m. 210, you will see that the beginning of this movement is not repeated there. What we have at the start of the piece, from mm. 1 through 24, is truly an introduction, a "once upon a time" lead-in. The movement has another, and much shorter, preface (again starting with the fanfare), in bars 25–26, though that one is clearly integrated into the thematic substance there under way.   210   1   25

I note here that a repeat of the exposition entails a rehearing of the curtain-raiser measures. I think that is too much of a good thing, and will urge instead that the performance go straight ahead into the development section.

The accent on the downbeat in the violin part in mm. 5 and 9 is supported by similar warmings of tone in the viola and cello. In mm. 14–21, on the other hand, the voices are involved in distinctly separate points of action; the accent marks there are placed very specifically, and should be observed. The forte in bar 23 will automatically produce some effect of accent from all hands; and in bar 24, viola and piano can share in the downbeat accent.   5   14   23

From mm. 25 through 49, viola and cello provide the motive force that drives the music. At first in 8ths, then triplets, the two players mark the passing half-measures with buoyant rhythmic figures. Play these below the middle of the bow, with the dotted notes (taken in one light, articulated upstroke) sounding like responses to the slurred, downbow couplets.   25

Around this rhythmic core, the remaining trio of players carry on their musical business. The bass at first provides connecting links between the piano's arpeggios and the violin's melodic response, then joins the two in simultaneous parley. The bass' alternation between pizzicato and *arco* adds a sonorous dimension to the ensemble. Both the plucked and bowed notes should be played with the same, forward-leaning melodic direction.

Schubert disguises a repetition of material by interchanging the assignment of parts between violin and piano (see mm. 38 ff.), adding ornamentations in the piano version to what had been more simply stated in the violin. The octave doubling in the piano's treble and bass, coupled with judiciously placed trills, adds to the mounting excitement, culminating at last in the piano's short spray of notes in m. 50, and the sforzando, chordal cap for the ensemble in the second half of that bar.   38

You must by now have realized the importance of the vivace aspect of the tempo. A lively two-to-the- bar is essential (even though the time signature is 4/4, without the salutary *alla breve* indication). In fact, the episode now beginning (mm. 51 ff.) must have the triplet repartée between high and low strings and the piano move along as though each measure is a single unit. The occasional 8th-note pulse in cello or piano-bass, or the syncopes in some measures of the string parts, all are swept along in the larger motion.   51

There is, indeed, a remarkable perspective in this music. From bars 51 through 63, your aural viewpoint is far enough back so that you hear in whole-measure bites. From m. 64, on the other hand, you seem to come closer, hearing the music pass in half-measure units, even though the tempo has not changed in the slightest. Partly, this is because of the half-bar dialogue between the two registers in the   64 piano part; the feeling is reinforced also by the two-to-the-bar rhythmics of the viola and bass. The more broadly spaced conversation of violin and cello bridges these divisions without obscuring them. The combined effect of these two rhythmic currents, as they flow around and past each other, makes for a wonderfully rich, yet airy, texture.

When the piano transfers the continuous triplets to its bass line as a background for the solo presentation of a second theme in the treble, you realize how constant the running motion has been. There are: garlands of triplet arpeggios in the introduction, 8th-note couplets under the first theme, level or arched triplet streamers since then. So much for past events. Looking ahead, you will find: more triplets, 16th-note tremolos, running passage-work in 16ths, long lines of dotted figures. All this seems to forecast, again, the watery setting that will be conjured up for the song variations in the fourth movement.

84 The E major theme that appears at bar 84 must be carefully handled. If played too squarely or slowly, it turns into complacent singsong. Keep it moving, flowing along on the current of triplets that supports it. When the strings join in, lines of half-notes merge with the triplet accompaniment. The half-note motion can help impel and direct the melodic overlay.

This episode closes with the eerie, verdant, eight-measure passage that floats on the piano's low tremolo. Observe the pianissimo dynamic, and don't let the measures drag. You are heading toward the rapid current of 16ths that runs from 114 bar 114. Once the 16ths start, they are supported by dotted figures that push each half bar. You aren't in a race, but there should be no hint of any backward drag here. Lean forward and let the music move.

Note how the writing inspects the various possibilities of shaping the 16th-118, 122 note flow: by two-measure units, as in mm. 118–21; in half-measures, bar 122; in quarter-beat array, m. 125; or in whole-measure descents, m. 126. Show these phrasing contrasts clearly in your playing.

125 The tattoos of mm. 125–32 must be executed by the strings with military precision; the violin will give the marching signals, and everyone will play the figures near the foot of the bow, so that drumbeat clarity will prevail. By way of 135 surprise, dusky and half-lit music returns for a few bars (135–40) before the energetic close of the exposition. Even that is marked by a momentary drop to quietness. The whole ensemble must rock from one extreme to the other in making these sudden contrasts. Exaggerate the differences, especially when reaching for the low-end dynamics.

The start of the development is a test of bow and keyboard control. Everything 180 from the double bar to m. 180 is cast in pianissimo. The point is reinforced by a *sempre* marking; and even so, there is a diminuendo over the last four measures of the passage. The low dynamic is especially important when the double-bass takes 165 up the half-note solo for six bars, starting in m. 165. The ensemble must play quietly enough to enable the double-bass to whisper its line. Should there be the least necessity for that instrument to force, it will sound like Papa Bear grumbling about his supper.

Through all these measures moves a current of gently propulsive figures, dotted quarter followed by lightly articulated 8th-note. Quiet though they are, these rhythmic fragments must be slightly warmed by the left hand (when, as is mostly the case, they are played by the strings), with just enough impulse in the bow stroke to define the predominance of the longer note. Whether in the strings or piano, the figure must always be shaped by a distinct, mental count of four, so that the time division is clear, with the short note always moving to the following long. Changes of pitch within the individual lines should be marked enough to delineate the harmonic shadings of the passage. Properly played, these rhythmic figures make up a transparent atmosphere through which the melodic lines are heard. Carelessly handled, they become a muddy background.

The mood changes radically at m. 181. I suggest that you pick up the tempo there. For one thing, despite all your care, the pace will probably have broadened somewhat in the preceding lines. Also, the writing from mm. 181 through 209 seems a bit too obviously bent on modulating inexorably back to D major and the recapitulation. Keep the triplets, dotted figures, 8th-couplets, and half-notes moving so that the harmonic machinery of the passage is not glaringly exposed. The chain of dotted rhythms, alternating between cello and bass in mm. 189–93, should be shaped so as to contribute to the four-measure swing of the writing.   189

Having arrived at the recapitulation so convincingly, you will perhaps be disconcerted to find that you are now playing along in the wrong key—the dominant, D, instead of the tonic, A. Rest assured: from the dominant, you will move to *its* dominant, for the theme at m. 249. That key is A major; you are thus   249
back at home without having to go through the usual harmonic U-turn in the bridge passage to keep you in the tonic.

Nothing much new need be said about the playing procedures in the recapitulation, for the section is a fairly straightforward revisiting of the events of the exposition. Take heed again to allow for a short breath after the downbeat of the last measure. And do play the final chord with both circumspect attack and slow bow stroke; there is tendency for the high A to hang shrilly in the air, leaving an uncomfortably sharp aftertaste to what has been a congenial musical excursion.

Andante. Even more congenial is the saunter through the harmonic landscape   II
of the second movement. You start in F major, a cool and shady contrast to the A major of the Allegro. For the gently plaintive second melody, you are in a slightly warmer F# minor. The closing episode brings you through D major to G major. Matters don't end there; the first melody reappears, now in Ab, a color transformation that somewhat mitigates the repetition. Consistent with the lines of motion in the first round of the movement, the second melody now makes its return in A minor. Again in consistent fashion, the closing material recurs a major third down from A minor, and—since this brings us to F—we close the movement in the tonic.

In accord with the easy swing of the melody, the Andante should be paced for a comfortable three beats to the bar, but fast enough so that the offbeat 8ths do not begin to poke through the metric fabric. The accent on the second beat of certain measures in the theme should be quite moderate. For the piano, this is more a matter of lingering slightly on the stressed note than of any significant attack on the key; for the string player, the usual discreet combination of vibrato and bow speed will serve.

A special charm of the writing is the friendly, uninhibited way all the instruments have of moving from solo to supporting role in the course of the first eighteen bars and in similar passages later on. It is not always easy to tell where the spotlight should shine. In m. 4, for example, as the piano solo falls toward its   4
cadence, the viola and cello rise in an 8th-note line that is really only connective tissue in the musical web, yet takes on melodic significance of its own. Even when

181

the violin steps forward as the undeniable soloist in the next measure, the continuation of the 8th-note strands in the lower strings vies with the top part for the listener's attention.

More of this amiability appears in the arched, dotted-rhythm figures in the third bar of each theme statement, and in the 16th-note triplets that adorn much of the second half of the theme in the piano. None of this can be played with metronomic rigidity. Use easy rubato to reflect the shape of the line and its progress **13** toward resolution. For the 1st violin, the rising triplet line at the end of bar 13 presents an interesting balance between the search for resolution and the pull of the ascending line against musical gravity. Here, the forward thrust of the first triplet should be modified in the second, to settle lightly and gracefully on the downbeat A of the next measure.

19 A similar play of forces is evident in mm. 19–23. In each bar, the piano cascades gently but irresistibly downward. The three upper strings, taking off from a massed downbeat, float upward through the rest of the measure. The changing sonority of the two strands of sound as they shift register fills these bars with a sense of space and breadth. This passage, by the way, like the similar spot at mm. **79** 79–83, serves as a pivot point in the movement, turning the musical camera away from the first theme and aiming its lens at the second.

24 And there we find one of those special themes, a sheer delight not only because of its melody, but (as is true also of so many of Schubert's songs) because of the setting in which it is presented. Each beat is embroidered in velvet tone by the piano and bass. The offbeat is marked not only by the piano's octave but by a silvery figure in the violin. Throughout the passage runs the rivulet of triplets in the piano-treble. Although the setting covers a three-octave range among the three participating instruments, it is basically a "horizontal" ribbon of sound, flat and low lying, with here and there a note change to mark the harmonic progression. Because of its serene profile, this scenic backdrop automatically suggests that a slower, more restful tempo is in force, though there has been no actual change in speed.

Outlined against all this, the viola and cello (truly an apt choice of voicing in this context, suggesting two serenading tenors) pour their hearts out in restrained and gentlemanly fashion. The occasional accent, the swell, the grace notes; the pressure of one or another major second (especially that on the downbeat of bar 33) in place of the usual spacing of parallel thirds and sixths in the duet; the sighing **33** turn in the viola part at the end of m. 33, countered by the fall in the cello line—all this should bring out the latent romantic in our two soloists and incite pensive reverie in their listeners.

36 At bar 36, the requisite contrast and conclusion emerge. In keeping with the prevailing quietness of the movement, however, this episode suggests a mild rain shower rather than any distant thunder and lightning.

Schubert overdoes the rhythmic and melodic repetition here. You certainly can't resort to any unseemly pushing of the tempo to rectify the matter, but please don't drag. First there are four pairs of measures in which exactly the same **43** rhythmic patterns alternate. Then, starting in bar 43, come six measures in which piano and violin answer each other with an identical arch of triplets. True, the first two of these have a major cast, the last four, minor. Still, I find that time hangs a bit heavy here.

At least try for the quietest possible frame, allowing for some fluctuation for melodic purposes. Even so, play ever less as you let yourself down toward G major and the triple piano at m. 53. From there to the change of key signature, play absolutely quietly. The supporting strings will need some activity in the left hand to keep the sound alive, or they will be left with muffled and indistinct rumbling instead of clearcut rhythms. Each beat of the dotted figure should start with some pulse, then slope off dynamically. Don't make the concluding 16th of the figure too short, even though it is marked with a dot. The resonance should endure enough to suggest that the sound merges with the 16th-rest.

53

Violin and piano should shape the last two measures of the section as though the movement is actually ending. It cannot, of course, close in G major; but the fact that, after a brief pause, the music shifts up a half-step to A♭ major and starts all over again comes as a surprise.

I have at last come to terms with this transposition. In my years with the Fine Arts—years in which I only heard, never performed, the "Trout" (there is no 2nd violin part!)—I felt some puzzlement at hearing this harmonic modulation. It was almost as though Schubert had somehow got hold of Irving Berlin's gearshift piano and was letting the machinery generate a bald-faced rehash of musical territory that had already been well explored. After leaving the Fine Arts, I had the experience of performing the "Trout," but as violist, at least ten times during a tour with another ensemble. As an active participant in the piece, I found myself enjoying the repeat.

Of course, with so clear-cut a harmonic outline as that described at the start of this discussion, the composer obviously knew what he was up to. As Malcolm Boyd points out, Schubert's transposed repetition gets him to the tonic, F major, at the start of the closing episode (m. 96). Then, by staying in that key to the double bar (instead of rising a fourth, as he does in the closing measures of the first half of the movement), Schubert achieves a firm harmonic ending to the movement.[4]

96

I could say that the sonority of new keys will awaken in your ensemble new perspectives on the familiar melodies and procedures. My own experience, though, tells me that this is not likely to happen. If you have played convincingly in the first half, do equal justice to the second. Play so beautifully that the 20th-century audience will have 19th-century time and attention span.

Scherzo. Presto. We are back in A major, and racing along. The writing is literally four-square, moving in four-measure units throughout the first section. There is, indeed, a two-bar extension (mm. 16–17) that rounds out the first group of phrases, Except for this, however, the writing and the desired speed of performance almost make it possible to count a broad, 2/2 meter for each four-measure block.

III

16

Despite the forte and fortissimo markings, the downbeat chords toward which the groups of three 8th-notes lead should not be played gruffly. At this tempo, there will be no time to recognize the pitch of the notes comprising the chord if the sound is crushed. Take it easy, too, on the sforzando chords; a brilliant, free-ringing sound will spark the flight of the phrase. The forte-piano groups should have just as much energy as their louder fellows, but played within a hushed frame that sets those measures well back in the aural perspective.

The repeated high Es of the violin (as in bar 6) should be harmonics, for the silvery resonance they provide. The viola's responding Es can only be played stopped, on the A-string, but the tension of that string, along with a touch of vibrato, will give these notes a suggestion of the violin's sonority. Under both, the accented, dotted-half-note chord of the piano must be lightly struck, then held so that the free ring of the piano strings will support the desired effect.

6

The strings should be using the lower half of the bow, taking the notes "as they come." This not only works out comfortably, but helps assure the lightness of the concluding quarter-note in each fragment. Notice, by the way, that the composer does not ask for a repeat of the first section, and in fact makes such a move a bit awkward on harmonic grounds.

42   Everyone on the alert for the start of the second section! The three lower strings must fire the downbeat chord exactly in line with the piano's arrival from the upbeat 8ths. Violin and viola, in turn, have to link their own 8th-notes with those of the piano, in one continuous metric chain. The galloping quarter-notes of the second four bars require the precise lineup of all five instruments; the top two strings must match their accented third beats to those of the piano. The whole process repeats over the next eight bars, except at a notch higher in pitch. Over the entire complex, the alternation between soft and loud in the successive, four-measure blocks adds depth and should be carefully observed.

59   Mm. 59 through 78 are all hushed, except for the brief, premonitory outbursts in the cello and/or bass. It is that duo that fires the shot (mm. 79–80) that ends the middle section of the Scherzo. This trigger must step hard on the heel of the piano's quiet notes of the preceding measure. A very, very slight breath may be taken on the second beat of bar 80 before violin and viola swing into the return of the opening measures.

After the repeat of the second section of the Scherzo, you may wish to broaden
103   bar 103 slightly, en route to the cadence of the second ending. This stretching must
Trio   be gauged partly in relation to the tempo you plan to take in the Trio. Some tradition has evolved of taking this section at a slower speed than the Scherzo proper. I find this to be dangerous, on two counts. For one thing, it tends to make the music a bit tedious in effect. If, as happens in some performances, each downbeat half-note is at the same time given a bit of pressure or accent, the result is an intolerable caricature of folk dance.

104   The accent marks in the Trio are carefully and sparingly used; put these emphases only where they are indicated, and with a light touch. It is important that the opening four measures be played as one smoothly descending unit, to maintain a convincing relationship to the mobility of the Scherzo.

The broadly flowing chain of responses between the piano and the high and low strings that starts the second section of the Trio must be smooth and quiet indeed. Light and easy resonance is required in this section generally, for example,
136   when the bass joins the violin and piano in mm. 136–45, or when the four strings present the theme after the grand pause. The strings, again, need a delicate touch in
159   playing the quarter-note chords of mm. 159–62, to keep the tone clusters from sounding dense.

In short, regard the Trio as a worthy companion to the fleet and trim Scherzo, not as some kind of bucolic, comic relief.

IV   *Tema. Andantino.* And now, for the fish course! As everyone knows, this is the movement the audience awaits through the entire composition and perhaps, for that matter, the entire concert. It is familiar, *gemütlich*, and even more fun than the song original from which the theme is drawn.

The tune itself is cheerful and lilting enough; but the supporting part writing has much to do with the infectious good spirits the *Tema* communicates to all within earshot. The three lower voices have simple, hearty rhythms. They fill the chinks of
2   the melody with engaging bits of business: the cello's little scalewise turn in bar 2;

that instrument's toe-tapper, dotted rhythms in bars 3, 6, and 7; and the viola and cello's neighborly, parallel-third sallies under the violin's sustained tones in bar 4 and in the first and second endings. The setting is both innocent and sophisticated—and obviously irresistible.

In the second section of the theme, the bass moves beyond a supporting role. The string group has now divided into two duets, made up of the outer and inner voices, respectively. The lineup of parts goes any of several ways, and it is only in mm. 15, 19, and 20 that all four strings march quite in step. All of this maneuvering, moreover, is in full evidence, for the piano leaves the field entirely to the foursome in the theme. It is up to the strings, then, to deliver the tune with all possible ease, free of strain and pretense, and without unseemly schmaltz.

In Variation I, the theme positively blossoms, sending shoots of melody in every direction. It is carried by the piano, amplified by an octave setting, and by strategically placed trills and turns. The string writing that surrounds the piano theme is so verdant, moreover, that it threatens to obscure that melody. The pianist should compensate for this by emphasizing the treble, the upper octave of the theme line. I suggest this even though Schubert has indicated *piano* dynamic level for the keyboard, the same as for the string parts. If I contradict the composer, it is only because he himself is inconsistent. He sets the violin part at pianissimo, while the cello—which replies to the violin at the lower octave in each measure—is set at piano. In view of the cello's innate sonority, this unequal marking creates an imbalance difficult to justify on musical grounds.

The idea of the piano's statement being set directly into the foliage of the string parts is even more firmly exploited in the second half of the variation. The cello now burbles on both beats of the measure. For its part, the violin fills in its second beats with trills on D and high A on the E-string. The constant leaping to and from these trills, in particular the high As, must be calmly and accurately carried out. Sickly intonation here can be heard for miles, no matter how much the violinist tries to hide.

One thing above all: play this variation quietly. The constant interweaving of the several lines shows to best advantage in a serene and transparent context.

Variation II is just as quiet, but goes to the opposite extreme in texture of part writing. The viola has the theme, closely backed by the cello, more sparsely by the bass. The piano offers quasi-improvisational commentary to fill the spaces created by the sustained notes or rests in the viola's solo line. A contest can readily develop between the violin's ornate, high-flying voice and the viola's statement of the theme. There is no need for this. If played in tune and with modest warmth of sound, the violin part will be heard to good effect, even though at quiet level. On the other hand, the viola need not belt out the theme, for the sonority of the register, the rhythmic breadth of the melody, and its very familiarity make it inevitable that the tune will prevail.

Still, the violin part should certainly have its place in the sunshine. Schubert must have communed with canaries to have known how to write such a line. It absorbs the theme, transmutes it into flights, roulades, tripping descents, silvery chromatics, chirping grace notes. It dissolves the tune, distills and reconstitutes it. The result is an inspired improvisation, captured in ink.

Restoring the improvisation to sound takes sure fingers and an agile bow. More than that, it takes willpower to bend the line so as properly to reveal its shape. After you thread through the narrows of the chromatic ascent in mm. 43–44, you

15

Var. I

Var. II

43

must take a bit of time to let the melody unfold in the open figures over the last three beats of bar 44. Schubert implies this by the accents on the B, A, and G in that measure. You can't just pound them in passing; some bemused lingering is needed.

46 After the steep descent of bar 46, you can't leap up through the first two beats of m. 47 as though no effort is involved. Again, Schubert points the way by composing an acceleration into the line: triplet 16ths on the first beat, four 32nds on the next. Also, the shape of the second half of the bar is relaxed, offering respite after the quick ascent.

49 The stepwise descent of bar 49 picks up speed of direction in the tumbling figures of m. 50. When you hit bottom on the low A at the end of that bar, you look ahead to a B—but that note is two octaves higher. You have to move the bow quickly to the E-string, obviously; but you must convey to the listener that some bold violinistic voyaging is involved. You can't linger noticeably at the start of 51 m. 51, for the viola has to proceed with the theme. Still, you are fully justified in imposing a rubato stretch over the first notes of the measure, suggesting a broadening of tempo without actually delaying your progress through the measure overall.

You will notice other such points in this variation, and your colleagues must respond to them with you. This is one of those areas that benefits from experiment in rehearsal. The violinist learns the notes at home; but it is in the give and take of the group rehearsal that the embroidery and the musical garment are merged with one another.

Var. III The pianist will be aghast when I say that I think Variation III is easier. What! With octaves between the hands throughout, and with sixteen fast notes to the bar? (*Really* fast, by the way. The ensemble has in all probability settled upon a slightly broader tempo to accommodate the warblings of Variation II. Just as probably, they will find that a brisk tempo is needed for the go-to-town spirit of the writing in the present episode.) Yes, this is undeniably a virtuoso part, but it can focus upon itself, without the player's having to give too much thought to what is going on in the other voices.

More dynamic variety is implied by the writing of the piano part than is indicated by the simple forte that stands at the start of the section. Play ebulliently, yes, but with inflection and breath-points. You have to convey a sense of fresh start 65 at the beginning of bar 65, for example, when the tune repeats, en route to the cadences of the first and second endings. You will no doubt allow for a bit of dynamic pullback, followed by a crescendo, for the chromatic ascent in each of the endings. These are obvious suggestions; you will exercise other options as you see fit.

Sometimes the succession of short, slurred groups builds tension, firing the 61 line into the longer, scalewise runs. This is true in mm. 61–62, for example. At others, the scale run itself tightens the spring, as in the long upward streamer of 68 mm. 68–69. Then it is the turn of the shorter groups to relax the pressure, as in bar 70. Don't override the difference in the lengths of the slurs; they are a guide to the punctuation of the line, the breathing that should be felt in the performance, even at high speed.

Let's not forget that the theme, in pristine (though rather athletic) form, is all the while being stated by cello and bass. These two might well think of themselves as momentarily transmuted into French horn and tuba. It seems obvious to me that Schubert is mindful here of the wind bands he must have heard in the Vienna of his time.

If, between them, the low strings and the piano play their parts with all possible shapeliness, the violin and viola can add to the fun by playing their offbeats as though hypnotized into a rock-steady metric pulse. All five parts must stay together, of course, but the players can exploit the difference in aspect between the two principal layers of the score.

In this movement, Variation IV seems to me analogous to the third variation in the slow movement of the "Death and the Maiden" Quartet. There, the loud, galloping motive reflects the overwhelming rush of Death, but also the desperate resistance of the Maiden. In the present case (and again, this aspect is missing in the song original), the loud, hammering triplets of the opening are, to my mind, a musical depiction of the trout's short-lived struggle against the pull of the angler's line. The sudden switch to D minor, after the major of the preceding sections, also contributes to the shock of the change of mood. The repeat of the first section of the variation allows for two outbursts, but the greater part of the variation seems devoted to a curiously amiable surrender by the fish to its impending capture. The shift to the cool color of F major adds to the sense of acceptance. Var. IV

I find the agitated, fortissimo measures to be the easier part of the performance. The piano and the upper strings have to play their triplets with force, but with some relief of the sound after the impact on the first note of the half-measure group. In the lower strings, observe the phrasing of two single measures followed by a two-measure unit.

The pianissimo phrases are more problematic. Bar 86 should be somewhat quieter than m. 85, otherwise the continued repetition of the familiar triplet figure in the violin part sounds trite. The arched line of the piano in bars 87–88 will profit from some rise and fall in dynamics, as well. 85

Be especially careful in the first four measures of the second section. The constant back-and-forth between piano and violin, abetted by the drone of Alberti figures in the viola part, can raise the image of a lethargic tennis volley. There are changes in direction within the lines, and also harmonic shadings that govern the individual melodic fragments. Take advantage of them, to mitigate the repetitive rhythms. 88

The next variation (V) will want a slightly slower tempo, not only to suit the character of that section, but to contrast against the Allegretto that will eventually close the movement. The transition to the slower speed takes place in the last eight measures of Variation IV, with the three upper strings pacing the change. 93

Part of the relaxation comes from the rhythmic pattern of the writing. In mm. 89–92, triplet motion figures strongly in the piano and violin parts. From m. 93, though, the dominant rhythmic pulse is in 16ths. This in itself might suggest an easing of time; the thought is reinforced by a return to D minor. Now in a very quiet setting, and strangely affected by its new placement after the F major passages, the key implies that we might well be heading into a subdued coda to the entire movement.

Instead, we find yet another view of the theme, Variation V, one that seems shadowed by the tonality of B♭. Don't move abruptly into this new scene; it won't work. You have to take a slight breath before the cello gives the upbeat of the variation, so that mental gears can adjust to absorb the new color. Allow, too, for the changeover from the dialogue between violin and cello (the close of Variation IV) to the new focus on the cello as solo instrument. True, there is a bit of commentary from the piano in mm. 105–08, and—at the very end of the variation—the Var. V

105

conversation with the violin. In the main, though, this episode belongs to the cello.

This doesn't relieve the accompanying voices of responsibilities. For one thing, much of the cello line moves in double-dotted couplets, with a 32nd as the second note in the unit. Wherever the 32nd occurs, it is heard against a 16th-note in one or more of the other parts. The difference between the broad 16th and the short 32nd must be preserved by all participants.

113   The phrasing of the individual lines also sets up interesting crosscurrents. In bars 113–20, for example, the violin plays four articulated 8ths, preferably in one bow stroke per bar; the piano complements this motion in the more liquid texture of 16th-notes alternating between the two hands (the onbeat stress of the left-hand notes identifies this texture as a disguised 8th-note rhythm). The bass, meanwhile, is spelling out octave quarter-notes in the shape of successive 8ths; and the viola is moving in a slow 16th-note tremolo, two quadruplets per measure. All these voices act in response to the shape of the cello solo. We hear the melody against a marvelously shimmering background.

121   The last seven measures of Variation V are again in transition, back to D major and the closing Allegretto of the movement. We ride on a harmonic escalator, from D♭ minor (to be equated with C♯ minor) to A major, thence to F♯ major, poising at the bar-line fermata to tip over into D major. This process can easily sound mechanical, so all hands in the ensemble should experiment with dynamic and rubato nuances. The audience must sense your response to the harmonic shadings that are flitting past.

128   The Allegretto is a lot of fun to play. Take care, though: except for its last four measures, every one of its bars—either in the piano-bass or in the pairing of viola and double-bass—has a tinkling, onbeat/offbeat, 8th-note rhythm that readily turns pedestrian. Keep this supporting line firmly in its place; play it very lightly and set the tempo at a speed that will focus on the quarter-beat, not the component 8ths.

In the piano and viola, respectively, the offbeat 8th is a triple or double stop. Play these with particular airiness, lest the supporting rhythmic line get a kick in the rear of each beat—a most unfortunate ending for the movement. Schubert shows where the emphasis should properly be placed. Look at the other element in the accompaniment, the sextuplet-and-two-8th figure that first appears in the treble of the piano (m. 128). The accent always appears on the second quarter-beat of the measure.

Unfortunately, this accompaniment figure, alternating between piano and violin, is heard so constantly that it demands some variety in shading, to avoid a hurdy-gurdy effect. Shade the accompaniment in response to the inflection of the theme.

In this closing section, strategically placed 8th-notes of the theme are embellished with a grace note. This suggests a hopping-dance character for the tune. To reinforce this impression, take a slight breath after the 8th in question. When that note is the third in a quadruplet, the fourth 8th should be lightly played.

148   When the embellished note is the last in the quadruplet (as in m. 148), the composer accents the note, implying that the succeeding downbeat should be played lightly. In short, don't spoil the lifting effect of the decorated note by falling with a thump onto the note that follows.

167   The coda in the last six bars of the movement needs little if any retard; just a touch, perhaps, in the third measure from the end. The diminuendo, along with the sustained chord on the last two measures, is enough to suggest the dwindling away of the sound.

Again, enjoy this movement on as sophisticated a level as you can. Your audience will appreciate a graceful approach to a treasured set of variations.

Finale. Allegro giusto. What does a "just" Allegro mean here? Think of a jogger's pace to gauge the speed. Look at the music starting in bar 3, imagine an exerciser's footfall on each quarter-beat of the bass part, and you will be close to performance tempo.

The sustained E in the viola, cello, and piano-bass that starts the movement is amusing: a chimed note that calls everyone to attention for the start of action. Use gentle impact and (in the strings) fall quickly away from the initial sound level to match the natural decay of tone in the piano. In the keyboard, this falling off will continue steadily over the opening six measures of pedal point. I think the pianist can sneak another impact on the bass octave when the treble makes its pianissimo entrance in m. 7. This will carry the sound of the pedal point through yet another four bars.

This is not the last chime to be heard in this movement. Meanwhile, start jogging. In the introduction, the bass and cello will take care of the metric pulse in their quarter-notes. The two upper strings and piano trade off on the melodic figure, itself a thinly disguised setting of a straight quarter-note succession. Observe the pianissimo marking well, for the hushed sound lends the simple musical procedures an air of mock profundity that is part of the fun.

In the movement proper, starting at bar 11, the introductory figure flowers into an eight-bar statement-and-answer phrase. All strings match step for the accented measure that is the apex of both units of the melody. That four-voiced bar is in low register, and the parts must be balanced to keep the sound clear and unchoked.

The piano's eight-measure response extends the harmonic process to round out the section. Though the part writing is now in somewhat higher register than before, the accented measures should again be gauged for transparency.

The repeat of the short section allows you to work up momentum before coming up short at a rerun of the introduction (m. 27). This time around, though, the preamble leads to the bridge passage of the movement. The bridge, in turn, is compiled of repeated, antiphonal blocks of sound, centering on interchanges between the piano and strings. The loud choruses (mm. 37 ff. and 53 ff.) should moderate their force in favor of clear resonance, especially since each passage begins with massed, unison-and-octave doublings.

The fourfold set of responses (mm. 64–79) between piano and strings—descending in dynamics, harmony, and register—gives you every chance to be tedious. Granted, the strings always have to utter a verbatim echo of the piano, though an octave down. Still, you should try your best to have the statement and echo cross-influence each other, as though in conversation.

The piano's accompaniment to the second theme, mm. 84 ff., sounds absolutely silly if it is simply pounded out. Even the mezzo-forte dynamic will not relieve the repeated, back-and-forth rocking of the dotted figure in the treble, or the left-right march in the bass. I admit that the accompaniment is meant to stay fairly steady, in contrast to the arched line and the offbeat accent in the theme line of the upper strings. But keep the piano figures in question (there are more of them to come, en route to m. 108) discreetly in the background. The piano's cascading triplets, as in the phrase at mm. 88–91, are of course foreground material, since they combine with the cello line to answer the melody of the preceding bars.

The string lines in mm. 108 ff. are a curious blend of accompaniment and

V
3

7

11

27

37

64

84

108
88

108

melody; the pairs of dotted 8ths should be played in one upstroke, with only the gentlest of articulations, so that the flow of the line is not unduly broken. Let the sound of the entire ensemble be exceedingly light and airy. Until m. 134, it should seem that the piano's commentaries emerge from the strands of sound spun by the string group. Overall, the passage should peak at, and recede from, m. 126 in the strings, 132 in the piano.

134

126

 As marked, the dynamics synchronize the string levels with that of the piano. I think, though, that it is more interesting if the strings follow the dictate of their own melodic shape. This leaves the piano in the clear to set its own arc toward a later climax and quick descent into the quiet music of m. 135—quiet, but difficult.

135

 The racing, octave triplets demand the pianist's concentration. Extending over four sets of repeated, two-bar units, the writing is quick to reveal any error. The strings have it easier, for they run alongside the piano with the slower strains of the jogging theme. From m. 155, the violin alternates the triplet phrases with the piano. In bar 156, by the way, play the E♮ with the second finger, the third extending slightly to take the G. This avoids a smeary leap-and-cross of the first finger from B♭ to E♮.

155

 From m. 171, the piano takes over the jogging line, leaving the triplet streamers to the alternate statement of violin and cello. Viola and bass are given lines of drumming triplets. These must be very quiet, for the resonance of the viola's double stops and the bass' innate power can easily overpower the melodic lines.

171

 In their triplet rhythms of mm. 194–212, the violin and viola should use the lower half of the bow. This allows for the natural, hinging action of the wrist, so that the successive triplet figures (slurred pair and single note) can be handled with an easy motion in a limited area of the stick. Otherwise, the bow will creep toward the tip, and the rhythmic line will eventually sputter and die out.

194

 In the codetta, mm. 213 ff., be guided by the decrescendo mark under the piano tremolos. The strings must follow suit, avoiding an explosive arrival on the downbeats of the second, fourth, and sixth measures.

213

 Should you make the repeat that is indicated at the double bar in m. 236? Definitely not! It's unnecessary, for Schubert, again with one of those gearshift harmonic changes, is about to move up a notch into E major, and to a carbon-copy repeat of introduction, theme statement, and all. He is now starting with the dominant of the original key, A. Thus, the same fall of a fifth that took him to D major to end the first half of the movement will now return him to the tonic at the end of the piece. In fairness to Schubert's sense of proportion, I must admit that he doesn't ask for a repeat at the last double bar!

236

 Further in Schubert's defense, I should quote Charles Rosen's observation about Schubert's procedure in this movement, of having the first half go from tonic to subdominant, and the second, from dominant to tonic:

> To Schubert, and later to Schumann, there was nothing absurd about an exposition that went from I to IV. The opening of the recapitulation in IV is also used more frequently by Schubert than by any other composer. It is significant that he abandoned both these procedures in his last works, in which the handling of classical form is at its finest.[5]

 There is little I can suggest, or that you can do, to make the second half of the movement sound significantly different from the first. Once the new harmonic color has sunk in, the listener will have a distinct sense of *déjà écouté*. Be of good cheer, though. If you have taken the movement at a good clip, observed the balances called for, and played with crystalline accuracy, your listeners will love every note of it.

Nonetheless, if you ever get to play the "Trout" ten times or more in one season, as I have, you will certainly find it to be one *big* kettle of fish!

PROGRAMME

MOZART

QUATUOR en ut majeur K. 465
« Les Dissonances »

Adagio, allegro
Andante cantabile e mesto
Menuetto : Allegro
Finale ; Presto

RAVEL

QUATUOR en fa majeur

Allegro moderato, très doux
Assez vif et très rythmé
Très lent
Vif et agité

SCHUBERT

QATUOR en ré mineur
« La Jeune Fille et la Mort »

Allegro
Andante con moto
Scherzo , Allegro molto
Finale : Presto

CHAPTER THIRTEEN

∾ Schubert ∾
Quartet in D minor, D. 810 ("Death and the Maiden")

In February of 1817, Schubert composed his setting of a poem by Matthias Claudius,[1] *Der Tod und das Madchen* ("Death and the Maiden"). It is a *scena*, through-composed (that is, with no repeats or additional stanzas), involving two characters—the girl and Death—and the piano accompaniment in which the song is framed. The music is deliberately simple: the eight-measure introduction by the piano is slow, in minor, with a melodic line that is all but unwavering in pitch—a dead march. The close, again for piano alone, is of similar vein, but now in major.

Between these end sections, there is first a faster-moving, almost stammering passage in which the maiden protests her unreadiness for death. Then, once more in the tempo of the opening and in a constant pianissimo, there follows the response of Death, who reassures the Maiden. The dronelike nature of the melody and its relentless rhythm tinge the consolation with an implacable edge, one that is only intensified by the pale sunlight of the piano epilogue.

When he composed his Quartet in D minor in March of 1824, Schubert turned again to the song he had written years earlier. He made it the subject of the slow movement. At the time of writing, however, Schubert had been suffering from syphilis since late 1822. The bouts of illness, coupled with an awareness of the then-gloomy prognosis for victims of the disease, may account not only for Schubert's choice of this particular song as the cornerstone of his quartet, but also of a theme-and-variations frame for its presentation in the work. In these variations, he realizes the implications of the original music and its text in a way that goes well beyond

---

SCORE: Franz Schubert. n.d. *Quartet in D minor, Op. posth., D. 810*. London: Eulenburg. Miniature score No. 11.

Left: Page from the program for the concert by the Fine Arts Quartet, Salle Gaveau, Paris, November 29, 1959.

the scope of the song itself. The impact of this Andante extends in fact to the entire quartet, for all of the movements are suffused with aspects of the same, somber message: the mortality of man. Alfred Einstein, in fact, points to what he feels to be a deliberate thematic linkage between the four movements.[2]

It is worth noting, by the way, that Schubert bases the variations movement only on the portion of the song devoted to the words uttered by Death. There are musical reasons for this, for the Maiden's recitative would not lend itself to the variation process. Still, the composer's decision is significant as a sidelight on his mental state at the time. And I think we will find in the variations that Schubert is concerned rather more with what Einstein calls "the savage threat" than with the concept of "death as the gentle friend."[3]

I   *Allegro.* All four instruments start this movement in rhythmic unison, on two baleful fanfares. In the first, fortissimo declamations, however, the melodic motion (so far as pitch is concerned), takes place in the two inner voices. For this reason, it was the practice in our ensemble for me, as 2nd violin, to lead both these fanfares, with the 1st violin taking over at the pianissimo in the fourth measure. The 1st may

5   wish to start that triplet with a downstroke; this makes the downbeat of m. 5 an upstroke. With all four instruments drawing this downbeat on the upbow, the desired effect of a very quiet sigh will be more readily achieved. Also, this bowing

7   pattern will place the accented halves in mm. 7 and 10 on the downstroke, again with desirable result.

14   After the fermata in m. 14, a long march begins to the full statement of the
41   theme, which will take place in mm. 41 ff. In dynamic level, this march rises, falls, rises again. A steady factor, however, is the triplet-to-long-note rhythm; this recurs constantly, with very little interruption, handed back and forth between the several voices. Adjust the balance so that this rhythmic current can be clearly heard, whatever the dynamic level of the moment.

41   With the full trumpeting of the theme, mm. 41 ff., there comes a liberal sprinkling of forzando marks; as always, the individual stress points must be graded according to their place in the melodic setting. In m. 42, for example, the emphasis on the second, third, and fourth beats must be progressively greater, reflecting the rise of the line and its motion toward the resolving long note in the next bar.

52   The second theme, mm. 52 ff., is really another manifestation of material already heard. The 2nd violin's triplet and dotted-figure response to the 1st violin line, as in the second half of mm. 52 and 53, must come forth clearly, as though in a
61   fulfilling echo. The quiet galloping in the viola part, mm. 61 ff., may be played with legato or spiccato stroke, as seems best to the ensemble. Whatever the choice, the violist must contrive to use the bow without creeping toward the tip, since the figure goes on for some measures. The cello figure in these measures should be played with a 16th that comes late and fast in the stroke, so that there is no confusion with the triplet 8th in the viola line.

66   In m. 66, the 2nd violin has to leap from the D to the E-string, while maintaining synchronization with the 1st violin's triplets. This only works if the 2nd sees the leap coming and angles the bow as close to the A-string as possible before the leap, to minimize the degree of arc to be traversed. Don't be late getting to the high A, and don't hit that note too strongly; either mishap will make it difficult to synchronize the rest of the measure.

Smooth string crossing is essential, too, for 1st violin and cello as they play the

running 16ths in mm. 83 ff. In many cases it is impossible to avoid leaping over an   83
intervening string, so adroit bowing will be needed to prevent awkward gulps and
stretches in the continuously moving line. The marching quarter-notes of the violins
in mm. 93–96 should not be played with anything like a *grand détaché* stroke. On the   93
contrary, the length of the stroke should be moderate, and the bow drawn slowly
enough to prevent a slashing sound; also, warmth in the left hand will help
produce a dramatic, while not overbearing, effect.

At mm. 103 ff., 2nd violin and cello carry one musical thread, the 1st violin   103
another, the viola yet a third, all within pianissimo. This passage must be played
with balance and utmost clarity, so that the listener can follow all three elements in
the web of sound. It scarcely needs saying, but the two-8ths/dotted-8th/16th figure
that appears in the three upper voices in mm. 115 ff., and often elsewhere in the   115
movement, should be bowed with the detached 16th included in the stroke. To do
otherwise will most likely produce a distressing gulp of sound. By the same token,
the two violins in mm. 134–37 should of course use only one stroke per half bar.   134

The octave duet of 1st violin and viola in mm. 128–31 (and again in mm.   128
286–89) will need some special practice. In the first two measures, the melodic arch
fits neatly within the bar lines. The offbeat accents in the second of these bars,
though, ripple the musical waters. Another half measure, and we come to the three-
quarter-beat-long figures of mm. 130 and 131. There is a feeling that the melodic   130
line is tightening in upon itself before steadying once again in bar 132. The
rhythmic compression of the writing must be observed, but judiciously, so that the
tightening does not become a spasm. Alert and sympathetic response in the chords
played by the 2nd violin and cello in the first three measures will help.

Again at the start of the development, the second violin has the initial figure,
and so should lead the attack. A few bars later (mm. 146–49) lies one of the   146
troublesome spots in this movement: the sequence in octaves between 2nd violin
and viola. This is not any more difficult technically than the similar duo for 1st
violin and viola back at mm. 128–31. Here however, in the middle register of the   128
quartet range, the effect can be rather murky and uncomfortable. The intonation
must be true, of course; of equal importance is the ease and control of the right
hand. The stroke should be in the upper half of the bow, the detached notes neatly
handled from the wrist. Whatever bowing may be agreed on for the second half of
m. 149, don't let yourself be surprised by this compression of the rhythmic pattern   149
at the end of the sequence.

The passage starting at m. 160 presents, in distilled fashion, one of the   160
challenging aspects of this movement: the ensemble repeatedly alternates between
loud, brazen proclamations and exceedingly quiet, distant-sounding phrases. To
make these abrupt and extreme shifts takes both technical and temperamental
control.

After the resounding chord on the second quarter of m. 186, the cello is   186
entitled to spread the second half of the measure. A touch of decrescendo, too, will
help make the transition to the stealthy pianissimo of the following measure. The
march to the fortissimo return of theme in bar 198 is a long one, so don't get loud   198
until you have to. The crescendo begins only in m. 192, and you have six measures
in which to make the rise.

On the whole, the recapitulation presents no new problems, though there is an
occasional reassignment of figure among the four voices. The coda, however, has
some hazards. After the long, low D of the cello in mm. 297–98 (a note which   297

should be sustained long enough for dramatic effect), the 2nd violin must lead the group into four measures of great suspense—the sensation should be one of almost stifling intensity. This mood returns after the loud interruption of mm. 303–04, bringing with it whole-note chords that can be quite troublesome in intonation; some painstaking rehearsal for true intervals and appropriate tone color will be needed.

303

Intonation is difficult also in the quarter-note chords in mm. 324–25. It may help if the 2nd violin, instead of changing fingers for the alternating sixths in that part, simply shifts one pair of fingers cleanly up and back to play the successive beats. I used this tactic myself; but I found that alert listening is needed, even in the heat of battle, to assure that the intervals stay in tune.

324

The success of the measures from Tempo I to bar 338 depends partly on the steadiness of the inner voices. Their dotted rhythms are the ticking of the musical clock in this passage. All three lower voices must feel the sudden drop to pianissimo in m. 333; it is like swallowing one's breath. In general, this movement, like the quartet as a whole, is a test of temperament and stamina.

338

II
Theme

Andante con moto. The tone of the ensemble should be quite cool at the start of the theme; use a very quiet left hand, slow bow speed, and very light contact with the string, at a point near the fingerboard. The essence of the line is the monotone tolling, reminiscent of a funereal bell; there are, however, narrowly restricted changes in pitch in one or another voice in these measures, and they should be projected just enough to be apparent.

Be aware, however, that these motions take place largely in the two quarter-notes that occupy the second half of each measure. It is important not to get "stuck" on the quarters. Our ensemble, I recall, once had an exquisite argument (and not for the first time) over the proper way of handling the quarter-note rhythm. I regret to say that I have forgotten how the discussion came out! However, on the basis of many performances of the work over the years, I can report my own view of the matter.

The theme progresses by the measure, *not* the half-measure. The march moves from one half-note to the next over an eight-bar phrase; the two quarter-notes in each measure are connecting links in the melodic chain. You defeat the structure of the musical line if you hesitate before the third beat, or between the two quarters. Further, even while bringing out the pitch-changes in the quarter-note pairs, you must still see to it that the half-notes predominate in the dynamic level. Please understand that the differences in level are to be scaled within a limited and very quiet frame, since the presentation of the theme must convey an extremely subdued mood.

4

The swell in mm. 4–5 can be marked with a slight and momentary warming of tone. Both the rise and the warming will be suitably increased in the first measures of the second section, but the descent from the forte measures must be marked and swift, so that the desolation of the theme will be rippled as little as possible. A bit of light may be admitted in the final cadence.

Var. I

If the inner voices want to regard the printed slurring in the first variation as a bowing instruction, they are welcome to it. I find that separate bowing is not only more comfortable, but better able to accommodate to the inflections that the 1st violin is bound to give its line. Those inflections, however, must not become too histrionic. For one thing, we have only just left the repressed lines of the theme itself, so a radical change in attitude is improper. For another, the tolling continues in the form of the cello's pizzicati; and finally, the constant flow of triplets in the inner parts suggests steadiness rather than turbulence.

None of this applies, to be sure, to mm. 33–40. Here the agitated motion of the solo line magnifies the crescendo of the corresponding spot in the original theme. Some regularity should still prevail, but it will surely allow for suitable inflection. All the more important is the subsiding into m. 41. In bar 40, by the way, the 2nd violin must be prepared for the sudden, monotone solo on the B♭s. It's a lonely feeling, but you are in control of the moment. You can inflect the repeated notes, especially in view of the decrescendo to the distant realm suggested by the pianissimo and the E♭ tonality of the measures that follow. 33

In Variation II, the cello has the solo, the 1st violin supplies elegant and athletic filigree; the viola takes over the rhythmic support function earlier supplied by the cello. The 2nd violin's dotted 8ths add a line that complements the cello voice; the 16th-note of the part, however, aligns with the corresponding note in the 1st violin part. In my own playing of the work, I found that it was necessary to add some strength to the 16th in order to have it function properly in duet with the companion violin line. Var. II

For the tempo in Variation III: the ensemble must feel free to set this noticeably faster than the original Andante. The galloping motif simply can't be held in check. As in the theme, balance the sound so that details of pitch motion can be heard, whatever voices may have them at the moment. Because the 2nd violin has the prime, moving line at the start of the variation, that instrument should lead the beginning and set tempo for the ensemble. Var. III

In the second section, the crashing musical gestures that alternate between 1st violin and cello, with the inner voices continuing the galloping motif, run headlong into the bar line at measure 89. To continue immediately after in pianissimo feels a bit like dropping off a cliff. For the inner voices, who have to play the fortissimo upbeat quarter of bar 89, it helps to make that upstroke a slow bow, so as not to be caught too near the frog for the pianissimo. 89

The tempo of the next variation will probably still be somewhat faster than that of the theme. This, after all, is an expansion on the sunny side (perhaps Death indulging in some promotional psychology?). The 1st violin's octave triplets suggest exuberant, bird-like warblings, an image that is reinforced by the grace-note figures in mm. 107–08 and 111. The solo is really embedded in the sustained lines of the three lower voices; their broad rhythms, however, should make it easy for them to give the 1st violin the room needed for its ornamental gyrations. Var. IV
107

The last variation moves directly into the return of the theme. This does not happen, however, until a final contest of wills takes place. The ominous drumming of 16ths in the three upper voices lies heavily atop the cello's insistent recall of the melody. At the climax of the movement, mm. 137–40, the 2nd violin must give full weight to its syncopes. In fact, there are four individual lines of activity going on simultaneously here; it is the friction between these lines, each demanding to be heard, that gives this passage its unusual intensity and excitement. Var. V
137

Elements of rhythmic variation still carry on into the restatement of the theme. It is not until the coda (mm. 161 ff.) that the spare texture of the opening returns. To let the energy of the movement flow completely away, the ensemble should try broadening the tempo gradually over the last six measures. This broadening applies especially to the pauses in mm. 168 and 170; allow breathing-time in these rests. Within the triple piano that governs mm. 161–70, try to scale the dynamics so that Theme
161

168

169 · mm. 165–68 constitute a first echo, and mm. 169–70 an even more distant reflection. For me, the crescendo in the penultimate bar evokes a bit of forward thrust, as though in reflection of some last ray of hope. To counter this, the diminuendo of the final whole-note must be both noticeable and rapid, and the tone itself must be sustained through skillful use of the bow, merging imperceptibly into silence.

III · *Scherzo: Allegro molto.* The speed of this movement should permit a broad count of one to the bar. This pulse is, in fact, heard in the accented, dotted halves throughout both sections of the Scherzo. It is important to play the forzandi or accents only where indicated. In the opening measures, for example, the viola/cello

2 · stress on the downbeat of m. 2 might draw the violins into placing a similar stress on their downbeat. This, however, would make it difficult for the accented third quarter to stand out sufficiently, and would degrade the intended effect of strong upbeat moving to strong downbeat, a prominent element in this movement. For both high and low voices, again keep in mind that the bow stroke should be focused, rather slowly drawn, and not slashing its way along. Whether at or between accentuated points, this treatment will yield grateful, yet energetic sound.

Take care not to thump notes standing at the end of a crescendo (for example,

8, 68 · the half-note in m. 8). So also, the Ds in m. 68 should be played, not barked. If the piano indications are properly heeded where they occur, the louder points of the writing will be able to stand out without forcing.

Trio · In the Trio, the printed bowing the score gives for the first measure of the 2nd violin is not felicitous. Even in the most skilled hand, such bowing must inevitably produce a crippled effect. It is better to take the notes on separate strokes. For all

79 · four instruments in the retard measures (79–82), bow the dotted-quarter/8th on a downstroke, the third beat, upbow.

The entire Trio, obviously, is marked by lightness and good spirits—the only extended, unalloyed stretch of such temperament in this quartet. It is important that the ensemble try to project this sensation in its playing. The retards must not be overdramatized; the loud-soft gradations should be apparent, but scaled within the prevailingly quiet level of the section. Demanding though it is, the 1st violin solo line should not parade virtuosity but serve rather as the bright edge to the more flowing melodic lines of the lower voices. There will certainly be some pullback in the last four measures before the da capo, especially to allow for the steep drop in

163 · register of the 1st violin at the start of m. 163. Keep this broadening within bounds, however.

IV · *Presto.* The break between the third and fourth movements should be kept to a minimum. Schubert does not ask for an *attacca* connection; still, the ending of the Scherzo and the theme of the finale display an evident relationship, which should be exploited by means of a smooth transition between the two. Moreover, this is a quartet of respectable length and does not benefit from between-movement fidgetings, on either side of the footlights. After everything that has preceded, it is time to get on with the last act.

I referred to the idea of the gallop in discussing the third variation in the second movement. It seems to me that a gallop is again suggested in the finale, this time faster in speed and pattern. Though 6/8 is a duple meter, the tempo must be such that there is time only for one beat to the measure, with a suggestion of an

7 · intense one-two count to underscore the sudden shift in texture in m. 7 and other such bars in the piece. Except for the natural highlight on the grace-note figures, the

8 · phrase moves irresistibly to the accented resolution in m. 8.

The bowing I am accustomed to starts with a downstroke on the initial, upbeat 8th, with the entire phrase played rather near the point of the bow. Except for the pairs of notes with printed slurs, all notes are played in separate strokes. However, the downbeat pairs in mm. 4–6 and m. 8 (as well as in all corresponding places in the movement) must be played as articulated, slurred downbows, for reasons that will be obvious to you as soon as you try the passage. A live left hand is needed to project the quiet line, especially to warm the principal tonc in the grace-note slurs. Attack the grace-note figure with some "bite" in the stroke, so that the decorative tone can be heard. It won't hurt for the ensemble to pay some special attention to one another in m. 7 and the like, to assure that the rattle of 8th-notes moves together.

What with the constant repetition of the rhythmic motive, important little melodic details may get submerged. The descending half-step pairs in the 2nd violin part in mm. 19–24, for example, should make themselves heard as part of the web of lines. Also, breathing-points and punctuations should not be lost in the constant motion. A block fortissimo such as that in mm. 31–32 will easily set itself off from the surrounding textures. More delicate is a spot like mm. 51–52, where the decrescendo should be followed by an infinitesimal breath to point up the contrast (both in register and in "dialogue") of the next two piano measures. The succession of measures from 77 through 81, on the other hand, may tend to break apart too much, owing to the forzando on each downbeat. In fact, the passage should move rather continuously to the culmination in its last measure. The same holds true after the fermata in m. 88. Note that the succeeding bars are thick with forzandi; the players will have to grade the accents in light of their decisions about phrasing. Indiscriminate hacking will dull the senses.

The passage from 110–23 is an exhilarating game of snap-the-whip, with the cello swirling the line, handing it to the viola, rejoining, then both throwing it to the violin duo for the final ascent. Another satisfying place: the violin duo at mm. 133–54, and again, mm. 173–94, with rhythmic support and stimulus from the lower voices. I should offer the following caution, drawn from reminders I have received in rehearsal as well as from the experience of many concert performances. The two violins switch roles in the two duos; whichever one has the sustained line should be careful not to luxuriate in the melody. Too great flexibility or broadening there makes real problems for the partner who is running and leaping in the line of continuous triplets.

The 2nd violin has a particular chore, starting in m. 252 (there is a similar passage from m. 610): sixteen measures, each centering on the theme's grace-note detail, with the high note of the figure varying between A and G# as the measures pass. The high notes will emerge without trouble, especially if encouraged with a bit of quick vibrato. The problem is to maintain the clarity of the quarter-and-8th figure in the first half of each measure, then to grab the string with the bow hair enough to make the grace note audible. Doing this so many times in a row takes concentration as well as physical control.

For all four players, the passage in mm. 282–317 offers several intricacies. First there are two five-measure units, each one nonsymmetrical, but alike in rhythmic pattern. The next unit, though, is an abrupt, telescoped package of three measures. After that, starting midmeasure, comes a three-and-one-half-measure unit. This does not make for easy counting especially for an ensemble still new to the piece. Even when accustomed to its performance, the player must be on guard against

4

7

19

31
51

77

88

110

133, 173

252

282

mental lapse here; it is too easy to slip anchor and leave a hole of gaping silence in the lineup. I suffered such lapse myself once in a concert, and can still recall the embarrassment I felt over the mishap. Fortunately, the ensemble responded like the pros they were, so there wasn't a full breakdown of the line.

389   From m. 389 to 445, Schubert converts his two-triplet figure, heard so often before this in detached bowing, into a slurred version. Moving from one voice to another, rising often to fortissimo level, this takes on a very ominous, snarling air. The fingering must be percussively intense to give the figure its proper edge.

636   The 2nd violin has the dubious pleasure of yet a third long sequence of grace-note figures (mm. 636 ff.), this time surrounded only by transparent, sustained chords in the other three voices, and finally left quite alone. The grace note is dropped after the first two of these solo measures, fortunately. If the player has been astute enough not to creep to the very tip of the bow, it remains only to pace four more measures into the return of the theme. Be it said that the 1st violin has almost as difficult a chore, with a longer stretch of it in solo exposure, in the earlier

302 transition that begins at m. 302. In both cases, incidentally, the lone voice should slightly bend the tempo of the line and diminish the sound in the measure or so before the reentry of the ensemble and the principal subject. Otherwise, it will seem that the return of theme is being taken very much for granted.

692   None of what has transpired to this point must be allowed to tire the group, for the last wind-up still awaits. The refrain proceeds as usual until m. 692; here it veers harmonically and leads into the Prestissimo coda. Much of the coda involves high-speed playing of unison-octave passages, an intonation problem in its own right.

725   I think, however, that the more troublesome spot in this regard is the long succession of accented chords from m. 725 through 738. This will take slow, quiet practice, so that fingers will still hold true when speed and loudness are restored.

747 The same holds true for the fortissimo passage, from bar 747 to the end. Much of this is rapid-fire, and in high register. With the double bar so close, don't throw caution to the winds and let intonation slip!

    A final word of caution: this quartet pulls a lot of emotional stuffing out of the players. If the ensemble offers this in the season's touring repertoire, the players will have to perform it numbers of times within a period of months. Stoking the temperamental furnace so that it is as intense for the fifteenth as for the first rendition—that's work. An uninvolved performance, however, will kill the Maiden before Death has time to lift a finger.

CHAPTER FOURTEEN

❧ Schubert ❧
Cello Quintet in C, Op. 163 (D. 956)

As studies in recent years have shown, Schubert suffered psychologically as well as physically in the closing span of his life. We need not go into his ailments and social and political disaffections in order to recognize that there is a dark side to his thinking. It shows in his music—as in the shadows that color the "Unfinished" Symphony, and in the wide-ranging exploration of sensations inspired by mortality (his own most of all, perhaps) in the "Death and the Maiden" Quartet. There is also, of course, a more optimistic strain to his musical personality. Both aspects appear vividly in one of his greatest compositions: the Cello Quintet. If I dare say so, it is a somewhat uneven work, but it contains chapters unique in our musical culture. Schubert never heard the Quintet; he composed it in September of 1828. On November 19, he died.

My own firsthand introduction to this work was associated with a somewhat humorous experience. A couple of months after I joined the Fine Arts Quartet, these many years ago, we were slated to perform the Cello Quintet at a prominent summer festival. Joining us for the concert was a European cellist who was then already a star of the concert stage and who remained a distinguished figure in the decades since.

When we met for rehearsal, it transpired that he had expected to play 1st cello in the quintet. We explained that, when a cellist (or violist, for that matter) collaborated with an existing quartet in the performance of a quintet, it was customary for the guest to take the 2nd part. Following some discussion on this point, our guest yielded but was careful to point out that, after all, the 2nd cello

---

SCORE: Franz Schubert. 1988. *String Quintet in C major, D. 956—op. post. 163.* Urtext. Ed. Martin Chusid. Kassel: Bärenreiter. Miniature score No. 287.

Left: Franz Schubert: Cello Quintet in C, D. 956. Braunschweig, Henry Litolff (c. 1895). Second violin part, first page of the second movement. Reproduced with permission from the collection of the Sibley Music Library, the Eastman School of Music, University of Rochester.

part was the more important in the Schubert! I was struck by this view, the more so when I found that experienced cellists—my own quartet colleague included—agreed about this. I leave it to my cellist readers to debate the matter further.

I   *Allegro ma non troppo.* As is often the case, the 4/4 meter of this movement is best regarded as a broad, two-to-the-bar count. Certainly, this approach helps in the playing of the long, sustained tones of the opening, but it is beneficial for the pace of the Allegro overall, carrying us through the phrases gracefully.

An immediate concern is the color of sound in the opening measures. How, and how much, vibrato was used in string playing in the first third of the 19th century may be open to debate. Many passages in the Schubert Cello Quintet, however, serve as prime testing grounds for the modern ensemble's ability to apply controlled use of vibrato to expressive musical purpose. At the very opening, the four upper voices sustain a chord from a piano beginning, swelling to forte for a new chord that immediately begins a descent back to piano and to a long exhalation on the original tonic. This looks innocent on the page, but draws on an entire complex of string techniques.

The first chord is best taken with an upstroke, starting at the very tip. The bow is drawn extremely slowly at first, in gentle contact with the string; the left hand is entirely calm in the early stage of the chord. As the speed and pressure of the stroke increase, so does the frequency and amplitude of the vibrato. If all players closely match the pace of gradation in bow and left hand, a unified play of tone color and loudness will emerge in the sound of the chord progression.

9   An even more rarefied, though brief, test is the pianissimo fragment in mm. 9–10, for the three topmost voices. In the intervening measures, a hushed, four-voice recitation sparked by two accentuated notes again shows the ensemble's ability to synchronize rhythm and blend character of sound. Moreover, these measures complete the path of the opening phrase to its target, the dotted half-note of m. 10. Don't stint this note, but let it breathe out completely and very softly.

11   At m. 11 the same process is repeated, now in different harmonic level, by the lower four voices, led by the 1st cello. The sonority has shifted, but—allowing for
16   changed inflection in this answering phrase (see cello line, mm. 16 and 19)—the low chorus must extend and mirror the interpretation of the opening ten measures.
20   Again, the goal of this second phrase is the long note in m. 20. The arrival of that target, however, is itself the point of departure for a conversation, low against high, based on the resolving, rhythmic fragment of 16th-note and dotted half-note. The
24   dialogue focuses momentarily on the unison fortissimo in mm. 24–25. (The 8th-note-to-quarter-note rhythm at the end of m. 24 should be clearly marked, to set it apart from the surrounding 16th-note figures.)

There is a sense that the music is seeking its direction, stepping forward
33   purposefully at last to what sounds like an actual beginning (m. 33). That, in turn, is quickly revealed to be a transition. In retrospect, we can now see that the entire opening has a curiously deceptive air about it. Though it seems to be introductory in nature, it is in fact the true beginning of the movement.

The energy that has been gathering in these measures is released at last by the emphatic figure (8th-note moving to accented dotted-quarter) in the 1st violin, mm. 33 and 35. The 1st and, following immediately after, the 2nd violin can each underline the force of the rhythm by lingering slightly on the long note. With the viola entry, third in line, the 8th-note pulse already established by the violins should still allow for a little rubato so that the viola can be heard as a consistent member of the trio.

In the course of the next measures, the same sequence of entries will recur twice. Avoid the mannerism of a full duplication of the stretches, but suggest them tastefully. Note, by the way, the wonderful effect of the compressed sequence of accents in the three voices in m. 37.

The series of detached 8th-notes in these measures sound convincing when played détaché, with light but energetic strokes in the upper part of the bow. These notes outline remarkable, unwinding springs of force, culminating in the triplets-to-accented-quarter figures of m. 38. Note, in that measure, that the cellos diminish to the third quarter, while the three upper voices have an accented arrival on that note. With regard to the cello lines, see that the fortissimo of these bars does not lead to crushed sound; also, follow the swell marks down, as well as up, and avoid an accent at the start of m. 38.

A most striking display of force is the ascending scale-run of the 1st violin in m. 39, a fuse to light the next, longer (nineteen-measure!) explosion. The two cellos cannot simply count dogmatically in this bar; their long note, and its decrescendo, must be shaped so that the move to, and through, the group of four 32nds takes place precisely with the arrival of the 1st violin at the final quintuplet of the scale-run.

Five players are made to feel like 100 in mm. 40 ff., with technical responsibilities to match. Whether assigned to sustained or agitated melodic lines on the one hand, or to the declamation of triplet figures on the other, the players in a given group must closely match style of bowing. Look at mm. 43–56, for example: at any given moment, the sound must come from two clearly defined sound ribbons, one reacting against the other. With accents occurring bar-by-bar in the upper voices, those players can avoid a coarse effect by drawing the bow slowly, once the accent has been stressed, and by using the left hand to warm and project the tone.

The cellos in these measures should balance their sound toward the lower octave (when the two instruments are not indeed in unison). Their accents, too (as in mm. 49–50), need to be moderate, and graded according to the musical context. The massed, triplet fanfares in the upper voices need not be screamed out, since they are in a more penetrating register and subordinate to the cellos' melody in any case. All hands can fall momentarily to a mezzo forte at the start of m. 47, to leave room for the crescendo in the next bar. The triplet voices in the following measures should yield, dynamically, to the duet in the viola and 1st cello. The entire ensemble, for that matter, ought to take advantage of every piano indication, both to relieve the pressure on the music and to enlarge the frame of contrast available to the group.

Mm. 57–58 offer a grand opportunity to rip the massed chords. Resist the impulse! They will be impressive enough if played for easy sonority. The downbeat of m. 58, especially, should be played so that the forte-piano tones of the cellos emerge graciously from the sound, with the 2nd cello making the chromatic descent (with intense left hand!) into the shadowed, pianissimo E♭ tonality of the second theme.

Allowing for an articulation at the end of its first six bars, the second theme actually extends over twenty measures (60–79). Special attention to the subtleties of so long a melodic statement is essential. The rhythmic pattern of bar 61 recurs two measures later, though in inverted direction and with new harmonic context. The changes call for some rubato shaping of the second half of m. 63, a process that is encouraged by the rhythmic stretching in the 2nd cello's dotted-rhythm figure at that point. You will note that this stretching is, in effect, augmented in bar 64 and further emphasized by the successive accent marks in both cello parts there. The

68 2nd cello carries the effect still farther in the three languorous measures, 68–70. The pianissimo (m. 66) of this second portion of the theme should be even more acutely observed than that of the first, though still lower descents in level will have to be made for the decrescendos in bars 68–69.

Some intensity of inflection must be given to the 8th-quadruplet in the 2nd
72 cello in the second half of bar 72. This is needed despite the sinking dynamic there, to help impel the 1st cello's progress toward the sustained A of bar 74. Beyond that, the theme must move toward the overall goal, the start of m. 78. Allow a suitably hushed, warmly played relaxation of time in the remainder of that bar. Note, by the
79 way, that the forte-piano of bar 79 should be quieter than that in the preceding measure.

81 By the same token, the violins' restatement of the second theme (mm. 81 ff.) might well be regarded as an echo, rather than a mere high-register duplication. Let the ensemble make it sound as though coming from a far distance; this second time around, present the melody in a changed and individual light.

Every instrument must be alert to the function assigned to it at a given
60 moment in the piece. From mm. 60 through 79, for example, the viola serves as the bass of the ensemble, and should lead the three upper voices in accompanying the solo of the two cellos. The instrumentation has been turned inside out. Rehearse the trio and duo groups separately, then put them together.

Note that the dynamic indication for all five parts here is pianissimo. The thin texture of the accompaniment will help assure proper balance, but the players must still adjust so that the cello lines predominate. In the two violin lines, the printed bowing will work well if each bar is taken upbow; if bowed up and down, bar-by-bar, the stroke will have to be an on-the-string, *portato* affair, rather too heavy an effect here. Alternatively, the players may elect to use upstroke on the second beat, downbow on the third, so long as the last 8th of the figure is light enough.

78 After a suitably hushed and lingering connection in mm. 78–80, the three lower voices take over the accompaniment (mm. 81 ff.). The viola and 1st cello should use separate strokes through the entire figure in each measure, for ricochet bowing will sound rather frivolous in this context. In both duet pairings (the cellos at m. 60, the violins at m. 81), there is neither 1st nor 2nd in the pecking order. The two lines are individual in detail and must be treated as equals.

100 Consider now the interesting deployment of forces at mm. 100 ff. The 1st violin and viola sing their hearts out in a duet; the 2nd cello keeps things going with motoric interjections that link into a distinctive bass line. The 1st cello acts partly as a third voice to the prevailing duo, while also filling out the 2nd violin's measure with a fourth-beat filigree.

It is the 2nd violin line that is problematic; the spiccato string-crossing pattern here can take on a gyroscopic force of its own, causing the player's attention to stray from what the 1st violin is doing. In fact, the 2nd is providing an ornamented duet voice to the companion violin part. The 16th-note patter must be played melodically, not allowed to snap wildly in the first three beats, especially when a dotted half-note in the 1st violin affords a dangerous sense of leeway. Nor can the 2nd take refuge in rigidly metronomic playing, for that would deny the 1st violin the necessary melodic freedom. Here again, rehearsal of the two groups separately

(2nd violin/1st cello; and the remaining trio), then together, should prove helpful.

When properly played, this passage is marvelous to experience, both within and outside the ensemble. Each player progresses individually, yet in league with the other voices. The listener has a sense of musical space much wider than can be measured by the actual pitch-range of the writing.

The players need to keep an eye out for each other across these reaches. For example, the triplet streamer of the 1st violin (mm. 123–26) is taken over by the viola and returned several bars later. The smooth joining of these lines involves more than private beat- counting. You can't make the triplets veer wildly, but do allow for some flexibility in the broader line they parallel (as in the 2nd violin, m. 125, and 1st violin and cello, m. 127). A gentle accommodation is all that is needed.

123

Maintain the sense of musical breathing space in such passages as mm. 138 ff., in related places in the development section at mm. 161 ff., and in later counterparts. These passages must have a light touch and forward thrust, especially when the five voices march in lock step (as in mm. 138–45), but even when only two voices have the assignment (2nd violin and cello in mm. 239 ff.). If not, the measures will sound like leaden and boring filler.

138

More than a third of the development is taken up with the march element, so my caution about a light and elastic tread should be kept in mind. The quasi-militant passages are connecting links between areas (such as mm. 181 ff.) where a more lyric and flowing manifestation of the rhythm dominates. Look toward these oases, and avoid a myopic focus on the left-right alternation of beats. Even in the lyric areas, you need a flexible swing from one accented half-note to the next, an easy move through the connecting streamer of quarter-notes.

181

Stay alert to musical opportunity. In mm. 181–90, for example, the 2nd violin's syncopated A♭s and the 2nd cello's drumbeats are not steps in a treadmill. Shade them in response to the 1st violin's soaring line and the broad figures of the viola-cello duo. The arpeggiated ascents of mm. 192 ff. in the 2nd violin are an inspired transformation of the preceding syncopes, not a parole from galley-slave servitude.

192

Try some experimentation with tempo. You may find that a very slight quickening will help frame the more brusque passages in the development, especially the long episode of mm. 239–57. The latter measure is the peak, not the end of the segment. From there to the downbeat of m. 262, the pace can be reined back gradually. The transition to the recapitulation is led, in the next few bars, by the 2nd violin and 1st cello.

239

Points I made about earlier events in the movement will apply also in the recapitulation. The roles assigned to 2nd violin and 1st cello in the passage starting at m. 100, for example, are given to viola and 2nd violin, respectively, at mm. 362 ff.—please observe the same precautions. A word about a prominent detail in the coda: the flares of 16ths in the cello, 2nd violin, and viola (mm. 416–25) should be strong but neither grating nor guttural in sound. Rub, don't scratch the string.

362

416

Before leaving this movement, let me raise the following question: should the repeat mark at the end of the exposition be obeyed? You will have to decide here whether the structural balance of the movement demands this repetition to a degree that outweighs the dramatic requirements of the writing. To my ear, the forzando chord that closes the exposition section has a much more convincing sequel in the surprise transition to A major (the opening of the development) than in the rather tame return to C major that is offered by a review of the exposition. Also, the magic stillness of the opening is most impressive at its initial hearing, when it emerges out of the silence of expectation. This stillness, incidentally, is replaced by an active background when the theme returns at the start of the recapitulation, a sign that Schubert himself attached special treatment to the movement's opening.

II

Adagio. If there be a Heaven, this is its music. To hear (and play!) the seemingly endless tones of the three inner voices is to think of infinite and timeless vistas. If you are the one drawing your bow slowly, slowly through twelve adagio pulses per bar, you will be very conscious of the passing of time. When you do the stroke properly, however—smoothly and as though with quiet inhale and exhale, with a feeling that it *should* last that long, rather than with a choking sense of dread at having to save bow—a calm exhilaration takes hold of you. The moving notes, when they arrive in the flow of tone, lend serene propulsion to the line. Hearing the birdlike utterances of the 1st violin above, and the resonant pizzicato of the melodic bass in the 2nd cello, is an unforgettable experience in performance.

2

In our ensemble, we started the inner parts upbow. Also, as at the end of mm. 2 and 4, we tied in some groups that are bowed separately in the print; with slight articulation to define the repeated pitch, this avoided any "gulping" of bow that might be encouraged by the printed slurring, and enhanced the sense of continuous flow that is inherent in the music.

Because the beginning of a plucked note has extreme definition, it is essential that the 2nd cello observe the 1st violin line at every moment, appraising the inflection of the rhythmic unit just played and gauging the shape to be given the music just ahead. The cellist can use incisive contact of left hand and string, along with vibrato, to extend the resonance of the pizzicato quarter-notes. He can also call upon dynamic shading, pulling the string more or less strongly, as the context may demand. As in the case of the harpsichord, however (where the sound diminishes irrevocably once the quill has plucked the string), the cellist's principal expressive device here will be the play of time. And through this, the low voice will inevitably influence, and be influenced by, the 1st violin line.

The violinist must think linearly, not letting the rests in the melody perforate the shape and direction of the total musical statement. The entire ensemble should be thinking in terms of an exceedingly quiet sound palette. Still, within the dynamic frame there will be shadings that no composer could adequately indicate in print.

15

For the 1st violin's high-register, *ppp* chordal pizzicati (mm. 15 ff.), experiment to find the spot along the string-length most favorable to the sound. The plucking stroke, in any event, must be "across" the string, rather than lifted, to prevent any suggestion of twanging. As with the cello pizzicati, the left hand must be applied firmly, and with sustaining vibrato.

For the inner voices, as I said earlier, the framing duet is a heartening and reassuring environment. Should these three players grow tense, though, the passing bars will seem endless torment. The bow will shake, the sound will grow skinny and tremulous. If, despite all care, you see that you will run out of bow before the printed change, by all means reverse the stroke, but do it so that the line is not interrupted before the appropriate breathing-points. If you guide one another toward the melodic punctuations as called for by the outer voices, the texture of the bowing will almost take care of itself. As in portions of Messiaen's *Quartet for the End of Time,* there will be a sense that this music should go on forever. But alas, no.

In the cathedral of Albi, near Toulouse in France, the apse is framed by a mural that rises from the floor into the heights of the structure. At the top is the realm of

Paradise. When the eye moves to the bottom of the painting, however, the torments of Hell are depicted in vivid and unsettling detail.

In Schubert's Adagio, the onset of the F minor middle section has the same effect. It is just a half-step up from the E major of the movement's opening, but the emotional distance is light-years long. The scoring of the first section of the movement had the 1st cello as part of the sustained, inner-voice group. In the new section, this instrument supports the 1st violin at the lower octave throughout. Second violin and viola provide ominous syncope and drumroll outcries, serving as a prominent background not only to the solo duo, but also to the 2nd cello, which assumes the role of a quasi-melodic opponent to the more sustained solo pair. All five join in chorus for the triple-piano gasps that close the section. In rehearsing what goes before, you might try separating into the trio groupings: 1st violin and both cellos; and 2nd violin, viola, and 2nd cello.

I am sure the ensemble will instinctively have made a shift in tempo as it moves into this middle section. If, as I see it, the end sections of the movement should move at about ♪ = 70, then this agitated center should be set at about ♪ = 94. Even so, this is a general suggestion, since musical events of the moment will call for some fluctuation of tempo within this stormy passage.

In the successful interpretation of this episode, much depends on balance. The duet lines peak frequently on sustained tones, which must be played with warmth and vibrancy, but not ground into the string. Overall, the climactic point is the fortissimo in m. 38. The dynamics that precede must be graded so that this loudest spot is playable without forcing. Also, the supporting voices have to scale their lines so that the solo parts are not obscured, being especially careful not to hammer excessively on the accented notes under the sustained tones in the duo melodies. At every dynamic level, the 16th-note triplets benefit from a brushed, "legato" spiccato, with the bow lifted only slightly from the string between strokes.

The major problem in this section is not technical, but musical. There are thirty-three long measures, without any break in the first twenty-nine. The solo line may have interruptions, though even the first of these does not come until m. 39; even then, the accompaniment bridges the gap and the solo voices resume on the same pitch as before, so that the line is continuous in effect. The same at m. 43. After that, there are no further pauses until those that fragment the four last measures of the section.

The solo voices and the ensemble as a whole have to lead the listener through Schubert's musical maze. Measure 35 seems ready to continue along the path set by the preceding two bars, but instead starts a three-measure migration to another harmonic level, where the melodic thread continues to wind. Again at mm. 46–47, a harmonic excursion seems to impend, but settles back for two bars. Then it takes off again for a longer voyage (mm. 50–53), only to bring us back to the same musical scene already viewed in m. 48, but continuing on now to end the section. I think this wandering process is deliberate on Schubert's part, intended to suggest the torment of the lost (or damned?). To maintain the audience's attention span, however, the ensemble should decide, among other things, how to grade the successive fortissimos so that the listener will be guided to one, not many, climax points in the section.

When properly presented, the total effect of this section is one of great anguish, shot through with musical thunder claps, and dying away at last to an unresigned silence. In the slow declamation of this close (mm. 58–63), obviously,

29

38

43

46

50

58

every entrance will need to be in response to a signal from the 1st violin. Don't trust entirely to group instinct, for each player may have an individual idea of how long a pause it takes to be dramatic. Further, give sustained, full value to every quarter-note and each 8th-note couplet, but extremely quietly.

64 After the experience of the middle section, a return to the serene light of the opening material is essential to the hearer's peace of mind. This is no simple da capo, however. The three inner voices resume their sustained, expansively moving lines. In the 1st violin part, though, the brief fragments that made up that instrument's original melody are now replaced by more extensive 16th-note streamers.

These are answered, more than three octaves below, by the 2nd cello. That line has now changed from its earlier, pizzicato commentary to a florid part, complete with 32nd-note drapery, all but outshining the solo violin. The cello part demands very sensitive and quiet playing. Avoid any rumbling of tone. Even more than in the opening section, the interplay of the two outer voices, from both ends of the tonal range of the quintet, takes all the alertness the players can muster. They need not rivet their gaze upon one another, but must listen for every innuendo of the other's line as it unfolds.

The 1st violin here has a succession of melodic units essentially alike in rhythmic pattern. Remember what you have just played; build the series so that it adds up to a meaningful line. (The responding cello has the same responsibility.) The task is like that in the opening section of the movement, though it is somewhat easier here: the gaps in the line are filled in, both by the violin melody itself and by the cello answers.

In the da capo section, as in the opening of the movement, the 2nd violin must not only lead the three inner parts, but also has to guide that group in responding to the inflections of the solo line(s). The synchronizing of the moving notes in the sustained lines must be governed by a quiet signal that extends over the entire 3/8 beat in question, as though the instruments themselves are being moved as a result of a broad, smooth flow of the players' breath.

Before the movement ends, Schubert simplifies the texture of the writing by having the 2nd cello revert once more to pizzicato support. The 1st violin, too, returns to the pattern of its first-section close: the gaps between brief utterances are filled by pizzicato chords. The atmosphere has become absolutely transparent and tranquil. In rehearsal, experimentation will be needed in the amount of vibrato, the choice of bow-grip in the alternation between *arco* and pizzicato, choice of string area for best sound, amount of arpeggiation, if any, in the plucked chords, and so on. A last point: in the final measure, the swell should be modest, and effected as much with coloration by the left hand as by bow pressure.

III *Scherzo: Presto.* I have always felt so moved by the slow movement of this quintet that I wished Schubert had chosen to leave this work "unfinished." As it is, the third and fourth movements must inevitably feel a bit anticlimactic. Since the audience may also harbor such an idea, it is up to the ensemble to make the Scherzo, to begin with, sound necessary.

Tempo is critical. Play the opening fanfare at a quite brisk Presto, in order to break the pensive mood of the audience at the close of the Adagio. The hairpin
20 swell in m. 20 underscores the pitch change in the inner voices. The four lower
53 parts must exercise restraint in mm. 53–56, so that the 1st violin is not forced into a screaming level in its high, forte line. Bar-by-bar stomping should be avoided by

both violins in playing passages such as mm. 65–69. True, Schubert has marked the 65
successive downbeats with accents, but these should be graded so that the line
moves to the peak of the phrase. Otherwise, visions of a buffoons' processional will
come to mind.

A touch of lightness is essential, too, in the playing of the unisons of the two
cellos, mm. 99 ff., as well as in the 8th-note lines of the viola and cello in mm. 65 ff. 99
So also for all hands in the full orchestrations of the theme, as at mm. 130 ff. There is 130
no need to suggest a field of romping Fafners. The 2nd cello should guard against
rumbling in the crescendo line around m. 40. 40

Whether in quarters or rapid-fire 8th-notes, avoid a choppy stroke with the
bow. It is important to exploit the quiet level of the dynamics, and to begin
crescendos no sooner than indicated. In general, the entire ensemble should
exercise discretion in this movement. Don't try to sound like an undernourished
symphony. Incidentally, it would be nice to avoid something that is heard at times
in performances: an awkward gap before the third beat in mm. 44 and 174. 44

As for the final, high C of the 1st violin part, practice target shooting so you
can arrive at the note with assurance, sounding neither tentative nor desperately
loud. Schubert also ends his exceedingly difficult Fantasy with a high C, though at
least there he approaches it with an arpeggio. Was he angry with Vienna's
violinists?

Once we have arrived at the Trio, the impressive solemnity of the dirgelike, Trio
4/4 measures seems to be an extension of the mood of the slow movement's center
episode. Here, the main precaution is to take the sostenuto at not too slow a pace;
something in the order of a solemn march tempo, *alla breve,* seems appropriate. The
musical discourse is written darkly and broadly enough and cannot endure
pompous stretchings. The pianissimo, low-register responses (as at mm. 9–12 9[221]
[221–24]) are especially vulnerable to any dragging. This is particularly so in the
triple-piano rumblings of the eight measures before Tempo I. When playing the
quarter-notes of m. 4 [216], avoid stomping on each beat; the effect is too ominous. 4[216]
Keep the line moving, and let the music speak for itself. Motion is needed also in m.
26 [238]; the 2nd cello has to be able to continue the line in the next measure. 26[238]

Despite the indication of "Tempo I" at the change of key, original tempo does
not return immediately in full force. There is a composed speed-up in the last four
measures before the da capo, and room must be left for it. The 2nd violin should
start this transition slightly below speed, so that a touch of acceleration can
underscore the sense of the passage.

Allegretto. The beginning of this movement is really touchy to carry off. IV
Coming after the Scherzo, the danger of anticlimax is compounded, especially since
the opening theme can easily sound square-cut and thumpy. Consider the *alla breve*
sign when setting the tempo, and take the Allegretto on the brisk side. Play for
lightness, and project accented notes and sforzati with left-hand intensity rather
than with excessive bow pressure.

Choreograph this music mentally for young dancers, and omit *Lederhosen.* The
first two measures of the opening phrases (whether four or six measures in length)
carry the weight of the unit, with succeeding bars subordinated, despite forzando
or accent. Stamping rhythms come to the fore in their own right in such measures
as 25–26. To my mind there is something a bit arbitrary about the blared, fortissimo 25
note that ends the opening complex in mm. 44–45. The effect is mitigated if the 44
decrescendo begins immediately after the loud impact and comes down rapidly to

the piano that follows. In general, look to the pianos, begin crescendos only when marked, and pace them carefully, so that the indicated fortissimos stand out against the surrounding level.

46   In the contrast theme (mm. 46 ff.), don't get hung up on the forzando in m. 49. The slightest of stretches will do, especially since three instruments are involved. A

54   light, moving touch is needed, too, in the duo for 2nd violin/viola in mm. 54 ff.

55   Bar 55, and its accent, is more prominent than the succeeding two measures; so

64   also, play m. 64 more quietly than m. 63, for it is really en route to the piano of bar

59   65. Conversely, the accented half-notes in the 2nd violin line in bars 59–61 should be progressively stronger: the B in the latter measure is the peak of the phrase complex

54   that extends from m. 54 to m. 77.

As for the 1st violin's spiccato in these measures, it must be immaculate and unlabored, putting no drag on the tempo of the duo lines. This treatment applies

85   also to the octave presentation of the same material in mm. 85 ff., compounded there by the need for the two violins to stay in sync and in tune with each other. When the same figure is asked of the duos of viola/1st cello, and of both cellos

107   together (mm. 107 ff.), the situation is trickier still, for the chain of triplets must be handed from one duo to the other, with the 1st cello serving as connecting thread between the two. In general, recognize that the triplet lines are secondary to the melodic lines they accompany.

123   A bit later, mm. 123 ff., the pace is slower (quarter-notes), in a short chain of measures that alternates between high and low trios. With the viola now the common link, the chain must shade down to pianissimo through the continuous shifts in register. The responses between high and low should suggest conversation, not mere echoes. Experiment with the inflection of the units and the gradation of accents and dynamics.

You will end the sequence with a pianissimo. The previous dynamic marking

122   in the score, at m. 122, is also pianissimo. This indicates that the players should insert a stronger sound level on the second beat of that measure, to be able to carry out the required diminuendo three bars later. The theme introduced by these

127   measures and played by both cellos (mm. 127 ff.; it returns in the same duo at m. 320) is an appealing moment of reflection in an otherwise rather light-minded movement.

187   The violin lines in the fortissimo starting in m. 187 should not sound scrubbed, and the quarter-notes in mm. 191 ff. need full length for sonority. So also, the half-

205   notes in mm. 205 and 209 benefit from a sostenuto quality. By the time you reach

227   m. 227, there may be a tendency to move the tempo briskly. Careful! The dotted

233   figures of mm. 233 ff. are coming and cannot be rushed. (Those figures, of course, will be played at the tip of the bow, with the dotted 8ths taken upbow.)

Perhaps the most demanding bit of ensemble business in this movement

250   occurs in mm. 250–52 and again a few measures later. In a patter of continuous 8ths, two voices overlap with another two—briefly, four move together—with the second two emerging for the final measure, still synchronized. Staying together is one thing; maintaining a satisfactory resonance in the succession of short notes in pianissimo is tougher still. Try for an effect that is rather nonchalant, neither timid nor parched.

401   Leave room for the final *Più* presto (m. 401) by gauging the tempo of the *Più*

370, 405 allegro (m. 370) judiciously. Watch out for mm. 405–06, where the 1st violin must flit gracefully to a high A. (This passage is an offshoot of such earlier acrobatics as those in mm. 191–94.) A last point concerns the closing note of the quintet. It is a unison-and-octave C for all hands, complete with appoggiatura, fermata, and diminuendo sign. Preceded by a triple forte level in the four bars that lead up to it, the decrescendo on this last note must not be overdone. If the bottom falls out abruptly, the effect will be disconcertingly like a rumba ending, not quite the thing for so serious a work.

A colleague has made me aware that, except for the mezzo-forte markings in the Trio, Schubert makes no use of halfway gradations in the Quintet. But with dynamic indications that go from *ppp* to *fff*, along with swell and diminuendo marks, both in print and sign, I think the player has more than enough room to color the music through loudness gradation. Further nuance is available through varying the quality of sound, both by action of the left hand and the use of the bow. I would again urge the ensemble, however, to explore the quieter levels sensitively: you are likely to attain a more extensive range of shadings there than at the loud end of the decibel scale.

PROGRAM

October 6

Quartet in E minor, Opus 44, No. 2 (1837–38) . .*Felix Mendelssohn*
    Allegro assai appassionato   *(1809–1847)*
    Scherzo: Allegro di molto
    Andante
    Presto agitato

Quartet No. 2, Opus 54 (1964–66) . . . . *Jean Martinon*
    Preludio   *(b. 1910)*
    Intermezzo
    Grave e Scherzo
    Epilogo drammatico

INTERMISSION

Quartet in B flat major, Opus 67, No. 3 (1875) . .*Johannes Brahms*
    Vivace   *(1883–1897)*
    Andante
    Agitato—Allegretto non troppo
    Poco allegretto con variazioni

October 8

Quartet in D major, Opus 44, No. 1 (1837–38) . *Felix Mendelssohn*
    Molto Allegro vivace   *(1809–1847)*
    Minuetto
    Andante espressivo ma con moto
    Presto con brio

Quartet, Opus 3 (1910) . . . . *Alban Berg*
    Langsam—Etwas rascheres Tempo   *(1885–1935)*
    Massige Viertel—Bewegter

INTERMISSION

Clarinet Quintet in A, K. 581 (1789) . .*Wolfgang Amadeus Mozart*
    (for Clarinet and Strings)   *(1756–1791)*
    Allegro; Larghetto; Menuetto E Trio
    Allegretto con variazioni

CHAPTER FIFTEEN

❧ Mendelssohn ❧
Quartet in D, Op. 44, No. 1

This quartet has long seemed to me to embody what J. M. W. Turner captured in his painting, *Rain, Steam, and Speed.* In the picture, produced just a few years after the date of the quartet,[1] a train slashes diagonally across the canvas, shrouded by steam and weather. Turner subordinates detail to his central idea, that of depicting overwhelming force and direction.

Mendelssohn gets the same effect musically, not, of course, by surrendering detail: fingers and bow have to work with engraver's incisiveness to project the notes the composer has written. But the unbridled energy, the forward thrust, the constantly renewed force—that is the stuff of this music.

I must confess that when I was much younger, though still old enough to know better, I complained in a classroom lecture about Mendelssohn's relentless propulsion in the opening movement of this quartet. Once he had decided to write a sonata allegro, I said, he should have settled down to business and developed his musical ideas in traditional ways instead of endlessly dashing about. Some of my students were perceptive enough to disagree with me, on the grounds that Mendelssohn here was up to something new. They were right, as I learned when I became member of a concert ensemble and had opportunity to play the quartet repeatedly.

The title of the first movement says it all: there are shades of difference in meaning between allegro and vivace, but they overlap in signifying "lively." Precede both words with *Molto* ("Very"), and you get the idea. Mendelssohn is in effect making excitement itself serve as the structural material of this movement. It's a ploy that works; when you hear this music, you don't think of analysis, or of

---

SCORE: Felix Mendelssohn. n.d. *String Quartet, D major, Op. 44, No. 1.* Vienna: Philharmonischer Verlag. Miniature score No. 348.

Left: Page from the program for concerts given by The Fine Arts Quartet at the Alfred Hertz Memorial Hall of Music, University of California Berkeley, October, 1967.

comparison with the ways of other composers. You are simply swept along by the energy of the writing. Also of the essence in this quartet is the sheer enjoyment of string playing. Mendelssohn simply refuses to let you regard the piece as a mere technical assignment; he makes you feel glad you are a violinist (or violist or cellist).

In performing this work, you have to convey contrasting episodes without letting the intensity of the music falter. This is true particularly in the first and last movements of the quartet. Think of a recording that is playing slightly above speed; neither the pitch nor the sound of the playback are significantly altered, but the musical events are quickened, linked, bridged by the speed-up. The expansiveness of Mendelssohn's line, wound up to the tempo this writing demands, is compressed just enough to produce ardent excitement.

Here are some points to watch. Dynamics: gradations, forte-pianos, and especially the quiet levels must be carefully observed. Delicacy of bowing: uninhibited scraping will turn this music to stone. Tremolos: there are a lot of them in the first movement, but they are disguised as 16th-notes. If the tempo is right, the 16ths will sound like a tremolo, but with the added force that comes from precise spacing and synchronization of notes, one voice to the other. The lines of 16ths must move toward emphases on the pitch changes, without thumping the bar lines en route.

I *Molto allegro vivace.* The three lower voices should give the starting signal with the 1st violin. This is so because the initial focus is actually in the middle-voice tremolo and the cello octave. The 1st violin line does not really take off until the
1 ascending quadruplet on the fourth beat of m. 1. Once it does, however, its flight is unstoppable; there is a remarkable feeling of continuity about this movement.

2 Note that the first solo statement extends from m. 2 (with upbeat) to m. 13. The violin touches down briefly at m. 5 and again at m. 9; each time, though, it is lifted by the rising quadruplet, until it finally glides to a rest in the dotted figures of mm.
10 10–12. Whether the figure be dotted-quarter to eighth, or dotted-eighth to sixteenth, the two notes should be taken on one articulated stroke, to avoid false accent on the short note.

13 The 2nd violin's 8th-note melody, starting in m. 13, takes over immediately from the landing-point of the 1st violin's line. It is important that all three lower voices play their 8th-note figures in these bars warmly, with truly melodic sense and flexibility. The two arches that span mm. 13–21 must be shaped so that they float airily on two-bar sweeps, up and down, not stepping ponderously on the
15 quarter-beats. Above this activity, the 1st violin commentary (mm. 15–17, 19–20) is a melodic bonus and should be played without any effort to predominate.

21 Over bars 21 to 30, the interest is divided between the slower-moving parts and the 8th-note line; the latter is actually an ornamented countervoice, to be
30 played in full awareness of that fact. A slight pullback is in order at measure 30, out
33 of which the 1st violin will restore tempo on the way to the forte G in bar 33. On that note, incidentally, the bow should be drawn slowly enough to produce warmth of tone; the stroke should be equally concentrated in the descending quarter-notes
36 that follow. When the 1st violin moves through its scalewise rocket (m. 36) to return to the theme, the cello's descending 8ths must help propel the violin into the fortissimo D of bar 37.

A solo role is thrust on each of the instruments in the rapid conversation of
45, 50 mm. 45–49. When all four join forces in the converging 8th-note lines of bars 50–51,

they should be ready to pull back appropriately from the faster pace that will undoubtedly have built up over the preceding measures. Be sure the indicated diminuendo takes place, so that the cadence on the downbeat of bar 52 is absolutely without accent. The viola solo that starts on the following quarter-note will deliver the proper stress on the first note of m. 53. A fresh conversation among equals will begin in bar 56, but now on a much calmer level.　　　　　　　　　　　　　53
　　　　　　　　　　　　　　　　　　　　　　　　　　　　　　　　　　　　56

　　The piano in m. 64 signals a moment of surprise; there should be no break　　64
from the preceding bar, however, only a sudden dynamic drop. At m. 71, the　　71
transition to the color and text of the F♯ minor theme is entirely in the hands of the violist; the two C♯s in this solo must immediately establish a hushed, *misterioso* atmosphere. A very slight and free broadening of tempo will help assert the mood of the passage. Don't rush; this interlude and its later counterparts provide a very necessary relief from the general excitement of the movement.

　　The dotted slurs that appear in mm. 71–88 are not a call for choppy playing.　　71
Interpret them by a gentle, *portato* stroke. The 1st violin should tie in the last quarter of bars such as mm. 72 and 73, to preserve a smooth line. Above all, underplay the pianissimo. The sound should be very distant, and should only begin to return toward the foreground from m. 93 onward.　　　　　　　　　　　　　　　　　　　93

　　Mm. 108–11: this is a magical spot, a *stretto* that is played out in a very quiet　　108
framework; combine "oomph" and restraint to create the intended effect. If necessary (and I think it can only help), listen to a tape playback of this passage to see if you are doing it well. The same goes for the massed 8th-note march of mm. 113–17; you want to be sure that it is indeed a march, and not a treadmill.　　　113

　　The 1st violin's 16th-note rise into the development (or the first ending, if the repeat is taken) is marked *con fuoco*; the fiery resonance is best achieved if the stroke is kept on the string, with a semilegato connection between the successive notes.

　　Much of the development section is cast in piano or pianissimo, with a few islands of forte projecting out of the surrounding terrain. Quick-moving and more broadly flowing lines move side by side, migrate through the several parts, or are suddenly interchanged among the voices. This kind of activity can best be followed by the hearers if the texture of the playing is transparent; observe Mendelssohn's dynamics and stress the quiet end of the sound palette. Note that a *leggiero* instruction appears twice, as well as several *sempre*s by way of reinforcement of the hushed approach.

　　The motive of the rising quadruplet is prominent in the middle area of the section; whether appearing in one voice or simultaneously in several, it must be played with nervous energy. This is especially important in such places as mm. 187–90, where the motive must be heard in a quiet context; the other lines must　　187
balance so that the figure can be heard without strain.

　　In the light of my own playing and coaching experience, I would caution the ensemble to check intonation carefully in mm. 206–13. The several voices are　　206
constantly in motion here, both in parallel and opposite direction, and there is much opportunity for cloudiness in the many chords that emerge. Rehearse the passage slowly, and listen carefully.

　　Later in the movement, work for transparency again in the interwoven part writing of mm. 303–14, and double check the intonation in bars 315–25. In the latter　　303, 315
passage, do not let the tempo lag; look for short breathing points in the lines (they may not occur simultaneously), but maintain excitement even by pushing forward a bit until the release in the fortissimo at bar 331. By that time, the head of steam　　331

will be so high that the pace will maintain itself right up to the culminating, high As
349 in the 1st violin part in mm. 349–50.
350   By the way, the two solo bars of the violin, descending through 350–51, carry a
harmonic surprise in the E♭–C♯ (where one might very well expect D–B). The tones
evoke some doubt in the listener as to the direction that the music will take, a doubt
that is resolved by the unsullied D major of m. 352–53. Clearly, the player should
treat the errant notes of bars 350–51 warmly enough to emphasize and exploit the
deception.
          If the 2nd violin doesn't take the lead and play with soloistic fervor in bars
354 354–59, I shall personally haunt that individual. Ardent playing is called for from
363 all three upper voices in the crowd scene of mm. 363–65. Try these measures slowly,
so that you can enjoy the crosscurrents of activity in the writing. When you play up
to tempo, don't lose the clarity of texture. For the listener, the fun of being made to
absorb this kind of detail at high speed is a reward of the concert experience.

II   ***Menuetto: Un poco Allegro.*** This movement is, of course, slower than the first,
but its ceaseless forward sway and long-spanned lines make it sound as though cut
from similar musical cloth. In the first section, interruptions in the line are so
skillfully bridged that the music moves in one seamless sweep from first upbeat to
4   the double bar. When the 1st violin rests on its sustained Ds in mm. 4–8, or its As in
mm. 12–16, the activity shifts to the inner voices' moving lines and to the broadly
descending cello part. The basic dynamic level is pianissimo; within that frame,
though, it is important that the swells and diminuendos be evident, for they
support the shape of the writing, the quick rise and more gradual decline in each
half of the section.
24   The second section barely pauses in m. 24; the pianissimo third beat should be
played with minimal separation from the preceding half-note—rely instead on the
drop in dynamic level to achieve the necessary contrast. If the opening was
25   pianissimo, this passage (mm. 25 ff.) should be doubly so, to capture the spellbound
mood of the writing. Note that the line swings repeatedly against the C♯–A figure
(mm. 26, 28, 32) before cresting on the D in bar 34. The two sforzandi and even the
36   forte (m. 36) of this passage should be moderated, so that the return to the theme, in
39   piano, at bar 39 is cast in relief. In m. 38, the merging of the decrescendo into the
piano third beat evokes the return. A very slight stretching of the tempo in mm.
36–38 will help point up this structural event.
54   In the codetta of the Menuetto (starting with the third beat of m. 54), the
pyramiding of the four parts creates the effect of a pedal point, slowing the pace of
the music without the need for any superimposed broadening.
Trio   The 1st violin's 8th-note entry into the Trio should emerge very smoothly from
63   the preceding D. In the first section of the Trio, the violin glides on the thermal
currents from the pedal-point chords in the lower voices. For properly exotic effect,
the 8th-note solo line has to unroll with just the right touch of rubato freedom. If
played squarely, the effect will be deadly dull; and the whole world will know
whose fault it was.
79   The first half of the Trio's second section is more difficult still, since the
flexibility has to be synchronized among the participating voices or handed off
from one part to another. Most telling of all is the *enchaîné* transition to the return
107 (mm. 107–12), where the relay has to be seamlessly coordinated with a diminuendo
and with some appropriate bend in tempo. Note, by the way, that the direction of
the oscillation is *not* the same in every one of these bars. The change should have

some impact in the way the voices respond to each other. That is, the chain is also a rather muted conversation.

Let me point out that, in mm. 101 ff., a reminiscence from the Menuetto proper surfaces for a moment against the current of 8th-notes. To balance the picture, the Trio idea returns to close out the entire movement. The cadential chiming of the last two measures is floated out against the sustained sound of the inner voices. Don't jar the silence that separates the Menuetto from the slow movement. Keep any necessary tuning to the absolute minimum and do it quietly. Also, avoid a long pause; you want to suggest that the continuity of the writing bridges every gap in the performance.

101

Andante espressivo ma con moto. In the middle quartet of this opus, the E minor, Mendelssohn will give this same instruction for the slow movement, but in German, translated freely as "Play it without dragging." In the present Andante, the burden of this message rests with the 2nd violin, who has to unfurl a long line of 16th-notes on which the more sustained line of the 1st violin can rest. The 2nd has to use musical judgment—in dynamic gradation, time spacing, and sound color (shading of vibrato and bow stroke)—to shape the line into the undulating, "espressivo" organism that it is.

III

I can recall rehearsals in our ensemble when my 1st violin colleague and I would have some difference of opinion about the relative importance of the two violin lines in this movement. You may well have the instructive pleasure of such dialogue in your own group. Let me stress that I don't (even secretly) think that the 2nd violin's 16th-notes are more deserving of projection than the 1st violin melody. The two lines are truly, however, different and closely interrelated facets of one lyric idea, and must be gauged as such.

Similar situations will arise often in the repertoire, and can involve any combination of voices in the ensemble. Each case will have to be discussed and decided on its merits; that is, you'll have to see how it sounds right to you as a group.

By way of underscoring my point: a few years ago, I had opportunity to play the 1st violin part in a summer workshop performance of this Mendelssohn quartet. In the slow movement, I was careful to insist that the 2nd violin treat its line as a full partner to my own. The effect was fine.

Don't take the articulation dots in this 2nd violin part too seriously. An archly pointed or, worse, a spiccato stroke will make for a frivolous effect that is quite out of place here. An elegant and flexible *portato* is more suitable and can give way to more energetic bowing in the bolder moments that are spaced through the movement. In playing its line, the 2nd violin must give constant ear to the 1st violin, and vice versa. The two parts must constantly reflect and influence each other.

One brief example: in m. 3, the 1st violin poises on the note, D, as though listening to the 16ths that are sounding in the 2nd violin. On the last 8th in the measure, the 1st violin joins the 16th-note rhythm; the line, through the first half of bar 4, must move as though it is a logical extension of the 16th-note melody played on the first three 8th-beats of bar 3. The 2nd violin, in turn, must play the four 16ths in the second half of bar 4 so that they conclude the musical shape of the violin duet immediately preceding. At the same time, the viola, in pizzicato, has to discern the inflection of the 2nd violin and fit its 16ths precisely to the upper voice. And all four must move into and out of the downbeat of bar 5 so the end of the first phrase

3

4

5

becomes the beginning of the second phrase. This may well mean that a slight, cadential broadening at the end of bar 4 will be followed by a subtle restoration of tempo in bar 5.

9 The bowed viola part, mm. 9 ff., is fully as important as the violin lines and is clearly in duet with the 1st violin right up to measure 24. As for the cello, precisely because it remains in pizzicato during these opening lines, the shape and texture of its harmonic support (I am tempted to call the line a melody in its own right) make it a distinctive and essential thread in the musical fabric.

25 In mm. 25–33, alone in the entire movement, all four instruments join in one ensemble texture. Still, even within the 16th-note rhythm that dominates here, differences in melodic direction or in placement of rests set the lines off from one another. Try to make the little individualities apparent in the playing; this will make 27 the absolute togetherness in mm. 27, 31, and 33 stand out in contrast.

34 In the brief conversation between 1st violin and viola, mm. 34–36, three identical measures offer a splendid opportunity to play uninterestingly. Avoid it; the voices should answer each other, not merely echo—note that Mendelssohn suggests a dialogue by asking for a crescendo and diminuendo in the course of the alternation. The progress of the exchange, and especially the viola's inflection at the end of bar 36, should lead gracefully into the second theme of the movement. There 46 is a larger discussion, again with much repetition of melodic figure, in mm. 46–53; the same cautions apply there.

56 The lamentation in bars 56–62 is not for the 1st violin alone, though it is most overtly expressed in the convoluted line of that part. It should be projected with equal intensity in the chromatic descents of the lower voices. The culmination of all 63 this takes the shape of the repeated upward flights of the 1st violin in mm. 63–66. These are impelled by the vigorous downbeat chords of the lower strings; remember that there are three of you playing these sforzando tone clusters, so don't overemphasize them.

You will find that the unison/octave descent in the three lower parts in mm. 68 68–70 can produce some fairly exotic colors of intonation, especially in the first three 16ths of the run. Look for some slow practice there. I suggest that the 2nd violin and viola clarify their unisons, then add the cello to complete the match.

80 Be careful, by the way, not to push forward unduly in the area of mm. 80–85 (the same for the earlier passage, mm. 25–33); just a touch of urgency will suffice. The composer, in any event, applies the brakes in the form of the four short, 86 dynamically contrasted segments starting in bar 86.

Mendelssohn makes a wonderful virtue of harmonic necessity in the way he 95 treats the recurrence of the second theme (mm. 95 ff.). Earlier in the movement, in D major, the theme offers a moment of radiance in this otherwise somber movement. Here, with the *cantabile* melody cast in the tonic, B minor, the contrast to the preceding version creates an effect of exceptional sadness.

In another display of ingenuity, Mendelssohn—having accounted for the structural balance of the movement by reviewing his musical subjects—reveals that the 1st violin's outcry, back at mm. 63–66, had more consequence than at first 122 revealed. Now, at m. 122, the violin picks up that trail again, leading quickly into the solo plaint of mm. 125–30. This, of course, must be treated with the cadenza-style freedom it demands. Be aware, moreover, that the cadenza continues, though now with commentary from the lower voices, until the final codetta. The lower parts, in fact, take over the cadenza, since the 1st violin secludes itself in the

extended trill that starts in bar 130. It is with some show of reluctance and   130
weariness that the violin resumes the lead; this is certainly evident in the composed
fermata of bar 143. Take care that the 8th-note at the end of that measure merges
smoothly, and without any suggestion of accent, into the decrescendo.

The violins must be properly imaginative in handling the repetitions of
material in mm. 144–51. These are nostalgic, pensive ruminations; maintain the   144
mood even through the last, forte exclamation of bars 150–51.   150

Presto con brio. The magically beautiful slow movement is followed by a   IV
finale that measures up, rather than merely providing a routine closer. For here is a
Presto that is a quartet player's dream: exuberant; well written for the stringed
instruments, though by no means a snap to play; carrying the ensemble and the
audience forward and out of the entire work with a feeling of well-being. The
"vigor" of the *brio* must be a matter of temperament, not a desperate chasing after
the fingers.

The principal theme is composed of three elements. First there is the four-note,
opening fanfare, which is continued in the sforzando phrases of mm. 4–6 and 8–10.   4
Be careful not to force the sound; the lines are in high register, and there are always
at least two of you playing it. (Where the 1st violin has a grace note, the ensuing
quarter-note should have a shot of vibrato to assure the clarity and resonance of
both tones.) Then there are the sweeps of triplets that connect and underlie the
fanfare phrases. Here you must work for clean synchronization and intonation. Use
short strokes, of course, but interpret the dots of the detached notes on the legato
side, to avoid an edgy sound.

Finally, there is the element that makes up two thirds of the opening complex:
the dotted-quarter/quarter/eighth figure. This pattern recurs innumerable times in
the course of the movement. Strung together in long series, even at full speed, this
figure can produce a disconcertingly singsong effect. As always, look past the
individual link to see where the longer melodic line is going. Treat the sequences in
cantabile fashion and resist the temptation to rush. The effect should be one of easy,
yet purposeful flight. The cello will help by providing a vibrant, harmonically
directed support. So also, the monotone triplets of the inner parts can lightly mark
the half bars, in reflection of the rhythmic shape of the outer voices. The sforzandi
in all four parts should be a very light reinforcement of the line, scarcely stronger
than the accented notes of the 1st violin. There is a brief resting point in bars 16–18;   16
this needs very gentle playing, easing down to the cadence in m. 18 without any   18
pullback in speed, since the flight must immediately resume. The diminuendo to
pianissimo in m. 25 should be obvious enough to suggest that the music comes   25
from a great distance on its way to the return of theme in bar 30.   30

It is soon apparent that the return is actually a bridge passage; the fanfare
element is extended and developed, with the attendant stream of triplets, until bar
45. At that point, the triplet figure becomes dominant, carrying us forward to m. 61,   61
where the second theme takes over. This subject offers a contemplative moment,
analogous to the contrast theme of the first movement. The theme is expansive in
rhythm, so the ensemble must avoid any tendency to slow the tempo. Play softly,
yet with each part making the most of its individual contributions to the
conversation. The viola will note that the *cantabile* instruction in that voice at m. 73   73
is equivalent to a "solo" designation. Again, don't wallow in the tempo; this is
lyricism at express-train speed.

Whatever indulgence you may allow yourself is countered by the urging of the

80 sforzando-and-piano phrases starting in bar 80. These pave the way for the 1st violin's long flight of triplets that closes the exposition of the movement. The success of this passage depends in part on the dexterity of the soloist and on the clean delineation of the subunits in that line (there are phrase articulations on the

92 downbeats of mm. 92, 96, 98, 100, and 102). It depends also on the alertness of the lower voices, whose broad rhythms punctuate and impel the solo line. Those parts

96 take on solo roles of their own in mm. 96 ff., where they must project their statements without obscuring the violin triplets.

102 The 2nd violin has to join those triplets at the octave, midway through bar 102. Since the 1st violin is already in full flight, it is up to the 2nd to listen alertly while holding the sustained, fortissimo A, so that the player can jump aboard the triplet line in immediate synchronism. There is no time for second guessing.

In the first two of the three pyramids that make up the very short development, be sure to maintain the piano until the crescendo and to drop back to

111 the quiet level after the forte in bar 111. The third pyramid sustains the forte, but each voice must still recede from its sforzando so that the successive entries can be heard.

In the return of theme, note the extension of the fanfare into the solos (1st

128 violin, mm. 128–29; 2nd violin, mm. 132–33) that are superimposed above the triplet lines; balance so that these can be heard without forcing. As mentioned above, the development proper is exceptionally brief; however, Mendelssohn

168 returns to development in mm. 168 ff. I regard this as the most challenging part of the movement. It offers a *misterioso* dialogue (the adjective is appropriate, even though the composer doesn't use it here) between the two elements of the principal theme. The intensity of the passage is raised by the pianissimo restraint imposed on it through fourteen measures of musical infighting, until a crescendo finally allows

189 the forte explosion at bar 189.

Throughout this episode, every member of the quartet is soloist; I need only point for example at the seething, two-measure outburst the 2nd violin has to

192 deliver in mm. 192–95. Even more demanding are the next eight bars, where every voice has to throw its fortissimo triplets into the racing conversation and just as quickly step over into a more sustained line.

A long series of the familiar, dotted-note figures leads to the second theme.

220 Some of this series (mm. 220–23) is set in pianissimo. Be especially careful there that the detached 8th-note that ends each half measure remains audible; otherwise, the listener may hear only a two-note, slurred figure, without the anticipatory note. I haven't mentioned it before, and I'm sure the ensemble would quickly decide this for itself, but—throughout the movement—the detached 8th should be bowed as an articulated note, in the same stroke as the preceding, slurred pair.

This finale is extremely well constructed; still, while there is no excess baggage, there is a generous amount of material. The ensemble has to pace its energy so that it has enough left to carry through to the end of the movement. One

254 might feel that the coda has begun at m. 254; in fact, this is only the start of the closing section of the recapitulation, corresponding to the earlier section that starts

270 at bar 88. There is again a whiff of coda at m. 270, though once more this turns out to be a last installment of the ideas treated in the passage back at bar 168, with every player again drawn into the soloistic repartee.

289 The spirit may quail upon arriving at m. 289, for the principal theme threatens

to rise in apotheosis yet again. Here, however, the coda does indeed begin. I think that Mendelssohn is having a last bit of inventive fun with the fanfare, apparently augmenting it in the march of dotted half-notes in mm. 293–98. In the peroration of the dotted-rhythm figure, bars 302–09, the currents of parallel and opposing motion in the several lines must be apparent through the excitement. Don't force the dynamics; save something for the fortissimo that ends the movement.

    293
    302

     As for the 1st violin, take courage for the closing triplet flourish that ends at last with the high F♯ in bar 314. Mendelssohn wrote more than two violin concertos, after all![2]

    314

schumann
PIANO QUINTET IN E-FLAT MAJOR, OP. 44

ernest bloch

dvorak
PIANO QUINTET IN A MAJOR, OP. 81

TOWN HALL
Friday Evening
at 8:30
February 1st,
1963

THE FINE ARTS QUARTET AND FRANK GLAZER

CHAPTER SIXTEEN

❧ Schumann ❧
Piano Quintet in E flat, Op. 44

No better opportunity could be found for reawakening in ourselves an appreciation of Schumann's artistic power and acumen than by specially listening to the strings next time we hear the Quintet. Schumann writes for these solo strings even more simply than for the orchestral strings in his concertos... yet every note tells, and the instruments are vividly characterized in spite of the preponderance of the pianoforte throughout.[1]

I quote this comment by Donald Tovey to counter in advance any suspicions harbored by the string players among my readers. Any misgivings we may have about our role in the Schumann quintet are groundless. We are not participants in a miniature piano concerto!

When we read that the work was dedicated to Clara Schumann, and that she gave its première performance in Leipzig in January 1843 (Ferdinand David led the strings), we might well suspect some favoritism toward the keyboard.[2] However, Schumann knew his wife's musicianship and artistic perspective and would not have expected her to tolerate any skewing of ensemble proprieties. As for the development section in the first movement, that is another matter. But more of that in a moment.

Allegro brillante. There are four accents at the start of this movement. A fifth accent, the most important, is missing: the stress on the downbeat of m. 3. Play that note without emphasis, after the four exuberant half-notes, and you will see that the bottom just drops out of the line. You will also want some extra pulse on the notes bracketing the bar line into m. 4 and on the upbeat that leads to the next

I

3

4

SCORE: Robert Schumann. n.d. *Quintet for Piano, 2 Violins, Viola and Violoncello in E♭ major, Op. 44*. London: Eulenburg. Miniature score No. 78.

Left: Broadside for the concert of The Fine Arts Quartet and Frank Glazer, piano, New York, Town Hall, February 1, 1963.

7   cluster of half-notes. As for the quarter-beats in m. 7, standing as they do at the height of this bold opening, a bit of melodic emphasis will not prove amiss.

    In print, the half-notes themselves carry identical, and consequently uninformative, accent marks. I am sure, though, that you will instinctively give the

2   fourth note of each group (mm. 2 and 6) a bit of extra pressure and length; those halves are the platforms from which you dive into the quarter-notes.

9   The string chord in m. 9 should not disappear after the forte-piano impact; slow the stroke, but sustain the sound to midbar, so that the chord merges with the first note of the piano treble. In every two bars of the transitional passage, mm. 9–16, one or more instruments of the ensemble state the thematic motive. That web of reiterations should be decorated, not obscured, by the 8th-note tracery in the piano part.

17   B♭, the first note of the transposed restatement of the theme in mm. 17 ff., will be lost in the harmony unless the ensemble adjusts balance to reveal that tone in the 2nd violin and piano treble. I note, however, that Schumann himself does not seem

21   overly concerned about this point. In m. 21, he omits the accent on the first note of the theme, the B♭ in the cello part. (The ensemble may wish to have the cellist restore the emphasis).

    Schumann expands the thematic upward seventh to an octave; by stacking two such leaps on each other, he gets the simple, effective fanfare of bars 25–26. With an accent on each of these half-notes, he reminds us of the opening. At the same time, by insisting on the octave, he directs us into the music of the passage that is now to come.

    Having brought us to the dominant, B♭, he might well have opted to introduce his second theme here. Not so. Instead, he lyricizes his initial theme, shifts it from G♭ major to E♭ minor and back, hints at a move to B♭ minor, but sidesteps to a bold F

51   major. Now, demure but determined, the second theme steps in (m. 51) and provides its own introduction. Here an E♭ is introduced to produce a dominant seventh on F, and thus to tilt the harmony toward B♭. The cello, however, is still

52   casting gazes back at the octave motive that has been displaced (see mm. 52 and 54).

    Second violin and piano are looking perhaps even farther back. Their E♭s, heard against the cello's F, remind us of the thematic seventh of the very opening.

    Schumann's second theme is warmly felt and warmly presented. There is sentiment enough. To overdrive that feeling in the performance will push toward sentimentality and mawkishness. The very retard of the lead-in to the theme, the measurement of any slight hesitation before playing the downbeat of the melody, must be carefully gauged. You can't charge straight into the tune, for that suggests indifference. On the other hand, you can't dawdle too long at the bar line, for that will imply emotional heartburn. Try several approaches; you'll see what I mean. And please don't laugh!

    A workable solution, I think, is to avoid a sudden return to full tempo, and

57   instead work into it in the course of m. 57. The first two quarter-notes in the second measure of each cello and viola phrase are dotted. This translates, of course, into a *portato* playing of those notes, not a sharply detached or staccato treatment. The articulation should be on the delicate side, so as not to block the progress of the melodic line toward the note of resolution in the following measure.

59   For no very good reason that I can see, the viola part is marked *espressivo*, while the cello is not. Such favoritism seems out of place, for both instruments are

equally involved in spinning the theme. In fact, I feel that the viola should avoid being too "expressive." The upward flare of that instrument's line counters the cello's downward leap. You don't want the dialogue to become a contest: *my* fifth has more feeling than *your* fifth! Besides, the greater intensity of the line should be saved for the cello's long climb and descent in mm. 65–73.   65

Under all this, the piano accompanies with a constant rhythmic pattern. The printed slurring is entirely within the bar (see mm. 59–60), thus fighting the implicit swing of the rhythm. Instead, you should slur the upbeat quarter to the first two quarter-notes of the following measure.

Sixteen measures (57–72) of this pattern will seem excessive unless you play   57
with a light touch and very discreet pedal. The piano here is very much in the crucial role of the song accompanist. Support the lyricism of the strings, move with them, don't obscure them. Your turn at the theme comes in the six-bar interlude, mm. 73 ff. (actually a repeat of the theme introduction, mm. 51–56). The change in   73
tone color is pleasing, especially since we get a break from the pulsating accompaniment figure.

Schumann now treats us to a repeat of the second theme, viola/cello dialogue and all. This would cloy, if it were not for the addition of the 1st violin's   80
commentary to provide some new sidelight on the melody. Even so, the unabashed repetition reflects an era when the pace of daily life was perhaps more relaxed than our own. I suggest that you keep the *a tempo* moving.

Schumann threatens yet a third span of the six introductory measures. In the fourth bar (98) of the phrase, however, he breaks off into a militant reminiscence of   98
the quarter-note motion from the first theme. If you make a very short break before the sforzando downbeat of bar 99, it will intensify the effect of that accent. Energy   99
will also come from the percussive and vibrant entrances on each half measure in bars 99–103.

I have played the Schumann quintet many times, and I think I know the score. Still, I have never been able to hear correctly the groups of three 8th-notes in the piano part in mm. 103–04. The strings have a sustained whole-note in m. 103.   103
Against this, the piano starts the measure with a half-note that suspends into the fifth 8th-note of the bar. I suspect that listeners, like myself, assume that the sustained note is still only a normal half-note, exuberantly played. They then understand the groups of 8th-notes as starting *on*, not off, the beat. Thus, when the downbeat of m. 105 makes its sforzando entrance, it sounds as though the ensemble   105
has completely eliminated an 8th-rest in order to jump onto the accent.

In view of Schumann's characteristic rhythmic quirkiness, this might well have been his intended effect. It makes me uncomfortable enough, though, to ask for a clarifying approach in the performance. Without being pedantic about it, you might try putting a slight accent on the second 8th-note of each of the three groups in mm. 103–04. More important: stretch the 8th-rest on the third beat of bar 104 ever so   103
slightly, to reinforce the sense that the three-note group will be starting with the offbeat 8th. Try this in rehearsal to see whether you think it helps.

After the sforzando entrance in bar 105, avoid making any stress until the downbeat of bar 107, and then only a mild one. You might introduce a slight   107
stretching in the remainder of that measure, to highlight the approach of the restatement of the principal theme, now in B♭, in bar 108. Once the theme appears, it   108
is given wings by the 8th-note line in the 2nd violin and viola parts. The ensemble should touch ground (by means of a slight accent) only on the downbeat of mm.

110 | 110, 112, 114, and 116. In the 1st violin and cello parts in bars 114–15, focus on the upper, moving edge of the line; take advantage of smooth string-crossing to minimize the drone side of the pattern. Let everyone drop the dynamic level slightly, just after the downbeat of the first ending, with a compensating crescendo to the start of the repeat. Also, steady the tempo in the ending, in order to introduce the return.

If, with or without a repeat, you are heading into the second ending, move directly into the accent on the second half-note of m. 116, after only the slightest stress on the downbeat. Up to and including m. 128, feel free to broaden the tempo somewhat. The lamentations of the piano and the sympathetic responses of the strings need breathing room.

And now I am in trouble, for I am afraid my perspective is biased. When I play the development section of this movement, I feel as though I am taking a deep breath, then swimming underwater as hard as I can. I come up for a quick catch of air in bars 146–47, and for more closely spaced breaths in mm. 154–61. From m. 162 to 170, I swim energetically along the surface; after that, it's under the waves again until bar 195, except for quick gasps in mm. 187–88. At last, from the vantage point of mm. 199–200, I can spy land again, in the form of the triumphant and clearcut return of theme in m. 207. A swift glide down the wave that starts in bar 202, and I'm on the beach, safe.

The view I have depicted is not only damp: it is seen through the eye of a string player. Let me try to do better. Schumann is obviously dealing with thematic material in this development. There are distinct statements of the theme in mm. 129–31 and 168–70. But these are islands surrounded by pattern work derived from the theme.

The texturizing of the melody begins by splitting the quarter-note element of the tune into the alternating 8ths of mm. 132–33. From m. 134 to 161, the piano treble is constructed only of series of 8th-note diminutions, either of the entire quarter-note melody or of its first half. What emerges from this musical fretwork (I would call it foam, but don't want to belabor the hydraulics) is the constant weak-strong pairing of 8th-notes.

If we number the notes in the bar from 1 through 8, the prominent pairs are 8–1 and 4–5. But the relative prominence of the pairs changes. Starting from the end of m. 133 to the seventh note of m. 135, the 8–1s are more important than the 4–5s. In the next two measures, however, the 4–5s are just as prominent as the 8–1s. In effect, we are now forced to hear the line by the half, rather than the whole, measure. The half- measure units are arranged in a rising sequence, countering the descending motion of the preceding two bars. A swell mark assures that this rise will be felt.

A lesser composer would have taken this four-measure process and block-printed his way into boredom. Schumann avoids this trap. After the next four measures (138–41), he takes a downward path in the second half (mm. 144–45) of the following set. He would have to do this at some point. If he were to continue to climb with each group of measures, he would soon fall off the upper end of the piano!

You will note that the piano-bass, in mm. 142–43, wins a new design element—a short-long, 8th to quarter—from the rhythmic process of the treble. The figure appears at various points in the development—for piano alone, for all five players, or for the strings—and always as a comment on the running passage work in the

Margin numbers (left column):
110
116
128
146, 154, 162
195
199
207
129, 168
132
133
138, 144
142

piano part. In bars 161–67, the comment explodes into broader, more belligerent form, impelled by tight grace notes and trills. Piano and strings hurl this version back and forth, making it the sole melodic material of the interlude.

    161

And interlude it is, for Schumann in effect runs through the development a second time (mm. 167 ff.), though now transposed into different harmonic areas. There is some change, also, in the sustained-tone background the strings provide for the piano solo. The fact that the piano is indeed the soloist is apparent in this entire development. Whether as support, commentator, or respondent, the string group always functions as miniature orchestra, as accompaniment to the piano.

    167

Judged as chamber music, this development is a failure (*pace*, Tovey), because it simply compresses the concerto apparatus into a size that will fit into the parlor. (Today we go to the other extreme: electronic playback expands the living room into the largest of concert halls.) The section comes off very effectively, however, if the strings recognize that they are accompaniment, and do not try to bloat their lines. Much of the piano's bass staff is part of the accompaniment group. As already noted, the solo 8th-note line in the treble part actually incorporates two components: fore- and background. Reveal this in the playing, with all due nuance, and the listener's interest will be unflagging. Above all, don't let the tempo sag. Take time for dramatic punctuation, but move along. Remember: allegro *brillante*.

Except for the predictable harmonic rerouting of the second theme, the recapitulation offers no change from the exposition, so earlier advice applies once more. It remains only to suggest that you add a modest decrescendo to mm. 320–24, and then a gradual buildup to a rousing forte at mm. 332 ff. Make no retard in the closing measures. Regard bar 337 as though it continues the resonance of the cadence in the preceding measure. You can permit yourself a slight broadening as m. 337 makes its way to the closing fermata.

    320

    337

In modo d'una Marcia. Un poco largamente. The piano's opening figure—to the downbeat of m. 2—returns at mm. 10 and 25. It is a background refrain, quiet, wistful, incomplete; it serves only to direct our attention to the several segments of the march. Don't make the refrain bold or histrionic. Keep it muffled and steady; count 8ths as you play it, so that the dotted rhythm does not become twitchy. The 8th-note in the figure gets full value, but is always subordinate in emphasis to the long note that follows it.

    II

    10

The same holds true for the upbeats in the march proper. A slight forward push can be given to the 16th-note couplets in the line; nothing flighty, just enough to suggest the direction that a short drumroll would have in an actual dead march. The funereal quality of this march is, after all, undeniable. Schumann is clearly playing the role of the brooding artist here, and you must allow him the pose. Some of the desired effect rests with the accompaniment. Play the piano chords with what I (as an innocent string player) would call a legato touch; the string participants in this underpinning of the dirge should use very modest vibrato and slow, sustained stroke.

In the second section (mm. 11 ff.), the 2nd violin can take a cue from the harmony as well as from the swell marks. A touch of angst is in order in bars 11–12, with a fall back into resignation in the rest of the phrase. The 1st violin can tighten the screw a bit more in the B♭ minor statement in mm. 15–16. A shudder is the appropriate coloration for the diminished seventh chord (third quarter of m. 18) that accompanies the precipitate statement of the viola. I think you can convey the feeling by giving the chord some sudden, sustained pressure. Let some of that

    11

    15

    18

19	emphasis drain also into the downbeat of bar 19.
26	In the tiny codetta, mm. 26–29, play so quietly that the audience will have to lean forward to hear you. The listeners at a concert should do some work for their emotional involvement in the proceedings!

An indication of tempo change is sadly lacking for the section starting in the

29 second half of bar 29. Here, all is life—a bit pensive, perhaps, but alive nonetheless. You simply can't play this music in the resigned lock step of the C minor episode. Not only is the melody ardent, but the accompaniment positively surges with vitality. The composer deliberately blurs the rhythm of the accompaniment by setting the 8th-note quadruplets of the 2nd violin and viola against the broad, quarter-note triplets of the piano. As a result, the background has a liquid quality that pushes against the restraining bar lines.

Still, the accompaniment must be synchronized and kept within bounds. The 1st violin and cello have their own melody to take care of; besides, their regular half-note progress gives way to sustained notes every so often. At those points, the accompaniment might spill over the dam. This is best avoided, I think, if the 2nd violin does some very discreet conducting. No flamboyant waggling of the violin, mind you, but just enough body English to convey the player's sense of the direction of the beat. This also involves the accompanists' alert reading of the solo lines that are being played by the outer strings.

Inspection of those outer parts, which move so innocently in half- and whole-notes, reveals some strange goings-on. The long slurs encourage you to gather the notes into expansive phrases. Play through the lines a few times, and you will find that they are actually written in a succession of four- and six-beat units (counting

30 the half-note as one beat). See, for example, mm. 30–31 and 32–34. The result is a changing of meters that enforces a sense of whimsy and freedom in the music. If things go right, the ensemble will feel itself borne along on a smooth, but irresistible, musical tide. Follow the swell-marks; they help.

The return of the march calls for a sudden reversion to the opening tempo.

60 Some of this can be effected in the pianissimo second half of m. 60. More can be achieved by broadening the pace of the half-notes in the second ending. The 1st violin completes the change by waiting just enough before playing the initial 8th-note of the march.

The march is complete in this return, except for the omission of the second

84 section repeat. Also, there is a new codetta (mm. 84 ff.), somewhat longer and even more suspenseful than the first one. This has to be played with all the restraint and sustaining power at your command. The ensemble accent in the second half of bar

88 88 should barely ripple the surface of the sound. There must be no advance warning of the storm scene that is about to be unleashed.

The energy of the *agitato* comes from the frequent clash of an accented second quarter against the basic two-to-the-bar pulse. Impetus is added by the constant play of off-*on* rhythms, derived from corresponding motives in the march melody. The entire section is plainly a strongly transformed variation of the march. In fact, you will find that the tempo of the *agitato* need scarcely be any faster than that of the march. The relation between Marcia and *agitato* is akin to that between the contemplative and dynamic characters, Eusebius and Florestan, that Schumann invented in his writing as musical journalist.

In the agitato, a duple rhythm in the strings is often set against triplet motion

99 in the piano, as for example in mm. 99 and 104. Emphasize this contrast; the friction

is another vital source of the energy of this section.

The Marcia returns (109 ff.), but now quite suffused with the temper and some 109
of the motive of the *agitato*. This is another one of those places where I must resort
to resting my right wrist against my knee. With twenty-three measures of intense
tremolo in the 2nd violin part, the player's arm gets to feel petrified if it is held aloft
throughout. Of course, free the arm for the sforzando in bar 125 and the swell in m. 125
128. Otherwise, try to save yourself for the return of lyricism in the next section of
the movement.

The violist, who is bravely—and loudly—declaiming the melody, has the
spotlight in this agitated version of the march. In the background, there is the quiet
turbulence of the 2nd violin tremolo and the piano's triplets. The comments of 1st
violin and cello are like distant and receding thunder.

You can all but visualize the shift of scene at m. 133 as the ardent theme 133
returns to center stage. The sense of a liquid flow of the music, already evident in
the first appearance of this episode, is even stronger here. Instead of broad, quarter-
note triplets, the piano now plays in a constant spray of 8th-note triplet
arpeggiations. In place of the C major setting of the earlier section, the present one
is in F major. Thus, when the march returns for the last time at mm. 165 ff., it starts 165
out in F minor.

It is not until bar 180 that the viola brings the harmony back to the tonic, C 180
minor. There is time now only for a brief leave-taking from the melody. The 1st
violin breaks off, in its statement, to move into the short coda. A last reminiscence
of the turbulent aspect of the movement surfaces in the outcry of the 2nd violin,
m. 187. The level is only forte, and is placed within a pianissimo surround; the 187
attack with the bow, then, need only be moderate, with most of the warmth coming
from the left hand.

The fade-out in the last six measures should be as atmospheric as you can
manage. When you rehearse the closing chord, try having the viola play harmonics
for its double stop. I think that adds an appropriate color to the sound. Now, if only
I could learn not to think of launching into Anitra's Dance at the double bar!
(Readers familiar with Grieg's *Peer Gynt* Suite will understand my reflex at the
sound of Schumann's cadence.)

Scherzo molto vivace. The indicated tempo of 138 to the dotted quarter will III
feel fast enough, especially if you think of each measure in one-to-the-bar fashion.
My experience has been that there is a tendency to start, or become, faster in this
movement. The speed has to be gauged according to the technical limit of the
pianist in playing measures such as 9–10, where the right hand has to pluck out 9
descending runs in octaves. There can be injury both to the line and the player if
frenzy sets in.

The ascending runs, both in the piano and the strings, end in a note marked
either tenuto or sforzando. Although the sforzando will require more attack than
the sustained note, in neither case should there be a desperate lunge into the tone.
Also, whether the note in question is quarter or dotted quarter, it should be held for
full value. Note, incidentally, that most of the ascending runs are immediately
followed by a descending line. The final note in one direction is at the same time a
connection to the return journey, and needs enough resonance to establish the link.

One of the difficulties in this movement is to play the musical Morse code of
measures like 25–26. It is tough for the pianist to maintain rhythmic clarity in the
rapid repetition of the full-fisted chord in the bass staff of such spots.

23 Another tricky bit: the short scraps of trill, whether in strings or piano, in descending passages, as in mm. 23–24. If you are playing up to speed, you actually have time only for one quick round trip to the upper neighboring tone whenever the trill sign appears. The string players can achieve the desired effect in their lines if they accent the principal tone slightly with the bow and vitalize the sound with a touch of vibrato.

44 The last chord before the double bar (m. 44) is an 8th-note. Despite the sforzando in the piano, don't hit this note too roughly or clip the sound too suddenly. The line should lift off into space, not bash itself against a wall.

44 This is especially important when you end the repetition of the second section of the Scherzo. In moving from m. 44 to m. 45, you are plunging from the key of E♭ to that of G♭ major—something of a mild shock, even to modern ears. Cushion the transition by slightly sustaining the resonance of the last, E♭ 8th-note of the Scherzo, and by catching a very short breath before taking the E♭ upbeat of the Trio.

Trio I There are sixteen measures in each of the two sections of this Trio. I can only imagine that Schumann was thinking back to childhood songs when he wrote a relentless selection of four-bar phrases to fill these sections. The result would have been unbearable had he not softened the regularity by the overlapping imitations in the string lines. The liquid accompaniment of triplets in the piano also helps greatly. The string players must do their part by letting the theme entries wind around each other in *cantabile* fashion. Take all possible advantage of dynamic shading within
47 the prevailingly quiet level. As for the *marcato* instruction in the viola part in m. 47 of the score: if it is meant literally, it can only be a mistake. It is completely out of place in this music. The line must respond, as an equal, to the lyric statement in the 1st violin, but I am sure the violist will need no urging in this regard.

The sudden return to E♭ with the reentry of the Scherzo somehow seems easier, now that we have had the experience of the opposite shift at the start of the Trio. And both experiences soften us up for the next jump, from the Scherzo into *Trio II*. There, we get a thorough drill in reading accidentals and in taking harmonic shifts in stride.

Trio II To begin, the 1st violin and cello play the 16th-note melody in A♭ minor. The inner strings take over with a restatement of the melody in E major. First violin and piano complete that statement, but jump to C♯ minor; a vehement return to A♭ minor follows. Then we are taken for a rapid roller-coaster ride, touching briefly on:

E flat minor
G sharp minor
G flat major/minor (though the 2nd violin matches the piano G flat with an
     F sharp, one of several such enharmonic matches in this section)
B minor
E minor
B minor
F sharp minor
C sharp minor
F sharp minor
E flat minor
G sharp minor
D flat minor
A flat minor (emphatically)

B flat major
E flat, and the return of the Scherzo.

Schumann makes this all work out, but it certainly keeps you guessing while it lasts. Here, eye and finger must react unhesitatingly to the many accidental signs as they fly past. Even more important, the ear has be thoroughly accustomed to the constantly unscrolling harmonic diorama.

As for staying in tune, *that* takes rehearsal. It would be difficult enough if only one player at a time had to navigate these lines. But there is a lot of doubling in octaves, both for the 16th-note passages and the broader rhythmic elements in the section. In all of this, Schumann is working up to his finest challenge to the ensemble: six lines (the four strings and the treble and bass of the piano) in mm. 189–93, racing in octaves and unisons. | 189

This passage will take some slow and alert practice. Not only do the strings have to think alike in their measurement of intervals, but they will have to match their intonation to the locked-in tuning of the piano.

A third and final return of the Scherzo is followed by the Coda. The *con brio* | 240
exhortation to the 1st violin—who now gets the lead-off spot in stating the theme— scarcely seems necessary. For one thing, the player who could come out of the Scherzo and charge into the Coda with anything less than full energy would probably not respond to any written prompting. Besides, the piano has just rung a two-bar tocsin of E♭ triplets, in octaves, that would galvanize any red-blooded violinist.

Piano, cello, and 1st violin, between them, fire the theme in repeated upward salvos. Adding to the excitement are the continued rolling of triplets in the piano, and fanfares from all otherwise unoccupied string players. But Schumann saves the best for his own instrument: the piano's mad dash, spanning four octaves and four measures, to the high E♭, followed by a splendidly tumultuous dive that ends on the lowest E♭ on the keyboard. The strings chase the downward flight of the piano and join with it as it rebounds into the cadence. Fun for all!

Allegro, ma non troppo. There are too many accent marks in the piano part at | IV
the start of the movement. Along with the *sempre marcato* instruction, the indiscriminate signs seem to call for a stiff-fingered attack on each note of the theme. (I can just see Chico at the piano in a Marx Brothers movie!) Further, it is too easy to infer that the accents continue on in both the treble and the bass even after the printed symbols no longer appear.

The music is better served if you focus on the sforzando marks. They show that the emphasis belongs on the high note at the start of the four-bar segment of the phrase. From there, with only slight and passing preference for the downbeats of mm. 3 and 4, the remaining stress point is the downbeat of bar 5; this note, | 3
however, is still subordinate to the earlier sforzando. Take a slight breath before | 5
playing the third and fourth quarters of bar 5, the notes that start the repeat of the phrase.

Astute phrasing in the early measures of the movement pays off when you get to mm. 10–13. There, the bar-by-bar spacing of sforzandi stands out in contrast to | 10
the broader groupings that have come before.

The strings must be circumspect in this opening, as well. With both violins and viola drumming away on the 8th-notes, a fairly threatening buzz of sound can be thrown up. Use bluff (but not *too* bluff) spiccato in the lower part of the bow; and play only loudly enough to reinforce the piano melody. The strings can come to the fore in mm. 10–13, then return to the background.

22   Play the 8th-note responses to the piano, in mm. 22–29, boldly but not roughly. The low register in which the passage is cast is prone to sound gruff if pressed too 30   hard. On the other hand, the strings' theme in mm. 30 ff. is high and bright; there the piano's supporting chords should blend in with easy resonance.

Though this finale is not so titled, I find it even more of a march than the second movement of the quintet. Whatever you can do to temper any sense of constant "left, right" will improve the effect of your performance. The phrase in 37   mm. 37–43 is a case in point. I recognize that the thumping accents here will be balanced by the smoothness and lightness of the music that follows immediately after. Even so, I think you should go easy on the half-bar accents in mm. 37–40, and leave room for the rise to the sforzando of m. 41.

43   In the complex of phrases from m. 43 to m. 77, try to maintain groupings of at least four bars, nothing less. There is a six-measure sequence from the middle of bar 51   51 through the first half of m. 57. Otherwise, the phrases are built of two measures 43, 57   answering two (see mm. 43 ff.), four answering four (see mm. 57 ff.), or four bars 69   repeated with changed texture (mm. 69 ff.). Link the units together as artfully as you can, so that the listener is not made overly conscious of the four-square writing.

77   At the start of the next section (mm. 77 ff.), you should give the impression 96   that the music flows rather continuously up to the middle of bar 96. True enough, the four-measure unit remains the building block; but the overall dynamic sweep from forte to pianissimo helps gather the component phrases together. Even the bemused, three-bar sigh at the end of this complex is a comment on the preceding action, not a separate musical event.

Mm. 96–114 offer a veritable oasis of irregular bar groupings and entry placements. This is a very quiet and dreamy conversation between the piano and the strings. Play it with enough freedom of timing in the responses to suggest an actual dialogue.

The raucous interjection by the viola in mm. 98–99 calls to mind either Schumann's own Florestan or some sudden appearance of the legendary Till Eulenspiegel. In fact, the viola is reminding us of the theme already heard in mm. 51–69; at the same time, the scrap of melody foreshadows the return of the theme in 114   mm. 114 ff. There, the theme moves from one string part to another, now in a new and sprightly version. It should be played on the string, in the upper half of the bow, in a crisply detached stroke, and very quietly.

Schumann gradually and adroitly changes the function of the theme. At first, it provides a rhythmic ostinato against a flowing countermelody—one that is heard only in this part of the movement and that, to my ear, is distantly reminiscent of 130   material from the first movement. From m. 130, the ostinato has taken over the 136   entire ensemble. In bar 136, the ostinato yields to the return of the principal theme of the movement. And we realize that we have been listening to an offshoot of the first three notes of the principal theme; this was true at mm. 51 ff. and 114 ff.

136   That melody is now (m. 136) welcomed back so boisterously that we think ourselves once more at the opening of the movement. The key here is G♯ minor, however, not the original G minor. Despite this harmonic state of affairs, it soon becomes evident that we are in fact involved in a recapitulation. We are given a review of the musical events of the first part of the movement, though it is not until 212   m. 212 that we get to hear the principal theme in G minor. Even that is an illusory

homecoming, for Schumann immediately veers away into E♭, a triumphant arpeggio fanfare (mm. 222–24), and yet other transformations of his melodic material.   222

The episode from bar 224 to 248 gives the pianist another chance for bravura display: a sparkling stream of 8th-notes, compiled of the treble syncopes and the onbeat quarter-notes in the bass. Here the strings for the most part offer a background of sustained notes, doubling lines that are already present in the piano part.   224

Strings and piano are on more equal footing in mm. 248–74. Now the principal theme is made the subject in a fugal texture, always with a counter-subject in 8th-note rhythm. I think the music will sound most interesting if the 8th-note line predominates slightly in the dynamic balance. The strings should use lower-bow spiccato in the passages of mm. 248–62. In the Eulenberg score, dots are omitted in the 2nd violin part for the 8th-notes from the middle of bar 250 through the second beat of bar 252. I feel this is an error, and that the spiccato should be maintained. In the viola part, the omission of dots in mm. 261–62 is more appropriate, for a transition to on-the-string playing helps the crescendo to the forte of m. 262.   248 250 261

The 1st violin's triple-stop chords in bars 267–74 are obviously to be played in alternating bowing, not all downstrokes. The latter would produce a very puffy effect; besides, the piano's chords—paralleling those in the violin—will lend enough incisiveness to the sound. In fact, both players should moderate the chords enough to let the 8th- and quarter-note lines project.   267

The comments about mm. 114 ff. apply again to the passage from mm. 274 to 286. As for the music in mm. 286–318—exercise caution! The writing here simply begs to be orchestrated for the full concerto apparatus, including winds and percussion. Don't even try to fill that bill with just five players. There are fistfuls of notes in the piano, and sturdy backup lines (half-, quarter-, and 8th-note) in the strings. If you press too hard here, you will stir up a thick pudding of sound. Let your ears advise you.   274 286

By the time you reach the choral fanfare of mm. 312 ff., culminating in the cliff-hanger, dominant seventh chord of bar 318, the ensemble blood pressure will undoubtedly have peaked. May I again urge moderation? I can easily imagine a Hoffnung cartoon that would show first aid and brandy being administered to the players during the grand pause that follows the chord.   312 318

One reason to keep some check on the sound and fury: after the grand pause, the piano has to start the fugal windup with a lone, middle register E♭. The note is bound to sound forlorn if the heavens have been stormed in the preceding bars. Moreover, even though the fugue is marked *sempre forte*, don't start too percussively. The tone would suffer, and you have to leave room for building toward the fortissimo that will arrive twenty-five measures later.

The fugue is great fun for the entire ensemble, but it is tougher than it looks. There are two subjects: the whole-note augmentation of the first movement's theme and the modified version of the finale theme. Spaced one-and-a-half measures apart, the two subjects together constitute a single entry in the fugue. Every six measures, there is a new entry. Allowing for the fact that each string part has measures of rest, the listener still is exposed to as many as six lines of melody at any one point in the passage. With the arrival of the fortissimo at m. 343, the fugue has become a juggernaut. And from m. 355 to m. 371, the *stretto* turns the pressure up still higher. The compression jams the two subjects together and reduces the   343 355 interval between the whole-note entries to two measures.

Accordingly, some slow and quiet rehearsal is in order. I suggest that you all 319 play through mm. 319–71 at mezzo-piano level, so that you can hear the entries calmly. Then, try raising each entry slightly above the surrounding dynamic level; those lines already in motion should immediately yield prominence to the new entries, so that the total volume can remain low. Gradually increase the loudness and speed of your play through, making sure that the succession of entries remains clear and audible. Finally, scale the entire passage up to performance tempo and dynamic level, maintaining proper volume relationship between the opening 343 section and the full-blown passage of mm. 343 ff.

When it comes to multiple climaxes, Schumann could teach Tchaikovsky a 371 thing or two. Here we are at bar 371, ready for a final cadence, only to launch into 378 yet another fanfare. This raises the curtain on a verbatim rerun (mm. 378 ff.) of the radiant piano passage, heard earlier at m. 224. And then, at last, Schumann releases the cavalry for the grand charge to the double bar.

You will note that the drone background provided by the piano is marked *sempre fortissimo*, while the melodic lines in the 1st violin and viola rate only a *sempre forte*. Experiment with the balance to see whether you want to adjust the dynamics here. In any case, all five members of the band are joined together for the 421 dash up and down the musical slopes to m. 421. From there to the end, the strings cheer the piano through its last arch of triumph. I'll say it again: this is great sport for all concerned. But please try not to let the sound get frayed at the edges!

SEXTUOR.

Ier Alto.

J. Brahms, Op. 36.

Paris, J. Maho, Editeur, 25 rue du Faubourg St. Honoré.   J. 971 M.

CHAPTER SEVENTEEN

❧ Brahms ❧
Sextet No. 2 in G, Op. 36

A string sextet is a splendid kind of ensemble. It has the homogeneous sound and the soloistic part writing of the string quartet. To these attributes are added the expanded sonority and textural possibilities that come with the additional voice in a viola or cello quintet. And it compounds that advantage by giving us a duo in each of the three tonal strands of the ensemble: violin, viola, and cello. Thinking back to what Mozart did with his viola quintets, I mourn the fact that he never thought to try his hand with yet a sixth voice, the additional cello.

There is, to be sure, some risk in the string sextet: the group is, by nature, unbalanced. In the orchestra, there are significantly more violins than violas, cellos and basses, in order to compensate for the greater sound output of the lower voices. Even so, the conductor has to assure that the appropriate parts can prevail in the given musical event. In a sextet, with one instrument on a part, the ensemble must give special attention to maintaining proper balance between instruments. The performance should not become a contest between shriekers and growlers.

If only with regard to the inherent question of balance in a sextet, I find it difficult to understand how Brahms could remark in 1865—soon after finishing work on his G major sextet—that he thought it "easy to play."[1] He said this in a letter to the publishers, Breitkopf & Härtel, and was perhaps trying to indicate thereby that the piece would have a wide market.

Looking back now over the entire chamber music output of Brahms, I suppose you could say that one or another of the works is more dense and convoluted in its part writing, more tortuous in its intonation problems than the G major sextet. "Easy," however, is a word that must be used only in a relative sense, and with

---

SCORE: Johannes Brahms. n.d. *Sextet in G. major, Op. 36, for 2 Violins, 2 Violas and 2 Violoncellos*. London: Eulenburg. Miniature score No. 236.

Left: Brahms: Sextet No. 2 in G, Op. 36. Paris, Hamelle (1908). First viola part, first page. Reproduced with permission from the collection of the Sibley Music Library, the Eastman School of Music, University of Rochester.

great reservation, in talking about Brahms' music. One thing I do know: easy or not, this sextet, with its intriguing range of colors and temperaments, is a pleasure to rehearse and to perform.

I   *Allegro non troppo.* The 8th-note pulsation that opens the movement in the 1st viola solo is a sound texture that proves crucial to the entire Allegro. Of 605 measures, precious few do not display this rhythm. In effect, it is a thematic strand in its own right, on which the remaining musical material is draped. Moreover, the opening 8ths, significantly, are cast in the form of a *bariolage*: the alternation of open G and stopped F♯ is heard as a kind of acoustic vibrato on the G. The G is what actually sustains the musical fabric; the 8th-note rhythm, important though it is, derives from the ornamentation of the central pitch.

The rocking, wavelike effect of the bariolage must have appealed to the composer, for it creates a wide-ranging musical vista. To set the stage properly, the violist should play the opening oscillation without angularity. The string-crossing should be as smooth as possible so that the alternate pitches—without losing the clarity of the rhythm—merge their resonances. That way, the flavor of the acoustic friction of the minor second, F♯ and G, will be captured, but without the rough throbbing that would result if the tones were played as a double stop.

3   Experiment to see whether the G should be underlined with a brief lingering on the first 8th-note, or instead, the pitch should be fully identified by the entry of the four companion voices in bar 3. Note the quiet level of the opening phrase and its restatement; preserve the hazy atmosphere throughout, moderating the
16   indicated swells, and implying a slight breath only at the end of m. 16 by means of a modest *calando* on the second and third beats of the bar.

A remarkable trait of this movement is the length of its melodic units. True, the units are for the most part constructed of four-measure building blocks, but the divisions between those subunits are bridged over by the flow that carries from
17   beginning to end of the larger structure. Thus, from bar 17 to 32 is the second major unit; bar 33 through 52, the third; 53 to 66, the fourth; 67 to 82, the fifth; 83 to the downbeat of 95, the sixth. All six sections together comprise the opening statement of the movement.

The shadowed harmonic shift at bar 33 provides the middle ground of the complex. Then the spreading of the 8th-note rhythm from one voice, to the violin
53   duo starting at m. 53, and especially the more energetic melodic profile of the rhythm in mm. 58 ff. provides the compression of force. In the sixth and last unit of
83   the complex (mm. 83 ff.), the energy is compounded: the two cellos alternate the 8th-note flow; the viola rhythms combine to emphasize the 3/4 pulsation; and the violin duo carries the melodic line up in a tight and exciting dialogue.

95   At m. 95, this excitement spills over into the transition passage. Here, the 8th-note rhythm takes the shape of cascading runs that succeed each other in the several voices. These lines are as important to the sense of the passage as the slower-moving parts that surround them. In fact, the 8th-note voices are actually rhythmically fractured versions of the slower parts, and must be played so that
119   point is made clear. At bar 119, the 8th-notes level out as though in a runoff from the cascades that have preceded. Here the octave duet between the 2nd viola's 8ths and the 2nd cello's quarter-notes is the focus of the action. The other voices offer encouragement from a bystanders' position.

135   When 1st cello and 1st violin take up the second theme (mm. 135 ff.), the 8ths retreat to an accompaniment role. The 2nd violin and 2nd viola now assume an

important support function, presenting elements of the theme in quasi-imitative fashion. At the same time, the 1st violin and cello frame the action with their full statement of the theme. The 8th-note tremolo in the 1st viola in these measures should suggest the sonority of double stops, rather than insist too ascetically on the clarity of the rhythmic pattern.

All this activity will finally deliver the 1st violin and 1st viola to the famous Agathe theme, A–G–A–B–E, starting at the upbeat to m. 163. (The Agathe in question is Agathe von Siebold, whom Brahms had met and loved in Berlin in 1858. The note, B♮, is called H in German musical practice.) This melodic figure offers the danger of imposing a false accent on the high note (the third beat of mm. 163, 165, etc.), something to be devoutly avoided. Bow that note with suitably short and light stroke, so it does not stick out. Brahms himself indicates the proper emphasis by the swell marks provided in the 2nd violin and 1st cello parts; they point to the downbeat that receives the last note of the Agathe fragment. Even this downbeat, however, is subordinate to the stress that should be placed on the first downbeat of the motto. This view of matters proves especially important in the sequential arrays of the fragment (as in mm. 169–71, 175–79); here, a succession of false accents will create the dubious effect of choral hiccups.

Mm. 180–212 are occupied with a running-out of the Agathe element; this is a tricky passage, since it can degenerate into singsong padding if the ensemble does not play with lightness and direction. The same holds true, to a lesser degree, for the first ending, which has to go through a process of some length in order to work its way back to the opening of the movement. The second ending is less problematic, since it moves quickly into the substance of the development section.

The opening of the development is restful. From bar 239, however, the pace of the action picks up. Even in the quiet, echo dialogue between the cellos, from m. 263 to 279, keep things going so that you gather the several statements into one coherent set. After this, the successive pyramids of the 8th-note tremolo figure, built on a chromatically descending bass line (mm. 283–99) need motion to make them link into a related series of events.

Brahms, in fact, seems to build this development in a succession of waves; for now a surge of figures drawn from the third bar of the opening theme carries us to the climactic point in m. 315. And from there (with the further compression of the thematic rhythm through diminution and hemiola) we are swept into the violin's chromatic descent, mm. 327–34, toward the recapitulation. For Brahms, this seems a fairly simple and obvious approach to the construction of a development section; it is, nonetheless, effective and in keeping with the nature of the movement and its material generally.

A note about the coda: from m. 575 to 596, as many as four voices move in a shifted meter. The upbeat quarter is suspended through the following half-note, so that the 3/4 measure is in effect moved back by one beat. The definition of the actual metric frame here should be left to the 2nd cello's onbeat, dotted half-notes and the 8th-note tremolo that is constantly heard. The offbeat voices must avoid any bar-line thump in their sustained notes.

In the 1st violin's arpeggio ascent, a few bars from the end, the bow strokes for the 8th-note couplets should start small, then flare out to fit the shape of the indicated crescendo. The final cadence places its stress on the third measure from the end; the remaining two chords should be solidly played, but not more loudly than the first.

163

169, 175

180

239

263

283

315

327

575

600

II   ***Scherzo: Allegro ma non troppo.*** This movement has a very strange way of interpreting its title. It is in duple, rather than triple, meter. Its tempo is marked Allegro, but the rhythmic flow, as much as the qualifying, "not too much," keeps the pace of the music down to that of a rather stately walk. And the tone of the writing is sober, far from levity and uproar.

In fact it is the *Presto giocoso*—in effect the trio of this movement—that supplies the exuberance and fun. A later parallel to this sextet movement is to be found in the second quartet, the A minor. There the shadowed Minuetto is set off against the sprightliness of the Allegretto vivace interludes.

1   As for the present Scherzo, however: note that the upper three parts have a line marked on the second quarter-note in mm. 1–3. Do not translate these into accents; the notes in question should be played with slow, sustained stroke, so that there is a gentle stress on the second half of the measure. These notes in the 1st violin have the added impulse of a short quiver of sound—a simple, one-loop turn to the upper neighbor.

The 8th-note pizzicato figures in the lower voices, at the opening as well as later in the movement, should be played melodically, not as mere background to the upper lines. Owing to the bar-by-bar shift of these figures from one voice to another, the resulting part demands conversational treatment. When, as in mm. 10   10–12, the rhythms overlap, the longer phrase lines should be made evident in the playing.

17   The marking at m. 17, *tranquillo*, is not informative enough by itself. I feel that there is a mysterious, enigmatic quality about this area of the movement. The triplet figures should be played very smoothly; the change of bow in each measure should be as legato as possible. Carry the listener to, and through, the peak of the phrase in the third bar of each four-measure phrase. Only in mm. 28–31 is there a bar-by-bar division in the writing.

21   The syncopes in the 1st violin and 1st viola (mm. 21–27) also require very smooth bowing. Both here and in succeeding measures of the section, there are rhythmic frictions between voices; play them, though, so that they are veiled and atmospheric, not confrontational.

34   The importance of this quietness in the Scherzo is demonstrated in the passage starting at m. 34. There, the four upper voices are involved in a somewhat turbulent, increasingly compressed sequence of statements. There are swell marks and a crescendo. The cellos respond to this and are eventually swept into the growing excitement. Note, however, that both low voices are played without swells. Until the wave of activity pulls them into the rhythmic and dynamic compression, they represent the carryover of the element of restraint that was established in the first section of the movement. It is important that the cellists maintain this role up 43   to m. 43. From then until m. 50, they join and impel the turbulence.

103   There will be a second forte point in this section, at bar 103. It is approached, though, in less excited fashion than the first instance. As I see it, Brahms wants to reestablish the basic, subdued tone of the Scherzo after that earlier outburst. The players must keep this in mind especially in the high, *sempre piano* passage from m. 108   108 to the double bar. Set up the greatest possible contrast to the approaching section.

121   The *Presto giocoso* needs to stand out against the dusky plateau that surrounds it. The Presto differs, not only in loudness, but also in its wildness. I think the spice of the Presto is intensified if the hemiola in the three upper parts is emphasized in

the playing, holding firm against the metric insistence of the lower voices. This means that the music will swing back and forth between hemiola and the basic meter through much of this middle section of the movement.

In a way, the Presto is a negative version of the Scherzo proper. There, the prevailing mood was restrained, with a couple of loud passages in relief; here, the general mood is boisterous, with some quiet passages offering contrast. In the context of the fast tempo of this section, the quarter-note triple rhythm of the quiet passages seems analogous to the 8th-note, *tranquillo* portions of the Scherzo. In these hushed Presto spots, however, the players should maintain the exuberance that marks the entire section.   164

The rapid-fire duet of 2nd violin and 1st cello in mm. 153–64 demands very clean, transparent playing. The cello should support these octave runs without submerging the sound of the violin. There is an accent at the start of each of the three descending phrases that open the passage; the duo should relieve the sound immediately after that impulse. Also, be sure to observe the lightness indicated by the dot on the last note of the figure. As for the other four voices in the ensemble, they should be playing incisively, but lightly enough to allow the duo to prevail.   153

Similar concerns about clarity and balance apply to the 1st violin's solo in mm. 160 ff. Here the starting dynamic is piano, and the violin line begins in the middle register of the instrument, so it is doubly important to check for balance as you rehearse the passage. The violin duo's octaves in bars 190–92 may benefit if the players think of a very slight punctuation at the end of m. 190, then a continuous run (though with a bit of emphasis on the downbeat of m. 192) up to the high B quarter-note.   160

190

Brahms is careful to compose the transition from the Presto back to Tempo I, but the players can help effect the return. Starting in m. 235, with the second set of responses between the violas and the other instruments, the pace should be slightly reduced. Then the pizzicato passage of the 2nd viola and 2nd cello can continue the pullback very gradually, with the augmented rhythm of mm. 247–50 completing the process.   235

247

The Animato coda with which the movement tosses its way out is obviously a sly comment on the two contrasting aspects of the movement. The melodic material and meter of the Scherzo are inoculated here with the temper, but not the unrestrained high spirits, of the Presto. Because of the rhythmic activity and the high-speed, imitative part writing in the coda, I suggest that the players go easy on the forte dynamic level.

Poco Adagio. Although they are not so marked, the successive sections of this movement constitute a theme and variations. Accordingly, I shall refer to the several areas of the movement as Variation I, II, and so on.   III

In the 1st violin part, there are swell and diminuendo marks over two measures of the theme; the two accompanying voices, on the other hand, have such marks for each half measure. Obviously, there has to be enough gradation of the successive figures in the accompaniment parts to reflect the dynamic shape of the solo voice. Note also that the 2nd violin has duple-rhythm figures against the triplets of the 1st viola part. There should be suitable rubato in both parts, without carrying matters to such extent that the triplets are distorted into dotted figures; the rhythmic friction between the two accompanying lines must be maintained.   1

The importance of heeding the dynamic markings of the opening lines of the theme is reinforced when you get to the closing four bars of the section. There, the   9 dynamic marks of top and inner voices are more closely matched. An apparent "opening out" of the theme results; the cross-grained intensity of the opening gives way to a more placid air.

The dolorous nature of the theme, both in its original version and in its guise in Variation I, makes the tolling 2nd cello part in that section an appropriate background to the violin voices. In fact, the cello line—along with its pizzicato extensions in the 2nd viola and 1st cello parts—is a solo in its own right, scarcely less important than the violin duo. The 2nd cello's detached triplet 8th-note at the end of each measure, incidentally, has to be played late enough to stand away from the corresponding duple 8th-note in the 2nd viola line. The rhythmic fillip that results is a necessary glint of relief in the overall solemnity of the music.

The dynamic swell in the 2nd violin and 2nd viola in the last measure of this variation is important. Not only does it close out the variation, but it sets the stage for the swell in the 2nd cello part. That voice, in turn, establishes the characteristic dynamic and rhythmic nucleus of Variation II. In that section, the antiphonal relationship between the 2nd cello and the chorus of upper voices must be exploited, with the chorus responding to the shaping of the cello line.

The emphasis in that low voice rests in the two figures that start in B, in mm. 25–26. The sense of ebbing away after that is reinforced by the more continuous writing in the third and fourth bars of the variation. Contrast and relief is offered by mm. 29 through the start of 32. Despite the increased rhythmic activity there, the quietness and the deliberate absence of any dynamic swells makes for a fascinating combination of placidness and agitation. The *più piano* instruction of the closing measures must be strictly observed in order to wash away any sense of turbulence that has been aroused in the preceding bars.

The forte that marks each entrance in Variation III really applies only to the upward octave leap that starts each part. The triplets that follow must be shaded dynamically to permit the next octave leap, in another voice, to make itself heard. As the lines pyramid, the overall dynamic should remain as close as possible to a forte, rather than piling up into a raucous jumble. The slurred writing in the closing measures of the variation calls for very smooth playing, to provide the needed contrast and runoff from the angular sound of the first part of the section.

The quiet close of the third variation is important too as preparation for Variation IV. That is actually a variation on the third variation, compressing and intensifying the agitation of mm. 37–40. The intensity of the fourth variation must not be allowed to flag in the dolce midportion (mm. 53–55). Through restraint and understatement, the quietness here emphasizes the nervousness of the music. Bow these measures in spunky fashion, with incisive, sparkling, clear sound. In bars 56 and 57, the two violins should consciously emphasize their part- and register-exchange; the shifting back and forth is reinforced by the activity in the lower voices, but each violinist must join solidly with the low chorus at the appropriate moments. The ultimate effect should clearly expose the high, long-short rhythms on the second and fourth beats of the violin parts. These will then link with the corresponding rhythms of the 1st violin in bars 59–60 to round out the passage.

Rehearse for clarity in mm. 57–60. The part writing is tightly interwoven. Don't let the voices mat into an impenetrable jungle of notes.

The transition (mm. 61 ff.) to Variation V is an elegant bit of musical business. Set against a transposed statement of the theme is a descending, syncopated inversion of the tune. Both yield place to an augmented statement of the theme; the

Var. I, 13

Var. II, 25

25

29

Var. III, 37

Var. IV, 49
37
53

56

59
57

61

augmentation is only apparent, however, for it is designed to relax the *più animato* of Variations III and IV into the Adagio of Variation V.

The three upbeat 8ths that lead into that variation must, of course, be equivalent to the 16ths of the new tempo. In the Adagio, try to evoke a pastoral feeling by weaving the strands of 16th-notes gently into one another. Play so that the shape of each melodic tendril is made clear; at the same time, though, listen to the overlapping figures in neighboring voices. Overall, aim at the focal points of the writing: the downbeat of m. 67; the third beat of m. 69; the midpoints of mm. 70, 71, and 72; the third beat of m. 73; and so on. The thread of pizzicato 8ths that runs through the variation as rhythmic underpinning should serve as a quietly motoric element, keeping the tempo from stagnating.

Var. V, 65

67

Maintain the sense of flowing tranquillity in the coda (mm. 78 ff.), and don't let your climb toward the forte climax result in too much thickening of the texture of the part writing. Also, avoid too hot a vibrato in the loud measures; you want an effect of noble and generous assurance, not ostentatious passion.

78

Poco Allegro. The movement opens enigmatically: the 16th-note patter is clearly to be an important element, but it serves here as an introduction to the other principal melodic component. That is the broadly flowing theme moving without interruption—except for the shaded interlude in mm. 15–18—from bar 7 to 22, and even beyond, on and up to the forte of m. 29.

IV

7, 15

As you play this thematic complex, make certain to shape it in accord with its structure. You may suggest a phrase breath at the end of m. 8; from there, however, the line should move steadily toward the piano of bar 15. In the next four measures, place the stress on the beat, as indicated by the lines marking the 8th-notes. The combination of line and dot should be interpreted in favor of the line; avoid too brusque a stroke on the 8th, for that will produce an accent rather than a sostenuto emphasis.

8

15

The original phrase resumes, arching over the next four bars. Don't hesitate in moving into the downbeat of bar 23, for the entrance there of the 1st viola's restatement of the theme will provide all the phrase articulation needed.

23

At m. 29, the running 16th-note element returns. By now, it is clear that this is the rhythmically energized source of the interlude of mm. 15–18. I feel that the omission of dots over these 16ths (so also at the opening of the movement) is deliberate. The composer does not want to encourage a spiccato treatment of these notes. Rather, the bowing should be legato enough to reveal the relationship to the sustained-tone music of the interlude measures. In fact, a suggestion of sostenuto pressure should be given the couplets at the start of the second and third beats of bar 29—and at analogous places in the following measures—to reflect the sound of the sustained 8th-notes in bars 15–18.

29

Practice the *enchaîné* series of 16th-note figures in the five lower voices in mm. 30–32 without the 8th-note appendages, to make certain that the connection between sextuplets is seamless. Then, add the 8ths; if the connections are still smooth, add the 1st violin part and check for balance and synchronization. Be sure that the lead-in to the forte at m. 33 makes a strong, but not rough, transition from the crescendo that has been built over the preceding one-and-a-half measures.

30

33

The 1st violin part in the next five bars seems to me to have come directly from Brahms the pianist. Even so, the string player must handle it with aplomb. The string-crossing must be smooth and very economical. Further, because of the detached note at the end of each slurred figure in mm. 33–36, the player must be

33

35 comfortable in having to start the successive sextuplets alternately with down- and upstroke. The octaves in the third beat of m. 35 must be played with exceptionally snug crossing and short strokes, so that the sudden change from the preceding bowing pattern does not come as too much of a shock.

Synchronization in these measures depends very much on the alert interplay between 1st violin and 1st cello; the latter must watch the pacing of the upper voice, which may well be indulging in some artistic rubato in order to carry off the 38 intricacies of the part. There is less problem in the violin duet in mm. 38–41, for the 1st violin part there is fairly straightforward.

44 The 1st cello should gauge the entrance in bar 44 carefully. Allow a bit of time for the sustained, forte-piano note of the preceding measure to settle down after the running activity that has gone before. Bars 44 and 45, in fact, should have a slightly relaxed tempo, providing a breather before the bustle resumes in the next three measures.

Part of the interest at this point in the movement lies in the pivoting back and forth between rushing and hovering passages. Starting at bar 38, there are two such 49 interchanges. The second of the floating passages, mm. 49–51, is truly pivotal, throwing us back to the opening for a repeat of the exposition, or—with only a changed spacing of chord in the second ending—carrying us on into the development. The ensemble should experiment with the pacing of these bars. Rigid counting of beats here will only deny the sense of reflection and hesitation that is built into the music.

Give careful handling to the three imitative entries of the violins and 1st viola that open the development section. The 2nd violin must yield prominence 54 immediately to the 1st in m. 54; and both violins, to the viola in bar 56. Each new voice must dominate in a sound fabric that never rises above the indicated molto 57 piano. And yet, details such as the figures in the violins in bar 57 must be heard clearly in the part-writing. Moreover, the melodic (though pizzicato) contribution of the cello in mm. 56 ff. should also emerge. The effect of hushed, rather conspiratorial dialogue in this passage can be very exciting to the ear.

66 Just as exciting is the imaginative play of sound in mm. 66–79. In the first four of these bars, Brahms seems to explore the mathematically possible combinations of voices available to him in the sextet grouping, as well as the spatial and register spectrum of the ensemble. He breaks off tantalizingly at bar 70, though he does suggest a continuation by using a slurred tremolo of 16ths as one of the musical threads in the ensuing measures.

His harmonic colorations in these bars is also tantalizing, threatening to carry us to Wagnerian depths—and yielding suddenly to the G major and the theme of 80 the recapitulation in m. 80. The development section has been short, but dynamic; take enough time in rehearsal to seek out all the shadings of these measures.

In bar 80, the first theme is marked *semplice,* corresponding to the *tranquillo* in the exposition. In a practical sense, this instruction means that the passage should be played in absolutely unforced sonority. The part writing is all in low register, and needs transparent, not guttural, texture.

117 Similar advice applies to mm. 117–19, at the end of the recapitulation. The sonority there is bold and brilliant; but the crunchy chords in bars 118 and 119 may invite too gritty an attack. Play musically, don't lift barbells. The 2nd viola is 120 particularly challenged by the chords in mm. 120–24; they are triple-stopped, yet in piano. The quiet level means that the chords must be rolled, not struck; but the roll

should be tight enough to avoid an arpeggiated effect. Experiment to find the area in your particular bow that works best here.

The lead in bars 129–34 belongs to the 2nd violin; not only does Brahms mark   129
that part *espressivo,* but the pacing of the transition to the Animato coda is entirely
under the control of that line. Only with the sustained trill in mm. 133–34 does the   133
violin yield the responsibility to the rest of the ensemble. No acceleration is
indicated by the composer. Nonetheless, the quickening is clearly built into the
writing of the 2nd violin part: duplet, triplet, quadruplet, trill—the constantly finer
fractioning of the metric beat compels excitement.

If you have achieved an exhilarating tempo at the start of the coda, hold it
steady from there on. There will be enough activity without forcing the issue
through further speedup. This coda is no ordinary closing passage. It is a highly
compressed review of the movement as a whole. At midpoint, bar 153, we again   153
hear the spatial plays of mm. 66 ff. A three-measure crescendo from forte has
brought us to a fairly loud level. Measure 153 opens with a forte-piano that still
resonates from the preceding loudness. Now in the course of two open-textured
measures, the ensemble has to drop to a pianissimo. The descent has to be dramatic
and definite, for the pianissimo provides the floor from which the final ascent takes
off.

That dynamic climb must be very carefully gauged. Brahms allowed only two
bars to come down to the pianissimo; he dictates a thirteen-bar spread to arrive at
the massed-voice fortissimo of measure 168. Another ascent takes place at the same
time. The 16th-sextuplet element triggers the final scene, starting as a single thread
in the 1st viola, m. 157. It flairs briefly into wider orbit in m. 160 and is joined   157
momentarily by the 2nd violin. Throughout, it must serve as a clearly audible,
animating force, even though the surrounding voices of the ensemble are
trumpeting out an expansive treatment of the first theme.

The broader melody seems destined to prevail over the close of the movement.
In bar 166, though, the two violas join in chorus on the 16th-note motive. The   166
impact of that duet is magnified by the fact that the two-string tremolos of the
respective instruments move in contrary direction. The effect here depends on
accurate and synchronized playing of the two viola parts; both performers must
play as though they are the solo of the moment, for that is indeed the case.

From the broad band of sound of the viola duet we move to the simpler, but
louder, octave duo of 2nd violin and 1st viola in bar 167. From there to the end, the   167
16th-note motive reigns triumphant. In measures 168 and 171–72, it must rule with   168
absolute unity in rhythm and intonation. The ensemble is parading its regimental
colors, and there can be no blemish to mar the exit.

Violine II.

Un poco più animato.

Allegretto D.C.

7380

CHAPTER EIGHTEEN

❧ Brahms ❧
Quartet in C minor, Op. 51, No. 1

Brahms was forty when his first published quartets appeared. Preceding them were songs, vocal ensemble and choral works, piano compositions (including his first piano concerto), the two orchestral serenades, and a number of chamber works—among these the first piano trio, the two string sextets, the first two piano quartets, the piano quintet, the first cello sonata, and the horn trio. With the string quartet, as with the symphony, he held back until relatively late in his productive years. It is known that he had made and destroyed many of his earlier efforts in the string quartet medium before satisfying himself with the two that were to become his Op. 51. At work on these pieces at least since the mid-1860s, Brahms was still asking for more time from his publisher, Simrock, in 1869. He cited as precedent the labor that Mozart had expended on the six "Haydn" quartets. Brahms must have known all six were composed in little more than two years. Still, the stature of those Mozart works was enough to give pause to any subsequent experimenter.

Of the three Brahms quartets, the C minor is my favorite. For me, its sweep and overt excitement wear more comfortably, over time, than the rather determined plaintiveness of the second quartet, in A minor, and the equally determined humor of the first movement and finale of the third and last quartet, Op. 67 in B flat. The claim has been advanced that the two quartets of Op. 51 are linked to each other, not only by thematic interrelationships, but by a complementary emotional cast of the pair:

> The first Quartet shows a struggle, a striving up to a point eventually attained. The epic that embodies this struggle is thus a complete thing in itself, a unified exposition of that struggle... But after that point is

SCORE: Johannes Brahms. 1926. *Quartett C moll, Op. 51, No. 1.* London: Eulenburg. Miniature score No. 240.

Left: Brahms: Quartet in C minor, Op. 51, No. 1. Berlin, Simrock (1873). Second violin part, last page of third movement. Reproduced with permission from the collection of the Sibley Music Library, the Eastman School of Music, University of Rochester.

attained... there may be a period of basking in that rarified ether. This the quiet and serenity of the A minor work represents.[1]

To my ear, the "serenity" of the A minor is rather disquieted, and certainly not without frequent shadow. That is another story, however; our concern here is with the turbulent emotion of the C minor.

I   *Allegro.* Brahms may have turned his mind not toward Mozart, but rather toward Beethoven's Op. 18, No. 4, in C minor, when working on his own quartet in that key. There is no literal resemblance, to be sure. But—as in Beethoven's case—Brahms' theme rises in several arches, the upward flights becoming more compressed as the theme complex progresses. Where Beethoven resolves the process in a flurry of solid chords, however, Brahms contents himself with only two. Here, as in all later instances in the movement, the chords demand a slow, rather sustained stroke, not only for quality of sound, but as a link to the musical line that emerges in the viola part immediately after. That voice exerts a mediating influence with its sustained, quiet octave, the tension further moderated by a pair of echo chords. For the performers, this means a quick conversion from the simmering-to-boiling attitude of the opening measures to the plaintive character of

11   the succeeding area (mm. 11 ff.).

A thread of turbulence underlies the plaintiveness, however: it moves in the dotted-quarter-and-8th-note figure (an integral part of the opening measures) that runs through the lower voices. As in the theme itself, these figures must be played for the firm edge of the 8th-note pulse, with no rounding off that might even remotely suggest the triteness of a triplet rhythm.

The clarity of the dotted rhythm is doubly important in establishing the contrast to the broad triplet rhythm of the solo lines. See, for example, the three

15   upper voices, mm. 11–14, and the three lower parts in mm. 15–18.

The 8th-note pulse plays a dominant role generally in this movement. Not only is it the stuff of the dotted figure, but it appears in drumming repetition as the undercurrent of the very opening measures. In either guise, and in varied application, the 8th is highlighted in almost every bar of the Allegro, and is presented, for the most part, in detached bowing. The stroke must be articulated, but judiciously so. Too pointed a spiccato, even in the piano passages, would be frivolous in this musical atmosphere. The space between strokes will vary according to the context of the moment and the vigor of the bow's motion. In general, though, the trajectory of the stroke will be low and of shallow curve, so that there is opportunity for sonorous and slightly sustained contact of hair against string.

Rather often, there are entrances of the 8th-note figures after an initial 8th-rest.

35   Whether, as in the case of the two violins in mm. 35–36, the entry is made over a running–8th pattern in another part, or takes over in relay fashion from a preceding

43   streamer of notes (see the cello part in m. 43), the player must always sound as though joining an existing, constantly moving 8th-note pulse.

At times, the motion in 8ths outlines a sustained harmonic texture. See, for

24   example, the violins in mm. 24–28 and the viola in mm. 32–40. There the spiccato must be especially broad and close to the string(s), to reflect the underlying continuity. Judiciously emphasize the changes of pitch that move the harmony, as in

32   the 1st violin's progress from E♭ to D♭, C, and C♭ in bars 24–28. In mm. 32–34, the viola functions as two voices, the cello being momentarily silent. Moreover, the

upper notes in the viola's oscillating figure provide the melody to which the violins' offbeats respond. Be sure that melodic edge is suitably shaped.

Passages in which melodic figures overlap closely in the several voices require special practice. In mm. 49–52, for example, the slurred groups of quarter-notes in the three lower parts demand clear inflection and dynamic gradation in each line. The listener must hear the individual horizontal threads, not just a succession of quarter-notes matting into a series of chords. In cases such as mm. 54–55, the situation is easier, since each of the four parts has its own distinctive rhythm; here, dynamic balance between voices will preserve clarity. At all such points, the instrument playing continuous 8ths has to be sure that the last note of each quadruplet joins melodically with the corresponding 8th-note in the voice that has a dotted figure.

It's tricky business, fitting this energy into the dolce moods that Brahms calls for at certain points. In mm. 61–66, for example, the 2nd violin and cello overlap their dotted figures to create a quietly bubbling ribbon of sound. This is punctuated by the offbeat quarters of the viola, whose notes must be breathily played, not overly pointed. All this activity is subordinate to the lyric voice of the 1st violin. When, in mm. 65 ff., that part moves into a convoluted, legato line of 8ths, the playing must still avoid rigidity and strain. Despite the rapid changes of register and close string-crossings, the 1st violin line should unfold with cadenza-like freedom. This can only happen if the lower voices follow alertly. Their half-notes have to fit to the pacing of the 1st violin line, while at the same time preventing any gross distortion of the 3/2 flow. Such an approach may sound self-contradictory, but you'll find that it works.

I hope you will enjoy Brahms' imaginative way of winning a constant 8th-note motion in these measures. Rhythms of dotted quarter-and-8th are played on the beat in one voice, off the beat in another. The overlapping of the figures produces the continuous 8th pattern. More than that, though: the offbeat voice is in effect playing a syncope. The result is an undulating texture that is quite different from that of a simple sequence of 8th-notes in several voices.

Whether the ensemble is moving through the first ending or on into the development, the transition measures (mm. 75 ff.) are led by the cello; the viola takes over at the change of key after the second ending.

In the second ending itself, the 1st violin's augmentation of the theme produces a hemiola. The violin is, in effect, playing in 4/4 meter. In bars 82–83, the cello is playing a hemiola of its own, as though in a measure of three whole-notes. With the two middle voices holding a pedal point, this mixture of slow meters creates a miraculous effect: if time does not stand still here, it has at least reached a point of great calmness. I would vote for pianissimo level, in order to reinforce the mood.

At mm. 92 ff., take care to achieve the chaining effect between the dotted-rhythm figures that overlap in contrary and parallel direction. The intended effect is an expansion of the rhythmic sequence of the original theme. You must not let the line, then, break into the individual rhythmic motives. Carry the listener through the entire bar. Also, when you make the shift to contrasting material (as at the end of m. 95) allow yourself only the slightest of breaths, to avoid a puffy effect.

In mm. 106–11, there are no fewer than six swells and decrescendos. The rise and fall must be moderate, so as not to induce a feeling of biliousness in the listener. In measures such as 114, where the violins have 8th-notes after a long note, play the

49

54

61

65

75

82

92

95

106

114

short notes easily, as though they fall away from the long tone.

118   Moderation is called for again in mm. 118 ff. This is the peak of the movement's storm, and the sound can get pretty rough if the players don't listen to themselves, especially in the bowing of the 8th-notes. The caution applies in
129   particular to mm. 129 ff., where Brahms asks for *marcato*. The bowing must be carefully gauged; these four measures can easily become an anvil chorus. If you listen to each other so that the melodic line carries through the measure—and beyond that through the four-bar phrase—you will be less likely to chop away at your own segment of the writing.

133   In the first two bars (133–34) of the change of key, Brahms has the cello and violins toy with the idea of returning to the theme. Then he threatens to delay the process by augmenting the lines of the three instruments. After two bars of this, however, he continues into the body of the theme, in the original rhythm, launching
137   the recapitulation irrevocably from m. 137. The players have to convey this composed indecisiveness, contrasting the strong three-to-the-bar feeling of mm. 133–34 with the broad succession of three whole-notes that stretches over bars 135–36.

     The most satisfying interpretation of this Allegro, both to play and to hear, will capture its robustness and its seething energy, but never grating, never at the expense of clear sound. Special care must be taken in the coda: Brahms asks for *crescendo ed agitato*, and compresses time by moving from a broad 3/2 to an *alla breve* 4/4. There will be every temptation to throw caution to the winds, to snort, gasp, and rip through the music. Don't do it; the music has quite enough tension and needs no exaggeration.

     The composed lessening of steam pressure in the last measures, by the way, is very much in the hands of the lower voices. Those three instruments, led decisively
254   by the 2nd violin from m. 254, carry out the broadening from 8ths, to triplet quarters, to four-quarter pulse. A gradual, slight spreading of tempo to reinforce Brahms' apparent intent is in order here.

II   *Romanze: Poco Adagio.* The 2nd violin, obviously, leads the start of the movement, in effect conducting what might seem to be the accompaniment to the 1st violin's solo. When you get to the 2nd violin figure that rides the swell on the
4   first two beats of mm. 4 and 5 (and again in mm. 10–11), however, you realize that the three lower voices have been playing a solo, to which the 1st violin solo is responding. Accordingly, 2nd violin and company should be playing just as expressively as the 1st, even though the instruction is not printed in their parts.

8   The fabric of the quartet is inverted in mm. 8–12. Playing in moderately high register, the cello is now acting as first fiddle. Nonetheless, the accompaniment—taken here by the three upper parts—again functions as a solo as well. The ensemble balance must reveal this interplay of purpose.

     Attention should be called to the dotted figure that plays so constant a role in this music. As with the related rhythm in the first movement, be careful not to make the figure round-shouldered; the underlying four-16th pulse must be apparent.

25   How to play the triplets in mm. 25 ff. and 75 ff.? To answer one question with another: how does one play the triplets in the *Cavatina* movement of Beethoven's Op. 130? There the composer uses the instruction, *beklemmt* (with the literal meaning, "straitened," or "with oppressed heart"), to describe the change from the assured calm that frames the movement. I believe Brahms intends the same kind of contrast here, though the degree of oppression is slightly less.

Then too, the passage is easier than its Beethoven counterpart. There, the triplets in the three lower voices have to provide a steady frame and background against which the 1st violin plays its duplet-rhythm lament. In the Brahms, on the other hand, all four voices stay together in most measures of the passage. Still, the ensemble will have to agree on the gradation of the many swells and the placement of the dynamic peaks. They also have to agree about the relative lengths of the onbeat rests that start successive triplets in measures such as 28 and 30. In addition, the players should experiment with an overall decrescendo that will grade the three printed declines within the bar.   **28**

The entire episode is an interesting ensemble problem, a rhythmic recitative for four, out of which emerges the brief solo recitative of the 1st violin in mm. 31–34. Rehearsing this kind of music can be one of the joys and challenges of quartet life.   **31**

Whatever emotional shadow colors the contrast section, the radiance of the ornamented return (mm. 49 ff.) of the movement's opening material completely   **49** displaces doubts. In mm. 55 through 63, the three upper voices must all play "first   **55** violin." Each of the three, in the chain of ascents in mm. 61–63, should play with   **61** warm inset on the longer note, followed by an immediate reduction in tone to allow the 16th-note figure in the adjacent voice to make its place in the chain.

The broader chain of quarter-note imitations in the three lower voices in mm. 64–66 is a pyramid of solos. Second violin, viola, and cello, in turn, step forward to   **64** duet with the 1st violin as it makes its three-octave descent. These three measures are a wonderfully simple, open-textured exploration of quartet space. They should be played simply, without excessive heat, to contrast with the rich sonority of the massed strings that wells up in the next passage.

The coda reviews the two opposite elements of the movement in smaller frame. At the very close, the brilliant light of mm. 92–93 emanates as much from the   **92** expansively rocking 8ths of the 2nd violin part as from the singing line of the 1st violin. The triplets and duplets must be played flexibly, with rubato that shows that the two lines are truly interacting with each other.

The coordination, in mm. 87 and 89, of the cello's plucked chords with the   **87** three upper lines is made easier by the fact that the chords are arpeggiated. Still, the players should watch each other to assure synchronization. This is more urgent in bars 92–93, where the cello chords are solid, and where contrary rhythms have to   **92** line up on each beat. In mm. 94–95, it is viola and cello who must lead each other.   **94**

As for the last measure, pizzicato and bowed notes start simultaneously. The 1st violin should give the signal; in such an exposed spot it is easier for the bow to synchronize with the plucked sound than vice versa. It will help, though, if the violinist prepares the signal by imagining mentally the approach of hair to string.

Allegretto molto moderato e comodo. The breadth of the solo viola line that   **III** opens the movement dictates the way the other three parts should be played. In the 1st violin, the couplets call for legato bowing, with slight lessening of pressure and speed on the second note of the pair, but with minimal separation between successive strokes. The player can choose to start downbow, to match the viola. So also, the 2nd violin and cello may want to take the accented, upbeat 8ths on the downstroke, following with an articulated upbow for the first three 8ths of the succeeding bar. (The bowings of mm. 3 and 4 can be arranged so that the accented   **3** fourth beat of m. 4 is again taken on the downstroke.)

No specific dynamic level is shown for the upbeat in m. 8. I feel, though, that   **8** from there through bar 11 you should play pianissimo. Second violin and cello, with their couplet 16ths, must be especially careful not to let the motion become loud and turbulent. Let the swells that follow carry the level back into the piano of bar 15.

15 The 1st violin, and then the inner voices, will enjoy what is, in effect, the free-meter writing in their lines in mm. 15–24. These are lyrical effusions on the central material of the movement. Leave it to the cello's repeated 16th-notes to maintain the 4/8 frame. Without distorting the pulse, the three upper parts should nonetheless move with the melodic events in their lines, and without stressing downbeats.

27 Somewhat the same sense of metric freedom, though to lesser degree, applies to the syncopations that two or three of the upper voices carry in mm. 27–36. These syncopes are simultaneous in the participating instruments. Even so, they are meant to wash across beats and bar lines in a liquid flow. Play them in *flautando* fashion, with light and rather broad strokes, in the upper part of the bow, and near the fingerboard. Stay together, but don't emphasize the changes of bow or the downbeats. The figures in the solo lines start with suspensions over the bar line in these measures. This, along with the syncopated background, gives the entire passage an eerie sway, one that is broken at last by the peremptory triplets and
37 crescendo in bar 37.

39 A *lusingando* passage follows next, mm. 39 ff. The instruction translates, literally, as "flattering" and/or various related meanings, depending on which dictionary you read. I don't know what to make of the application of the word here. It is apparent that Brahms is extending the idea of the couplets of the opening measures into a broader, triplet-motivated line. He emphasizes the effect by weaving the rhythm alternately between 1st violin and viola, then between the two violins. For both duos, the tricky part is to move together into the continuous sextuplet measures and to stay with each other in a free, yet synchronized, voyage through that garland of parallel sixths.

45 The 2nd violin has the individual responsibility of receiving the motion of the violin-viola duo at the end of m. 45, balancing the impetus, tipping it over through the syncope of m. 46, and then launching into the new voyage with the 1st violin. Don't spend too much time practicing the passage with a metronome; this is very sophisticated ensemble playing, far removed from dogmatic counting of beats.

86 In the trio section, *Un poco più animato,* the inner voices, and especially the 2nd violin, can have a high old time. To look at it, the alternation of stopped and open A in the 2nd-violin line would seem to be a dog of a part. Actually, like Bach and Haydn before him, Brahms knows how to enjoy the sound of *bariolage* (the term for the alternating stopped/open sound on a bowed instrument). So, though it must be played piano, as marked, the line must also be played with gusto, and with enough energetic string crossing to project the difference in timbre between the open A and stopped D-string. The same applies to the octave oscillations in 2nd violin and viola, and to other 8th-note rhythmic offshoots of the bariolage idea. None of this should mask the importance of the rusticated melodic line, mostly assigned to the 1st violin, that overlies all the activity.

135 After the hubbub settles down, the *bariolage* returns in the 2nd violin, now in solo splendor, accompanied by the pizzicato chords in the other three parts. It is left to the violinist to control the transition back to the tempo and mood of the da capo section.

146 The role of the initial upbeat of the return, coming after two beats of an

incomplete measure of 3/4 time and introducing the return of the 4/8 opening, would seem to be ambiguous. In effect, the upbeat here is acting simultaneously as a third and fourth beat. On paper, it looks wrong; with proper shading of tone and tempo, it sounds just right. In many years of playing this work, I never felt this to be an awkward transition—which shows what artful ensemble cooperation in the shading of tempo and phrase can do.

Allegro. The first three measures look back to earlier points in the quartet: the forte portion incorporates the dotted rhythm and arch-shape of the first-movement theme and the stepwise climb of the second-movement subject; the *poco forte* melody reflects the interval sequence of the *espressivo* melody (m. 11) from the first movement. It might also be said that the slurred couplets in mm. 3 ff. trace back to the accompanying rhythm in the third movement's opening, but the motoric 8ths of the first movement suggest the more striking parallel. [IV] [3]

In fact, the temper of this finale not only reflects that of the first movement, but raises it to a higher degree of intensity, if that is possible. This prompts me to ask again that you express the emotional heat of the music through a warmly robust manner of playing that is never carried to the point of a rasping or forced sound. Even on the finest of instruments, excessive force will coarsen and actually inhibit the sound, as though pressing it back into the box of the instrument rather than letting it breathe out through the *f*-holes.

The danger of forcing is greatest in the groups of slurred quarters (for example, mm. 33 ff., inner voices); if the inevitably slower bow speed is coupled with unrestrained pressure, the tone will immediately degrade. There is less danger in the detached 8ths and slurred 8th couplets, often assigned to the 1st violin but also taken up in other parts as well (as in the 2nd violin and viola, mm. 13 ff.). Just don't play them with too choppy and vertical a stroke. [33] [13]

Whether the 8ths are slurred or separate, there are a lot of them. Don't let yourself get hypnotized by the motion; look for the phrase behind the activity. As an illustration: the 1st violin has no fewer than forty-eight consecutive, slurred pairs of 8ths in mm. 21–32. Be aware that you are playing three phrase units, each four bars long. The first two, rather smooth in outline, carry you up in two melodic arcs; the third, bolder in the couplet interval, ends with a downward plunge across the fingerboard. [21]

Then you head into eight measures of athletic, cross-string playing. Stay near the foot of the bow, and play with a broad and gentle spiccato, maneuvering snugly from one string to the next. Emphasize the continuity, not the angularity, of the line.

When a dot appears above a note, please read it with the ear as much as with the eye. In the limited arsenal of notational signs, the dot can represent both staccato and spiccato. Even when the sign is supplemented by the verbal instruction, the player must judge the particular shading of sound and texture most appropriate to the musical situation.

In bars 18 and 20, for example, the detached quarter-notes in the 1st violin part actually arpeggiate two half-note double stops. The violin should play the quarters just broadly enough to suggest the underlying half-bar motion, without blurring the separation of the successive tones. By the same token, the three lower voices need enough breadth on the first and third beats to support the action of the solo part. [18]

Another example, mm. 41–45: the dots, the forte, the successive entries of the four parts can encourage a rivalry between voices that lends the passage the sound [41] of a military contest. The two lowest parts, especially, must recognize that the violins have embarked on more lyric pursuits. Don't overplay.

50 The few measures of *dolce* (50–53) are the first break in the storm. Let all hands, including the solo 2nd violin, take advantage of the chance to relax the tension. A few bars later, you'll all be slugging it out. That's what it can feel like as the four of you deal with the short, slurred groups of 8th-notes in mm. 58 ff. Resist frenzy. Play for smoothness; the figures themselves will provide all the intensity that's needed,

62 especially when the rhythms overlap (as in mm. 62 and 66).

68 Both violins give the thematic battle cry in octaves in bars 68–69. This can sound fairly shrill. Again, lean toward the lyric; and remember, the dynamic is only forte.

As in the first Allegro, the greatest musical test of the ensemble comes in

71 dealing with the two quiet oases of the finale: the episodes at mm. 71 ff. and 162 ff. (Brahms raises the ante the second time around by calling for *mezza voce* and *dolce ed espressivo*, rather than for a simple *poco tranquillo*.) The sudden turn from the general fury of the preceding lines to the somewhat more subdued emotional lyricism of these passages, and the equally swift return to musical fisticuffs (as at

192 m. 192), will show the resilience and collective wit of the players. I think the ensemble is justified in taking a slightly broader tempo for these passages. Avoid too great a slowdown, however; the composer has already given the music a broader rhythmic flow, one that needs little reinforcement other than in the graciousness of the playing.

83 In the *agitato* return to the sterner plane of the movement (mm. 83 ff.), the 2nd

86 violin's half-notes and dotted figures (mm. 86–93) benefit from a moderate approach. With the doublings and octaves, they tend to sound shrill and edgy. Again, the peak of the crescendo is only a forte.

98 The interweaving of corrugated lines—for violin and cello in mm. 98–100, and

106 for all four voices in mm. 106–08—will take some slow and careful combing out. In view of the compressed writing, it's no wonder that these spots feel awfully gnarled and twisted in performance. You almost heave a sigh of relief when you are safely past them. I don't ask that you play cautiously here, only that you practice until there is a touch of nonchalance in the mayhem.

One of the most climactic passages in the finale is the descent from the

180 triumphant outcry in m. 180. The entire ensemble is in high register here. Listen carefully to be sure that the group sound is free, not strangulated. Find just the right balance between the speed and pressure of the bow stroke to achieve the proper resonance. Above all, the style of bowing must be an expansive legato. The feeling of breadth should be maintained even as the diminuendo takes place.

224 A particular danger point for sound in this movement occurs in mm. 224–30. There, with the safety of the double bar already in sight, the performance can run aground on the jagged boulders of the chords. The peril is the greater because, for full vigor, the chordal pairs in the upper and lower duos should be taken with successive downbows. Both for the benefit of the resonance and to reduce the amount of bow that must be recovered between strokes, take a gliding approach to the string, slowing the bow after the stroke begins.

The very end of the quartet requires circumspect treatment. The ensemble is

231 likely to take Brahms' *stringendo* marking at face value and sprint for the double bar at a furious clip. Well and good, but note that, along with speed, there is still the singing, melodic element of the slurred groups of quarters. Even in the jumping line

of the 2nd violin's 8th-notes, allow for astute use of rubato and dynamics to reveal the lines of melodic motion that are built into the ribbon of tones. As for the last measures, from 239 on, there can be no designated "leader" in the group; all four control this tumultuous exit.

239

A general hint: Brahms does not simplify the texture of his writing in his fast movements and passages. Use enough slow-speed practice, separating into pairs and threes as needed, to sort out linkages and interweavings among the parts. Work toward a clean and flexible performance. Also, keep in mind the limit of loudness that is commanded by the small group; extend the dynamic palette by exploiting the quiet side of the range. Less is often the road to more.

Poco a poco più mosso.
sf p
cresc.
f e con fuoco
cresc.
Allegro non troppo ma con fuoco.
ff
cresc.
p
Poco accellerando
ff
cresc.
ff cresc.
sempre accell.
8
f f f

CHAPTER NINETEEN

❧ Tchaikovsky ❧
Quartet No. 1, in D, Op. 11

It was in a motel room in Tucson, many years ago, during the afternoon of a concert day. I suppose I should have been practicing. Instead, I found myself getting a music history lesson, Hollywood style. The TV was showing a movie about Tchaikovsky. The scene: Cedric Hardwicke (Russian prince), overcome by the experience of hearing Tchaikovsky conduct the Pathétique Symphony, has sent his daughter backstage with the deathless line, "Go, he is worthy of you!" She, standing in the wings with Tchaikovsky's valet, asks the good fellow what he thinks of his master. "Oh," replies Valodya, in the thickest of Russian accents, "he is the best!"

After witnessing so hilariously wrongheaded a scenario, I was fortunate not to have to deal with a Tchaikovsky quartet on our program that evening. On the other hand, I think that both the composer and I might have survived. Happily, his music speaks convincingly on its own behalf, despite all the efforts of misguided popularizers.

Chamber music forms only a small part of Tchaikovsky's work-list. The Quartet in D (the first of three completed quartets) was written for a concert of the composer's music, presented in March of 1871 in Moscow. The work—and especially its second movement, the Andante cantabile, based on a Russian folk song—made a hit. So popular did the slow movement become, in fact, that Tchaikovsky himself grew a bit irksome about it. (Ravel was later to have the same reaction to the inordinate vogue of the *Bolero*.)

Moderato e semplice. Surely, this is not the opening of a string quartet: a piece for accordion or harmonium, some such instrument or its Russian equivalent, or

I

SCORE: Peter I. Tchaikovsky. n.d. *Quartet in D major, Op. 11*. London: Eulenburg. Miniature score No. 161.

Left: Tchaikovsky: Quartet in D, Op. 11. Moscow: Jürgenson (c. 1903). First violin part, last page of first movement. Reproduced with permission from the collection of the Sibley Music Library, the Eastman School of Music, University of Rochester.

227

perhaps even for a folk chorus, but not a quartet. How else account for the absolute rhythmic conformity of all four voices, or the utter subordination of the three lower voices as they move in harmonic support of the 1st violin melody?

I admit that the effect is as convincing as it is intriguing. To carry off the passage, though, the players must surrender to the atypical sound of the music. The four bows must move as one, and—with due allowance for the structural requirements of the phrase—each measure of music should seem impelled by a fresh supply of air from some instrumental bellows. The rhythmic pattern of the opening, identical for each of the first fifteen bars, seems the kind that would come naturally from the alternate expansion and compression of a wind chamber.

13   If you follow the printed bowing (and I can suggest nothing more suitable), odd measures will start on the downstroke; even measures, on the up. This will hold true until bar 13; there, because of the additional slur in the third beat of the preceding measure, the 1st violin will start with an upstroke, as also in mm. 14 and 15.

5   The *poco cresc.* in mm. 5–7 should be quite modest, for the harmony (certainly at the end of m. 6) suggests a distant, rather than closeup, perspective. As for the
12   crescendo marked in bar 12, that should start from the far-off point of the
15   pianissimo that began in m. 9. I find it a bit jarring to take the mezzo forte of bar 15 at face value, especially since there has to be a quick fallback to piano at the end of that measure. I would reserve a fuller dynamic level for the activity that starts in
16   bar 16. The rhythm of the opening, as well as some of the chordal texture, remains in force. But the zephyr of 16th-notes that runs from one voice to the other suggests a freer, more open atmosphere than the intimate, hothouse air of the movement's beginning.

An interesting problem in bowing awaits the violins in this passage. The rhythm of the opening is retained; but its dynamic level is extended all the way to
23   forte (m. 23). The original, clinging and confined bowstroke, then, will expand to take almost the entire length of the stick. Try not to lose the clinging effect, however. You have to enlarge the musical photograph without distorting the image.

Both lines of motion in this passage—the 16th-note tracery and the broader rhythm of the theme—must balance so that the two can be heard equally. Work toward maintaining this balance throughout the shifts in dynamic level specified by the composer.

29   When you get to the second theme of the movement (mm. 29 ff.), you find that Tchaikovsky insists on his initial premises. The new theme divides the 9/8 meter in its own way. Even so, the new melody's close kinship with the first theme shows in two respects: a breadth of motion, underscored by the *largamente* instruction; and the insistence on bar-by-bar phrasing in its first two measures. There are, indeed,
31   longer phrase units, as well as the passing diversion of a 12/8 measure (bar 31). But there is much rocking on the triplet, *long*-short, *long*-short motion. Take advantage, then, of every melodic fluctuation you can find in each voice to avoid being hypnotically lulled by the rhythm. To be sure, there is enough skydiving in the
34   16th-note line of the 1st violin (mm. 34–41) to divert the listener's attention. That line, however, is partly decorative in nature and cannot mask the activity of the broader lines in the lower voices. Let every player, then, stand and deliver intelligently.

There are some awkward spots in the writing, from a string player's point of view. Note, for example, the finger-twisters in the 1st violin and viola parts, from
34   m. 34 through 44. Only clever choice of positions and delicate string crossing can

make such lines flow smoothly. Fortunately, the writing is less athletic in the approach to the *Poco più mosso* of m. 47. You will probably want to make some acceleration at least in the course of bar 46. The *più mosso* must move along briskly, especially to produce something in the order of a vivace in the fortissimo passage of bars 51–56. 47 51

The *a tempo* that appears in the middle of the first beat of both the first and second endings is properly sudden. It is an instantaneous change of scene, dropping you from the wild leaping of the preceding measures back into the tranquil pulsations of the opening. 57

The return to D major through the last beat of the first ending comes as a slight shock; it makes you suspect that the composer simply felt he had to have a repeat, and so chopped in a return. There is a more comfortable feeling when you move forward through the second ending into the development. There the composer lets you linger for a moment longer in A major before turning you toward F major (m. 62).

At that point, the actual start of the middle section, trouble awaits— Tchaikovsky's trouble. He seems not to know quite what to do with the development process. He fastens on the ascending scalewise figure of the *Poco più mosso* (see m. 47) and adds a new, plaintive bit of melody that is used fitfully from mm. 68 through 83. From there on, the stage belongs to the scalewise fragment and the thematic rhythm. The two together mount a rather orchestral assault march until the reprise steals in at bar 104. Make the best of things: think of the 1812 Overture, or of some imagined ballet scene, work up a good head of steam, and play with dramatic conviction. Your listeners must be led to accept the sound and excitement as a replacement for deeper musical invention. If they haven't heard the quartet too often or too recently, they will love the deception. See to it. 47 68 104

It is only fair to point out that I am not the only one to have had some problem in dealing with this development section. Gerald Abraham praises Tchaikovsky as being "no mean contrapuntist; the first movements of the D major Quartet and the Serenade for strings... show him as a complete master of the art of fluent, effective part writing." Even so, he maintains that, to develop Tchaikovsky's preferred melody, consisting of "clear-cut, balancing phrases... is to ruin it."[1] David Brown describes Tchaikovsky's process here as "extending the development by simply repeating in transposition a very substantial stretch of music..."[2] Still, I must not conceal from you that Andrew Porter considers this development to be "of an extraordinary richness."[3] In any event, let your inspired playing vindicate Tchaikovsky's thinking.

Coming out of the development, the scalewise figure and a longer extension thereof (mm. 112 ff.) continue into the recapitulation; there they serve as a filigree above the thematic pulsations in the lower voices. Be prepared for the rather brusque detour (bars 128–29) that steers the harmony to the tonic, D major. As in the exposition, the composer calls for pianissimo at this point of transition. Because of the abrupt harmonic turn here, the dynamic must be taken very seriously, and with all possible *misterioso* approach. This applies especially in the playing of the bit from the second beat of bar 129 to the downbeat of the following measure; you have to make the musical sleight of hand come off effectively. 112 128 129

In the 16th-note traceries this time around, mm. 141–44 are the difficult ones for the 1st violin, though still not as problematic as the corresponding measures in the early part of the movement. Once again, though, the critical task is to make 141 these runs unfold with flexibility, in whatever voice they appear. The runs must adorn, not hang heavily on, the more broadly moving lines.

145   A tough choice faces the viola, incidentally, on the third beat of m. 145. Either take the last four 16th-notes on the D-, A-, D-, and G-strings, respectively; or else follow the even more awkward alternative of playing the sextuplet in second position and taking the last, low A with a backward extension of the first finger.

161   A very touchy spot for intonation is bar 161, where the octaves between the two violins must remain true despite the 1st violin's voyage to and from the high B. For clarity, I suggest that the upper voice use: fourth position from the second 8th-note, with an extension for the F♯ (or else arrange to play the figure from a start on the A-string, already in seventh position); 7th position from the following E, with extension for the high B; and sixth position for the remainder of the measure and the downbeat F♯.

160   The *giusto* of the Allegro (m. 160) must be carefully interpreted, so that the
170 measures move fleetly but still leave room for the acceleration to begin in bar 170. Tchaikovsky does not say where the speedup should end. I think that the swirl of
171 bar 171 should pick up the pace set by the preceding flourish, with the pulse
173 quickening yet again through the following bar. By m. 173, the speed will be fast enough to please anyone. The violins get to test their octaves at full tilt in these bars; my earlier fingering suggestion may serve effectively here. For all possible *brio*, the ensemble can push up the throttle yet another notch for the last four measures. Enjoy!

II   *Andante cantabile.* This is a fairly simple, exceedingly familiar movement—which means it's not easy. Avoid oversentimentalizing the tune; the folk-song melody does not bear such treatment well. As it is, the muted sound of the ensemble creates enough of an exotic atmosphere. If your tempo is conducive to the gentle pulse of the quarter-beats, the tune should unfold clearly and honestly.

     The melody is built on two four-bar units, but don't assume that matters will necessarily proceed in squared-off manner. The third bar of the first group is a 3/4 measure. Moreover, the slurring and punctuation of the tune in these opening bars divides it into five beats followed by four. Another interesting touch of asymmetry
17 appears in the second melodic complex, starting m. 17. This phrase leads off with a four-bar unit; and, at bar 21, we assume we are beginning a second four-measure group to balance the line.

22   To my ear, though, the descending quarter-note line of mm. 22–24 continues;
24 the cello couplets in m. 24 bridge any gap and propel the music into bar 25. The phrase moves on, through five measures in which melodic turns are echoed between violin and viola; and it ends only in the pensive cadence of the violin in
30 bars 30–32. If played so as to reveal this structure, the promise of a succession of four-bar units in the movement's opening gives way to something more interesting.

     Fortunately, Tchaikovsky does not carry through on what at first threatens to be a repetition of the entire opening complex of phrases. Instead, after reviewing
50 the first sixteen bars of music, he has the 2nd violin play a lone, syncopated series of Fs; this serves as the pivot around which the harmony swings to the key of D♭. The cello has much to do with defining that key. But that privilege comes at the risk
54 of utter stupefaction, for the cello has no less than twenty-six measures of the same, pizzicato, four-note figure. This is followed by another seventeen measures of tonic-and-dominant to render the player soporific. For safety and sanity's sake, the cellist might number the measures of the series, until familiarity makes it safe to fly on automatic pilot.

Bar-numbering is also advisable insurance for the two inner voices in this passage; the offbeat sighs with which they respond to the outer voices in most of these measures are even more sleep-inducing than the cello line. The very best antidote the three lower voices can find, of course, is to become engrossed in what the 1st violin has to say.

That player, now liberated from the sober strains of the opening, is pouring out the *molto espressivo* music of the middle section of the movement (mm. 56 ff.). The muted sound of the ensemble now creates an intensified aura around the impassioned utterance of the solo. By responding to the changing nuances of that line, the lower parts can make their own measures come alive. 56

The solo will probably want to linger slightly in approaching the fourth 8th of m. 58 and in savoring the quarter-rest at the start of the next bar. Restfulness will again prevail in mm. 61–63. The harmonic and dynamic change at bar 80 will undoubtedly evoke a slight surge in tempo as well. In all such cases, the accompanying voices will move with the inflection of the melodic part. Don't yield too much, though, or the four of you will end by circling around each other. 58
61, 80

The three pianissimo measures (94–96) that lead to the return of theme demand not only extreme quietness, but some diminuendo and *calando* as well, to avoid any suggestion of abrupt falloff at the end of bar 96. The theme itself is cleverly reorchestrated. At first, all three upper voices fortify the melody at the unison. The piano dynamic of the opening is retained, with *espressivo* now added. Be sure that the total level remains piano, for the triple voicing can easily give the tune an inappropriately brassy quality. If properly hushed, the melody will have a very effective air of nostalgia about it. 96

In any event, much of the "expressive" nature of this restatement comes from the quasi-improvisational wanderings of the cello line. The viola soon joins the cello in this decorative procedure, with the result that the theme flowers into the forte climax of the movement at mm. 125–26. The players ought to build toward the intensity of this moment all the way from the crescendo at bar 110. Measure 127, the dramatic grand pause that follows the loud outburst, should be stretched a bit, to set the scene for the even more histrionic exhaustion of the two pianissimo phrases of mm. 128–37. 125
128

Bar 136 has two bowed 8th-notes in all four voices. Play them as fairly short, articulate notes, to prepare for the sound of the pizzicato 8th-note couplets of the three lower voices in the next episode. 136

In that passage, the second theme—formerly the vehicle of some palpitating emotion—appears in more contemplative vein. The 1st violin is instructed to play the melody entirely on the G-string, to reinforce the "very expressive" nature of the sound. Tchaikovsky does not say when this stipulation ends, but it is obvious the player should be free to use other strings from bar 153 on. 153

There should be freedom, too, for the ensemble to pace the rests and entrances in mm. 167–78; provide for the steady draining away of energy that marks the end of the movement. The suspension on the D (mm. 178–79) in the 1st violin part must also be sustained according to the player's best judgment. That note is the true end of the movement; moreover, the *morendosi* ("dying-away") ascent that the violin makes in the last measures can only begin when the performer has—figuratively, at any rate—summoned enough energy after the suspension to float upward toward the high B. The 2nd violin will lead the musical amen of the last two bars, pacing the entry and resolution to suit the 1st violin's final utterance. 167
178

III
1

Scherzo: Allegro non tanto. Did Tchaikovsky deliberately omit a dot over the detached 8th-note at the start of bars 1 and 3 in the lower voices? If so, I suspect it might have been because he recalled the breathy sound of the first movement's opening. The 1st violin, though, is clearly instructed to play its 8th-note with a sense of lift; accordingly, I think the accompanying parts should do the same. My advice, then, is for all four players to begin with an upstroke, here and at the start of the third bar.

This writing has a brazen quality, as though trumpets and cymbals are sounding from the wings of the stage, and the ensemble should work to suggest that sonority. In the second section of the piece, the alternate forte and piano of the first eleven bars should be very clear-cut in contrast, as though on- and offstage bands are playing to one another.

45

It is important, too, to set the mezzo forte of mm. 45 ff. distinctly below the preceding forte. You want to underline the dampening effect that the new harmonic color has on the exuberance of the D major phrase just ended.

53

I recall that our 1st violin was in the habit of playing the first measures of the solo cadenza, mm. 53 ff., on the G-string. This color, coupled with the appropriately emphatic lingering on the B♭ at the start of m. 54, produces rather too guttural an effect for my taste. I find the lighter sonority of the D-string more suited to the nature of the tune.

Trio

In the Trio, bring out the interesting play of rhythm and meter. The writing is clearly in 3/8, even though sparked by the melody's accent on the second beat of the bar, as in mm. 84, 86, and so on. That accent, in fact, combines with the surrounding accents in the viola part to emphasize the 3/8 pulse. The viola, however, is actually playing a 3/4 metric pulse, starting with the offbeat entrance in bar 82. All this, moving against the steady 16th-note oscillation of the cello part, makes for an intriguing mix of rhythmic currents. The effect is even more beguiling when the viola gives up its accentuations in mm. 91 ff., leaving the listener to imagine the continuation of the rhythmic current. The pianissimo at m. 99 throws the entire process into a distant and completely unaccented plane, and draws the listener even more strongly into the web of the music.

84

82

91
99

I trust you will play the Trio at a good clip, faster than the *non tanto* of the Scherzo proper, for Tchaikovsky repeats the entire metric game he has contrived. This carries the section to needed length, but outlasts the interest of the musical material. A brisk tempo will help gloss over the composer's self-indulgence. You will, however, have to decelerate gradually over the last five measures of the Trio in order to prepare the way for the broader tempo of the da capo.

57

The composer asks you play a diminuendo through the last twenty-four measures of the "second time" (see m. 57) through the Scherzo. I suggest that you close with exceeding quietness, but no retard. This will suggest that the music has not ended, but continues very far off—even if we can no longer hear it.

IV

Allegro giusto. Tchaikovsky must have enjoyed writing this movement! The themes are bright and lively; the frame of the movement is sonata allegro, but the development process is more assured than in the first movement. And, as though in homage to the memory of Haydn, there is a humorous, slow rumination point before the run that closes the quartet.

Don't be misled by the look of the printed score at the start of the movement. The piano dynamic is right enough, contributing to the light and mischievous air of the tune. The notes, though, are printed without dots, which might lead the unwary to try playing the theme on the string. No matter how gentle the bow stroke in such an approach, the legato effect will make a sticky mess of the melody. Use the lower half of the bow and begin with an upstroke, tying the first two 8th-notes together in a bouncing, lifted stroke. The last 8th of m. 2 should also be hooked into the same upstroke as the preceding, slurred couplet. Arrange the bowing so that the half-note that ends the phrase (bar 8) will come on an upbow. This will deliver you to the lower part of the stick to start the second phrase of the tune.

Work out further bowings to match the temper of sound with which you have begun the movement. Be sure the sudden, chordal outbursts (the second beat of mm. 16 and 26) are resonant, not barked: use a lively left hand, not too much bite at the start of the note, and a rather slow stroke, rather than a slash.

The entrance in bar 18 is the first of many in this movement that starts on an offbeat; all hands must come in after an ensemble rest. Whether the silent beat is an 8th or a quarter in value, the leader (in most cases, the 1st violin) should give a small but definite signal on the rest itself, with the note that follows sounding as a reaction to the preliminary impulse.

In a closely spaced series of such entrances, as for example in mm. 34–37, don't assume that signalling the first of the set will suffice, with the remainder falling into place automatically. After a number of performances, that might prove true. You probably will choose, though, to let each bar have enough signal to trigger the rhythmic fragment. That way, you can tease the spacing of the figures; an absolutely straight count misses the fun of the writing.

For clarity in the 1st violin line in mm. 44–47, I suggest that bars 44 and 45 be played in the fifth position, with a clean third-finger shift to the E♯ at the start of m. 45 and a change to sixth position at the second half of that bar. The G♯ on the downbeat of bar 46 is played with the extension of the third finger (no smeary shift here!). Starting with the second 8th-beat of that measure, there are four ascending quadruplets of 16ths. Except for the last of these groups—which obviously starts on open A—each quadruplet should be played with a fingering of 1–2–3–4, to avoid any shifting within the figure. The same need for clean fingerings applies to the corresponding figures in the lower voices.

Under no circumstances should the 2nd violin try to avoid string crossings in mm. 51–65. The brilliance of the E-string, contrasting with the color of the open A or other drone notes in this passage, is essential to the sonority here. Play in first position throughout and cross strings economically so that the liquid effect of the writing is achieved. The bold drumming of the cello part, half of it on the open A and D, will contribute handsomely to the sound, especially if played with a bluff, spiccato stroke.

One of the most engaging aspects of the movement is the offhand, suspenseful way the composer leads us to the second theme. First, there is the dwindling away of the five F major chords in bars 77–79. At that point, a rhythmic chorus begins in all four parts. The chant is just two measures long; when you hear the two measures in their six-fold repetition, you think the figure will go on forever. Just as the seventh turn begins, the second theme enters in the viola. Play the repeated pattern with enough spice to make the listener think that the rhythmic refrain is going to be the center of interest; the entry of the theme itself must come as something of a surprise and a musical bonus.

The violins, in fact, are made to overlook the surprise, for they continue the rhythmic chant, rising eventually to forte, while the viola and cello, in turn, concern themselves with the new theme. In so doing, they must translate the composer's *largamente* into expansive bowstrokes, boldly applied to the string, for this theme is as bluff and hearty as the first is delicate and pointed.

In fact, it is the first theme and the rhythmic pulse that win out; they, along with the racing 16th-note element, take over the closing lines of the exposition. The 1st violin will again have to seek out nonsmearing fingerings for mm. 130–41. I suggest that the first four bars be played entirely in third position, with an extension to take care of the high D–E♭ at the end of the first and third ascending groups. You may find it convenient to take the C (second 8th of bar 133) in fifth position on the D-string. This will enable you to reach the F (downbeat of bar 134) cleanly, with an extension of the third finger. That will put you in sixth position, where you should remain, right through the first 8th of m. 138.

Measure 155, in the second ending, can be played by the 1st violin with a touch of rubato on the first two 8th-notes, to help point up the emphasis on the quarter-note that follows. After this, the chain of sprightly 8th-notes should proceed without any diversionary activity until it reaches the cello. That player may be permitted a bit of philosophical stretching of the pace, from the second 8th of m. 162 into the following bar.

The development is based on the first theme and the running 16th-note line, along with a plaintive, dotted-rhythm motive that is freshly introduced. The predominant level in this section is piano and pianissimo, even though louder points are reached. In the 16th-note streamers that move from voice to voice, play as smoothly and liquidly as possible, though with shape. For example, in the cello part at mm. 184–86, the first bar is played "straight," with a bit of emphasis on the first and fifth 16ths to mark the metric pulse. In bar 185, the cello emerges from a background into a solo role. The line there merits some dynamic flair and thrust toward the middle of the bar; this will help the melody peak before it dies away in the course of m. 186.

As for the other ingredients in the developmental brew, they flicker past in individual voices or in several at once. Sometimes they displace the 16th-note streamers; at others, they are heard through that drapery. Whether in the form of commentary (as in mm. 199 and 201) or actual thematic statement (as in the 1st violin, mm. 205–08), these bits and pieces of melody should be played with spirit. They have only the passing instant in which to make their impact on the listener.

From m. 224, the viola and cello, and eventually the 2nd violin, have the job of racing toward the first stage of the transition to the recapitulation. The actual shift again takes the form of a passage in rapid-fire 16ths, doubled at the octave. Here (mm. 245 ff.) all four voices are involved, and the notes are detached rather than slurred.

The instruments, from high to low, must join each other on the fly. This works only if a steady pace is maintained throughout. Keep the stroke short and on the string, with pressure as light as is consistent with the fortissimo dynamic. As the lower voices join in, the dynamic balance of the four voices should shift to favor the lower edge of the ribbon of octaves. For fullest excitement, a slight drop in the fortissimo level is advisable at the second 8th of m. 247, to permit a rise in loudness as the line swoops up to the reprise at bar 250.

In the recapitulation, the cello has the second theme all to itself, in the brilliant upper register of the instrument. At bars 329 ff., the 1st violin will again have to find fingerings that allow the runs to be played unsmeared. This is the more

130

133

138

155

162

184
185

186

199
205

224

245

247
250

329

necessary since the register of the runs is now even higher and more exposed than was the case in the exposition.

In a marvelous bit of musical business, Tchaikovsky carries the ensemble up, in a fine frenzy of agitated figures, coming to a screaming halt at the edge of an extended pause, mm. 386–87. The ensemble will have to gauge the length of the break for best dramatic effect. A very quiet Andante follows; its slowness produces an augmentation of the rhythmic pattern that originally introduced the second theme. Here, the pattern runs out of steam in a protracted cadence on the dominant.

386

Now, at last, we get the real finish: an Allegro vivace that must be played as fast as clarity permits. Second violin, be on the alert for some rapid string crossing in bars 402 and 406. Viola and cello bear the brunt of the action in their agitated lines in mm. 409–15. Practice slowly and, when full speed becomes possible, don't let pride of ownership trap you into a gruff rendition. The entire span of voices should be heard, with the prominent edge granted to the 1st violin.

402
409

That hardy soul should contrive to play bars 420–23 in seventh position, with the D that starts each measure taken on the A-string. There is obviously no time for the shifting that would be required to play these figures entirely on the E-string. A final caution: the triple-stop chords for the inner voices and—in the four bars before the last chord—in all four parts, must all be taken with short downbows. Play comfortably near the frog, angle the stick so as to parallel the plane of the strings involved, and use a short, rubbing stroke.

420

The cello's four-string chords at the end will clearly need a slight roll, if performance speed permits. In any event, be sure to sound the three bottom notes of the chord, so that the bass is well represented.

PROGRAM

October 12, 1954

Quartet in E-flat major, D. 87 (Op. 125, No. 1)   Franz Schubert
(1797-1828)

    Allegro moderato
    Scherzo: Prestissimo
    Adagio
    Allegro

Quartet No. 1, Op. 7   Bela Bartok
(1881-1945)

    Lento
    Allegretto
    Introduzione: Allegro — Allegro vivace

— Intermission —

Quartet in E minor, "From My Life"   Bedrich Smetana
(1824-1884)

    Allegro vivo appassionato
    Allegro moderato alla Polka
    Largo sostenuto
    Vivace

*

Leonard Sorkin, violin   Irving Ilmer, viola

Abram Loft, violin   George Sopkin, cello

CHAPTER TWENTY

❧ Smetana ❧
Quartet in E minor
("From My Life")

From mid-1874, Smetana began to suffer from deafness, a debility stemming from the illness that was to result in his death ten years later. By the winter of 1876, he had completely lost the hearing in his left ear and was not responding to attempts at treatment. From October through December of that year he wrote the Quartet in E minor.

According to his own account, the work is both programmatic and autobiographical. He did not specify detailed connotations of the successive musical events. The movements, however, relate to his early artistic ambition and point of view; his enthusiasm for dancing in his youth; his nostalgic recall of his first wife, Kateřina Kolářová; and the blighting of his musical aims by his tragic deafness.

Writing to his friend, Josef Srb, vigorous champion of Czech music, Smetana explains that

> I did not intend to write a quartet according to formula and in the forms so familiar to us. As a young student of music theory I worked enough in that vein to understand and master it fully. For me the form of each composition determines itself according to circumstance. Thus, my quartet created its own form.[1]

Allegro vivo appassionato. Despite Smetana's apparent disclaimer, he is in fact adhering to familiar forms, for the first movement is cast in the mold of the

I

SCORE: Bedrich Smetana. n.d. *Quartet in E minor, "From My Life."* London: Eulenburg. Miniature score No. 275.

Left: Page from the program for the concert by The Fine Arts Quartet, Lutkin Hall, Northwestern University, October 12, 1954.

sonata allegro. But it quickly becomes apparent that he uses the quartet as a vehicle for a tone poem, a musical play in four acts. You don't really need the composer's subtitle to tell you this. The players are there to let the elements of the principal theme progress in ways that vividly suggest the stage or, nowadays, the screen. It is easy to think of the music as a setting for dramatic action, intensifying the impact of the plot on the viewer/listener.

The musical elements that will figure prominently in the first "act," and again in a final reminiscence at the end of the quartet, are all announced in the first theme. The ensemble chord that starts the piece has the resonance of the violin's high E to set it off. Later versions of the chord will be in less open placement and tonality; in every case, however, the ensemble must work to give the sound of the chord a vibrant, excited, free-ringing resonance.

Next, there is the sustained-note pedal point. In whichever voice it appears, it must have a live and transparent glow, so that it supports rather than smothers the action of the parts it accompanies.

1   The same applies to the other pedal point: the tremolo, 8th-note oscillation. This appears first in the two violins, but will migrate to other parts as the movement unfolds. The composer could scarcely have used the static equivalent of these tremolos (that is, sustained double stops in the instruments in question), for that would have had a truly deadening and thickening effect. It is clear that he chose the oscillating texture precisely for the shimmering sonority it lends the music. These figures must be played, then, as though they are composed realizations of vibrato tones. In view of the built-in waverings of the line, only a moderate amount of actual vibrato need be added. Nonetheless, the left hand must have life in it, and note changes must be duly projected.

59   As early as m. 59, by the way, you will see that Smetana has other uses in mind for the tremolo figure, for there he applies its rhythm to a winding figure of peculiar melodic beauty, one that helps in the transition to the second theme.

A fourth and very important element in the theme complex is the rhythmic sequence of a short note thrusting toward a long. This pattern is presented in various proportions. In the opening viola statement, there is a gradual rhythmic speedup, with the long note represented successively by a whole-, half-, and quarter-note, and with the short note also contracting from an 8th- to a 16th-note. This produces an irresistible acceleration, especially because it is coupled, in the first phase of the theme, with falling intervals that add the force of gravity to the line.

This brings us to the fifth element: the triplets. Once the melodic line has picked up speed, raced through the low point of its trajectory, and started its uphill swing, its rhythm contracts still further, from duple 8th-notes into triplets. Linked with a fresh burst of tightly paced, short-long figures, the triplets bring us to a new chordal shout. And this triggers the restatement of the theme in a new harmonic context. The triplets themselves will continue to play an important and very evident role as the Allegro progresses.

First things first, however; let's have a look at the actual state of affairs as the quartet opens. In my long years as a quartet 2nd violinist, I enjoyed the role for the inside view it gives of the chamber work, and for the way it collaborates with each of the other voices in the ensemble. There were times, though, when I wished I had stayed with the viola, the instrument I played for a decade before reverting to the violin. The opening of the Smetana E minor invariably made me nostalgic.

What a shot for the violist, starting the piece with that bold, roistering melody! 4
On the other hand, what better choice could the composer have made? There is a
pungent, virile force in the viola sound, when played for full output, that exactly
suits the peremptory, seething energy of this theme. The melody has a theatricality
that is matched only by the way the composer introduces it. It would be one thing
to leap immediately into the melody on the heels of that first, chordal whoop from
all hands. But to follow that outburst with a pianissimo, tremolo pedal point for
four measures, during which the violist must keep the boilers stoked before
launching into the theme—that's dramatic writing.

I don't suggest method acting as a prerequisite for playing a quartet.
Nevertheless, the violist has to enter the frame of mind that makes it possible to
tear (not rip!) into this tune. You can't take a laid-back attitude, either physically or
mentally, and still give this melody the impetus it demands. I have already pointed
out the composed acceleration in this passage. It's up to the violist to give this
speedup a supplementary forward push, with a willing assist from the violins.

A compensating pullback in tempo takes place in the viola's 8th-notes in bar 16
16. It should not be so abrupt or noticeable as to suggest the sudden aging of the
ensemble, only enough to permit a solid entry into the fresh chordal impact on the
downbeat of m. 17. Whatever adjustment remains necessary to settle back to tempo 17
can be effected by the length of the rest in bar 17 and by the pacing of the violins'
8th-notes in the second half of that measure. I would not find it amiss if a very
slightly faster tempo than that of the opening is now in force, to reflect the
increased excitement level of the second statement of the theme.

The idea of quickening actually dissolves the end of this restatement, carrying
it more rapidly into the contracted rhythms and, from there, into an extended surge
of triplets. In bars 31–36, in fact, the triplets hold the solo role. All this activity 31
carries us into a passage that is both an apotheosis of the theme (mm. 37 ff.) and the
prelude to the second area of the exposition.

As in the traditional sonata allegro, there is a bridge passage (47 ff.) to effect 47
the transition; here it has aspects of an operatic/cinematic shift of scene, carried out
in full view of the audience. The characters in this musical drama seem to move
past and around each other to take up their places for a new phase of the action.
There are the ominous remnants of the triplets in the low voices in bars 47–48; and
the viola's threat of resuming the theme in mm. 57–58 and 63–66. The violins 57, 63
convert the landing at m. 47 into a brief version of the pedal point. And they
descend from that platform into a quiet valley of sound, passing en route through
the dolce transformation of the tremolo (see mm. 59–62). 59

In a passage like this, the ensemble have to act in concert with one another (no
pun intended); with such assertive parts, though, each player must be self-
motivated. This is even more true in the second theme. The 1st violin part is 71
marked *espressivo*, but will draw only part of the listener's attention. Although viola
and cello offer rhythmic background, they have melodic figures that set the two
voices off from one another; and the 2nd violin gives support to the 1st, but with a
musical personality of its own.

The three upper parts coincide rhythmically in bars 76 and 80. Mostly, though, 76
the listener has to be alert to the contrary rhythms and shifting lineup of the
instruments. This passage has a richness of texture much greater than would be
imagined from the look of the printed page.

The 2nd violin, from mm. 71 through 90, surges from a subordinate role into 71 what seems like prominent melody. In these same measures, the viola will feel less in the spotlight, especially when playing the long stretch of sequential rhythmic patterns. Still, within the repetitions, changes of pitch emerge to mark the harmonic progression; also, wider flares in the line lead the way to a sudden and brief

82 resumption of the instrument's early, solo function (mm. 82–84).

I doubt that the cello can resist the flow of events, though the bass line is the least melodic of the four parts here. The cello shares, for example, in the swells and

80 declines of the other parts; and in m. 80 the placement of the dynamic marks is adjusted to suit the specific shape of the instrument's rhythmic line.

The thematic 8th-note element, now carrying an ornamentation of the

73 underlying melodic thread of the current passage, surfaces in mm. 73 and 78 in the

85 1st violin, and in the violin duet in bars 85–86. At bar 91 it becomes the solo line, to be passed in dreamlike conversation among the three upper voices. The players have to practice their emotional flexibility here; nothing short of physical response

81 will sustain the rapid transitions from the viola's nostalgic outburst in mm. 81–82, to the resumed quietness at bar 83, the momentary surge a few measures later, the

91 distant pianissimo at m. 91, and the sudden shift to forte and fortissimo soon after. This is the kind of passage where your toes tense up inside your shoes and grab at the floor as the excitement of the music builds.

The last flare-up in the exposition rests partly on the 2nd violin; the 8th-note

101 figures in that line from m. 101 on are only arpeggiated expressions of a series of double stops. Even so, the vigor of the constant oscillation and string crossings make this voice the prime mover in the ensemble action. The score is deceptive here, for the part in question, alone among the four voices, lacks swell or accent marks. Nonetheless, the line is perhaps the most expressive in the bunch at this point, and must be played accordingly.

Some of the same advice goes for the cello part here. Despite the sequential rhythm in successive measures, there are harmonically significant note changes in the figure, so the line should be played for its melodic, as much as for its support, aspect.

111 In the transition (mm. 111–18) to the development, the cello leads by sounding a rhythmic fragment—short-long, short-long—that has figured in the bass line since the start of the second theme. The rhythm probably traces back to the viola's declamation at the movement's opening. Although the cello line is marked pianissimo, as against the piano of the three upper parts, I urge the player to shape the line with the dramatic intensity it deserves, for it is indeed the solo of the

115 moment. Take special advantage of the *più piano* in bar 115; the swell and diminuendo over both cello exclamations there demand some spread in time. This will be reflected in the response of the upper voices and in the cello's own

117 continuation, in low register, in m. 117. The *più piano* event, in effect, foretells the printed *rallentando* that follows.

Smetana struck musical pay dirt when he fashioned his urgent opening theme. He mines its rhythms, its characteristic falling intervals, its mounting pressures at almost every point in his exposition. In writing his development, he did not settle for some academic exercise. Instead, he boldly continues to exploit the dramatic potential of his initial musical idea. The development section is a storm scene in which elements of the first theme race past as though whipped by gale winds. Further, with the timing of the skilled playwright, Smetana holds the scene to just the right length. He lashes the excitement until he reaches the climax at the

fortissimo at m. 163, then drops quickly to the change of key and the reprise. The   163
entire section is just half the length of the exposition. Significantly, there are no
repeats in this movement; they would be impossible, for Smetana has built a
continuous musical narrative, with no U-turns.

One roadmap of this movement that I have seen says that the development
deals only with the first theme, and the recapitulation, only with the second. This is
true, but I think the situation is even more unusual than that: development and
recapitulation are telescoped into each other. The first theme is pursued so
exhaustively in the development that there is no possible room for restatement of
the idea; it is for this reason that Smetana falls directly into the second theme to
start the recapitulation. Further, the turbulence of the development calls for relief,
and this too is provided by turning at once to the quiet, second subject.

Some idea about tempo management is essential to the successful performance
of the development section. Tempo may be officially restored at m. 119, but we are   119
still involved in a transitional phase until the last 8th-note of m. 122 and the   122
entrance of the 1st violin. There is then a natural push forward to bar 129. The surge   129
would continue farther, but the cello entrance starts the process anew, even if at a
higher harmonic level.

With the return of the solo to the 1st violin at the end of m. 134, things   134
definitely pick up. The violin's threefold, compressed shouts in mm. 135, 137, and
139 build an irreversible force. Matters are whipped along by the inner voices'
triplets. From m. 139 to the *sforzando fortissimo* of m. 143, the tempest must howl.   139
And from there, in turn, a truly long journey begins, extending without hindrance
to m. 157. A constant stream of triplets, carried by one voice or another,   157
accompanies and incites the frenzy of short-long figures in neighboring parts. The
sustained pedal-point element, now a kind of bellowing in the storm, is heard for a
time, until it gets swept away by the rush of quicker rhythms.

The most heroic role is reserved for the viola, which lashes about, back and
forth across the fingerboard, in mm. 151–56. Harmonically, this passage is   151
composed of three successive pairs of measures; all must be swept together. Take
only the slightest of breaths to mark the divisions; the punctuation will barely be
discernible in the hubbub, anyway.

The speed should be at least as great in the next six bars, but the apparent pace
may seem to broaden somewhat, since each bar is repeated identically before the
next pair of measures takes over. Impose a very slight broadening in the course of
bar 162, in order to land with proper emphasis on the gigantic F minor chord of   162
m. 163. That downbeat itself needs some breathing room, which is provided by a   163
slight spreading in the low-voice triplets at the start of the measure. There follows a
two-bar plunge, straight down to m. 165 and the composed restoration of calm that
takes place over the next four bars.

Still harking back to its original role, the viola now tries to sound the call for
continued agitation. It succumbs, however, to the more peaceful mood of the other
voices and is carried into the reprise.

The second theme is not all sweetness and light here, any more than it was in
the exposition. There is, for one thing, the rumble of viola reminiscence in mm.
189–91. Then too, the *tranquillo* line of 8ths of the three upper voices in bars 199–204   189, 199
turns loud, muscular, and agitated in the next measures, urging the broader violin
melody to lead the way to a fairly blustering climax. In short, don't relax entirely in
this second theme area. It is calm only by comparison with the wilder parts of the
movement.

217   The transition (mm. 217 ff.) to the coda promises a more lasting peace, despite the muttering in the cello part (again, the solo belongs to both the upper and lower edges of the ensemble). The coda itself, however, decides matters by siding with the predominant tone of the movement. Viola and 1st violin echo each other in the
242   characteristic thematic motive (mm. 242 ff.)
251   The last word, though, belongs to the cello. From bar 251, that instrument has combined the theme rhythm and the sustained pedal point. A similar merger is implied by the pairing of the inner voices' tremolo 8ths and the violin's pizzicati in
259   mm. 259–60. The final distillation is manifest in the cello's pizzicati in the last two bars. Though now at triple-piano level, the cello's exit remark, the closing short-long, must be given an inflection and resonance that distantly recalls the agitation of the original viola statement.

II   ***Allegro moderato a la Polka.*** I have a love-hate attitude toward this movement. It is an extremely effective piece if played well. Still, I was always a bit apprehensive when we had to play this Allegro, because of the great opportunity it gives the ensemble to play out of tune. More of that, later on.

First, a few other cautions are in order. Watch out for the sforzando chords on
1   the second quarter-beat of mm. 1 and 5; these and corresponding chords later in the movement can very easily sound strangled. Be sure to relieve bow pressure and speed immediately after the attack, so that the resonance can sail out freely.

These chords are immediately followed by a series of 16th-note figures in octaves. There are also figures composed of a 16th couplet followed by an 8th-note, both in separate and slurred groupings, presented either in single voice, or by all four in unison and octave. Slow, quiet, careful practice is strongly indicated, for a general malaise of intonation can already spoil the effect of this part of the movement—the easy part!

3   Please exercise restraint in landing on the sforzando 8th-note at the end of m. 3 (and in all such spots later on in the movement). There are four of you leaping down to the B♭, whereas only the viola and cello go on to play the low C on the downbeat. Listen for good sound and for proper relationship between the up- and downbeat 8ths.

39   The viola theme in mm. 39 ff., "like a trumpet," should have an outline as clean as though played on a valved instrument. Smetana instructs that the melody be played entirely on the C-string. I shall assume that the player's instrument is small enough, hand large enough, and agility great enough to present the tune without smearing. The maneuver is: move to fifth position on the second quarter of bar 39; play the C and F in the next three beats with second and fourth fingers,
41   respectively; and shift to third position on the second quarter of m. 41, with the C played by the extended fourth finger. A similar approach should see the 2nd violin through its presentation of the theme immediately after. The G in the fifth position (mm. 48–49) can be managed with third finger. For suitable projection, both the viola and violin should play as close to the bridge as acceptable sonority permits.

61   The 1st violin, in *its* turn with the theme, can extend back from the F in bar 61 to play the D with the third finger, and shift to third position only on the second quarter-beat. You will no doubt want to make refined shifts from the F to the C♯ in
63   bars 63 and 65. Please do avoid a mucilaginous voyage from the F to the high G in
67   bar 67! Slow the bow stroke immediately upon leaving the F (to parenthesize the shift), press lightly with the sliding finger and land on the G with the third finger. You can then play the high B♭ with the extended fourth finger, and make your next

shift (either to fifth or fourth position) on the downbeat of bar 69.   69

    In mm. 75–78, all necessary shifting by any of the four instruments should take   75
place only after an 8th-note, never after a 16th couplet. Whichever instrument has
the cross-string, 16th-note quadruplets from m. 39 to m. 66: play them melodically,   39
balancing between moving line and drone, and marking harmonic changes
tastefully.

    In measure 78, by the way, Smetana makes life unnecessarily difficult for the   78
2nd violin by asking for a simultaneous B♭ and C (on the G- and A-strings,
respectively). The solution is for the 2nd to trade the C for the 1st violin's B♭.

    Now, for the troublesome trio section: let's consider the cello part first. In
mm. 85–136, make due allowance for the dynamic gradations and accentuations   85
that are indicated. Also, provide whatever shadings of pace that melodic
considerations may dictate. In general, the second and third 8th-notes in each
measure will stand in the background, as though an echoing runoff from the
downbeat.

    During this same section, the viola part cooperates with the cello in providing
the response to the downbeat pulse. The 16th-note couplet on the third pulse of the
measure will get the slightest of stresses. In effect, the viola couplet flows into the
cello's upbeat couplet. You want to create some ambiguity. The downbeat 8th is
theoretically the strong beat of the measure; but Smetana has marked the downbeat
with a dot, indicating a lift. That shifts the emphasis back onto the cello's upbeat
16ths.

    All this creates an irresistible, swaying sensation. If anything is needed to
complete the effect, it is forthcoming from the violins' dotted-quarter wheeze (sigh,
exhalation, hum?) after the first 8th-rest of each measure.

    This trio is the section that brought out all my insecurities in rehearsal. The key
of D♭ is not the easiest for intonation, especially when four are playing together,
with double stops to boot. I urge the ensemble to give some solid practice to these
measures, so that the performance can be relaxed, assured, and enjoyable.

    You might, all four, try playing—slowly and quietly—only the chordal
groupings that line up on the second 8th-note of each measure, omitting all else.
When you have combed and fine-tuned the succession of chords into reliability, add
the intervening notes, dynamics, and performance tempo.

    Although there is no indication of a change of speed at m. 85 in the score, there   85
is a *Meno mosso* at the corresponding passage, mm. 195 ff., later in the movement.   195
Besides, it seems impossible to charge ahead in the music of the D♭ section at the
original, polka tempo. Choose an appropriate *meno*, then, at m. 85; you will have to
pace the upbeat 16th-note couplet in m. 84 so that it makes a quick transition to the
new speed.

    Intonation problems increase in mm. 118 ff., when the 1st violin starts adding a   118
fourth 8th-note to its motion, so pay some special attention to this passage.

    If you have occasion to read the book, *Smetana*, by Brian Large, be advised
about an error therein. Large translates from Smetana's letter to Srb (cited above), as
follows: "the third movement (the one which, in the opinion of the gentlemen who
play this Quartet, is unperformable)..."[2] Not so! What Smetana actually wrote was:

> The middle section: *Meno vivo*, in D♭ [that is, precisely the trio section of
> the *second* movement, discussed above], is the part of this quartet that
> performers claim is absolutely unplayable. A purity of intonation is

ostensibly unattainable. I am recalling in sound here my memories of the aristocratic circles in which I spent many years.[3]

This last is an ostensibly innocent comment about his earlier years, when he saw service as a dance pianist. It is intriguing that he submitted for Srb's evaluation an easier, alternative version of the parts for the upper three instruments in this section. Smetana himself expressed preference for the original and difficult version, and it is apparently that which we conquer in our performances today. The trick, of course, is to make it appear not only predictable, but effortless, right up to the

136 dreamy exit chord in m. 136. Incidentally, the "long pause" printed there refers to the length of the fermata, and does not demand any prolonged silence after the chord has died away.

Don't let down your guard in the *Più allegro* that follows. The cross-string figures of the 1st violin need to be carefully matched with the accompanying chords in the lower voices.

153 There is nothing new to tell about the return proper (mm. 153 ff.). In the final chord of the section, bar 192, the 2nd violin will again have to trade the top C for

230 the 1st violin's B♭. Make the same switch for the chord in m. 230, by the way.

195 The intonation problems in the *Meno mosso* (m. 195) will have been partially settled by the rehearsal of the earlier counterpart. In any event, the transition to

209 more active motion in all four parts—it starts in bar 209 and is fully effective by m. 215—eases the situation.

231 Viola and 2nd violin, between them, will control the nostalgia of mm. 231–34. In the closing *Più mosso*, the two violins are asked to play their octaves "with force." The sound will benefit, however, if the balance allots more of the force to the 2nd violin. At the very end, the ensemble's two-16ths-and-8th figure can be broadened slightly to create an air of finality.

III ***Largo sostenuto.*** The cello cadenza that opens the movement can be thought
2 of as making a slight acceleration, extending from the F in m. 2 to the D♭ in bar 5. Linger a bit, not only on the quarter-note F and D♭ in mm. 2 and 3, but also (very little) on the first B♭ in m. 4. Whatever speedup you have made in the first four bars
5 must be countered by a deceleration in mm. 5–6.

A restrained, rather simple approach will serve the theme better than a sentimentalized treatment. Don't neglect the contribution made by the chromatic
13 and harmonic motions in the inner voices. The heat can be turned up in mm. 13–14, especially in view of the flaming E♭ tonality that is to prevail in the next two bars.
17 Cooler sound returns with the piano in m. 17.

It is then the 1st violin's turn for a cadenza. The composer spells the phrasing
18 out for you: the swell marks denote the second half of m. 18 as one unit. The sequential rhythm pattern of the two halves of the next measure makes that the next unit, though you can impose a bit of acceleration within the measure. Mm.
20 20–22 constitute one arch of melody, moving forward to the peak in the high F♭, then easing its way down to the B♭–B♮ ending.

23 In the theme restatement (mm. 23–26), attention is divided between the 1st violin solo and the now more elaborate ornamentation of the inner voices. Moderate tempo and temperature should prevail. On the other hand, the blood will course more hotly in the next measures, to carry you to the first exultant shout—the
30 B♭s in mm. 30–31.

That there are three such shouts, with identical aftermaths following each, is potentially embarrassing. You are in danger of sounding like a troupe of ham actors. Be guided by Smetana's markings: the high B♭ in m. 31 and the octave E♭ in bar 35 each are given only a sforzando, albeit in a fortissimo context. It is only the octave F in m. 39 that is granted a fortissimo of its very own. Note, too, that a *Più mosso* appears in bar 32. I would regard this as an instruction to swirl things along until you get to the peak in bar 39, then steady yourself slightly on the way down to the stentorian Fs in bar 41.

The 2nd violin will allow a suitable pause, to let the dust settle, before taking the pianissimo upbeat into m. 42. The ensemble may also find a slightly slower tempo to be appropriate for mm. 42–45, by way of transition to the E♭ interlude. Here the focus is not only on the new (though subject-related) theme in the 1st violin, but in the pizzicato arpeggiations in the cello part.

The veering away from the E♭ tonality, starting in the second half of m. 50, seems willful to the ear. The 1st violin must fit the mood, as though pulling the ensemble into new harmonic paths. The three lower voices give some harmonic advice of their own in mm. 55–57, under the sustained tones of the solo. The 2nd violin should underscore this by leading appropriate pauses in these bars. The rest on the first half of m. 57, in particular, needs some extra time; so also, the figure in the second half of that bar can be spread. This will give the 1st violin a chance to start the upward swirl of mm. 58–59 with proper deliberation.

The chords in mm. 60–63, many of them containing eleven tones, run the risk of sounding very chunky. Rehearse the ensemble bowing style (slow, rubbing, not over-pressed) so that the passage is resonant, not noisy.

The composer writes *espressivo* in the cello part in bar 66. This is too late. The line begins two measures earlier, in the 2nd violin. Even though in pianissimo, that instrument—and the viola in the next bar—must prepare the way. It is, in fact, exclusively a two-part conversation until the cello upstages everyone.

The cello has a noble time with the theme in mm. 68 ff. On the other hand, I don't think a 2nd violinist could ask for a better part than is provided in these same bars. Tranquil it may be, but that won't prevent you from responding sympathetically to the cello theme (and even stealing the scene here and there!). If you do your job right, the flutterings of the 1st violin will seem to be inspired directly by the inflections and emphases in your line. The entire passage from m. 68 to m. 83, in fact, is that most intriguing ensemble phenomenon, wherein every instrument is at once soloist and accompanist. The music must be rehearsed—and heard—so that the fabric, and not any one thread, of the musical cloth is the center of attention.

The same holds true for the simpler texture of the coda. There the 1st violin, despite the beautiful tracery of the part, plays second fiddle to the viola, the 2nd violin, and—just before the cadential measures—the cello. But most of all it is the interplay between voices that sustains our interest.

Vivace. This movement has a strange principal theme. The triplet fanfare appears at the opening, at strategic points during the course of the Vivace, and at its end. It seems to act, however, as a musical pointer to call our attention to other signal events in the movement, rather than to itself. A word about the playing of the first, fortissimo fanfare: the emphasis belongs on the downbeat of m. 1, m. 4, the downbeat of m. 5, and m. 8. The accented triplets are set back in prominence, coming toward the foreground in mm. 3 and 7.

Our first real focus is on the 16th-note theme that starts in m. 9 and is handed around from viola, to 2nd, to 1st violin. This theme, with its vigorous zigzagging between adjacent strings, can give pause even to the most stalwart of players. But consider the way the line is written. The melodic streamer begins with a pair of solid double stops. After that, the 16th couplets represent double stops that are spelled out melodically. When the "horizontal" double stop crosses strings, the slightest deflection in the angle of the bow will suffice to present the hair to each of the notes in turn. With such short notes in rapid tempo, it is understood that the bowstroke will be effected by hand, not arm motion.

Above all, don't rush! Nerves or exhilaration, or both, can easily push ahead in the third and fourth measures of your statement. That means your successor will have Hobson's choice: either to seem pedantic by hauling back on the tempo, or to take your speed and run with it. With three theme statements in sequence, the

23 ensemble might build up a terrific head of steam by the time it arrives at bar 23. Then you will all have to dig in your heels as you careen down the two-bar scale. Rehearse the passage until it has spirit, not frenzy.

25 Be sure to observe the piano level of mm. 25–32. Use a gentle spiccato and play well down into the lower half of the bow, to assure that the tempo will be on the held side. Also, use enough imaginative rubato to temper the repetitive rhythmic

35 patterns in the passage. The three sforzandi in measures 35–36 should be broad, not pointed in attack. You want to suggest that two long notes are moving into and through the triplet that announces the second theme.

The score assigns a *scherzoso* mark only to the two violins. That won't do, for the lower voices are part and parcel of the effect. A soggy rendition of the cello line will hang on the upper lines like an albatross. And the viola, even before it takes

41 over a more active part in m. 41, provides indispensable zing with its strummed pizzicati. Assuming that enough steam is ascending from the lower regions, the 2nd violin can sail into the 16th-note rhythms with gusto. Impetus builds in the four

37 quadruplets of mm. 37–38, bubbles over in the compression of the couplets in bar 39, and dances through the detached notes in m. 40. Above all this, the 1st violin can't help but perform some Bohemian equivalent of a Highland fling.

The point is that the whole second theme area, from m. 37 to 72, is for quartet players who are having a whale of a good time. This doesn't involve grossly overt smiling or body English. Just make music of such verve and wit that all in attendance believe their chairs ready to whisk them down the aisles of the hall.

The violist will need a very limber left hand for the convoluted figures in mm.

49 49–72. Much of the passage can be managed in half position. Bars 63–64, however, must have been written for a contortionist. If you have a large hand and a small viola, you might try the following: a big stretch from first-finger C♯ to third-finger F♯, and the equally strenuous extension of the fourth finger to reach the E on the G-string. My own vote is to split the 16th-note quadruplets in these measures into slurred couplets, and jump across the G-string to snatch the E on the D-string. The

69 2nd violin passage in mm. 69–72 is fortunately a bit less athletic.

73 The 16-note couplet theme returns for an extended run in mm. 73–124, and

147 will appear again in the shorter passage, mm. 147–60. There is no new technical difficulty here. The length of the passages, though, brings a musical danger with it. The ensemble must arrive at a relaxed and nonchalant way of playing these measures. Concentrate on realizing the dynamic shadings of the lines. More than enough agitation is built into the writing itself. If the four of you settle in for dogged survival here, you run the risk of sounding like an outsize, treadle-

operated, musical sewing machine. Go easy, too, on the sforzando couplets (as on the downbeat of m. 87), or on the massed chords in mm. 97–98 and the like. 87, 97

The *Più mosso* of mm. 195 ff. is not just fast. Here you want to be a bit over the edge of frenzy. When you reach the four repeated measures, 215–18, the ensemble must be playing in a manner to suggest accurate, precisely synchronized hysteria. Run straight ahead into the sforzando fortissimo chord on the downbeat of bar 219. If possible, the 1st violin should play the high E as a harmonic, the better to prolong the resonance of the chord in the ensuing silence. 195
215
219

Stretch the grand pause a bit, to heighten the suspense of the audience. The score does not tell you how loud to play the sforzando attack in the three lower voices at the *Meno presto*. It should be loud enough to have shock value, dropping immediately to pianissimo. The tremolo in the inner voices needs nervous rapidity in the right hand, and enough vibrato in the left to intensify the sound.

The high, ringing, harmonic E in the 1st violin is foreshadowed, by Smetana's own account,[4] in the long tone of the viola theme, back at the start of the quartet. The composer emphasizes this connection by repeating that theme at various levels in the *Meno presto*, and always with a sustained tone to reflect the high E. That resonance, as is now well known, was the persistent tone that plagued him in the early stage of his deafness. 224

Several of the sustained tones are marked by a strong attack in the accompanying parts. Those insets should be of savage intensity.

The remaining lines of the quartet are given over to reminiscences of the second theme of the first movement, alternating—then merging—with the first theme of the finale. The dramatic approach demanded by this close is clearly implicit in the writing. If you need any coaching here, a quick visit to the nearest movie, live theater, or opera house will do the trick. As I said at the outset, this quartet is drama in the guise of chamber music.

Friends of Chamber Music of Miami
Presents
The Fine Arts Quartet

Leonard Sorkin, *Violin*   Bernard Zaslav, *Viola*
Abram Loft, *Violin*   George Sopkin, *Cello*

with

Seymour Bernstein

Pianist

PROGRAM

MENDELSSOHN
(1809-1847)

QUARTET IN F MINOR, OPUS 80
> Allegro vivace assai
> Allegro assai
> Adagio
> Allegro molto

FAURE
(1845-1924)

QUARTET IN C MINOR FOR VIOLIN, VIOLA, CELLO AND PIANO OPUS 15, No. 1
> Allegro molto moderato
> Scherzo-allegro vivo
> Adagio
> Allegro molto

INTERMISSION

SCHUMANN
(1810-1856)

QUINTET IN E FLAT MAJOR, FOR PIANO AND STRING QUARTET OPUS 44
> Allegro brilliante
> Un poco largamente
> Molto vivace
> Allegro, ma non troppo

GUSMAN PHILHARMONIC HALL
174 E. Flagler Street, Miami, Florida
Thursday Evening, February 21, 1974
8:30 o'clock

Management: Melvin Kaplan Inc.
85 Riverside Drive, New York, N. Y. 10024

The Fine Arts Quartet: Artists-in-residence at the University of Wisconsin, Milwaukee

RECORDINGS: Everest
Vox
Columbia
Decca

CHAPTER TWENTY-ONE

❧ Fauré ❧
Piano Quartet No. 1 in C minor,
Op. 15

The young Gabriel Fauré was appointed organist at the church of Saint-Sauveur, in Rennes, Brittany, in 1866. He was twenty-one years of age and had graduated the year before from the École Niedermeyer in Paris. A biographer describes what happened in Rennes in 1870:

> The young organist of the Saint-Sauveur having left a dance at dawn and not having had the time to return home to change his clothes, conducted the first morning mass in evening dress, wearing brightly polished shoes and a white tie... putting an end to his career as a provincial organist.[1]

Fauré returned to Paris and to a long career as organist, teacher, musical administrator, music critic, director of the Conservatoire (both these last, late in life)—and of central importance to him, composer.

He wrote the C minor piano quartet in 1876–79, right after the first violin sonata. Before these two works, Fauré had written the first twenty-one of his many songs, a few sacred and secular vocal works, his orchestral suite, Op. 20, and several piano pieces. The importance of the piano in the C minor quartet is evident; the part offers a florid, yet crystalline, setting for the ensemble, appears very often in solo role, and combines both functions in many of its passages. Conversely, the strings, though treated with due regard for their individual timbres, are frequently massed to provide a unison, quasi-orchestral background or response to the piano voice.

SCORE: Gabriel Fauré. 1979. *First Piano Quartet, Op. 15*. Ed. Robert Orledge. London: Eulenburg. Miniature score No. 1403.

Left: Program for the concert of The Fine Arts Quartet, with Seymour Bernstein, piano, Miami, February 21, 1974.

I
3

Allegro molto moderato. The piano's offbeat 8th-notes should collaborate with the string parts in moving the opening phrase, first to the G of the third measure, then to the accented D of m. 4. By this, I mean that the offbeats should not deliver a pedantic reminder about the tempo that has been set on the metronome, but rather should accede flexibly to the drive of the melodic voices. The fuller writing for the piano in the succeeding measures needs absolutely unobtrusive playing, to match

12

the pianissimo of the upper lines. In m. 12, the forte applies more to the strings than to the keyboard, for the latter is still en route upward to the peak of its line at the

18

fortissimo to come. At m. 18, the rolling sextuplets of the piano part ornament its doubling of the viola line. The more distinctive contribution is in the bass; doubled at the octave, it should act in concert with the lower strings to support, not cover, the theme in the violin.

Fauré, a keyboard player himself, asks much of the instrument in this movement: technical finesse in playing the intricate traceries written for it, coupled with restraint in carrying out the background role that is often its assignment here. Yet at a moment's notice the pianist has to throw off reticence and step into the

14
33, 22

spotlight in bravura or lyric fashion. Note the passage at m. 14 ff. and the forte sweeps at mm. 33 and 36, or the brief responses to the strings, as in mm. 22 and 24. Whether in or out of the spotlight, the piano often has many notes to the measure. Sometimes they ripple easily between the hands or lend themselves to crossing of hands; at others, very deft leaps are required. Whether the rapid passages involve arpeggiations or scalewise runs, it is important that the traceries be cleanly played, and without the blurring effect of excessive or misplaced pedalling.

The melodic structure in this movement makes great use of rhythmic

62

sequence. See, for example, in the close of the exposition, mm. 62–65. Applying the elements of the opening theme, itself a study in sequences, these bars repeat rhythmic figures without embarrassment. Herein lies a performers' stumbling block. If the players thump contentedly away on the repetitions, the four measures turn pedestrian and seem longer than they are. The second measure should be even quieter than the pianissimo of the first, and the crescendo should bring with it a slight freshening of tempo, carrying the line into the forte crest of the phrase in the fifth measure. Similar tactics should be applied at many points in the movement.

The overall tempo should not be too slow. At its start, the movement is rather grand, and the piano writing, moving from the opening 8ths to the 16th-note textures of the ensuing bars, lends a salutary bubble to the proceedings. The air of activity, though, will not suffice. The ensemble has to be willing to swing with the musical context.

The instructions of Fauré (or his editor) are not always helpful to the

38

performer. At the second theme (mm. 38 ff.), for example, each of the strings—viola, violin, and cello, in that order—is told to play both *espressivo* and *très également*. I don't know what to make of this. Coupled with the alternating-8th-note accompaniment in the piano, the "evenness" becomes quite disconcerting by the time the cello makes its entry. Did the composer actually intend to create background music for a tearoom? I hope the ensemble will bend the instruction enough to avoid this impression.

The exposition, development, and recapitulation sections in this movement are of equal length (discounting the coda). Allowing for the harmonic excursions that are expected in the development, Fauré here essentially passes his already stated musical ideas in review. He saves his thunderbolt for the fortissimo-cum-tremolo

passage (mm. 153–58) that leads at last to the return of the first theme in the tonic. I   153
have given a lackluster idea of the proceedings, hoping that the ensemble will get
the point. You must take advantage of every opportunity the composer gives you.
At m. 72, for example—the start of the development—the piano part introduces   72
broad triplet rhythms as accompaniment to, and part of, the first theme. All in the
ensemble must play the passage as though the triplet element has revealed a
surprisingly new aspect of the already familiar tune. When the writing permits
brief outbursts of passion (mm. 95 and 125), rise to the occasion. Consider the   95
development to be a series of abstract musical images, shadowed and lit by the
passing harmonies. Play so that listeners will respond with perceptions of their
own. You don't want the audience to sigh with relief at the arrival of the return.

The Federation of the Friends of Fauré will be after my scalp, for I seem to
have given a damning picture of this movement. That is not my intent. I enjoy
playing this quartet, and audiences also seem to like the piece. It has its own
strength, which is gentler and intellectually less rigorous than that of a Beethoven
or Brahms, and it must be performed on its own terms. The coda of the movement
phrases all this better than I can: sober, calm, self-assured, and without pretense.

Scherzo: Allegro vivo. The prevailingly shaded atmosphere of the first   II
movement demands a chaser. Fauré provides the follow-up in fine style in this
Scherzo. If, moreover, he places his own instrument in a rather subordinated role in
the opening Allegro, such is not the case here. In roughly half the movement, the
piano part is predominant; for the rest, its traceries provide a sparkling background
to the string lines. With the strings muted in the middle, B♭ section, the piano line
there offers a bright edge to the sound even when it provides quiet accompaniment.

The idea of starting the movement with the strings' harmonic, pizzicato   1
accompaniment is a clever stroke. Two three-bar units, harmonically
complementing each other, make up a rhythmic ostinato that manifests itself in
various guises through much of the movement. Combined with the fast tempo and
the pianissimo level (the hushed dynamic is very important), this ostinato makes
for a wonderfully racy, forward-leaning feeling, especially since each three-measure
phrase unit peaks and drops in its last bar. A bit of an accent on the downbeat of
m. 3 and a lesser stress on the downbeat of m. 6 in each six-bar unit will probably   3
happen automatically, helping the direction of the line. These points of emphasis in
the string parts make an effective counterfoil to the piano melody as well.

The ploy of moving to 2/4 meter (m. 19) tightens the pace without increasing   19
the tempo. Alternating the two meters, or overlaying them one above the other, as
necessary, sustains the breathless energy of the music without whipping it into a
frenzy. The players will have to cultivate a peculiar blend of intensity and
relaxation as they run through this musical landscape. Rehearse for lightness,
clarity, synchronization. Note that, in the cadence of this section, the fortissimo
impact is on the high-register chord, two bars before the change of key; the
sustained unison in the final measure must not be pounded. The same holds true
for the cadence at the movement's end.

If the tempo is fleet enough in the middle section (mm. 222 ff.), you will   222
experience uncanny feeling of weightlessness. The accompaniment, now in the
piano, is again heard first, and is once more cast in a three-bar grouping. The piano
part contracts to two-measure units to support the four-bar phrases of the string
solos, phrases that float as though on air. The zephyrlike sensation is especially
strong when triplet streamers are passed up through the trio of strings.

263   When the piano has the theme, as at m. 263, there is an accent on the second beat in the second and fourth measures of the phrase. The same should apply in the string version, even though the use of swell marks there only suggests the effect.

250 (Note, however, that there is a sforzando on the second beat of m. 250.) The marks are somewhat ambiguous and inconsistent in this section, but the ensemble can make the necessary assumptions. Be sure to capture, also, the shadowed nuance of

295 such passages as m. 295 to m. 327. In general, the mixture of bright and dark in this entire trio section is something special in the chamber literature.

372   The pianist's roller-coaster run (mm. 372 ff.) to the return is bravura in a saucily nonchalant manner. This alone, if carried off with appropriate wit, is worth the price of admission.

III   *Adagio.* Fauré should have been a chef. To serve up musical dishes of such contrasting flavors in one composition! The Scherzo, full of sparkle and high spirits, is now followed by a movement of unrelieved darkness. I know there is a contrast section (starting at m. 27) that extends through almost half the Adagio. To be sure, that contrast episode has a consoling, rocking accompaniment, provided by the piano both to the strings and to its own turn with the melody. But the music sheds only a subdued, moonlit kind of glow. Even so, this middle section of the movement demands a slightly more moving tempo than the surrounding portions. Some of this mobility will come from the triplet-duplet sequence of rhythm in the piano; a faster beat will probably be found necessary as well.

    The open and close of the movement call for a true Adagio, slow enough to accommodate the funereal tone of the music. Twice the opening strain rises from an initial piano to a forte, only to drop back into a stifled pianissimo, and eventually into the quietness of the transition to the middle section. In this opening, the piano moves in broad, tolling rhythm. To match this mood in their sustained notes, the strings need physical control, even to the extent of breathing very slowly, in order to keep their sustained tones free of nervous flutter.

64   For the pianist, special difficulty is more likely to attach to the constant stream of 32nds Fauré dictates for the return section (mm. 64 ff). Except for three forte moments, everything is cast in piano, pianissimo, dolce, and dolcissimo, with an occasional, cautionary *sempre* as well. Holding the dynamic level down, while still producing a singing tone in the wave of 32nds and highlighting those notes that form part of the overall melody—not easy.

    A word about the final cadence in this movement: the strings are in triple piano, and the viola has a three-string chord to play. Owing to the quiet level, that chord will have to be rolled, though as neatly and economically as possible. The ensemble will have to be guided by that roll in synchronizing the last two notes.

IV   *Allegro molto.* After the closed in, hothouse atmosphere of the Adagio, the finale gives room to breathe; that is, if you can breathe quickly. The piano triplets, the dotted rhythms in the strings, the frequent passing of the line back and forth between the instruments, all contribute to the feeling of racing, of flight.

    In playing the theme, the strings must take care not to hit the quarter-note downbeat that follows the dotted rhythms. Undue impact there will break the swing of the line toward the half-note that ends the thematic unit.

26   Again, as in the second movement, the rolling 3/4 meter tightens at a couple of points (as at m. 26) into 4/4 meter, as though the speed has made the runner stumble forward momentarily before regaining stride. Note that, though mm. 26–27 are written in 4/4, they are actually—because of the part writing—heard as a

succession of 2/4 bars. The abridged metric frame, along with the shift to a detached, rather than slurred, dotted rhythm accounts for the feeling of speed-up; this sense must be transmitted in the playing.

A more extended interruption, the brusque, stamping figure (see m. 39 ff.), 39 appears from time to time. Though obviously derived from the basic material of this Allegro, this material seems also to refer back to the quartet's opening melody.

I think that the momentum of performance will carry the ensemble safely through the passage of mm. 70–87. Note, however, that Fauré takes you up three 70 identical melodic ramps to intermediate landings before making the final ascent to the high B♭ in bar 84. From there the quicker descent takes place. If all, piano and 84 strings, clearly project the subtle differences in chordal and intervallic detail in the preliminary landings, the sense of the whole passage will be apparent. It would be a good idea to play through mm. 72–73, 76–77, and 80–81 slowly and in direct 72 succession, to observe the effect of the differences in the writing.

The major contrast element in this movement is first encountered at m. 95. It is 95 lyricism viewed at express-train speed. Here the pianist needs agility and wit in equal measure. Keep the acrobatic treble crystal clear, but hold it to a pianissimo. It is an ornamental garland around the thematic lines in the strings and the countermelody in the bass. The same holds true for the 1st violin at mm. 116 ff., 116 when that instrument trades roles with the piano-treble.

There is a strange sense of finality when the ensemble alights on the sustained E♭ chord at m. 146; but the composer cannot abandon us so soon—and on the 146 relative major, at that. Actually, here you launch into the part of the movement that is hardest to interpret: 58 measures given over to a landscape dotted with the stamping figure first heard at mm. 39 ff. The strings will do what they can to project 39 the harmonic differences in the recurring appearances of the figure. It is up to the piano, however, to sketch the broad outlines of the terrain, for the melodic continuity is entrusted to that instrument. The harmony moves, but so gradually that it is hard to overcome the repetitiousness of idea. Two suggestions: keep the tempo going enough to preserve the overall perspective of the episode; and second, let the strings rehearse these measures alone for the appraising ear of the pianist, and vice versa. This way, the two elements can advise one another, and at the same time can discern how their facets of the writing can collaborate effectively. Don't just play the passage repeatedly and verbatim and hope that it is making a point.

For the passage from m. 208 through m. 235, I suggest that the quartet try 208 omitting the running triplet work of the piano-treble. Add the piano tracery only after you are sure your way of playing the sustained lines can sustain interest. Again, from m. 236 to m. 270, be sure that you are not lulled by facile playing of the 236 successive blocks of activity. Be sure you are building the cumulative wave that will carry you to the return.

I would strongly advise taping and hearing the entire complex, from m. 146 to 146 270. Do you find your attention wandering when you hear the playback? If so, the ensemble is probably playing with unrelieved excitement and loudness.

Apply careful judgment also to the triumphant passage from mm. 310 to 342. 310 As for the piano cadenza in the latter bar, give heed to the composer's instruction, *a piacere*. What should "please" you is to play the arpeggio sweep both freely and with due attention to the A♭s, lingering dramatically on the low G♭, proceeding with panache to the A♭ that tops the first wave, then swooping down through the middle C and up to the fermata at the end of the bar. Try playing the line several different ways for the approval of your string cohorts—and then surprise them with your improvisatory flare at the concert!

343   The coda: forgive me if I tell you that I invariably think of fluttering ballerinas when I hear the piano's measures at mm. 343 ff. At any rate, heed Fauré's *leggiero* very seriously, playing within a modest dynamic frame until forte really takes over

399 at m. 399. From there to the end, let fervor prevail—with two caveats: take the

429 dynamic drop truly suddenly and strikingly at m. 429; and try to exercise enough

440 tempo restraint so the strings can play their tremolo 16ths (mm. 440–42 measures before the end) with some clarity.

Violoncell.

CHAPTER TWENTY-TWO

❧ Dvořák ❧
Piano Quintet in A, Op. 81 (B. 155)

The English writer, Alec Robertson, not one to mince words in expressing an opinion about a composition, waxed enthusiastic about the Dvořák Piano Quintet:

> It is simply one of the most perfect chamber-music works in existence... Here there is not a note too many—and there are plenty of notes!—the melodies are of the greatest beauty and freshness, and a joyous springtime happiness flows through the music.[1]

I heartily agree with these sentiments. The work engages the performer upon first acquaintance. Moreover, it has the power to inspire the ensemble anew after a period of separation. Truth to tell, though, this is not a piece that I would like to play week in and week out; the drain on my reserves of passion would be too great! To perform the quintet every so often with a fine pianist, however, is one of the rewards of a quartet player's life.

Composed in August to October of 1887, the Piano Quintet was both premièred and published the following year. In 1890, after repeated performances in England, it was introduced in New York.[2]

Chamber music figured significantly in Dvořák's output throughout his productive years; he wrote a viola quintet in 1861, when he was twenty. His last ensemble work was the string quartet in A flat, Op. 105, completed at the end of 1895. The list of his extant chamber pieces comprises: no fewer than fourteen string quartets; the two (if we include an earlier effort, from 1872) piano quintets; the bass quintet and viola quintet; four piano trios (including the very familiar Op. 90, the *Dumky*); the string sextet; the two piano quartets; the Terzetto for two violins and

---

SCORE: Antonín Dvořák. 1989. *Piano Quintet, A major, Op. 81.* Prague: Supraphon. Miniature score No. S2357.

Left: Piano Quintet in A, Op 81. Berlin: Simrock, 1888. Cello part, first page of the second movement. Reproduced with permission from the collection of the Sibley Music Library, the Eastman School of Music, University of Rochester.

viola; the sonata and sonatina for violin and piano; the character pieces for violin and piano, as well as those for cello and piano; and so on.

This impressive body of music fascinates us by its melodic richness and variety, its rhythmic vitality, its imaginative harmonic coloration, and the equally subtle textures of its part writing.

I *Allegro ma non tanto.* In the piano's two measures of accompaniment that begin this quintet, note the upper line in the bass clef. The 8th- and half-notes are both marked with a dot (as in the following bars of this accompaniment line). These might be interpreted as instructions for light playing of the notes in question. I think, rather, that they are articulation marks, with the intent of making the rhythmic pattern clearly heard. That articulation is important, because it gives edge to the contrast between the triplets in the treble and the dotted-quarter/8th-note/half-note rhythm in the lower part.

Here and elsewhere in the movement, the 8th-note should be played a bit on the late and short side, to make certain it does not get rounded off into anything like a triplet value. Without this rhythmic friction, the short introduction would ominously suggest that we are about to hear an all-too-comfortable reflection of some kitsch operetta.

17 The dotted rhythm in the cello solo needs similar treatment, to confirm the nobility of that line. When the 2nd violin takes over the solo (m. 17) with its own, more fiery version of the theme, be sure to play the grace note early enough so that it is not swallowed up in the ensemble sound. The other instruments should go easy in that measure in general, so that the sustained A in the 2nd violin and cello can be heard.

19 The 8th-note couplets in the piano here (and in other instruments soon after) should swing through the bar, as is indicated by the swell mark in mm. 19 and 21. In the fortissimo passage that follows, combine the bass line's syncopes and the upper parts' dotted rhythms for driving force, avoiding any half-measure, treadmill effect.

25 Be sure to relieve the loudness after the fortissimo that starts at bar 25. The
29 eight bars at mm. 29 ff. are only forte, and there should be no need for the 2nd violin to force the middle-register solo in the first four measures of that passage.

37 Bars 37–60 constitute a harmonic and melodic diversion, ranging from *ff* to *pp* in level. A glimmer of the principal theme emerges in the piano's *espressivo* line at
53 mm. 53 ff. In general, though, the entire area should—with proper attention to the passing scenery—be traversed without undue histrionics, to get to the more serious
61 business at m. 61. There, the 1st violin restates the theme, now at an ethereal level, three octaves above the cello's original statement.

The keyboard's accompaniment is set at the same dynamic, piano, as the solo violin. That, I feel, is a mistake. The pianist's part here is no more important than that of the three lower strings; those are marked pianissimo, and even so should be played with restraint. There must be no need to thicken the violin melody. Second violin and cello should play their parallel-octave lines exceedingly quietly. The viola, too, should use very light bowing, one modest stroke per measure. Moreover, quiet as everyone may have been before, let all shrink the sound even more for the
71 atmospheric pianissimo in the mm. 71–74.

These maneuvers will probably have broadened the tempo by the time the
75 ensemble gets to m. 75. Don't hesitate to pick up the pace immediately at this *leggiero*; the repeated dactyl rhythm of the accompaniment and the running triplets

of the piano's melody demand fleetness. The addition, at m. 79, of the viola's dotted rhythm adds to the impetus.   79

On the other hand, the rather histrionic gestures in mm. 90–92 (I can just see Sarah Bernhardt swooning gracefully here) act to stop the motion, so that a slightly broader tempo can be established for the second theme. Give these few measures some attention. The cello's lone, pianissimo response to the quartet unison of the preceding bar, and the keyboard's brief chord on the downbeat of m. 92—these have to be very carefully paced and touched. The pianist may want to arpeggiate the chord slightly, and add a hint of pedal in order to spread the resonance.   90

92

It is up to the violist to gauge the proper length of the pause after the piano's chord, before starting the second theme. The sequential, half-bar rhythms in that theme can sound sticky and awkward. Though the level is only mezzo piano, the violist should swing through the five measures of the theme with a certain bravura. The pianist's accompaniment to the theme (8th-note couplets for both hands, on the first and third beats of the bar) should be smooth in texture. In effect, each keyboard couplet links to the couplet in the succeeding beat of the viola theme.

The same relationship holds true between the piano and the 1st violin's statement of the theme (mm. 98 ff.). There, however, the situation is eased by the continuous 8ths in the piano treble, and by the broad triplet rhythm in the inner voices. The opposing rhythms must be clearly maintained, so that the distinctive texture of the blend can be achieved.   98

Dvořák gets mileage out of the second theme by repeating it four times (either in whole or in characteristic fragments) before reaching m. 119. The piano's interlude, in mm. 103–10, is cast in G♯, as against the prevailing C♯ minor. Take advantage of the harmonic coloration here and the shifts in orchestration generally to underscore the variety in the repetitions.   119
103

Once past bar 119, don't spare the horses. A sense of breadth is built into the piano's arpeggiations in mm. 121–22 and 125–26. Even there, the bravura rubato can be effected without slowing the tempo. Overall, neither the musical material nor the temperament of this closing section of the exposition can brook any dragging of the speed. Let the excitement whip things along until you are safely past the second ending.   121

As for the first ending: note that it is fully eight measures long. It takes time to let down steam enough to effect the return to the opening of the movement. Even then, the sudden lurch from C♯ minor to A major is not entirely convincing. My own preference is to skip the repeat and move directly into the development. There, it takes Dvořák even longer to make the harmonic and temperamental transition, but it is more smoothly done—and it brings you to new experiences.

Viola, play very gently in your two solo statements in the mm. 175–80. You are responding to the piano's declamations each time, and there should be a fine, moonlit glow about your sound.   175

In the *tranquillo* at m. 181, the violins may feel they are affecting gypsy airs by playing their rapid triplets against the smooth 8th-notes of the piano and the sustained theme of the lower strings. Don't be self-conscious; hold the triplets down to the indicated pianissimo and they will add a quiet spark to the texture. I feel that a return from the *tranquillo*'s presumably more restful tempo should start at m. 197, so that the music is already in full swing at the forte, four measures later.   181

197

For me, the development turns awkward at mm. 221 ff. Here begins a fourteen-measure shouting match between the string team and the piano.   221

Experiment with this passage to keep it from sounding like opposing fan clubs at a Czech soccer game. At least keep it moving so that the audience doesn't have time to score the rounds. Some discreet urging is needed also in the modulatory maneuvers that follow. You want to arrive, with audience attention span intact, at **279** the *tranquillo* (I think that *misterioso* should be added) at m. 279, to build from there through the long 8th-note fanfare to the triumphant return of A major.

259 You will, of course, have to ease off from m. 259 to the start of the *tranquillo*, but not too much. The interlude moves in broad rhythms, so has its expansiveness already built in. Besides, the *tranquillo* itself arrives with an excitement factor of its own—the drumming 8th-notes in the string parts.

The recapitulation probably poses no new problems. The melodic material is reviewed and the appropriate harmonic adjustments made (the second theme now in F♯ minor rather than the earlier C♯ minor). There is, however, a very exuberant coda, with the theme blaring out in fortissimo; only a Berliozian brass band is lacking.

414 During rehearsal in my quartet years, I had been known to utter a raucous "Hurray!" at this point (m. 414). On one occasion, while backstage before a lecture concert, my friend the cellist suggested that we both sound this battle cry during the actual performance. As we approached the spot, we eyed each other in mutual encouragement; and I thereupon found myself giving the shout in solitary splendor! It was my privilege to give a red-faced explanation between movements, while our cellist stifled hilarious mirth.

Anyway, this coda is a lot of fun for extroverted players and listeners.

II *Dumka: Andantino con moto.* The players had better be extroverted for this movement, for there is a lot of public weeping to be done herein. The *dumka*, much loved by folk and art composers in Slavic Europe in the 19th century, was generally melancholic or lamenting. This Dvořák example is definitely a case in point. After a short, warm-up preamble by the piano, the viola begins the plaint, with an encouragingly mournful interjection from the 1st violin at midpoint. Viola, then violin, continue the lamentation, with the piano keening softly away in a background commentary that can't help attracting attention to itself. The piano part sounds like an adaptation of zither music, a thought reinforced by the arpeggiando chords of the measures that carry us to the first contrast section.

44 A *dumka* is supposed to alternate contrasting moods; the *Un pochettino più mosso* (m. 44) not only "moves a bit faster," but brightens the musical thought. Take first things first, though—the accompaniment in this section. In typical Dvořák fashion, this is a rhythmic mosaic: pizzicato 16th-note figures interlaced between viola and cello; offbeat 8ths in the piano treble; and 8th-note triplets in the piano bass. Some discreet metric emphasis from the viola will reassure the pianist, and will help synchronize the three background voices. As for the two violins, the parts are absolutely even in interest and register.

64
70 In the G minor section (mm. 64 ff.), the piano takes the solo role. Starting with bar 70, there is another troublesome accompaniment texture, this time involving all four strings. Sixteenth-note couplets are distributed between cello on the beat, and the other three in response. The printed bowing ties the two notes of the couplet together in a kind of controlled ricochet stroke. The players might experiment with a detached bowing. Be on your guard, for this passage can sound like a brood of forlorn chickens. Stay together, try for an effect of continuous 16th-notes, and maintain the integrity of the rhythm against the triplet 8ths of the piano-bass.

With the refrain of the sad *dumka* melody (*Tempo I*), it is the cello's turn to play the tune (mm. 94 ff.). This leaves the violins free to take over a version of the complementing tune that had originally been the lot of the piano. That player now retreats to a simple chordal support, while the viola, more than ever, zitherizes in a tremolo commentary on the entire procedure, yielding the task to the piano in the second half of the refrain. Some rubato quivering in the tremolos will indicate sympathy with—and encourage the intensity of—the lamentations of the other strings.

94

The second contrast section, a Vivace (mm. 128 ff.), is a transformation of the refrain theme. The variant is most effectively bowed if it starts with an upstroke in each entry, tying the sforzando downbeat to the articulated 32nd that follows; this sends the line off with a fine snap. The analogous figures (with or without the 32nd-rest), when used in repeated series later in the section, must be bowed as their position in the measure dictates, with the 32nd-note always tied to the note preceding. Controlled savagery should be unleashed for the fortissimo climax at the end of this section (mm. 160 ff.), with the indicated *stringendo* taken quite literally. The downbeat chord of bar 185 ought to suggest the impact of a collision between the ensemble and an immoveable object. Some slight pause before the piano begins the transition will prove therapeutic for both the player and the hearer.

128

160
185

In the refrain, Dvořák chooses to give the piano a background figure that derives from the Vivace theme. I wish he hadn't, or at least that he had not insisted on using it throughout this section. As it is, the pianist will have to be artful to keep the line from sounding like an uninspired pattern taken over from some mechanical instrument. The 2nd violin, too, will need imagination to keep some life in the offbeat pizzicato responses that fill most of this refrain setting.

To tell the truth, the composer's need to rehear, at the end of the movement, everything he did at its opening is a bit much. By this point, the *dumka* themes are so familiar that one longs for some lyrics to liven the proceedings. I shouldn't complain, though. So much does Dvořák enjoy his theme that he sees to it that every member of the ensemble—including the 2nd violin!—gets a crack at it before the double bar arrives. And I must confess that, though I find the movement slightly overgenerous, audiences seem to lap it up and ask for more.

Scherzo (Furiant): Molto vivace. This movement does not display the hemiola mixture of 2/4 figures within 3/4 measures that characterizes the dance-derived *furiant* found elsewhere in Bohemian music (including other works of Dvořák). What it does have is the speed and exuberance of the typical *furiant* movement. The Czech word, by the way, does not connote "fury"; rather, it means an unrestrained and frivolous person.[3]

III

In any case, you could never be furious in this Scherzo; the movement is too full of high-spirited good humor to permit such a view. The melody flings its way up to the downbeat of mm. 2, 3, and (especially) 4, then goes through the roof in m. 6 before reversing course and handing the tune over to the piano. To the energy of the subject is added the rhythmic sweep of the countermelody, carried in the opening eight measures by the viola, then given to the violins. All this calls for precise yet unstrained bowing, held within a small, manageable circuit of motion. One or more instruments are called out of the group to play the broader, secondary subject that is first hinted at by the viola line in mm. 9 ff. Turning on a musical dime to switch characters this way is part of the fun of this movement.

2
6

9

Twice in the Scherzo (the fortissimo at mm. 50 ff. is the first occasion), the cello

50

has the dubious pleasure of flailing away in a cross-string passage worthy of the Haydn cello concertos. The first time around, this is followed by a contrast section, one that does not recur in the da capo conclusion. Here the piano and first violin must contrive to suggest bell-like sounds (at least, that is what the passage suggests to me). The ensemble may wish to relax the tempo a bit, as well.

In this section, Dvořák seems so intent on having the 1st violin devote itself to the bell-sound accompaniment that he never gives the melody in this section to the lead violin, but only to the viola, 2nd violin, and piano in succession. Even closer to a bell-like sonority is the ringing, *bariolage* passage—rapidly alternating the stopped and open-string A—assigned to the 2nd violin. This forms part of the background for the piano solo, just before the return of the principal melody, prior to the change of key.

142 In the *Poco tranquillo*, the "trio" of this movement, the bell sound continues in various guises: the on- and offbeat chords of the piano and 1st violin; the tinkling, introductory measures of the 2nd violin and viola; the recurring high Fs of the piano measures under the sustained chords of the strings; the duple-rhythm
193 chiming of 2nd violin and piano at m. 193, to name a few examples.

Woven through these sounds are references to the principal melody of the
181 movement, and a spate of measures (mm. 181 ff.) that exhibit the duple-meter hemiola typical of *furiant* pieces. The hemiola is embedded in the piano part; whether it is revealed depends on the player's interpretation. The overlapping of treble and bass figures makes it possible to hear the measures as made up simply of continuous 8th-notes; thus, the composer's intent is a bit ambiguous. There can be
329 no doubt about the contraction to duple meter in the final measures (329 ff.) of the movement, after the abridged da capo section has run its course. There, strings and piano mark the two-beat units, with the indicated accents underscoring the point.

IV ***Finale: Allegro.*** The piano must be slightly predominant in the opening measures, since it is the only instrument supplying the impression of continuous 16ths (the result of the interweaving of the onbeat and syncope 8ths in its two staves). This effect is important; Dvořák not only brings it back literally at several points in the movement, but derives from it 16th-note patterns of various kinds.
13 One among them, a convoluted line of 16ths (see the 1st violin part, mm. 13–15), is an essential part of the principal subject and of the fugue that forms a prominent episode in the development section.

Relentless motion, in fact, is so constant a force in this movement that it is doubly important to capture in your playing the dynamic gradations and contrasts indicated in the score. Without such contrast, you may still have a good time rattling around, but the listeners' concentration is bound to wander. There are some
120 moments of built-in relief: the six measures (120–25) written in quarters, both onbeat and syncopated, before the current of 16ths returns; the two fanfare
150, 160 measures at mm. 150 ff.; the cadential measures, 160–62, that preface the ensuing
216 theme statement; the eight measures (216–23) leading to the aforesaid fugal
374 passage; and a few others, notably the broad, half-note oases at mm. 374–81 and
394 394–401, that precede the triumphant, last rush of the coda. Take advantage of all these points of relief. The music and the onlookers need them.

With all the activity in this movement, you might not notice whether you fall into an oom-pah, left-right kind of playing. Guard against this, for the effect is not only laughable but tedious, reducing the music to the level of cabaret
224 entertainment. The danger is perhaps greatest in playing the fugato (mm. 224 ff.),

where the ensemble can become engrossed in maneuvering through the twisting lines. Perhaps that episode will be helped if you think of Mendelssohn while playing Dvořák; the flavor is different, but there is some affinity in texture and spirit. Keep up a good head of steam, and use a light touch, leaving room for the loud and boisterous passages. In fact, this approach will prove beneficial not only to the fugato but to the entire Allegro.

On the subject of speed, be advised by the musical situation at hand. The transition to the coda, for example, starts from a blazing fortissimo (m. 366) and sinks, over the course of eight measures, to a pianissimo setting of hymnlike nature. It is up to the piano to lead an appropriate broadening as it moves from continuous 8ths, to quarters, and finally (along with the ensemble) to half-note rhythms. This broadening certainly need not be much, for the change in pace is composed in the writing; still, some supplementary spread is in order.

Whatever pace is established upon the arrival of the *tranquillo* at m. 382 may be maintained until the final pianissimo. From there until the last fortissimo is the place to accelerate, not simply to the original tempo, but to one that will carry the ensemble flamboyantly to the finish line.

366

382

The WINNETKA CONCERT SERIES

in cooperation with the
Midwest Music Foundation

presents

THE FINE ARTS QUARTET

LEONARD SORKIN, *Violin*   IRVING ILMER, *Viola*
ABRAM LOFT, *Violin*   GEORGE SOPKIN, *Cello*

Skokie School Auditorium, Winnetka

Wednesday, March 25, 1959 — 8:30 P.M.

PROGRAM

Quartet in G major, Opus 54, No. 1 . . . . *Haydn*

    Allegro con brio
    Allegretto
    Menuetto: Allegretto
    Finale: Presto

Quartet in F major, Opus 96 . . . . *Dvorak*
("American" Quartet)

    Allegro ma non troppo
    Lento
    Molto vivace .
    Finale: vivace ma non troppo

Intermission

Quartet in G minor . . . . *Debussy*

    Animé et très décidé
    Assez vif et bien rythmé
    Andantino, doucement expressif
    Très modéré; très mouvementé et avec passion

Recordings:
    Concertapes Stereo Recordings
    Concert-Disc Stereo Recordings

FINAL CONCERT — Wednesday, May 6, 1959

Program to be announced

For ticket information — The Winnetka Concert Series
P. O. Box 88
Wilmette, Illinois

CHAPTER TWENTY-THREE

❧ Dvořák ❧
Quartet in F, Op. 96 (B. 179)
("American")

If truth be told, the views of the performer and the audience do not always coincide. Ask the typical concert goer which of Dvořák's chamber music works comes most quickly to mind and the answer will probably be the "American" Quartet. That is not as likely to be the response of the informed musician. I believe, nevertheless, that the Quartet in F merits our full respect.

Dvořák wrote fourteen string quartets, from Op. 2, in A, of 1862, to Op. 105, in A flat, of 1895 (completed after the Quartet in G, Op. 106, which also dates from 1895). In the roster of these works, most professional ensembles would rank Op. 96, the work under discussion here, lower than, for example, the E flat, Op. 51 (1878–89), or the final two, Opp. 105 and 106.

This attitude of the fraternity is reflected by the English musicologist, John Clapham. In his important biography of Dvořák, Clapham says of the Op. 96 that "it hardly qualifies as one of the composer's best products." At the same time, he acknowledges its great popularity, attributing that to the quartet's "remarkable freshness... lively rhythms, its predominantly major keys, its appealing Lento in D minor, and [the fact that] it makes no great demands on the listener and is easy on the ear."[1]

Easy on the ear the work may be; it is no snap to play. Its writing is rather more open in texture than is the case in the larger, more imposing quartets in Dvořák's output. That very quality, however, makes it doubly important to perform the piece with great clarity and neatness. Many clever twists of rhythm and

---

SCORE: Antonín Dvořák. 1984. *Quartet XII, F Major, Op. 96.* Supraphon. Miniature score No. AP 1381.

Left: Program for the concert of The Fine Arts Quartet, Skokie School Auditorium, Winnetka, Illinois, March 25, 1959.

phrasing underlie the apparent simplicity of tone in this music. The ensemble will need all the alertness and technical polish it can muster.

But there is much more to this work than its challenge to the performers' abilities. The music is written in a way that makes us focus on the supporting, background lines as often as on the melodic overlay. Three of the movements (all except the third) start with a rhythmic-pattern introduction, like the keyboard preamble before the entry of the voice in an accompanied song. The subordinate matter is the first thing we hear.

Subject and support, foreground and background, vie for prominence in this work because they are closely related in substance. Think of the pitches that are sounded by the black keys on the piano: F♯–G♯–A♯–C♯–D♯. Lower the entire set of tones by one half-step, to F–G–A–C–D. This gives you the pentatonic (that is, five-tone) scale that underlies the material of this quartet.

In a perceptive article, David Beveridge states that, in the "American" Quartet:

> pentatonicism plays an important role—perhaps a more important role than in any other example of Western art before Debussy... None of the important themes in the American Quartet contains exactly the five notes of the pentatonic scale, but all of them come close. Most include a sixth note at one point or another, while a few are limited to only four notes (F–A–C–D). In places pentatonicism permeates not only the melody but the whole texture, placing severe restrictions on the harmony. The key scheme for [the successive movements of] the quartet, F–D minor–F–F, allows use of the pentatonic scale at the same pitch level in all the movements, but within movements one finds pentatonic melodies in A, F minor, D♭, A♭, and A minor as well.[2]

The Quartet in F was one of two works (the other, the Viola Quintet in E flat, Op. 97, also called the "American") composed in June of 1893, while Dvořák and his family were on vacation in the Czech community at Spillville, Iowa. The composer was then in the United States for the first of his two periods of service as the director of the National Conservatory of Music in America, in New York City.

There seems little evidence to support the idea that this pentatonic emphasis in Op. 96 could have come from Dvořák's having been exposed to any American Indian music during his stay in America.[3] The focus traces rather to his own accustomed use of such interval patterns in his earlier compositions, long before his visit to the United States.

In any case, one could justifiably think of changing the nickname of the Quartet in F to "The Pentatonic." Though perhaps less esoteric in its procedures than the Allegro of Haydn's "Quinten" Quartet, the Dvořák example is just as single-minded in its devotion to its chosen palette of intervals.

I

3

Allegro ma non troppo. I don't think Dvořák is trying to be ambiguous at the start of this movement; it's simply that he wants to have the first theme emerge (m. 3) out of some timeless mist of sound. That suggestion won't help the two violins and cello, who have to converge successfully on their way to the theme. As a homely remedy, I suggest that the three instruments play straight 8th-notes a couple of times: F, A, and low F, respectively. In so doing, the 1st violin should give its downbeat signal; the 2nd, the third-beat pulse; and the cello, the fourth quarter of the measure. These signals should be small but incisive (in keeping with the pianissimo dynamic of the opening) and will serve not only to key the players in question, but will also orient the viola for its solo entrance in the third bar.

When the pattern of entries is clear to all concerned, switch to the 16th-notes, as written, to see that things remain comfortably in place. Assuming that the sonorous background is now not only suitably tremulous, but reliable, the viola can take center stage with a properly robust statement of the first theme. In bar 6, the swell in the 1st violin should emerge directly from the crescendo of the viola line, so that the violin's 16ths gradually dominate over the cadential F of the lower voice in the second half of the measure.   6

As the dynamic marks indicate, the 1st violin's restatement of the theme is not only in more brilliant register, but is to be played with correspondingly greater force than the neighboring parts. The accent marks are now reinforced by forzandi, for example. The deliberately placed pizzicato notes of the cello part make that instrument very clearly a duet voice against the violin line.   7

In mm. 11–14, be sure the 16th-note quadruplet played on successive beats by the several instruments are heard as a continuous chain. So also, the dotted-rhythm figures in violin and cello and the interplay of 8th- and quarter-note rhythms in the inner voices should make up supplementary threads in the musical fabric.   11

At mm. 17 ff., the instrument playing the rhythmic 8th-note quadruplets has to use enough articulation of stroke so that a firm (not inflexible) metric spine supports the melodic voices. Note that the dynamics are carefully marked to make mm. 18 and 20 dominate the part writing, leading to the flash of activity in bar 21.   17   18

As an example of the flexibility in timing required by this kind of music, note that, in mm. 21–25, the first two bars are active and need full tempo; the third measure has a hesitant turn of melody and harmony that asks for a slight pullback over the second half of the bar; and the last two measures afford a rhythmic road along which the tempo builds back to full steam. I can't spell out the amount of these deviations; but you must let the music breathe, experimenting to find the degree and rate of bend the context may require.   21

I think you should also be sensitive to what you might call the tension factor. Starting at m. 26, for example, the first half bar thrusts forward, the next measure and a half rests; bar 28 pushes again (the turns on the violin couplets help spark the musical engine), while bar 29 settles back. Mm. 30–31 gather energy; bars 32–33 stoke the fires, both by the offbeat accents and the vigorous tattoo of rhythms in the lower voices; and mm. 34–35 simmer the energy more expansively.   26

The entire span from m. 36 to m. 43 effects the gradual release of this force. Note that the rhythmic undercurrent in the cello part and the syncopes of the 2nd violin occur only in the first four of these bars; the second four are dominated by broader rhythms and by great relaxation of sound and speed.   36

The *in tempo* at m. 44 should be read intelligently. It is incongruous to play this music fully up to the speed of the movement's opening; also, there has to be room for the push toward the forzando of m. 47 and the ebbing away at the end of that measure. All the way to the *molto rit.* in m. 59, in fact, each player will have to push and pull the time as needed. At bar 51, for example, the viola will maintain speed or even move ahead in the first four 8ths of the bar, while the 2nd violin will relax the pace slightly over the quadruplet in the second half of the measure. In the quintuplet over the first half of m. 49, the 1st violin will have to generate a microcosmic swirl of time, rather than count the five 16ths arithmetically over the two beats. Again in that instrument, the triplet on the third beat of bar 57 cannot be counted rigidly, especially after the little eddy of time occasioned by the grace note   44   59   51   49 that introduces the figure. In all such detail, the surrounding voices will have to be alert and give room or take up slack, whatever the current in one or another leading part may dictate.

If you look at the score pages of this movement as a piece of graphic tapestry, you will see that the rhythmic detail dominates the visual aspect of the writing. You almost have to ferret out the thematic and melodic frame on which the music is draped. For example: the last four measures of the exposition test your ear and your judgment. Clearly it is the theme in the 2nd violin that predominates in bars 60–61; the 1st violin then, in mm. 62–63, echoes its partner's rhythmic pattern. In those same measures, though, the broader rhythmic figure of the 2nd violin is scarcely less important in the musical fabric. For that matter, the liquid tremolo of 16ths that runs through the viola part in these bars has figured prominently from the very opening of the movement. It's not easy to distinguish skeleton from sinew in this writing.

The rivalry and merger of background and foreground continue at the start of the development. Both violin lines in bars 64–67 carry out an accompaniment function, but they have interesting detail in their own right.

The tremolo of the 2nd violin moves in opposite direction to that of the 1st (the crossed motion lends added vibrancy to the combined sound of the two instruments) and is occasionally sparked by a large leap. Both violin parts should be played as though they are melodies, not just spelled-out tremolos. Be aware that, after the half-note in the viola part in each of bars 65–67, the violin lines are left exposed in quasi-solo role. It should not sound as though the stuffing is suddenly heard through a hole in the musical upholstery. Stand ready to be heard at a moment's notice, to beautiful effect.

These same measures undeniably put the viola very much in the spotlight. Make the most of both the repetition of figure in the second and third bars, and of the unexpected appearance of the A♭ on the second beat of m. 67.

In bar 68, the tremolos of viola and cello directly reinforce the half-bar movement of the violins. In the next three measures, the tremolos move on each quarter-beat, along with the chords that are being sounded in one or the other violin line. Chords and tremolos should be rehearsed alone (that is, without the melodic voice of the moment), for synchronization, intonation, and clarity of sound.

In bars 72–75, the 1st violin is marooned unless the lower voices give proper support; each of the first two measures is fired with the help of the 2nd violin and cello inset. The syncopes of the 2nd violin in m. 74 must start out with determination, for that rhythm dominates until the outer lines start moving at midbar. From the upbeat to m. 76 right on through m. 79, our attention is directed to the rhythms of the bass line. The octaves should be played with all the artistry and shading that a skilled timpanist might bestow on such a line.

In m. 76, the 1st violin has a line of G♯ 8th-notes. Are these only background, along with the 2nd violin syncopes, to the active figures in the cello and viola? Partly so; but the violin 8ths are also a rhythmic solo, an articulated version of a whole-note that swells inexorably toward the obviously melodic quarters of the following bar.

At bar 80, I suggest that the three top voices practice the first four measures slowly, to assure that solo and rhythmic accompaniment fit well, without having to be nailed into synchronization by the cello pizzicati. In mm. 84–89, the four instruments should rehearse by twos and threes, checking for intonation.

The famous battle call in the 2nd violin at bar 96 should sound virile, not desperate. It is deliberately marked to be played on the G-string for the rich tone color such placement can produce. The combination of line and accent on each of the quarter-notes in the first bar of the melody clearly calls for a sustained stroke that is fired with vibrato and bow-speed impulse at the start of each note. Practice finding the first note with assurance, so you can play the tune without nervousness. Most important, please avoid any forcing of the sound. This spot can stick out like a sore thumb if not adroitly handled.

It takes control, again, for the 2nd violin to back the 1st in the pianissimo statement of the theme in mm. 98–99. Small, incisive strokes, as well as assurance in playing the reversed stroke on the second and fourth beats will help. In the next two bars, the violins should use very little bow for the first slurred group, enlarging the stroke with each half measure, but only as much as needed for good sonority. Otherwise the "creep" of bow may contribute to a frenzied air in the duet. You want to arrive at the fortissimo of m. 102 in a blaze of dignity.

At bar 106 the inner voices have two measures in which a slurred triplet precedes a detached triplet, with a swell extending through all six notes. Avoid the natural tendency to use more bow on the slurred, strong-beat group, for this will produce a rise-and-fall over the two beats. You'll want to save bow on the slur, then progressively increase the stroke on each of the three detached notes.

At the recapitulation (bar 112), let the playing show that the dynamic level has been scaled down from that of the opening. As for mm. 121–22, if the violins interpret the slurred, staccato markings in the first two measures literally, I'm not sure I want to hear the effect! I could possibly conceive of doing the first beat of the figure on an upbow, the two notes of the second beat hooked on one downbow, and the concluding 8th on a light upstroke. The figure will work quite convincingly, however, if the first four 16ths are played on separate, spiccato strokes.

The legato version of the same pattern in the 1st violin part in mm. 123–26 and in the 2nd violin right after, is again printed with a half-bar slur. And again, I vote against it. Perhaps Dvořák intended that the suspension of the fourth 16th into the dotted 8th of the second beat rub against the metrically stable cello line. The accent on the second and fourth beats of the violin part, however, breaks the suspension; you might as well, then, change bow at the same time. In any event, the inner-voice syncopations and the broadly flowing theme of the cello combine into a wonderful panorama of sound, a restful oasis in the movement.

Starting at m. 129, the violins lead the way back to the real world—and the bridge passage of the recapitulation—at bar 133. At m. 138, the 2nd violin can most comfortably realize the intended effect by removing the larger slur on the fourth beat of that measure, playing each 16th couplet on a separate stroke. In the next bar, again play each couplet—whether of 8ths or 16ths—on a separate stroke. This approach will help the 16th couplets project as they should through the quarter-note resting points in the 1st violin part. Note, by the way, that the writing is different at the corresponding spot earlier in the movement (m. 26), where the printed bowing works well.

Also different is the accompaniment texture that surrounds the cello solo at m. 160 ff. Once again, the upper voices will need some group practice to make the 16th-notes merge into a smoothly continuous pattern. A last danger lies in the violins' octaves, four bars before the end, where the 1st violin will have to find a reliable fingering that avoids any smeary shift.

96

98

102
106

112
121

123

129
133

26

160

I have written at length about a movement that is actually rather short. What with its many textural details, this Allegro takes some doing. When all its mosaic particles are made to fit neatly into its melodic frame, the result is worth the effort.

II   *Lento.* Both because of its slower speed and its more open texture, this is technically easier than the first movement. Still, it has its own problems and demands. Much of the melodic presentation in this movement falls to the 1st violin and cello; and, owing to a great deal of high-register playing, the low voice will perhaps feel the heat of the spotlight more intensely.

In such slow and expansive melodies, both players must make special effort to interrelate the successive musical events convincingly. For example, when you play

9   bar 9 in the 1st violin, you must have in mind bar 5, the corresponding element in the melody. The higher pitch and dynamic level of m. 9, and the changed ornamental detail on the last beat, are "explained" by their relation to the earlier

6   measure. Another point: shape the composed acceleration at the end of m. 6 to lead inevitably to the forzando on the succeeding downbeat.

Though at the lower octave, the cello follows the violin solo with an identical restatement, but not a carbon copy. Put enough individuality into the second statement to justify the use of the time! A little concert by the outer voices, presented during rehearsal for appraisal by the other two players, will help set the

19   perspective. The violin solo starting at m. 19 is answered and reflected in the cello

31   solo at bar 31. At the latter point, both voices are in close-order duet, which makes the result easier for the protagonists to judge.

43   From mm. 43 through 81, the duet is between the two violins. Here the 2nd

47   violin reflects and echoes the 1st, but must still evince some solo sense. Bar 47, for example, focuses more on the 2nd violin, certainly for the first half-measure. The

51   same is true at m. 51; after that, at bars 56, 58, and 63, and so on. Approach the B♭ in

49   the 2nd violin at mm. 49 and 68 via a discreet slide on the A-string, to provide a soulful touch in the pianissimo echo. Don't overdo the glissando portion of your shift, however; use a light-fingered glide, moving the bow slowly and lightly until the finger is near the B♭, so that only the last part of the voyage is heard by the audience.

70   From m. 70 through 81, the solo truly belongs to both violins. And from there almost to the end, it is the cello that carries the theme from high to low and on to its last repose. But it is the viola that leads the ending in the *morendo* measures, carrying out the implication of whatever preliminary retard the cello may have made.

The ornamental traceries of this movement are an integral part of the music. For one thing, there is the constant undulation of 16th-note couplets: constant, that

82   is, until m. 82. There, its sudden disappearance from the fabric of the sound has an electrifying (and, to me, almost ominous) effect, as though the lifeblood of the music has been stilled. Of course, the pulse endures in the form of the 8th-note rhythm. Even here, however, there is a deliberate drying of the sound: the alternation of bowed and plucked rhythm gives way, eight measures before the double bar, to pizzicato alone (the tremolo accompaniment is far enough removed that the plucked notes stand by themselves).

Pizzicato is used in the cello part from the very start of the movement, but as support to the aforementioned, wavelike writing. There are actually *two* waves, for the couplets in the viola part are carried on a bed of syncopes in the 2nd violin. Throughout the body of the Lento, the wave couplets are paired with some counter-rhythm. When the syncopes drop out, the pizzicato frame remains. The pizzicato itself breaks off, and a drumlike commentary takes its place (m. 31). In short, the wave rhythm and its accompaniment are revealed as the aural canvas on which the movement is painted. By the final three measures, the melody has faded away, and, as at the start of the movement, we are left with the canvas itself. 31

Though simple enough in outline, the Lento is—if I may summon up a hackneyed term—a marvelous evocation. It is the center of gravity in this quartet.

Molto vivace. In its own way, this movement continues to divide our attention III between line and background: four measures of melodic interest in the foreground; four of constantly rotating rhythmic pattern, heard as though in the distance; four bars of melodic line again; and yet another four of rhythmic pattern, now set higher in register. Starting at bar 17, a fragment of the opening melody is spun into a 17 tuneful succession of its own, like a bird call. At mm. 21 ff. a more overtly melodic 21 line is set off against the call. From here to the *Fine* at m. 48, we continue to hear melody and matrix as two elusive aspects of one musical organism.

For all this to work, everything must be played cleanly, and dead in tune. Fourths and fifths abound in the writing, and they villainously betray any flaw. The texture of the writing is so transparent, moreover, that error shows all the more readily. This is one movement you will want to rehearse slowly—and without too much vibrato to mask inaccuracies—to assure that all notes fall into place, both in pitch and timing.

Unless the 1st violin has spider fingers and mental frets, I think that best control of the passage from m. 21 through 28 is achieved in seventh position, with 21 crossing to the A-string and with quick shift back to 6th position on the note, E, for the end of each phrase.

Note that accents are placed to form their own pattern within the 3/4 pulse. Play them precisely as indicated, and avoid accidental emphases that muddle the clarity of the intended effect.

A word is needed about the viola's rhythmic tattoo in mm. 21–28 and 33–40. 21 It's trouble enough to have to play the alternate measures in reverse stroke, but to have the fourth measure trip you up with an eccentric, extra slur is a bit of devilment. Practice the passage slowly until you can command the pattern smoothly. You will amaze your friends and confound your rivals.

This movement is a scherzo with two trios (though not so marked, that is what the F minor sections at bars 49 and 149 represent). The movement is also a kind of 49 theme and variations, for the trios expand on the melodic idea of the opening section of the movement. There is a double da capo; the first return is actually written out, from m. 97 through 148. There are changes in the assignment of parts 97 and in melodic detail to keep this from being a verbatim review of the opening section. Owing to the interrelationship of material in the successive portions of the movement and the length occasioned by the twofold return, Dvořák does not ask for any further, sectional repeats.

In the first trio, the greatest technical problem is found in the rhythmic background figure, first heard in the violins starting at m. 57. Keeping the figure 57 clear and articulate at performance speed is tricky. The bowing should hook the first two notes, with the rest of the measure taken as it comes. This results in starting each measure on the downstroke, which is not only a comfort but also helps in projecting the accent. Don't use too much bow on the quarter-note at the measure's end, but try to keep the stroke pattern focused near the tip of the bow.

The figure is played with finger- and wrist-motion of the right hand, and only as much involvement of the arm as is absolutely necessary.

94 The 2nd violin must not be taken by surprise in mm. 94–96, at the end of this section. The pattern changes, and the player is left to flutter the tune away with nervous couplets at the tip of the bow. You might want to think of the three bars as one big 9/4 measure, with a very slight retard towards its end. The bowing, after hooking the very first two notes, is all in reverse, with each 8th-note taken on the upstroke. More than ever, focus the stroke in the fingers and wrist. The 2nd violin and cello should play these measures together slowly, to fit the cello's 16th-note couplets neatly into place in the last two bars.

106
113 In the return section that separates the two trios, the cello has some rapid-fire pizzicato rhythms to play at mm. 106 ff. Luckily, there is at least a quarter-rest between salvos; try to catch your breath! At bar 113, practice the first four bars slowly, to merge the lower- and upper-voice rhythms smoothly. The same for the three lower parts in the next eight bars,

125
144 Check the rhythmic mosaic again in mm. 125–36, for the placement of the two participating teams is now reversed. In bars 144–48, be sure the viola's *bariolage* fits the cello solo, for the latter will most likely want to broaden its line somewhat as it approaches the fermata.

149 At m. 149, the 1st violin should consider writing down- and upbow marks at the beginning of successive measures. If you get confused about the direction, you'll find the triplet pattern turning into a confused tremolo. The cello part in the
173 remaining measures before bar 173 corresponds to the 2nd violin part at m. 81, and the same procedural suggestions apply.

For the triplets in the three lower voices at bar 173, the hint about marking the bow direction at the start of each measure is again relevant. Confusion in any one voice will muddy the rhythmic waters and might also jar the other players' handling of their lines.

Dvořák must have enjoyed the engagingly simple permutations of his theme in this movement. It's fun to play, too, once you are comfortable with the little rhythmic gears that make it run.

IV ***Finale: Vivace ma non troppo.*** The bowing of the rhythmic pattern at the opening calls for: hooked downbow for the dotted 8th and 16th; upstroke for the single 8th, down for the suspension across the bar line, and (most comfortably), one
2 bouncing upstroke for all three separate 8ths in measure 2; and so on. Get the pattern neatly and reliably in hand, then let the vivace fly!

In the 1st violin melody, hook the dotted figure on a downstroke, take the 8th-note couplet on one bounced upstroke, and use separate strokes for the four 8ths in the second measure of the figure. The melody should, of course, be played below the middle of the bow.

29 Everything is introduction, up to m. 29. The two isolated, upward thirds in the 1st violin at that point do not recur at the corresponding spot later in the movement
234 (m. 234). In this first statement of the theme, the thirds are like tentative, whistled attempts to get started with the melody. Suggest the whistle effect by playing lightly, in a quasi-harmonic tone; I could suggest a discreet slide from the A to the C—but I don't dare.

The principal theme is marked for nonchalance; note how often Dvořák pulls the line back to pianissimo, or quickly down from a forte-piano. He wants the tune to sound casual, a bit innocent in its excitement. Make sure the ensemble balance

allows for this quietness in the solo. The outburst at bar 65 must again drain away 65
quickly, so that the even more restrained theme in A♭ can make its point effectively.

The cello pizzicato line under that theme is so vigorous that it may be hard to
hold it down. It makes a fine, drumlike foil to the solo. If you want to have some
extra fun with it, try playing it in three-measure groups; it seems to lay out very
nicely that way, in ten units that comprise the thirty-measure total that ends at m.
98. The ensemble will have to decide whether this cross-grained approach, moving 98
against the clear, two-bar units of the three upper parts, sounds convincing.

The passage from m. 99 through 122 is a shift of scene, returning us to the 99
principal theme in F major. You will need very snug string-crossings in mm. 111, 113
and 114 to maintain speed in the 16th-note quadruplets. The chords in the violins
and cello in the next five measures should be taken with short downstrokes, near
the foot of the bow. If the angle of attack is right, the chords will sound without
rasping.

Mm. 146–78 again shift the scene, with the pianissimo, chorale-like tune from 146
bar 155 on serving as a kind of preview of the A-minor scene to come. That episode 155
is divided between the chorale at m. 179 and the sprightly transformation thereof at 179
bar 199. 199

There, the bowing in the 1st violin should have the second and third 8ths of
the first measure on one upbow; in the third bar, both notes of the dotted figure are
taken with one hooked downstroke, with similar arrangements in later measures.
Take advantage of the *Meno mosso* pace to preen the notes of this tune as archly as
seems proper. Throughout this episode, the 1st violin will be fitting its actions to the
statements of the principal line in one or another of the low voices.

Mm. 234 through 309 offer a compressed, kaleidoscopic review of ideas and 234
keys from earlier in the movement. From bar 310 to the end of the movement, we
are dealing with the coda. This is led by the 1st violin up to m. 325, and then by the 325
viola to bar 333. The same two voices, in succession, take the lead again from m. 343 343
to 356.

There is some jockeying for position in the next four measures. The 1st violin, 363
however, is in control for the last twenty bars of the piece. The triple forte of the
final twelve bars is orchestrated fully enough so that none of the four instruments
need press too hard; let the ensemble sonority ring out freely.

KAMERMUZIEKVEREENIGING   ROTTERDAM

OPGERICHT in 1907   *   Seizoen 1959-1960

FINE-ARTS QUARTET (U.S.A.)

Leonard Sorkin,   1e viool   Irving Ilmer,   altviool
Abram Loft,   2e viool   George Sopkin,   cello

SERIE A — Zondag, 11 oktober 1959
Museum Boymans-van Beuningen, aanvang 2,30 uur

1. KWARTET in C (K.V.465)   W. A. Mozart
        (Dissonanten-kwartet)
        Adagio, allegro/Andante   (1756-1791)
        Menuetto/Finale

2. KWARTET in F   Maurice Ravel
        Allegro moderato (très doux)   (1875-1937)
        Assez vif-rythmé
        Très lent/Vif et agité

PAUZE

3. KWARTET in Bes, opus 130   L. van Beethoven
        Adagio-allegro/Presto   (1770-1827)
        Andante con moto, ma non troppo
        Alla danza tédèsca (allegro assai)
        Cavatina (adagio molto espressivo)

SERIE B — Dinsdag, 13 oktober 1959
Museum Boymans-van Beuningen, aanvang 20 uur

1. KWARTET in G, opus 54 No 1   Jos. Haydn
        Allegro con brio/Allegretto   (1732-1809)
        Menuetto/Finale

2. KWARTET in g, opus 10   Claude Debussy
        Animé et très décidé   (1862-1918)
        Assez vif/Andantino
        Très modéré-très mouvementé

PAUZE

3. KWARTET in C opus 59 No 3   L. van Beethoven
        Introduzione-allegro vivace
        Andante con moto, quasi allegretto
        Menuetto/Allegro molto (fugue)

Volgende concert: JANACEK QUARTETT
Voor Serie A en B
op zondag, 8 november '59 in het A.M.V.J. Gebouw (ingang
                    Schouwburgplein) aanvang 2.30 uur.

CHAPTER TWENTY-FOUR

✑ Debussy ✑
Quartet in G minor, Op. 10

Debussy wrote his quartet almost 100 years ago. Like every artist, he must have hoped for wide acceptance of his brainchild. I wonder, though, whether he could possibly have imagined the popularity and longevity this quartet would enjoy. The course of music in France during preceding generations would scarcely have encouraged his optimism.

Musical taste in Paris, the arbiter of French culture, during the 19th century had been oriented more toward vocal music and opera—the grander the better—than toward abstract, instrumental composition. The piano was indeed a fixture of the well-appointed household, but it was fueled by operatic transcriptions and potpourris more often than by serious fare. Dedicated amateur chamber music players set themselves to the reading of the Haydn and Mozart quartets, or to the unending flow of publications disguised as ensemble music but actually written as solo melody and subordinate accompanying parts. This kind of composition could satisfy the ego of the accomplished amateur soloist; it also could serve as an avenue of collaboration between the invited or hired professional (who, in many cases, was the author of the piece) and the amateur participants. An extreme and amusing reflection of this kind of spotlight writing appears in a quartet of the celebrated cellist, Friedrich Dotzauer. The title page proudly declares that the works are for "CELLO, two violins, and viola."[1]

As the century unfolded, musical initiates gave less time to personal music making, turning instead to the enjoyment of performances by professional ensembles. Especially popular were subscription concerts organized by the famed violinist and chamber musician, Pierre Baillot, and others. Until midcentury, the programs of these concerts focused on the classic repertoire, eventually venturing

---

SCORE: Claude Debussy. 1969. *Quartet, Op. 10.* Ed. Irene Alberti. London: Eulenburg. Miniature score No. 210.

Left: Program for concerts by The Fine Arts Quartet, Boymans-van Beuningen Museum, Rotterdam, October 1959.

275

even into the late Beethoven quartets. By the '70s, music of Schubert, Mendelssohn, Schumann, and Brahms had been added. French composers were given entrée, first in the short-lived series of the *Société des quatuors français,* then—in the nationalistic aftermath of the Franco-Prussian War—more significantly in the concerts of the *Société national de musique.*[2]

Even with the stimuli of these and other avenues of activity, the attention given by French composers to chamber music in the 19th century was rather spotty. The output would in any event seem smaller because composers tended increasingly to write single works of greater length, rather than the traditional opus of six compositions. There is, of course, the ever-bountiful Georges Onslow to reckon with, to the tune of thirty-five string quartets (along with much other instrumental output). How much food for today's listener is to be found there, or in the more discreet ensemble productivity of such composers as Henri Reber, Guy Ropartz, Alexandre Boëly, Félicien David, Guillaume Lekeu, or Édouard Lalo—to name them in no particular order of chronology or importance—is something for the musical gourmand to determine. Clearly, however, the one work of 19th-century French chamber music that has fixed itself prominently in today's concert programs is the string quartet of Claude Debussy.

The String Quartet in G minor was composed in 1893; alone among Debussy's compositions, it bears an opus number (10) and also is labeled "First," though there was to be no other. As student at the Paris Conservatory, Debussy had won the Prix de Rome at the age of twenty-two. In Vienna and Bayreuth, he had drunk the Wagnerian waters without becoming addicted. During a term of service as musician to Mme. von Meck, the Russian patroness of Tchaikovsky, and later from music heard at the Paris Exhibition of 1889, he was stimulated by the writing of Glazounov, Rimsky, Balakirev, and others. At the Exhibition, also, he heard the Indonesian *gamelan* orchestra, with its exotic sounds, rhythms, and interval structures.

Disparate the influences on Debussy in these years may have been. This quartet, however, reflects his ability to merge diverse ingredients into an eminently coherent work. Partly, the unification comes from a clear thematic linkage: the first, second, and last movements are obviously bound together by adherence to the motive that is pronounced at the start of the quartet. The same idea is more circuitously present in the material of the slow, third movement.

Though the Debussy quartet looks back to inherited devices and forms (the first movement is modeled on the sonata allegro), the total effect of this work is unlike that of any that had come before. The influence of the piece, in turn, can be seen in the quartet writing of Debussy's successors, starting as early and as clearly as the quartet of Maurice Ravel (1902–03). Even before composing the quartet, however, Debussy in 1892 had already begun the work that, from its première in 1894, would mark a watershed in contemporary musical thought: the *Prélude à l'après-midi d'un Faune.* Our concern here, though, is with the way of performing the quartet, a work that retains its youth and freshness after the passage of a century.

I   *Animé et très décidé.* One thing is central to the Debussy quartet: the colors and textures of its sound. If you look at the score, its visual impact alone will transmit some idea of the aural palette (since I am blending metaphors, I might as well say, "aural flavors") that await you in the work. In the opening *Animé,* the rich

13   grittiness of the first measures shades off into the 16th-note wash in mm. 13 ff. In

26   mm. 26–38, the brusque opening theme is studied in dynamic shadings and

distances: piano, pianissimo, forte, and gradations between. The rivulets of triplets that sweep through the lines from m. 39 through m. 59 are obviously inspired by, but differ in texture from, the 16th-note texture heard a few moments earlier. 39

As you begin the movement, you find that there are twelve measures in the statement of the first theme. This, you might think, would guarantee against any squareness in playing the phrase. Consider several points, though: for one thing, the number of times that the note, G above middle C, occurs in the 1st violin part during these measures: no fewer than fifteen, to say nothing of an additional three, an octave higher. Clearly, this pitch is the structural axis of the tune, but it must recur with enough shading to keep it from becoming a spear of sound aimed at the listener. Debussy must have been aware of this danger, for he was careful in his marking of the tone: with line, accent, dot, or none of these, as the melodic context warrants.

What about the ornamental triplet that ends each of six of these bars; or the fact that the rhythmic pattern of the second measure of the piece returns, with little modification, in bars 6 through 12? You are right to say that this kind of repetition is an essential character of the opening (and actually of many points later in the movement). Once more, though, observe that Debussy tries to guard against treadmill recurrence: a steady diminuendo shades the rhythmic sequence from m. 6 on; also, the lower voices in these bars move rather variably, changing rhythmically within the individual lines, shifting a rhythmic pattern from one voice to another, and maintaining some independence of linear direction. Only in three out of the twelve bars do all four voices move with identical rhythm. One of these homogeneous measures (m. 5) stands at the peak of the line; from there on, individuality reigns. Another detail: in bars 10–12, the syncopated figure becomes an ostinato in the cello part; the three upper voices, though, abandon it for the first half of m. 11, rejoin in chorus with the cello in the second half of the bar, give it up again in m. 12, with the viola taking it over as a transitional figure at the end of that measure. 6

5
10

Why do I burden you with this dissection? To stress that Debussy, through dynamics, texture marking, and astute part writing, makes it very difficult for the ensemble to play this opening badly. Still, you could spoil it if you ignore or minimize the subtleties he has built into these measures. In fact, the violist alone, singlehandedly, can at the very end blunt an elegant beginning by plunging stolidly through the final syncope in m. 12. There must be a very slight but noticeable languishing there, both in time and decrescendo, to carry the quartet into the following measure. 12

The 16th-note waves that follow demand absolute unity in rhythm, dynamic gradation, and accentuation from the three participating voices; you want the effect of one line that, like a stroke of the artist's charcoal, has been padded into a broader ribbon. Special care is needed where the lines of motion diverge, particularly at m. 25; there, be alert to each quarter beat, the more so since you are likely to want some bending of tempo before the piano downbeat. Watch out for the mm. 26–38. Rhythmic sequence is quite noticeable there, especially because the four voices move pretty much in a block; a suitable touch of pallor in the pianissimo of the third and fourth measures, a slight raising of level at the fifth measure (even though not indicated), and definite marking of the forte measures as the target of direction, all will help. 25
26

In the next passage (leading up to the *en augmentant* of m. 51), flexibility in the 51 triplet lines of the 2nd violin and cello is essential; without appropriate ebb and flow of tempo, especially to underline the swells, the accompaniment figures will freeze the melodic voices into a very repetitious, hurdy-gurdy effect. In fact, from

26   m. 26 all the way to the change of key at m. 61, Debussy is exploiting a succession of wave patterns. If the players refuse to let themselves float in this musical sea, it will immediately sound like desiccated padding.

63   At m. 63, the tempo is marked *Un peu retenu* for the second theme of the movement; there follows a retard, just before the faster tempo of the cello's quotation of the opening theme. The slow-down might be regarded as a reinforcement of the contrast between the *retenu* and the original tempo. I would suggest, though, that it is just as much a receding from a momentary surge of tempo that should instinctively have taken place in the third measure of the *retenu.*

69   In the next *retenu* (m. 69), on the other hand, the third measure is only the start of a broader progress toward the full resurgence of the *Premier Mouvement*, and so falls into place in the gradual acceleration, or—to use the composer's term—"tightening" of the tempo.

75   The fortissimo statement of the theme at the *Premier Mouvement* (m. 75) is changed from the opening, not only in tonality but in orchestration. Where it had been robust and deep-toned, it is now cast in a brighter, fuller, edgier coloration. It is introduced by a correspondingly craggy measure of massed triplets; and the triplet rhythm, now spun out in strands of varying density, breadth, and articulation, serves as the support and frame for the development of the theme. The original tempo having been regained at the fortissimo, Debussy makes no other

97   indication until the *En animant* at m. 97. He obviously relies on the players to respond to the rubato needs of the intervening phrases—and so shall I. Suffice it to say that, once the *En animant* has arrived, the cello should whip things along, so

101   that the *Toujours animé* (m. 101) is effectively at Presto speed. At the F♯ major section (m. 103), Debussy himself utters the magic term, *Tempo rubato*. The ensemble worth its salt will respond without reserve; and once again, much of the flexibility of tempo will rest with the voices playing the triplets. Their task is complicated, since they also have to highlight those tones in the triplet figures that reflect the broader lines of the solo voice(s). It should be quite clear that rubato refers here not only to a certain time-freedom within and between voices in the confines of a measure or phrase, but also to the freedom to shift tempo overall, as the musical moment

109   dictates. Thus, starting at the *più forte* (m. 109), make a definite acceleration to the fortissimo, then a gradual slowdown to m. 119.

    There is a tricky spot for ensemble at m. 136. This forte, just before the *Retenu*, comes at the end of four bars of acceleration and proceeds at full tilt, with all four

137   players running in rhythmic unison. At the downbeat of m. 137, they must react to the "hold it!" command by playing the succeeding triplets at a markedly slower pace. This takes rehearsal, of course; but also, it takes alertness and instantaneous adjustment to the lead of the 1st violin.

138   The return of theme, at bar 138, has none of the subtle detail of the opening; it is a brusque, impatient, and abridged version of the beginning, serving mostly as a

145   transition to yet a larger transition, the *Animé* that starts in m. 145. The core of this passage is the augmentation of the first theme, presented successively by the outer voices. The expansiveness of the solo rides on the equally broad playing of the accompanying triplets, whether they be slurred, detached, single-, or double-stopped. The same holds true for the relationship between second theme and

background at bar 161. Here the *Tempo rubato* is a spice that flavors the new, half-measure garlanding of the triplet rhythm. Further excitement derives from the bravura turbulence with which the triplets roll across the fingerboards of the violin and cello.

Since both inner voices take over the melody, starting at m. 163, it will be up to 163
the 2nd violin to lead, especially in the augmented triplets in m. 169, as well as to
start the gradual acceleration in m. 171. The remaining measures of the movement 171
are physical enough to assure that there will be sufficient signalling to guide the
four players to the supersonic speed of the *Très animé* (m. 183). (Has any group ever 183
really matched the indicated metronome mark of 138 to the half-note?).

The two measures of accented, quarter-note triplets leading to the *Très animé*
are immediately transformed into the 8th-note version that follows (a tremolo, in
effect, owing to the tempo). In practice, there is no problem of synchronization in
these 8th-note couplets. Do, though, make a real descent to a pianissimo.

The two violins must carefully match fingerings and intonation in their unison
approach to their high G in m. 191. That note has a nasty habit of hanging in the air 191
in the abrupt silence, revealing to the world at large any discrepancy in pitch. Don't
hit the note too hard (there are two of you playing it), and try for a cool vibrato, for
too intense a resonance will muddy the unison.

Assez vif et bien rythmé. The second movement is perhaps the musical chef's II
masterpiece in this quartet. At the beginning, as well as at several points later on, a
wonderful mixture of sound flavors is layered together: a bowed line; a line of
steady pizzicato triplets, constituting a drone; a third line of irregularly spaced
triplet groupings, interspersed with occasional duplets; and a drone bass of
drumlike, duplet rhythms enlivened with resonant chords. My guess is that this
kind of passage most closely reflects Debussy's recollection of the *gamelan* music he
had heard at the Paris Exhibition.

Reserved for one point in the movement (at the fortissimo, m. 33) is a splash of 33
color produced by massed pizzicati in all four voices. The middle section of the
movement is awash in the liquid tremolos of the middle voices, which abruptly
turn into spiky jabs of sound when taken over by the violin duet in two passages
(mm. 64–67 and 78–82). There is a reflection of this, though now in altered texture, 64
in the accented, mono-level outbursts of mm. 140 ff. Near the end (mm. 164–67), 140, 164
Debussy enjoys the side-by-side comparison of bowed and pizzicato settings of
identical melodic figures.

Back to the start of this movement, though: I don't know about other 2nd
violins, but for myself, I was always happy that I could put the bow down on the
ledge of my musicstand for the first fifty bars; the four-bar rest at mm. 51–54 is time 51
enough to take up the stick. To play the constant stream of pizzicato triplets in the
first ten measures of the part hangs heavy if you have to fight the weight of the
bow. I sympathize with the plight of the 1st violin and cello, who have no similar
break, but they at least have short rests and broader rhythms to ease the situation.
Another hint to the 2nd: take advantage of the rests in the two retard measures
before your *a tempo* solo of mm. 37 ff.; you need to recover quickly from the effort of 37
playing the fortissimo triplets in mm. 9 through 34.

Having issued all these therapeutic suggestions, let me hasten to say that the
entire opening should have a relaxed edge to its vigor! Remember that the
ensemble is applying an exotic twist to an adaptation of the first-movement theme,
one that was exotic enough to start with. The audience should feel energized, not

frozen with anxiety for the ensemble. A further point: the quarter-note, F, in this opening's bowed theme is marked with a line, not an accent; sustain, don't hit it; the emphasis should have the allure of ambiguity.

54 The first phase of the middle section (mm. 54 ff.) offers a fairly straightforward augmentation of the theme. A tremolo figure now serves as background, with pizzicati in the bass to offer another element of connection to the opening section. After the initial sforzando stings, the inner voices should play their 16th-notes liquidly, not hammering the fingerboard, so as to reflect the sustained quality of the solo line. The louder, more active tremolo passages assigned to the two violins are another matter. Here the consistent accentuation, along with the unavoidable string-crossing, makes for a turbulent effect. Try to preserve as much of a horizontal approach to the bowing as you can; if the figures get too choppy, the two lines tend to fall out of alignment.

86 In mm. 86–89, the three upper strings (but especially the two violins) should try to play the spiccato triplets with a low-lying stroke, so that the transition to the
90 on-string notes of the mezzo-forte measures (90–93) does not come as a shock. In
100 the *en diminuant* measures (100 ff.), I suggest that the inner voices use one articulated downstroke for both of the first two notes in each measure; the repeated pattern may not sound quite alike in successive measures if the printed bowing is used. Under the 1st violin's E major statement of the theme, the lower voices must be ready to push forward in the successive half-measures of the crescendo bars, should the 1st violin part so move.

The return of the opening section is much transformed, especially by being recast in a 15/8 frame, which the dotted bar line splits into triple and duple subunits. As I hear it, the swell and sforzando in the duple "bar" have the effect of tightening that unit, setting its brevity off more strongly against the 9/8 portion of the measure. You should follow Debussy's lead and not surrender entirely to a
168 straight, five-beat rendition. Note that in the return of the 6/8 meter at the *Même mouvement*, the overlay of upper voices against cello in the second measure suggests a compression of the music immediately preceding the metric change.

At the very end, the pizzicati are the last traces of a sound that has evaporated into thin air. For the last two notes, the strings do not really need to be plucked; if the finger is touched to the string and pulled away, enough resonance will be produced. For the onlooker, the sound will be seen, as much as heard.

III **Andantino, doucement expressif.** For me, this is the center of gravity of the
107 quartet. The closing lines, from m. 107 to the end, have always been an especially moving experience, no matter how often I have played them; but the entire movement has a quiet intensity that strikes home.

As far as timbre and texture are concerned, the Andantino offers an interesting contrast to the second movement. Some of Debussy's textures look alike in print in both movements. In the Andantino, however, we hear the patterns in a kind of slow-motion-photography way. Just as a visible gesture looks quite different when spread out and slowed down in time, so also, familiar sound-patterns have a completely altered impact on the ear when we are made to hear the figures in an
107 expanded frame. When we get to the close of the movement (mm. 107 ff.), we are actually moving in the original tempo. Yet, there is something so arresting and tremulous about the sound of the passage that player and listener feel themselves suspended in a kind of endless time warp. Marvelous!

1 At the start of the movement, a sense of space is very skillfully created by the

shifting, equivocal harmonies that lead us in three directions within the first five measures. We are also pulled into the "depth" of the sound through the contrasting tone colors Debussy uses. The 2nd violin part is marked piano, with swells—the first measure dominated by the resonance of the open G, the second, by the closed and hushed sound of the A♭. The sustained breath of that tone is rippled by the cello's far-off pizzicati.

Now there is a repetition of the 2nd violin figure, but this time in the viola, and without the retarding influence of the swells. The sonority of the viola changes the coloration even of the open G. A deviation in the viola's second measure turns us in a new harmonic direction. Finally, an unexpected deflection of the viola's harmonic course by the pianissimo statement of the theme in the 1st violin turns us still farther away. We are at once lost and assured.   3

The 1st violin will want to delay the entry of m. 5 slightly in order to suggest that the fermatas of m. 2 are still remembered, and to emphasize the faraway aspect of the new turn of events. In these measures, we see that accompaniment voices can be subordinate without being submerged. Only two examples: in mm. 5–6, the slowly moving tones of the viola are as important as the quicker line of the 1st violin; in m. 7, the sustained tones of the 2nd violin and viola in the second half of the measure are an essential support to the 1st violin figure and should be sufficiently marked before deferring to the solo line.   5

Before leaving the start of the movement, I offer some technical advice to the three upper voices: in the 2nd violin's first measure, the tone of the open G can be warmed very slightly by a slow oscillation of the hand, even though no finger touches the string. The swells themselves should be colored by a corresponding increase and decrease of vibrato speed. The pianissimo A♭ in bar 2 should have little or no vibrato; and the viola echo in bar 3, without swells, can be generally restrained in its vibrato coloration. As for the 1st violin part: within the pianissimo frame, vibrato can and should be used, but constantly graded to suit the melodic requirement; for example, apply a bit more to the notes marked with lines. In this kind of writing, vibrato is closely bound up with the gradation of dynamics, accentuation, and emphasis. Just be sure that you control the amount you use, and gauge it *for* the music, not against it.

The first and last sections of the movement are not only muted, but are cast predominantly in shades of piano and pianissimo. It is vital that these nuances and contrasts be fully exploited in performance; the lone forte (m. 22) must not seem to be isolated in a muddy, nondescript tonal landscape.   22

In the middle section, *Un peu plus vite,* the triple-piano chords in mm. 32 and 35 need special attention: the viola must obey the decrescendo marked for the tone that suspends into the measure of the chord, so that the note becomes an inherent part of the cluster; in playing the chord itself, all bows must move very slowly and lightly, just grazing the strings, while the left hand imposes little if any vibrato. The chord should sound as though composed entirely of harmonics.   32

The passage (starting at m. 41) for the two violins, leading into the viola solo, should do just that; these are transitional measures and should be played sensitively but not pompously, and certainly without dragging. I interpret the fact that the violins' accompaniment to the viola solo (mm. 48 ff.) is cast in pianissimo, while the three-voice background to the cello solo that follows is marked piano, to mean that the cello line should be louder than the viola solo, even though both are marked piano. This seems logical because we are en route to the more agitated solo,   41

48

62   in octaves, for 2nd violin and cello, that begins at m. 62. The dynamic markings for this extended solo passage are enigmatic: at m. 62, we are instructed to "get louder gradually"; nevertheless, the piano marking of m. 62 is repeated at the head of mm.

66   66 and 70. I rely on the instinct of the players to set the successive pianos on a slightly higher, more excited level.

      As for the acceleration instruction (*serrez le Mouvement*) at m. 62, it should certainly apply up to the beginning of the 1st violin solo in m. 76; there, however, a slight broadening, or at least a stabilization of tempo, should take place. Also, it does not seem likely that the peak tempo will be literally maintained during the

99   octave duo of 1st violin and viola in mm. 99 ff. Some preliminary relaxation is in order here, in preparation for the retard that will return us to the *Premier Mouvement*

107   at m. 107. (Incidentally, a checkup on the intonation of the octaves seems to be a ritual facet of Debussy quartet rehearsals.)

      I cannot think of the cello solo that leads into m. 107 without imagining a

103   slight suspension on the A at the end of the m. 103, prior to the descent through the

107   next bar. As for the coda in mm. 107 ff., there is no more sanctifying passage in the repertoire. Overheated playing here would be quite out of place. For me, the simple

113   8th-note line in the 2nd violin in the first two measures of the *Un peu retenu*, played against the soaring line of the 1st violin, holds unaccountable wonder. Scarcely less so, the breathless spell of the four-measure close. As with the slow movement of the Schubert Cello Quintet, it seems inconceivable that any music should follow after this cadence.

      To be flung from the slow panorama of sound images of the third movement into the blurred rush of patterns and ideas in the finale is a shock. The stark contrast of the change heightens the intensity of the impressions we get from the last movement. In fact, I think that Debussy's most striking achievement in this quartet, even beyond the imaginativeness of the textures he creates within each chapter, is the sense of balance he contrives between the four very different movements that make up the work.

IV   *Très modéré.—Très mouvementé et avec passion.* Debussy himself must have recognized the difficulty of breaking the spell of the slow movement, for he provides a transition, a kind of musical air lock, to lead into the finale. My choice of title for this movement recognizes this situation; though *Très modéré* stands alone at the start of the score, it is the *Très mouvementé* that is the true finale, even though it does not arrive until the thirty-first bar of the music.

15   You may decide to let the cellist, who starts the acceleration alone at bar 15, lead it until the forte, when the 1st violin will take over. Even though all four

19   instruments move together in mm. 19–20 of the *En animant peu à peu,* control of the

29   next four measures shifts to the two low voices. Again, in mm. 29–30, the cello will govern the pacing of a dramatic and suspenseful pause. The *Très mouvementé* proper

45   cannot really be said to attain its full speed until m. 45, for the first fourteen bars of the section are held in check by the two forte cadences. After m. 45, the drumming 8th-note lines will move things along.

      There ought to be a slight bending of tempo to shift the musical viewfinder to

69   the violins' F major solos at the pianissimo (mm. 69 ff.). The 2nd violin's four

82   measures of rhythmic sequence (mm. 82–85), soon after, seem to reach forward, so an appropriate speedup is in order, to be continued by the 1st violin right up to the

90   fortissimo in m. 90. From there, a gradual and slight relaxation is indicated by the music; not too much, though, since the cello will be augmenting the theme anyway.

At m. 106, the rhythmic pattern shrinks to normal size and the tempo will instinctively pick up, running steadily until the retard of mm. 121–23. (Note, incidentally, that the Eulenburg miniature score is misnumbered in its mm. 115–23; I adhere, nonetheless, to the numbering given.) 106
121

The call for the original tempo (*a Tempo I*) at m. 125 is puzzling. The 1st violin melody is greatly extended, so you don't want to stretch the pace unduly. Still, the character marking is *doux et expressif*, and the line will not sound "gentle and expressive" if it is being thrust ahead at the speed of the *Très mouvementé*. On the other hand, to identify the *Très modéré* of the introduction as the desired tempo would put a terrible drag on this passage. The 2nd violin, whose figure provides the motive force in these bars, will have to use judgment, setting the pace but also responding flexibly to the inflections of the solo line; so also for the viola when it takes over the rhythm. 125

On the way into m. 141, the 2nd violin will have to lead the inner voices in a suitable transition to the *Tempo rubato*. It is impossible to run headlong into the double bar and then suddenly to affect a freely swaying tempo. The 2nd violin will continue to influence matters in the first eight measures of the *Tempo rubato*, since so much of the 1st violin's solo moves in syncopes. 141

The *a Tempo* of m. 145 does not come fully into its own, I think, until its twenty-first measure, when the 1st violin arrives at its forte, high F in m. 165. Whether the tempo should be maintained unabated in the fortissimo, m. 181, is a question. The passage is marked, "with passion and very sustained"; even though the 1st violin line is hugely augmented here, the 2nd violin is moving in fairly agitated quarter notes, with the cello triplets going even faster. My experience has been that, from the fortissimo up to m. 216, the music benefits from some broadening of tempo. This, however, is the last breather you get; from here to the end of the movement, there is no time for apology. 145
165
181

216

For sonority, Debussy orchestrates some double stops into the parts along the way. None are more athletic than the octaves for the 2nd violin, starting at m. 240, owing to the sizeable leap needed to play the second measure of each set. It should be noted that the half-note rhythms, in mm. 248–51 are not accented, whether in octaves or no, even though the heat of the moment may blind the player to that fact. 240

248

In mm. 258–59 and again at mm. 266–67, the 2nd violin must try valiantly to make its response to the 1st violin statement robustly audible, even though in a lower and less brilliant register. In mm. 270–75, that player again has to make sure to be heard while engaging in the broken-field running the part imposes. Both inner voices must look to the synchronizing of their parts in mm. 270–71, 275, and 279. Synchronization is the concern of all four voices in mm. 286–88; the upper three parts actually line up with each other, while the cello must play the broad triplets in its part emphatically enough so that they add contrast, not uncertainty, to the total effect. 258, 266

270

286

At m. 289, let everyone recognize that the spotlight is on the 2nd violin for four measures. As for that player, to appear suddenly in the demure and yearning melody, fresh out of the seething waters of the preceding measures, is another one of those rapid changes of character a performer remembers. For all three lower voices, the passage from the E major signature (m. 299) through the downbeat of m. 318 is always a breathtaking experience. The 2nd violin and viola, particularly, are kept very busy grabbing at the swashes of tremolo as they rush past. 289

299

Possibly the greatest playing challenge of the entire quartet comes at the very end. Everyone has been pelting away at the triplet figures in *Très vif* tempo since m. 326, in a brilliant peroration on the original theme and on its second-movement modification. The 1st violin has been dancing some light fantastics up on the E-string. Even the cellist has finally been pulled into the rhythmic rapids. Then the 1st, after a short rest and three measures of pawing the ground, has to make a brilliant, three-octave run, splendidly alone, up to an exultant, sustained B. It's a blazing finish to a rather helter-skelter movement, a closing flourish that makes the violinist appreciate all those hours of scale practice.

I feel a bit contrite about calling the finale "helter-skelter." Nonetheless, I can recall the first time I had to perform the Debussy in concert. It was one of thirty-nine quartets, most of them new to me, that I had to play in a weekly broadcast concert series soon after joining the Fine Arts Quartet. At no point did I feel more apprehensive than when about to go on stage for the Debussy; and my concern was most of all for its finale. It is technically demanding, of course. What really concerned me, though, was the thought of having to respond at high speed to the variety of musical events and episodes that are flung at the players in the course of the movement. Even now, after years of performing the piece, I still find the finale exhilarating, to say the least.

It is one thing to pass some of the textures and timbres of this quartet in review. Realizing them in performance is another. In rehearsal, be alert to the aural possibilities of each segment of the work. Help each other to get beyond mere accuracy of note rendition. In a pointillist painting, each tiny dot may be perfectly formed; it is the color created by the juxtaposition of many dots, however, that creates the intended impression on the viewer. So also in the Debussy: make sure that the notes merge into the colors and textures of sound that you discern in the music. Experiment with touch and speed of bow stroke, dynamic balance, fluctuation of tempo, and especially gradation of vibrato.

Rehearsing the Debussy will sharpen the ensemble's ability to evaluate tone color. Don't shrink from trying various approaches to the shading of a given passage. I think that, even after years of performing this quartet, you will still be surprised by the vivid nuances that you can evoke from its pages.

SOCIETA' FILARMONICA - TRENTO

Lunedì, 14 dicembre 1959 alle ore 21

4° CONCERTO SOCIALE

THE FINE ARTS QUARTET

Leonard Sorkin - *violino*   Irving Ilmer   - *viola*

Abram Loft   - *violino*   George Sopkin - *violoncello*

PROGRAMMA

Hindemith	- Quartetto op. 22 Nr. 3
	Fugato (sehr langsam - molto lento)
	Sehr energisch - Sehr glitzernd (molto energico, e scintillante)
	Mässig - Rondò (gemächlich und mit Grazie - moderato, comodo e con grazia)

Haydn	- Quartetto in re magg. op. 64 Nr. 5
	Allegro moderato
	Adagio cantabile
	Menuetto: allegretto
	Finale: vivace

Beethoven	- Quartetto in la min. op. 132
	Assai sostenuto - Allegro
	Allegro, ma non tanto
	Molto adagio: Canzone di ringraziamento di un guarito alla Divinità (in modo lidico) - Andante (sentendo nuova forza)
	Alla marcia, assai vivace
	Allegro appassionato

Durante le singole esecuzioni non si può accedere alla sala

Prossimo concerto, mercoledì 13 gennaio 1960

La Pianista ELSA TRIANGI

Dopo il concerto funzionerà servizio di autobus cittadino

Tip. « La Reclame » - Trento

CHAPTER TWENTY-FIVE

✒ Hindemith ✒
Quartet No. 3, Op. 22

In a very small hall... we can readily discern the most involved melodic lines, the most complex harmonies, and the most intricate rhythmical patterns, because we are in closest spatial connection with the source of the sound. And besides, the instruments... can make use of the most refined subtleties of technique, because nothing will get lost, and the performers can transmit their production as directly as in intimate talk. The composer, writing for such conditions, enjoys the greatest possible freedom to develop his technique into the most esoteric realms.[1]

These perceptive thoughts about chamber music were written by the composer, Paul Hindemith, in middle age, in the light of decades of prolific output in various musical categories, and of his own experience as performer. From the age of nineteen he was second violin in the quartet led by his teacher, Adolf Rebner, at the Hoch Conservatory in Frankfurt. During his military service in World War I, Hindemith was himself 1st violin in a regimental quartet, and later—once again in Rebner's quartet—moved to the viola, which was henceforth his principal instrument. In 1921 he formed the Amar-Hindemith Quartet. It was this ensemble which introduced both his Quartet No. 2 (1921), and the present work, Quartet No. 3, Op. 22, which dates from 1922.

These works began the long list of his published chamber music, which was eventually to include six string quartets, sonatas for a wide range of instruments (the last is for tuba and piano), and ensembles of various kinds, including the late Octet for winds and strings. String Quartet No. 3 is in five movements: a slow, central chapter framed on either side by paired, contrasting movements.

SCORE: Paul Hindemith. 1923. *3. Streichquartett, Opus 22*. Mainz: Schott. Miniature score No. 3435.

Left: Page from the program for the concert by The Fine Arts Quartet, Trento, December 14, 1959.

I

1

Fugato. Sehr langsame Viertel. ("Fugato. Very slow quarter-note.") There is no time signature at the head of this movement (nor for any save the third movement, where a parenthesized 6/4 sets the metric frame). Hindemith wants the freedom to move variably within each measure. Within the first ten bars, the groupings of quarters are: 5, 4, 4, 4, 5, 4, 4, 4, 4, 4—not very irregular, after all. The melodic line, moreover, is so clearly constructed that you can quickly feel comfortable with the free-meter process. Besides, this is visually easier to live with than having to read changing time signatures on a measure-by-measure basis.

The tempo range indicated by the composer (quarter = 58–69) serves as a qualifier for his verbal instruction, "very slow quarter-note." In my own experience with the work, metronome 58 to the quarter-note is too slow, making the line break apart on each beat; a speed of at least 69 is more appropriate. Even so, you will have to use your own judgment in pacing the "more lively," "much livelier," and "Presto" measures that occur later in the movement, where no metronomic guides are offered.

Either no, or else a minimal and carefully graded, vibrato should be used for the opening measures. A fitful, sporadically lively left hand is bound to make this opening sound sickly. At any rate, Hindemith himself calls for "warm" playing by

A − 2

m. *A* − 2, and we can assume that the temperature can be raised during the *poco crescendo* of the two preceding measures. *Gehalten* ("held," "steady"), the instruction

B − 3

at m. *B* − 3, should be understood to mean sostenuto, without any adjustment in

B − (5–4)

tempo. The pace arrived at during bars *B* − (5–4)—the instruction there is, "push forward a bit"—should be firmly maintained, with the bow stroke just as firmly legato.

B

In the first three bars of *B*, the chromatic descents in the viola part and the cello's more steeply falling figure are only slightly subordinate to the 2nd violin's statement of the theme. Let the voicing be heard through the quiet dynamic level here, with the individuality of the part writing projected yet more clearly in the measures that follow.

C − 7

The "livelier tempo" of mm. *C* − 7 ff. is led very definitely by the 2nd violin through the first measures of the passage, with the flourishes of the 1st violin part fitting to this frame; the dominance moves to the viola part in the two bars

C

following. Again in the "much livelier" passage starting at *C*, the 2nd violin must offer very definite leadership to synchronize the three lower voices. Be especially

D − 8

clear in leading the *molto ritenuto* in the two bars at *D* − 8; the three-within-four groups of 16ths here are tricky enough when played in steady tempo, and more so when moving within the context of a slowdown. Control returns to the 1st violin

D − 6

only when that instrument floats downward through the cadenza of mm. *D* − 6 ff.

The pizzicato line provided by the cello under the return of the opening theme,

D

mm. *D* ff., is very much a melody as well as a supporting bass, and must be played with shading and rubato to match its importance. You will note that, while the 1st violin line is marked pianissimo, the composer's instruction to the cello is simply, "very soft, but definite." In fact, through the fourth measure of *E*, the cello part is the broadly framed solo that is decorated by the upper voices; in the three bars that follow, the violins are, in effect, spelling out a bowed continuation of the cello voice.

E+11

In the last eight measures of the movement, the sound must be ethereal; move toward the fingerboard and play, figuratively, with one hair on the string. The performers' aim here should be to lull the audience—and themselves—into an utterly restful state. Don't look ahead until you have to.

Schnelle Achtel: Sehr energisch. ("Fast 8th-note. Very energetic.") It is   II
important to obey Hindemith's call for *Folgt sofort II* ("proceed immediately with
movement II") at the end of the first movement. The shock of the sudden shift from
ppp to *ff*, and from other-worldly to savagely guttural sound will be weakened by
any but the briefest pause, and cannot endure any fidgeting on the part of the
players. Hold the bow still at the tip after the final, long downstroke of movement I.
The 1st violin, finishing a measure earlier, begins a slow and very unobtrusive
preparation for the new attack, even as the lower voices are drawing to the close of
their note. Then, with quick and tightly unified inset, begin the fortissimo of
movement II.

The repeated, downbow 8ths of the second movement theme are taken with
incisive wrist strokes near the frog of the bow, and certainly as close to the bridge as
decent sound permits. The swell and receding of mm. 2 and 3 (and corresponding   2
measures throughout the movement) are essential, and must be strongly marked.
Prominent in much of this movement is the short swirl of 32nds; see m. 7, for   7
example. The swirl should always be played incisively, with percussive impact of
the fingers against the string.

Another critical point: always emphasize the thematic contrast between a
broad 3/4 measure and a tight 3/8 bar; for example, as in the second and third bars   *F*+2
after *F*. The quarter-beats need not be hammered, because the expansiveness of the
measure is of paramount importance. On the other hand, each 8th in the 3/8
measure should be strongly marked, even though the dotted notes would seem to
indicate utter lightness of touch. In furiously drumming measures (for example,
m. *F* + 8), where Hindemith puts an accent mark on each note of every triplet, play   *F*+8
as though you mean to strip the bow hair of its rosin.

From the sixth to tenth bars of *G*, the metric frame is 3/2, governed first by all   *G*+6
three lower parts, then by the cello alone. This broad swing of the beat must be
made evident, for it generates the retard into the *a tempo—grazioso* of letter *H*.   *H*

In the quiet interlude of the movement that takes place there, the 2nd violin
leads the band, leaving the 1st (and later, the cello as well) free to play a lyric,
Hindemithian ditty. The solo, as well as the accompanying lines, reveal aspects
derived from the basic theme of the movement. The long-slurred units, first in the
viola, then the 2nd violin, should make themselves felt, even within the
pianississimo level. As for the short, rhythmic pulses (for example, 2nd violin and
cello at letter *H*), these must be played as legato as possible, even when string   *H*
crossing is involved, without any hiccup effect in the sound of the 16ths.

The hammered 8ths of the theme's first measure are called into play, very
cleverly, in the *Ruhig (ein wenig langsamer als vorher)*—"Quietly, a bit slower than   *L*
before"—passage that closes this interlude/development section of the movement.
Then, voice by voice, starting with the viola, all the ingredients and the original
tempo of the theme are restored. The return to tempo is spread over a span of ten
measures, from *M* + 4. Viola and cello will have to resist any temptation to   *M*+4
telegraph the acceleration in the preceding seven bars. If they take Hindemith's
instruction, *etwas trocken* ("rather drily") to heart, and play their lines with a dash of
irony, they will not sound stodgy in holding to the slow speed. Once the "gradual
return to the first tempo" starts, the pacing can ride on the 8th-notes, which appear
in one voice or another in every bar. With the unison 16th-note rhythms in the   *N*−5
accelerando measures, control is in the hands of all four players. So it remains in the
fury that is unleashed at *N*, for the players are absolutely dependent on one   *N*
another.

P − 6

I can't help feeling some frustration in arriving at a combination of triple forte and the instruction, *Wild* ("savagely"), at m. *P* − 6, only to have the cold water of a diminuendo and retard thrown over me after a mere four measures of rambunctiousness. In fact, however, the unwinding process continues right on, up

Q, P

to *Q*. Don't mistake the instruction "Still flowingly," at *P*, as a sign to let down the tension too quickly. It is up to the violins here to exploit the vigorous profiles of, and the friction between, the two lines of their duet.

The massed, Presto review of the theme that closes the movement is tricky because the four instruments must hurl themselves through the measures in unison; any mishap will be glaringly apparent. Watch out especially for the two triplet measures, five bars from the end. Very firm fingering and a suggestion of accent on the start of each triplet will help promote clarity. I have always been a bit puzzled by the final measure, where the foursome seems to join in a robust, almost barbershop-quartet-style cadence chord. Is Hindemith kidding himself—or his listeners?

In his Sonata for Violin and Piano, begun in 1923 and completed in 1927, Ravel paid homage to a jazz inspiration by labeling the second movement, *Blues.* Hindemith, I think, got there a shade earlier; the third movement of this quartet is

III

titled, *Ruhige Viertel. Stets fliessend* ("Quiet quarter-note. Always flowing.") For me, though, it has a blues-in-Berlin flavor. Moreover, in temper at any rate, it seems related to the music of the first movement, adopting a *mit wenig Ausdruck* ("with little expression") air in place of the earlier theme's *sehr weich und innig* ("very softly and inwardly").

It is strange that Hindemith relented enough here to provide a time signature of 6/4, only to apologize for it by enclosing the number in parentheses. Perhaps the composer was only signalling the player that, here at least, there are no metric surprises in store?

The entire movement is played with mutes. The dynamic level rises from the initial *ppp* to a full and, at one point, extended forte, before fading at the close to a quadruple piano. This takes place as the composer extends and applies the

1

components of his theme: the slurred and convoluted 8th-note figure of m. 1; the more linear melody of mm. 2–3; and the pizzicato, quarter-note background pulse. In its own way, the loud peak of this movement, straining against the damping effect of the mute, is as intense as the more raucous points in the companion movements. Despite the *weich* ("tender") in the composer's instruction to the three

G+2

lower voices for their four-string pizzicato chords at *G* + 2, they must also give full heed to *und voll* ("and full"). The 1st violin's high-register proclamation of the theme needs ample resonance in the supporting voices.

Some performance hints that come to mind: the initial 8th-note figure of the theme seems to combine melodic and drone lines. I think, though, that the "floor" of the figure is important in its own right, and is only interrupted and ornamented by the rising tones. The stretching between the two diverging lines of the figure is melodically important, and should be exploited by very smooth string crossing and by some rhythmic flexibility (within the confines of the composer's call for "little

B

expression"). Certainly when all four players are wailing away with this figure at *B*, the restriction on expression no longer applies.

C−1

The transition from the triple-piano pizzicato of the 2nd violin to the equally quiet bowed notes of the viola (m. *C* − 1) must be hushed, to be sure, yet have enough projection so that the listener can follow the action. You can't simply leave a hole in the sound.

The violins, in their quiet duet before letter *D*, and the viola in the solo passages between letters *C* and *E*, must sound neither skinny nor whining. No matter how high the lines go, the effect should be warm and relaxed.

D—7

This movement, with its slow, steady unfolding and continuous sound, has always been for me the center of gravity in this quartet. There is only one full pause, and that a very brief one, at m. *E* − 1. The movement can exert a kind of hypnotic effect, carried through to the very end, when the pizzicato quarters fade into nothingness.

E−1

Mässig schnelle Viertel. ("Moderately fast quarter-note.") No matter where the ensemble finds its tempo, within the narrow bracket offered by the composer (quarter = 80–88), the details of this movement will inevitably veer widely in speed. Much of its length is given over to cadenza-like passages: for cello alone; cello against background; cello and violin; 2nd violin and viola; viola and cello. In fact, the entire movement seems to be a cadenza for quartet, turning the spotlight on the several facets of the group, but standing the group on its head and focusing especially on the cello.

IV

Please keep this idea in mind throughout. The duo passages must be treated with as much artistic freedom as those that star the solo cello. The *a tempo* marking at *B* is simply a restorative after the broad cello retard in the preceding measure— and by no means a sign that the viola and cello 16ths to come should be played squarely in time. If any confirmation of this fact is needed, consider the two wild surges of consecutive fifths in the viola part, a technical flourish that is all the more brilliant because it is easier than it looks! Hindemith also exhorts the viola—his own instrument—at letter *C*: *bariolage, brillant*. He asks for a "brilliant" (I would prefer to translate it as "dazzling" or "flaming") rendition of the stopped-note/open-string alternation. In short, this movement is as flamboyant a display of quartet virtuosity as anything you might find even in the tiny repertoire of quartet concertos.

B

B+3

C

At the end of the movement there is the instruction to proceed directly to the finale. In fact, the reverberation of the last chord of the fourth movement still hangs in the air when the viola launches the *Rondo* with a resounding F♯. To that player: don't crush the note; try to sound like a wooden trombone, while dwindling to the pianissimo that begins the movement *Gemächlich und mit Grazie* ("Comfortably and with gracefulness").

V

There is balance and symmetry in the overall structure of this quartet. The essentially quiet first movement serves as prelude to the wild second movement. Now the even wilder fourth movement raises the curtain on a finale that is quiet overall.

This last movement is based on two contrasting elements: the legato, lyric line, heard immediately in the viola part, and the sprightly and pointed countermelody, presented by the cello. Both elements, in whatever voice they may appear, must be played so as to project their respective characters, or the music's contrast will be dulled. The movement is as much variations as rondo, for the successive episodes seem to deal only with transformations or extensions of the original ideas.

At *E*, 1st violin and cello would do well to imagine some slightly exotic, courtly dance, the two instruments pacing delicately around one another. When this dance reaches *F*, it is as though the 2nd violin stands in the middle of the company, cranking out a wheedling accompaniment; repetitious that line may be, but it needs to be played with some archness, the recurrent G♯s vibrant, the 16th-note couplets

E

F

F+4   crisply fingered. Starting in the fourth bar here, let the three lower voices take care not to overpower the 1st violin with the drumming 16ths.

G−9   The cello's ascending chromatic line at m. *G* − 9 should converge cleanly against the opposing violin lines. Two measures later, the 2nd violin and cello ostinato demands neat finger and bow action to provide proper background for the viola solo.

G+4   Hindemith carries his insistence on the central idea of the movement pretty far: at m. *G* + 4, the 1st violin pirouettes in the top line; the three lower voices grind out the once-lyric theme in chords that each contain five consecutive pitches of a whole-tone scale. Don't take my use of the word "grind" too literally. You will note that Hindemith has written lines over the quarter-notes. Clearly, he means this to be a chordally expanded (I was tempted to say, smeared) version of the basic tune.

H−3   Three bars before *H*, the offbeat accents should not be hit so hard that the melody is rendered grotesque. The stress marks are intensifications, but they do not countermand the "flowing" instruction given several bars earlier.

L   All ends well. True to the movement's title, the opening duet of viola and cello returns in literal restatement at *L*, before a rather sardonic coda closes the quartet. In the final measures, see that the trills played by the upper voices in answer to the cello melody are smooth, not calisthenic in nature. For me, the piece really ends with the airy, pizzicato chord three measures from the double bar. I suspect this was the case for Hindemith as well, and that he added the fortissimo tag as a kind of bluff reassurance to the audience.

This finale is fun to play: the four members can see that the musical cards are constantly being shuffled and re-dealt, in various guises, to all participants. Audiences, however, seem a bit disaffected by the Rondo, perhaps because it may strike them as anticlimactic after the fireworks of the preceding movement, and especially because of the enigmatic tone of its ending. Strangely enough, I found this quartet to be most coolly received by listeners in German concert halls. In any case, I think the work is a solid contribution to the repertoire, and one that should figure more often in concert programs than has been the case in recent years.

PROGRAM

String Quartet (1931)   **Ruth Crawford**

    Rubato assai
    Leggiero
    Andante
    Allegro possibile

               (Played without pause)

Quartet No. 3 (1968)   **Karel Husa**

    Allegro moderato
    Lento assai
    Allegro possibile
    Adagio

        Commissioned by Mr. and Mrs. Lee A. Freeman
        for The Fine Arts Music Foundation of Chicago.
            Pulitzer Prize in Music, 1969.

Intermission

Five Pieces for String Quartet, Op. 5   **Anton Webern**

    Heftig bewegt
    Sehr langsam
    Sehr bewegt
    Sehr langsam
    In zarter Bewegung

Concertino for String Quartet   **Igor Stravinsky**

Quartet No. 3 (1927)   **Bela Bartok**

    Prima parte: Moderato
    Seconda parte: Allegro
    Ricapitulazione della prima parte: Moderato
    Coda: Allegro molto

               (Played without pause)

CHAPTER TWENTY-SIX

⚬ Crawford ⚬
String Quartet (1931)

The composer Ruth Crawford Seeger (1901–53) is virtually unknown here [England] and in her native America. Yet, in the early 1930s, she was recognized by the American avant garde as one of its most original and innovatory representatives... The neglect she has suffered is undoubtedly due to the effective cessation of her composing activities after 1933; yet the few works she produced up to then use many techniques not fully explored elsewhere until the 1950s and 60s, most notably by the "accepted" European avant garde.[1]

The undeserved obscurity that has surrounded Ruth Crawford is now gradually being lifted. Even so, far too few performers and ensembles have had firsthand experience with her music. As the work under consideration here demonstrates, she must be numbered among the significant American composers of the 20th century.

The Crawford quartet is a model of contemporary chamber-music writing. In ways that still sound stimulating after the passage of more than half a century, its four movements explore and expand the sounds and techniques of the string quartet. The work is interesting both to play and hear, and completely honest in its workmanship. Its candor is reflected in its length: scarcely ten minutes, overall. It wastes no notes, yet is absolutely complete in its brevity. Every ensemble will benefit from giving careful rehearsal to this piece, whether or not they can bring it to performance level.

The composer herself once said of the quartet that "it should have months of

---

SCORE: Ruth Crawford. 1941. *String Quartet 1931*. Bryn Mawr: Merion Music, Inc. Full Score.

Left: Page from the program for the concert by The Fine Arts Quartet, Western Washington State College (now Western Washington University), Bellingham, April 3, 1970.

295

rehearsal, due especially to its rhythmical and dynamic difficulties. Of course, music which is thought horizontally is usually more difficult than that which is thought vertically."[2] Her comment, however, was in response to a 1938 performance, when little rehearsal had been allotted the piece.

In the decades since, performers have had to learn, comprehend, and present many contemporary works whose technical demands approach or exceed that of the Crawford work. Also, our ability to absorb and understand nonconventional musical sounds and melodies has been greatly expanded. Consequently, the Crawford composition is not as daunting to players as it undoubtedly was in the years immediately following its creation. The quartet, nevertheless, remains a very challenging experience. I think you will find that the hard work is worth it.

Ruth Crawford, daughter of a Methodist minister, was born in Liverpool, Ohio. She moved to Chicago in 1921 to study piano. As a result of her work there in theory and composition with Adolf Weidig, she gradually turned her emphasis from piano to composition. In New York in 1929, she became a student of Charles Seeger, composer and musicologist. Her experiences in New York confirmed her already strong interest in the work of avant-garde composers in America and Europe.

She spent the year 1930–31 in Europe, as the first woman to hold a Guggenheim Fellowship in composition. Work on her string quartet was completed during her stay in Berlin and Paris.

Crawford and Charles Seeger were married in 1932. In ensuing years, the interest of both was directed, partly by concern for the social upheavals of the '30s, toward the folk music of America and of the world. In addition to family obligations (raising four children) and piano teaching, Crawford devoted herself to preparing folk music accompaniments, arrangements, and transcriptions. Her plans to return to the writing of serious music were cut short by her untimely death in 1953.[3]

I *Rubato assai.* A footnote on the first page of the score states, "The melodic line, as indicated by 'solo' in each part, must be heard continuing throughout the movement." You won't be able to take this instruction literally. For one thing, two contrasting threads run through the movement: the solo line, of broad rhythmic flow and large intervallic motion; and another of tight-knit, quick rhythms.

For the most part, the composer directs attention to the designated solo by marking it a notch higher in dynamic level than the surrounding parts. Even so, the difference in loudness does not conceal the intrinsic interest of the subordinated line, especially since the composer sometimes highlights a voice by making it louder, yet not giving it the benefit of the "solo" marking.

At the start, for example, the cello part, *piano ma ben marcato*, is a close contender for attention against the *mezzo piano cantando* of the 1st violin's lyric solo.

6 And when, in m. 6, the 2nd violin takes over the solo function in *forte marcato bruscamente*, it seems not to be a continuation of the 1st violin's singing line, but rather to be bringing the agitated melodic idea into the foreground.

Let me draw your attention to a few melodic connections that you can see in the first area of the movement. I hope these will lead you on to pursue a detailed investigation of the score, to find other part relationships. You won't necessarily plumb the composer's thought processes by such an inspection, but you will gain appreciation of the devices and techniques that sprang from her concept of the work.

Compare the first two 1st violin solos (mm. 1 ff., mm. 8 ff.); they are almost identical in pitch sequence. Note that the beginning of the viola part (m. 5) is the reverse of the line that the cello plays in mm. 1–2; and that the continuation (mm. 8–9) of the viola part is a direct imitation of the same source. The cello provides the connecting link between the two viola segments by playing a segment from its opening line, first in reverse, then in forward motion, in mm. 6–7. The 2nd violin's brief outburst in mm. 6–7 starts over again in m. 13, but this time continuing on. 1, 8
5

6

Crawford marks the 1st violin as solo in m. 8, then finds it necessary to label it that way again in m. 16, owing to the competing action in the lower voices in the intervening bars. Again, after designating the cello as the soloist in m. 28, she does not affix the title again until m. 43, in the 2nd violin part. The territory between is open to all four voices. 16
28
43

Even more homogeneous texture is evident in mm. 44 through 49, with agitation pervading all participating voices. The turbulent element prevails for a time, but the sustained idea returns in m. 50 and builds quickly to its own epitome, the stentorian trills in the three lower voices, mm. 52 through 58. From here to the end of the movement, pedal-point lines gradually soothe and quiet the brusque factor. 44
50
52

In short, this is a movement in which there is no accompaniment, but rather a dialogue between distinct musical identities, placed variously in foreground or background, and important whatever their position of the moment. The pacing of the music is skillfully ordered, building gradually to a climactic point two-thirds into the movement, then unwinding to a quiet ending.

As in much conventional music, but to a higher degree, each player has to change attitude quickly. You move from the sustained, lyric role, where flowing bowstrokes and warm sound are required, to a more spiky, edged mood, calling for contained, precise bowing and deft string crossing. Along with this, the latter passages demand rhythmic agility, for beats are likely to be divided into three, four, five, six, even seven parts in quick succession. The performed line must combine accuracy with the effect of improvisatory freedom.

Individual practice will make you familiar with details of your own part. You will want to get into ensemble rehearsal fairly quickly, however, to see how the parts and rhythmic units fit together. I would suggest a few slow run-throughs, section by section, through the movement. Leave out the accents at first, to avoid confusion about the rhythmic patterns.

Even in slow practice, try to use the kind of contained stroke that you will need when playing up to speed. Your slow rehearsal needs to be a slow-motion duplicate of your eventual performance. Otherwise, you will find that the moves you are making at reduced speed won't work when you return to full tempo.

Use especially concentrated bowing in the *marcato* areas of the line. Much of the time you will be at the middle or in the lower half of the bow. The many accents, sudden rests, catches of breath, and intervallic leaps compel you to play where you can focus the bowing motion toward the hand and fingers.

If you find yourselves freezing up and making scratchy grunts of sound, go back to slow playing so that you can study the kind of motions you are using. The music must sound vibrant and agitated, not cramped.

Leggiero. It is surprising that Crawford did not carry the footnote instruction for the first movement over into the Leggiero, for the idea of continuity is even more apparent here than in the opening Rubato. In character of melody, the II material seems to build on the texture of the agitated element in the first movement. Here, though, there are not the many changes in the rhythmic fractioning of the beat; instead, the division of the quarter into two 8ths or four 16ths is consistent throughout.

In many measures the sound is thinned down to two or three parts. The fabric of the music is never torn, however, for a break in one voice is overlapped or taken over by concurrent activity or a fresh entrance in another.

Extremely agile bowing is needed in this movement, because the lines are built mostly of 16ths and of short, sustained notes that often start in midbeat. Also, the transition from one voice to another is often marked by either a forzando or accent in the entering and exiting parts. The total effect is one of telegraphic urgency, with the stream of sound throwing off sparks and bursts of energy, subsiding and regenerating with great suddenness.

25   One of the fascinating spots in this movement is the passage from m. 25 through m. 39. The 1st violin hangs aloft on a high C; far below, the cello sustains its lowest D♭. Within this frame, and starting very high, the two inner voices skitter their way down to their lowest range. As the descent progresses, the outer voices close in, so that a sense of contraction and condensation of sound space is conveyed.

57   The high-register twittering of the two violins in mm. 57–74 is bound to need a deal of slow practice, both to nail the notes in place and to fit the two parts accurately to one another. Stitching all four parts together through the movement as a whole will take patient work. In your focus on notes and synchronization, don't forget that you must balance to let the solo spots emerge as designated in the score.

The composer calls for a *giocoso* attitude at several points in the three lower voices. I doubt, however, whether the ensemble will feel anything other than intense concentration when playing this movement. If your stroke is sprightly, your sound clear and unstrained, I think you can rely on the listener to imagine the jocularity.

III   *Andante.* As the score dictates, the entire quartet is meant to be played without pause. The first two movements, in fact, are bridged by a sustained note in the cello; that note ends with the fortissimo chord, from all four voices, that fires the Leggiero. A grand pause separates the Leggiero from the Andante. Still, with the cello line evaporating in a final spray of 16ths, and the Andante starting with the triple-piano entry of the viola on a sustained, low C♯, the *attacca* effect is well supported.

The Andante is worlds away from the preceding movements in spirit. It carries the sustained-tone element of the first movement to extreme lengths. A headnote dictates that bow changes in all parts be masked throughout, and that the constant dynamic swells and releases be finely graded.

75   Except at the climax of the movement, the dynamic fluctuations are always overlapped, so that the long tones of the several instruments merge into a continuous stream of sound. The surface of that stream is continuously rippled, as a result of the very deliberate placement of the dynamics. Crawford's special concern about this is not fully indicated in the movement's headnotes. In the previously mentioned 1938 discussion, a listener asked, "How is it possible to perform the slow movement... when there is no pulse?" It is surprising that the composer did not demur at this. She did, however, reply as follows:

The slow movement... is done best when it is conducted. But, with sufficient amount of rehearsal, it can be done without. This movement is built on counterpoint of dynamics. The crescendi and diminuendi should be exactly timed, and no instrument should reach the high or low point at the same time as any other.[4]

Crawford's reference to a conductor probably relates to the score's indication that the slow movement can be played by string orchestra, with double bass. Though I have not heard such a performance, I imagine it would be most impressive. From experience, however, I know that the Andante can very well be controlled by a quartet—without conductor! The music does indeed have "pulse," even though that is deliberately blurred. In part this blurring comes from an occasional change of meter, though the change is always simultaneous in all four voices. Much more of the haze effect derives from the composer's specified overlapping of the swells in the several instruments.

The viola starts alone, triple piano, on the second half of m. 1, playing a line   1
that rises and falls gently over the space of each two half-notes. The cello enters on the downbeat of m. 3, a minor second up from the viola part; the cello line also   3
oscillates dynamically, but out of phase with the viola. Taken together with the characteristic resonance of the minor second, the quiet dynamic friction immediately lulls the ear. The switch back and forth between clusters of measures in 3/4 and 4/4 time, starting in bar 5, helps slip the listener's moorings a bit more.   5

The 2nd violin enters in m. 13, but on the fourth quarter of the bar. As a result,   13
the dynamic peaks now fall on three successive quarters. With the entrance of the 1st violin on the second beat of m. 19, the four voices peak in turn on each of the   19
four quarter-notes of every measure.

The close intervallic spacing also continues, but with more layers of tone; in m. 20, for example, we find the superimposition of three minor seconds, formed by the   20
notes C, C♯, D, and E♭. These and other dissonant combinations in the movement are built so gradually and steadily, however, that they present themselves to the ear as completely normal and acceptable. The constant ebb and flow of the overlaid swells, in fact, lulls us into a feeling that we are afloat in a sea of consonance.

There are momentary forte peaks at the midpoint of the movement, but the major outbursts occur later on, especially in the close lineup of the four instruments in mm. 74–76 and in the tightly spaced forzandi of the succeeding, double-speed   74
passage. The pace in these measures (77–87) is intensified by strong acceleration.   77
The laminated swells have returned in the three upper voices at work here; owing to the speed, the dynamic spurts are concentrated around the forzandi, as is indicated by the shape of the swell marks. A brief postlude resumes the original tempo, and the movement ends, as it began, in the two lower voices.

Since you are acting as your own conductors, you will have to rehearse giving, and watching for, very discreet signals. It is easy to get lost or hypnotized in the constant surges of the sound. Ideally, I would want to play this movement from score, rather than from the individual parts. Page turns, of course, are a problem, especially in music that relies on constant rubbing of one voice against the other. In any event, try to rehearse with the score until you have absorbed the sound and the way your line fits into the overall texture. Then you should be able to play effectively from your individual part.

The bowing will also take practice. You need control to manage the constant legato. The instruction for the movement, in practical effect, asks that each instrument sound as though it is maintaining a single, endless stroke. Within this continuity, you need constant gradation of speed and pressure of stroke to give accurate shape to the swells and the general dynamic profile of your line.

You might think that the experience of floating in this undulating lagoon of sound would be a restful one. The metronome mark, however, is pretty fast (116 to the quarter-note). It's no simple matter to keep moving while holding your place and making sure that your dynamics are not dislodged by the activity in neighboring lines. Placing the intended climaxes, joining forces for the major outburst and the pullback to the renewed quiet of the close: these take as much concentration and self-control as anything else in this quartet. In some ways, in fact, I think this is the most difficult movement to put together. But again, what imaginative sounds are evoked!

You and the audience may be in a trance by the end of the Andante, lulled by the low, pianissimo C/C♯ of the viola and cello. But the fortissimo-forzando A♭ of the 1st violin at the start of the fourth movement will snap you to attention.

IV   *Allegro possibile.* This movement is a musical equation, literally written by the numbers. Once again, it seems to take off, even if only distantly, from the same kind of texture contrast evident in the first movement. The organization of contrasts is at once simple and complex. To begin with, the ensemble is divided, in quasi-concerto fashion, into a solo 1st violin and a tutti group composed of the three lower voices. The solo moves from one detached note, to a pair, to three, and on up to a slurred group of twenty. At the same time, it progresses gradually from fortissimo-forzando to pianissimo. From midway in the movement, it makes its way back up the dynamic slope and also reduces itself steadily, returning to a final, single note.

The other three parts, muted, moving always in simultaneous rhythm and at octave spacing from one another, progress from a pianissimo, slurred streamer of twenty notes (note the number!) through ever shorter groupings, dropping one 8th-note with each new entrance. As the groups grow shorter, the dynamic level rises and forzando emphases appear on the last notes of rhythmic clusters.

57   One sustained note (mm. 57–60) marks the midpoint of the movement for this "orchestral" group (as it does for the solo violin as well). Thereupon the process reverses, both receding in loudness and increasing the number of notes per musical event, ending at last with a group of twenty slurred, pianissimo notes.

The tempo is so fast that the listener is not likely to recognize the numerically ordered scheme of the parts. Less obvious still will be the pitch organization of the three lower voices. The composer George Perle points out that these are built on "a ten-note *ostinato* figure whose recurrent statements are regularly modified... by a cyclic permutation of the whole figure, with each new statement of the *ostinato* beginning on the next succeeding note of the original set."[5] You can see this by counting successive sets of ten 8th-notes, skipping over the rests as necessary to complete a given set.

Further, "at that point in the first half of the movement where the series of cyclical permutations restores the original form of the *ostinato*, the latter is transposed up a whole step."[6] You will find this transposed set starting on the third

21, 35 8th-note of m. 21. Permutations of this transposed set continue until measure 35. From there until the midpoint of the movement, the regularity of the set is altered.

At the midpoint, a melodic reversal begins. Look at the phrase of twenty notes

60   starting on the second 8th in m. 60 of the 1st violin part. You will see that the phrase

is a mirror image—but transposed a half-step up—of the phrase in mm. 55–57. (Do   55
not include the G that leads into bar 58—that is part of the midpoint note.)
Compare the notes in the three lower voices in m. 63 with those in m. 54, and you   63
find the same relationship exists. This precise correspondence will prevail for the
rest of the movement.[7] The 1st violin will have the last word, with a couplet, then a
single note fired in accented, fortissimo salvos.

These and other structural details of the quartet yield to the practiced eye of
the composer and the theorist. Even without such insights, the performer and
listener will sense the firm organization of the work. The features we have noted in
the last movement may seem to be fairly cut-and-dried maneuvers. I can assure
you, though, that the "possibile" speed (no metronomic guide is given, but fast is
fast!) gives this music tremendous excitement. The racing notes; the occasional long
note, which sounds blared, even when muted or at medium dynamic level; the
opposed progression of the solo and tutti—this is heady stuff.

For all hands, exquisite technical control is needed to attain anything
approaching maximum speed. In the tutti group, the leaps and contortions in the
line are demanding, especially since any deviation will show glaringly in the
rhythmic and pitch lineup of the three voices. For the 1st violin, the swooping of the
line and the often free-wheeling succession of rhythmic groupings make for pretty
acrobatic stunt flying. As for the listener, a cleanly played rendition of this
movement comes across as a very sophisticated and virtuoso distillation of some
classic jam session.

Many years ago, I was told by a New York concert series manager that
"chamber music is dying." With the irrepressible zeal of the performer, I replied
that I would like to play at the funeral service. It is now decades later. I am happy
to report (the line is Mark Twain's) that the rumors of the demise are greatly
exaggerated. With treasures such as the Crawford quartet to play, I am confident
that chamber music will endure yet a while.

FINE ARTS QUARTET

LEONARD SORKIN   1er violon
ABRAM LOFT   2me violon
IRVING ILMER   alto
GEORGE SOPKIN   violoncelle

Quatuor en do majeur K. V. 465 . . . . MOZART

    Adagio - Allegro
    Andante cantabile
    Menuetto - Allegretto
    Allegro molto

Quatuor No 5 . . . . BARTOK

    Allegro
    Adagio molto
    Scherzo
    Andante
    Finale : Allegro vivace

Quatuor No 4 opus 18 en do mineur . . . . . BEETHOVEN

    Allegro ma non tanto
    Scherzo - Andante scherzoso quasi allegretto
    Menuetto - Allegretto
    Allegro

DIRECTION: M. CASETTI-GIOVANNA - GENÈVE

CHAPTER TWENTY-SEVEN

❧ Bartók ❧
Quartet No. 5

The string quartet preoccupied Bartók throughout his productive career. Two such works, no longer extant, date from 1896. A third, in F, was written in 1898. However, the series of his string quartets now so firmly entrenched in our chamber music literature begins with Quartet No. 1, Op. 7, of 1908. The individuality shown there was to persist and grow in the quartets to come. His sixth and last, composed in 1939, is a landmark in our musical heritage, a searing editorial on human ways in our century.

As with the works of the great chamber music composers before him, each of Bartók's quartets carries its own stamp and personality. Structural and procedural similarities may link them, but each fulfills its own premise. They all have in common a sense of economy. No matter how long the work, there are no superfluous notes.

A giant among the six quartets is No. 5. Like the Fourth Quartet, this one has five movements, arranged in the form of an arch. Quartet No. 4 centers on a slow movement; the Fifth Quartet, on the other hand, puts a fast movement in the center, framing it with two slow movements; outside these, in turn, are the two large, fast end movements. The arch idea is reflected also in the extended "mirror" procedures of the first and last allegros: the musical events of the first part of the movement are presented in reverse order and with melodies inverted (literally turned upside down in shape) in the second half of the movement. Further, there are the internal symmetries of the second, third, and fourth movements, and the common structural frame of the second and fourth movements, to say nothing of thematic and harmonic relationships within the quartet as a whole.[1]

SCORE: Béla Bartók. 1939. *5th String Quartet*. London: Boosey & Hawkes. Miniature score No. 78.

Left: Page from the program for the concert by The Fine Arts Quartet, Théâtre de la Cour St. Pierre, Geneva, March 18, 1958.

Bartók received the commission for this quartet from the Elizabeth Sprague Coolidge Foundation in 1934, then proceeded to write the piece over the span of only one month's time.[2] The feat is astounding not only for Bartók's rigorous working out of musical ideas that is so evident, but also because he made important revisions in the composition, especially in the third movement, within the month.[3]

The playing demands in this work are formidable but realistic. The parts fit well on the several instruments. In performance, however, problems of coordination, synchronization, and flexibility reach a level unusual in the repertoire. Still, this quartet has become meat and drink to the modern concert ensemble, and to its hearers.

I   *Allegro.* Bartók is quite clear in his dynamic and accentuation markings, not only in this movement but in the entire quartet; his instructions should be heeded. Wedged notes must be more sharply and cuttingly emphasized than accented notes; and accented tones must be clearly distinguishable from nonaccented. Further, the players should be careful not to insert accents on their own. Bartók uses his accents to contribute to the shape of an individual line, as well as to construct specific stress patterns that emerge from an interwoven fabric of two or more voices. The patterns are important, and should be heard as they are notated. So also, please carefully observe the loudness relationships between successive phrases and sections, and between the several voices of the ensemble.

On paper, the opening is quite straightforward: all four instruments play boldly, in unison and octave. There are interruptions, however; consequently the 1st violin must signal to assure that the several entrances are precisely together. Once

4   the quartet splits into upper and lower pairs (mm. 4 ff.), the overlapping patterns of the two duos provide a constant metric beat that guides synchronization. The turn

13   at the end of m. 13 can be correctly placed by means of a signal from the 1st violin on the fourth quarter of the measure.

Bartók is kind to the players: though at times he constructs his part writing in contrary and changing meters, he does so as much as possible without changing his metric signature or bar-line placement. Instead, he indicates metric groupings within the given part by inserting dotted bar lines as needed; for example, in the

14   treatment of mm. 14 ff., a dotted line and an accented note start each metric unit.

15   Singling out the 2nd violin part starting in m. 15, we find the following sequence:

19   5/8, 7/8, 6/8, 7/8, 9/8, 5/8, 5/8, 6/8, 5/8, 2/8, 3/8, 10/8. From m. 19, the viola metrics fall into line with those of the 2nd violin. Since 1st violin and cello follow their own paths all the while, it is fortunate that the players do not really have to read the metric subgroups too zealously. Count 4/4, stress the accented notes as they occur, and Bartók's musical scheme will fall clearly on the ear.

25   At m. 25, upper and lower duos form again, their independence asserted by barred metric patterns; yet both pairs sound interlocked in an exhilarating, free-

36   metered dance. It is not until m. 36 that Bartók signals the realignment of the group by running a dotted line across the four staves. Even so, the two pairs of instruments remain in staggered syncopes until the next measure.

44   In the second-theme area of the movement, mm. 44–58, meters change simultaneously for all four voices, moving from the central 6/4 pulse through 8, 5, and 4 quarters. The 8/4 measures themselves are divided (via dotted bar lines) symmetrically into 3/4, 2/4, and 3/4 units. Together with pedal-point chords and resonant pizzicati, the flow from one meter to another creates appropriate atmosphere for the undulating, chromatic melody. For the players, this and the

corresponding episode later in the movement (mm. 132–46), are the only easy moments. Still, the transparent and lyric nature of this theme will test the players' musicality. 132

Play the melody as though you are enjoying and inventing it at the same time. You will note that it winds its way continuously from one voice to another until *D*; here is where the ensemble idea of "four players acting as one" will be defined in action: the personality of the melody, as it is established by the 2nd violin at letter *C*, must be maintained and expanded during its wanderings in this section. Straight playing, here above all, damages the piece severely, by denying the movement the substance of its principal contrast element. *D* *C*

The pace picks up immediately with m. 59, where the development section begins. The opening tucket, raised now to E from its original B♭ (it had visited C, back at m. 37), is sounded; then the race is on, with elements from the exposition section expanded, played off against each other between voices, and piling at last into a vortex of sound at the *mosso* passage, mm. 104 ff. 59 37 104

As an illustration of the use of accent, note mm. 82 ff.: the wedge is reserved for the last notes of triplet runs. At *E*, however, the violins end on an unstressed note, while the wedge in the two lower voices kicks those two parts into a vigorous dance step. In succeeding measures, line, wedge, and combinations of the two send a patterned thread through the ribbon of sound woven by the viola and cello parts. The violin parts, meanwhile, though seemingly more melodic in nature, are presented without accent of any kind, the instincts of the players shaping the line in other, equally subtle ways. When the two duets switch roles in m. 97, the accentuation also moves from the lower pair to the higher. 82 97

A strident (the instruction is Bartók's) apotheosis of the pitch, E, follows from m. 112, leading at last to a fortissimo statement of the tucket a step higher still, on F (at letter *F*), with the pungent support of the lower minor second, and the attendant restatement of the opening theme, now in inversion. 112 *F*

This is the pivotal point in the movement. After this, as I mentioned at the start of this chapter, the material of the exposition is reviewed in reverse order and in inversion, with the second theme appearing at letter *G* and again requiring specially attentive performance. In the recapitulation process, the opening fanfare is at last restored to its initial B♭, in a blazing, high-register setting (letter *I*). The coda of the movement, *Allegro molto* (letter *J*), positively whirls the four players through a summary of the melodic ideas. *G* *I* *J*

Here, as well as at many earlier points in the movement, one would doubt the players' ability to remain oriented in the wild swirl of events. I can only say, from personal experience, that some slow-speed rehearsal will make the pattern of the interweaving of parts familiar to the ear and the reflexes. The ensemble will learn who has to give what signal, and when. To a degree unsurpassed in any other work in the repertoire, the Bartók Fifth makes the four of you rely absolutely upon one another. This is definitely music written for fully equal partners.

Adagio molto. You will probably find it desirable for each member to give a discreet signal when handing the line on to the next player in the course of the first two measures. This is most necessary for the two violins, for in each of their parts the half-note trill moves directly to the resolving 8th; in the case of the cello and viola lines, the turn itself signals the resolution. In mm. 6–9, the three upper voices have the job of fitting their isolated couplets expressively into the line that is spun out among the several voices; this is soliloquy and colloquy in one. II 6

|10|The sustained tones in the three lower voices, mm. 10–24, should be colored|
|15|with minimal, if any, vibrato except in the swell and diminuendo area, mm. 15–19,|

The sustained tones in the three lower voices, mm. 10–24, should be colored with minimal, if any, vibrato except in the swell and diminuendo area, mm. 15–19, where the warmth of tone should be graduated to match. Very slight but clear signalling by the 2nd violin (actually nothing more than an extension of the motion of the bow changes) guides the trio of players through the sustained tones from mm. 10 through 24. For the 2nd violin's tremolo in mm. 26 ff., the bow stroke should be as small and rapid as possible; that player's left-hand fingernail pizzicato in mm. 32–33 (see Bartók's footnote) should, of course, be played by flicking the string from right to left; the reverse is theoretically possible, though not comfortable to imagine. In any case, it would not produce the short and strongly accentuated interruption of the trill called for in the score. The 16th-note couplet in the 1st violin at the start of m. 34 should be plucked by the right hand, for sonority; there is time for this if the bow is retained in playing position, with the index finger extended for the pizzicato. The A♭ alone is actually plucked, with the open G, of course, sounding as the result of the quick and decisive lifting of the first finger from the string.

The close-order, imitative writing from C to D is another instance of egalitarian writing: the web must be spun by eight hands under the control of one collective mind, right on through the end of the wide-ranging scale in mm. 43–45, where each player almost literally hands the melody to the neighbor next in line. With the acceleration and *rallentando* spelled out among the four players, the direction and gradation of tempo in this section must be revealed by the motion of instrument, bow, and body. The amount of movement can be so slight as to be scarcely apparent to the audience, but if all members of the ensemble show what they are playing, there will be no need for formal signalling.

Mm. 46–50 in the three lower voices should be treated the same as mm. 10 ff. The signalling in mm. 52–53 is like that at the start of the movement. For the successive entrances in Tempo I, each player is left to move alone, though all four are, in effect, acting out the beats of the tempo. As for the cello's *perdendosi*, the effect should be as close to exhausted death as the player's dramatic sense can afford (without overt histrionics, please).

Scherzo: Alla bulgarese. The subtitle of the movement is reflected in the time signature: 4 + 2 + 3 is not just an arbitrary way of dividing a count of nine 8th-notes; it produces a rhythmic twist quite unlike 3 + 3 + 3. The cello's pizzicato establishment of the rhythm in the first two measures is in itself enough to intrigue the listener. In order to fix the pattern, the cellist must be careful not to shortchange the 8th-rest at the end of the bar. It will help if the cellist mentally sings the 2nd violin's opening measure of music while playing each of the first two bars. When actually launching the tune in the third measure, the 2nd violin will shape the inflection properly by putting a mental stress on the first 8th-note of the middle couplet of the bar. The other players must then mirror the inflection as the tune passes from one instrument to the next.

Each statement of the tune takes off from the impulse of a downbeat in some other voice. The fact that the tune's *own* downbeat is silent, however, gives the melodic shape a fine flip. In fact, the players can soon feel at home in the pattern; it may be old Bulgarian, but it shouldn't phase anyone who has heard good jazz. Matters are so much under control, in fact, that scraps of the tune can flutter out in mm. 12–13, with the melody regenerated by the cello alone in m. 14.

The contrast theme, mm. 24 ff., is distinctive not only in melodic outline but especially because it begins strongly on the downbeat of the measure. The forte outburst over three measures should be wild in effect, but with a weather eye out for the meter. The initial tune continues as a melodic ostinato, so the metric count must be steadily maintained.

Mm. 27–29 will take some slow rehearsal by the three lower voices, to fit the overlapping melodic arches reliably into place. The players now also have to learn to play the tune with the indicated swells. And all three must arrive solidly and together on the downbeat 8th-note of m. 30, in order to give the 1st violin a safe start on a newly introduced figure. That player, in turn, must be sure to hold steady on the last three 8th-notes in bars 30–32, though some solid rhythmic instruction will come from the strongly accentuated lines of the 2nd violin and cello in those measures. Note the wedged, downbeat 8th-notes here, lecturing us on the anatomy of the theme.

In mm. 36–41, all four players will have to play with dogmatic devotion to the meter: the three upper parts, in order to stay together; the cello, to hold a somewhat erratic line firmly to the pulse of the other voices. The cellist's 16th-note couplet at the start of mm. 38 and 40 has to be tightly played in order to fit into its assigned metric slot. From m. 42 to 49, the cello is like the big hand on the metronomic clock, tolling the downbeats for the gyrations of the upper voices. The 2nd violin needs furious concentration in these measures, both to hold fast to the rhythmic fragmentings of the line and to give clear indications to the partner voice, the viola. In practice, this applies to both players, since they will have to lead each other. The duo of cello and 1st violin should practice the pedal point in mm. 47–49, to match the sound and projection of their left-hand pizzicati.

In carrying the musical relay into the *pochissimo rit.* of m. 62, the 1st violin must not slow down too much, for the cello still has to finish out the calming (Bartók's instruction) of tempo in the next measure.

In the Trio, Bartók moves into a pattern based on ten 8th-note units: 3 + 2 + 2 + 3. In the straight 8ths of the 1st violin part, this becomes a motoric pedal point that parallels a sustained pedal in the viola. Starting in m. 5, the 2nd violin plays a plucked, rhythmic ostinato that, on the one hand, highlights corresponding tones in the other violin's racing line and, on the other, previews the rhythm of the impending viola solo.

In m. 9 the viola at last presents the subject of the section, a kind of whistling tune. The player must be careful to adhere to the composer's unaccented version of the tune; any inadvertent stress on the quarter-beat that represents the sixth and seventh 8th-beats of the measure will give a distorted rhythmic view of the pattern and will tend to shorten the beat unduly. The quarter-note must be held to full value, but with a casual air, whether in the viola or cello portions of the line.

The moving pedal-point figure finally boils up in all three upper voices; and when the flurry subsides, the whistling tune reemerges, only to transform itself, subtly but quickly, into an augmented version of the Scherzo theme. Because of the speed of the trio, this augmented view is already halfway to a resumption of the Scherzo tune proper, which soon makes its reappearance, complete with original tempo and 4 + 2 + 3 metrics.

Bartók marks this, *Scherzo da capo*. It is not, however, a simple revisiting of the first section. To cite one facet: Bartók highlights the initial episode with left- and right-handed pizzicati in the cello and violin parts. Attention should be given these in rehearsal to make sure they can be heard through the surrounding part writing.

22	Another added attraction: the 2nd violin in mm. 22–26 has a wonderful new bit of business (the composer marks it *espressivo*) as it floats languorously through a sequence—not counting the initial upbeat—of 4 + 9 + 10 + 4 + 4. The vignette is quickly over, but it is an unforgettable moment.
48	Still another great spot starts in m. 48. Here, Bartók is winding up the Scherzo and working his way to the coda of the movement. The cello is lashing itself into a frenzy in a high-register solo line. To offset this, the three upper voices (though at this point it is not easy to separate upper from lower) join in jaunty lock step: starting after Bartók's comma, and including 8th-rests, we have 2 + 2 + 2 + 3 + 2, 4 + 2 + 2 + 2 + 3, 3 + 2 + 2 + 2 + 3, 5, 4, 5, 4. In cold print, this sequence seems completely arbitrary, but in the playing you get an indescribable feeling of clear-headed intoxication.
58	With the *Agitato* coda, mm. 58 ff., there comes a performer's dilemma (at least for this performer). In countless playings of this quartet, I found it very difficult to avoid feeling that I was, at last, from m. 58 to m. 65, playing in straight 9/8 meter, even while seeing the familiar 4 + 2 + 3 grouping on the page. I always felt guilty about this, but a look at the score page will show that Bartók, by overlapping his stated metric group in all four parts, makes it difficult (perhaps undesirable!) for the ear to try to unravel the web of voices. A conventional 9/8 becomes a sea anchor that enables the player to survive the passage. Let my readers make what use they will of this confession and advice.
75	In mm. 75–80, the swells must be played so that there is no involuntary suggestion of an accent at the peak of the crescendo. Move smoothly up and down. This, by the way, applies as well to earlier such measures in the movement.
86 88	As for the very end of the movement, the viola will be exceedingly *espressivo* in mm. 86 ff. (a whiff of *Pierrot Lunaire*?), the cello suitably militant in its snapped pizzicato of m. 88, and the 2nd violin sufficiently coy in its exit statement of the theme.
IV	**Andante.** In the opening measures, each instrument must direct the force of its pizzicato series to the ensuing downbeat. Only thus will the slurred grouplet have enough resonance to reach the listeners' ears. (Once again, let me urge firm pressure of the left hand, and vibrato to match.) At that, the two violins will have to add a suggestion of left-hand pizzicato in order to reinforce the second and third notes of their descending slurred figure. In each instrument, the 8th-notes must be played so that they move toward the resolving, slurred group.
5	It goes without saying that in the 1st violin and cello, mm. 5 ff., the glissando must start immediately upon the plucking of the string if the slide is to be audible. On the other hand, concern about sonority should not make you rush the glissando; try to preserve the rhythmic placement of the written pitches. The 2nd violin's
15	*arpeggiando* pizzicati on the downbeats of mm. 15–18 must be directed with special emphasis to the E-string, so that the top note of the octave is suitably projected.
22	In m. 22, the *poco slargando* seems to indicate that the 2nd violin is ending an episode. Accordingly, it is advisable to observe a slight comma before launching into the *Più andante* of the next bar. The bowing indications in this new episode are problematic. Certainly the simultaneous ricochet for all four strings gives the desired, eerie drumroll effect in the quiet measures. However, when we compare the score with the individual parts, a question quickly arises. In the three upper voices, the parts agree with the score in showing a (ricochet) slur over the notes in
23	mm. 23 and 24, and in giving a *simile* instruction for the recurrence of the figure in

the measures that follow. For the cello, though, the part differs from the score. The score implies ricochet for m. 26 by using the *simile* instruction. But m. 25 is shown slurred into the ricochet of m. 26, a technical impossibility since there is no opportunity to lift the bow and bring it down onto the string to initiate the bounce.   26, 25

The solution would seem to be to take m. 25 on an upstroke, with the bow then thrown onto the string in the downstroke direction for the ricochet in m. 26. The printed, individual cello part, however, muddies things by omitting the slur in m. 24. This leaves the cello to play spiccato while the upper voices play ricochet, which would destroy the dry, rattling effect that should be forthcoming from the ensemble. The contradiction is compounded, since in m. 26 a *simile* in the cello part has that instrument continue to play the detached bowing, further marring the ensemble effect.   24

The answer is: let the cello indeed take upbow in mm. 25 and 28, so that it can join with the other instruments in the ricochet. The viola should also take upbow in m. 31 in order to play the ricochet in m. 32. Here, by the way, is another doubtful place; both in the score and the part, the viola is shown playing a sustained tone against the accustomed rattle in the other three parts. This must certainly be a mistake, for it goes against the pattern that is otherwise adhered to throughout the passage. For sonority and force, all four instruments should use detached bowing from mm. 32 through 36 and 37, where the dynamics swell and recede. (Note that the detached notes in the sextuplets sound more appropriately stern if played as three couplets rather than as a pair of triplets.) Then the two lower voices, in their pianissimo accompaniment in mm. 39 and 40, can resume the ricochet bowing for atmospheric effect.   25
    31

    39

I hope that my lengthy argument will help shorten ensemble discussion when the foursome come to deal with the passage. Inconsistencies of notation aside, we may assume that the seemingly impossible bowings in the score are Bartók's phrasing, rather than actual performance instructions. In that regard, the third quarters of mm. 25, 27, and so on, should be held long enough to suggest their connection to the ensuing, drumming figures, even though a slight break will be needed to allow for the preparatory lift of bow from string.   25

In any event, the detached bowings I have suggested seem to prepare for the furious drumming (octuplets, now) of mm. 60–62, which unleashes the musical flood of the *Più mosso, agitato.* En route to that section, be aware that the moody, 32nd-note swirls of the *Più lento* are preparing for their louder counterparts in the storm to come. By way of savoring the drama of that event, be sure to play the pianissimo bars (mm. 54–56) extremely quietly, letting the crescendo wait until called for.   60

    54

Against the rumblings of the lower voices, incidentally, the two violins will want to bear down with the bow on the glissando turns in mm. 76–79, so the audience can hear the effect. Throughout this *agitato,* let the lower voices balance so that the screaming rivalry in the violin duo can be heard above the waves. Take note again that swells, where marked, should not be topped with an accent, and that dynamic balance will have to be made—even in a fortissimo context—so that the rise and fall can be apparent. See to it, also, that the last bars of the episode, from m. 77 on, make a smooth transition down to the quietness of the *Tranquillo.*   76

    77

My longtime friend and colleague from Fine Arts Quartet years, George Sopkin, tells me that there are two ways to play the ascending glissando in the cello part in m. 92: pluck the open C- and G-strings, then immediately throw the first   92 finger onto the vibrating strings and begin the glissando; or, in a kind of micro-position, put the first finger on both those strings at the saddle of the fingerboard, playing the E♭ with the second finger. For the closing pizzicati of the movement, he suggests playing only the last beat of m. 98 on the three lower strings, switching then to the upper three strings for the remaining glissandi. This approach is to avoid the tight, dry sound that would result from going up to the high register on the low strings.

The bowings for the three lower voices in mm. 95–97 are, in the three measures successively: detached octuplet; ricochet sextuplet; and, for the better execution of the *col legno,* a sextuplet viewed as two triplets rather than as three couplets.

Finale: Allegro vivace. As at the opening of the quartet, the beginning of the finale should indeed be counted by all hands, but for assured synchronization, each of the four utterances of the introduction should be signalled by the 1st violin. Even if paced metronomically, the effect is that of a free declamation.

Before proceeding, let me stress again the importance of playing the accents in the degree and placement given by the composer. The patterns they construct are an essential element in the sound of the music. They are not mere ornaments of the line; rather, they serve such musical ends as highlighting pitches important to the outline of the piece, and marking out directions of motion within or between sections.

Now, on to the *Presto* (letter *A*). It takes determination for the three upper voices to launch immediately into the tempo after the comma in m. 14, rather than working up to the speed over the first two bars of the section. The three upper voices begin together and, with only the briefest pause for the comma, have no time for a preparatory signal. Therefore, the players must have their *Presto* tempo ingrained in order to get off the starting blocks simultaneously and at speed.

The movement as a whole imposes some intricate, close-order drill on the four players; Bartók groups them in every conceivable way, and the alignments must become as familiar to the players as the specific notes themselves. You have to know beyond any doubt what signals you have to give, where to look for signals from your colleagues, and what part(s) to listen to in any given passage. Otherwise, you will flounder, a fatal condition in a piece of such complexity. Mark your part carefully.

You have to be on guard, too, for high-speed changes in physical and emotional attitudes in this movement. For example, the rough knockabout between upper and lower pairs in mm. 55–62 is suddenly replaced in mm. 63–72 with lacy strands of sound overlapped in the four parts. The players have to assume new personalities for these quiet measures. Just as quickly, they have to revert to brusqueness for mm. 75–82, and then switch back to the hushed vein for the passage that follows.

By m. 150, when the shouts of the introduction are revisited, the inertia of the tempo, as well as the head of steam that has built up in the ensemble, will assure that the fragments of declamation synchronize automatically, without signal from any corner. Note, however, that the upbeat placement of the opening has now been replaced by a downbeat location of each fragment. Moreover, Bartók emphasizes the point by putting a wedge over each starting note. Intervallic relationships are also being highlighted in this way, so do as the composer asks.

In the *Più presto, scorrevole,* on the other hand, there are no accent marks of any kind until m. 266. The composer is layering the voices into a kind of musical thatch, which should not be marred by carelessly intruded splinters of sound. You will note that when the accents do return, they effect, among other things, the ascending chromatic scale, from A to its octave, in the violin parts in mm. 275 ff. 275

Things are now moving at a furious pace. Don't lose your place here, or you will probably be embarrassed for a long time. There is every chance that, once having fallen out, you could be groping all the way until the grand pause in m. 347. 347 The stuff of nightmares would be to try to fake your way back in and somehow be left hanging with an unintended solo in the measure of silence. Worst of all is the fact that one player's uncertainty in so close-knit a web of voices and events could unsettle the entire ensemble, resulting in a grand and public pandemonium. Again, please don't get lost!

The entire section from m. 202 to 349 will benefit from slow, repeated run- 202 throughs, both in portions and overall. That way, you will get the sounds and sequences of events into your ears and muscles.

There is a longish grand pause before the *a tempo* in m. 351. The effect should 351 be such that, starting with the accented downbeat in m. 348, a four-beat measure is 348 counted, each pulse representing one measure of the *Presto*. The *a tempo* comes in as part of the fourth beat of this composite measure. Unfortunately, the 2nd violin part has a page turn at this very spot. The solution: have the bottom corner of the page dog-eared; count the four "beats" dogmatically; turn the page with the left hand, so the bow is held ready for the next entrance; and have mm. 351–56 memorized so 351 that you can fall right onto the melodic line by reflex action. Exactly the same situation befalls the viola at the next break (mm. 356 ff.), with the same kind of 356 remedy.

The violins and cello should practice the synchronization of the *col legno* grace notes and the cello's glissando inset, going into bar 369, especially since the spot is the beginning of an acceleration. For that speedup, a bit of rehearsal by viola and cello will help. Both in the score and 2nd violin part, that instrument is lacking an *in modo ordinario* (that is, in regular, or bowed, fashion) instruction at m. 380. Be 380 advised: don't try to play the passage *col legno*; you'll hurt yourself! More seriously, the ensemble should balance carefully in that passage, so that the *oscuro* ("obscure," "dark"), low-register violin part can be heard. In general, the entire passage, right up to m. 457, is difficult to keep steady, what with the speed, the contrasting part 457 rhythms, and the exchange of figures among the voices. Slow practice, with gradual approach to playing speed, will help.

The *Allegretto capriccioso* and its lead-in (mm. 482 ff.) must be played archly, 482 indecorously; Bartók's call for *poco rubato* should be heeded, even more so in the 8th-note scales than in the glissandi, which can more readily express capriciousness. From my experience, the whimsical attitude should be maintained in the glissandi even into the *Risoluto* passage that begins in m. 528. Time enough 528 for stern sobriety when the unison trumpetings of mm. 544–45 arrive. The musical tobogganings will then carry the group irresistibly forward to the craggy chords of mm. 673 ff. I can't imagine any quartet failing to give utmost bite and force to these 673 chords, and especially to those in mm. 691–92. 691

Now for the *Allegretto, con indifferenza*: why "indifference"? Much ink has been M expended about the significance of this passage in the quartet. I have even heard it said that the inane, scalewise wandering of the melody is Bartók's satiric look backward over many years of piano teaching at the conservatory in Budapest. The satire is there, I believe, but not about teaching; instead, I concur with some who have written that he is casting a new and quixotic sidelight on the thematic idea he has so thoroughly and imaginatively exploited in this finale.[4] He finally chooses to reduce the idea to absurdity. This notion must color the nonchalance with which the two violins play the tune.

N

    Then it is back into the saddle for an ever faster thematic dash to the double bar. It is with a severe pullback, the *slargando* of the last four measures, that Bartók finally nails the theme down, a defiant response to the capricious and clownish episodes heard earlier.

    For me, Bartók's Fifth Quartet is analogous to Beethoven's Op. 59, No. 1: when you finish either quartet, you know you've played. It's like climbing a musical Mt. Everest.

TWO CONCERTS COMPRISING THE ENTIRE CYCLE OF SIX QUARTETS BY BELA BARTÓK

28th March.

Quartet No. 3 (1927)

  Prima parte : *Moderato*
  Seconda parte : *Allegro*
  Ricapitulazione della prima parte : *Moderato*
  Coda : *Allegro molto*
    (Played without pause)

Quartet No. 2 (1917)

  Moderato
  Allegro molto capriccioso
  Lento

INTERVAL

Quartet No. 5 (1934)

  Allegro
  Adagio molto
  Scherzo: Alla bulgarese
  Andante
  Finale: Allegro vivace.

7th April.

Quartet No. 1 (1908)

  Lento
  Allegretto
  Introduzione: Allegro – Allegro vivace

Quartet No. 6 (1939)

  Mesto – Vivace
  Mesto – Marcia
  Mesto – Burletta
  Mesto

INTERVAL

Quartet No. 4 (1928)

  Allegro
  Prestissimo, con sordino
  Non troppo lento
  Allegretto pizzicato
  Allegro molto

RECORDS: Saga, Musicaphon/Barenreiter, Concert-Disc/Everest, Vox, Decca.

Founded in 1946, the FINE ARTS QUARTET is one of America's foremost ensembles. This Quartet is well-known to European as well as Canadian and American audiences. They frequently appear on the National Broadcasting Company, the American Broadcasting Company and the Canadian Broadcasting Corporation. In addition to its many other activities, the Fine Arts Quartet has established, in its annual Chicago concert series, one of the most significant chamber music sounding-boards in America. As a highlight of its year-round activities at the University of Wisconsin, Milwaukee (where the four musicians are faculty members), its Summer Evenings of Music Series has, since 1955, been the centre of a festival of the arts-in-integration that has become a focal point of interest for artists from all parts of the country.

VAIL & CO. LTD. LEEKE STREET, LONDON, W.C.1

CHAPTER TWENTY-EIGHT

✒ Bartók ✒
Quartet No. 6

I still recall the mixture of disbelief and anger I felt in reading a particular concert review of the mid-'50s (the American metropolis and the critic shall remain charitably nameless). The commentator maintained that the quartets of Bartók were then already obsolescent! It is now more than a generation later. The Bartók quartets are still going strong, and will surely long outlast both the reviewer and me.

Happily, the opinion of that miscreant scrivener is far outweighed by the view of scholars, the performing fraternity, and audiences: the six Bartók quartets are regarded as classics, not only of contemporary music, but of the entire range of Western musical culture.

If I had to name the most significant of the cycle, I would have to choose the Sixth Quartet. When I hear it—and certainly when I perform it—the work exerts overwhelming impact on me. I hear in it the mental anguish of a keenly sensitive spirit who laments the evil that men do to one another. The Bartók Sixth is not only a consummate musical structure; it is a musical editorial on the pestilence that had befallen the world Bartók knew. Like the composer's Second Quartet (1917), the Sixth Quartet (1939) was written in wartime. I have always felt that the shadowed air of the Second Quartet reflected Bartók's grief over the events of the First World War. With Quartet No. 6, there can be no doubt. The titles of the movements, to say nothing of the sound of the music, are in desperate protest against the Nazi laceration of Europe in the 1930s.

The Sixth Quartet has the Mesto ("Sad") theme as its essential thread.

The theme of this work, which is stated at the head of each movement, in successive one-, two-, three- and four-part settings, generates each of the

SCORE: Béla Bartók. 1941. *Sixth String Quartet*. London: Boosey & Hawkes. Miniature score No. 25.

Left: Page from the announcement for the Bartók cycle given by The Fine Arts Quartet, Wigmore Hall, London, March–April, 1970.

movements, with the entire fourth movement functioning as its most direct and complete expansion.[1]

Bartók seems to have decided on this structural frame only in the course of working on the composition. From a study of the sketch full score, a scholar has deduced that the movements eventually titled Vivace and Marcia were laid out first. The Mesto theme (not yet so labeled) appeared—already in three-part guise—as the introduction to the Burletta. The opening of what we know as the last movement figures in the sketch as the introduction to a finale of rather lively, folk-dance nature.[2]

Bartók had started work on the quartet in Switzerland in the summer of 1939. Darkening events in Europe sent him back to Budapest in late August. There the pressures surrounding the onset of war, as well as Bartók's preoccupation with other work, kept him from continuing with the quartet until November, in which month he completed the piece. "But the 'tempo giusto' of the village dance, conceived in Switzerland, was now replaced by the... mourning song for the murder of Europe."[3] That is, the Mesto theme grew into the entire closing movement. At the same time, if not before, Bartók decided to use the theme as introduction to the first two movements as well as to the third.

In October of 1940, Bartók sailed for America, where he was to spend the last five, still productive, years of his life. In the summer of 1988, his remains were returned to the Hungary he loved.

I   *Mesto.* As in the Smetana quartet, "From my Life," the violist takes center stage to open this Bartók work. The spotlight role here, however, has some drawbacks: the performer is completely alone; the dynamic level is rather restrained; and the tempo is slow. Above all, the mood of the music is truly "sad." The player, therefore, cannot let go, cannot invoke self-confidence by dint of bold sound and free-swinging bowing.

Add to this a sense that you are about to make one of the most meaningful and poignant musical statements in the repertoire, and none could blame you for feeling nervous. This condition is most likely to manifest itself in a trembling sound on the long notes of the tune. The very profundity of the music, however, carries with it the best antidote for the jitters.

Before you start to play, close your eyes for a moment and think of the first notes of the melody. Steep yourself in the melancholy that is embodied in the theme. With this focus, you will very likely forget even the possibility of nervousness.

Give yourself a slow, full, three 8th-note upstroke with the bow, all but playing the D-string as you move your right wrist through the air. Glide smoothly onto the string to start the downstroke. You already have the tempo firmly in mind, so you can concentrate not so much on your sustained, opening G♯, but rather on your first goal of motion, the B in m. 2. As soon as you start that note, look ahead immediately to the succeeding A♯, and beyond that to the next resting point, the D in bar 3, and to the pivotal C♯ in the following measure.

From this, your musical horizon must expand greatly: you alight, in passing, on the E in m. 5 and the F𝄪 in m. 6, and push on to the C𝄪 in bar 7. I would suggest, incidentally, that you change unobtrusively to a downbow after the opening quarter-note in bar 6; this will mean that you take the long C𝄪 on an upstroke. Devote the entire stroke to that note, so that you can use the increasing weight of the stick to sustain the crescendo to the frog of the bow.

Move smoothly into a downbow with the D♯. Break the slur smoothly again in bar 9, after the sustained E. You will arrive at a downbow for the accented A♭ in the cadence of the closing two measures of the theme. (Note, by the way, that the C♯, E, and A♭ each mark a new and lower dynamic level. Don't grade these levels into a continuous decrescendo; instead, preserve the composer's terraced dynamics.) The final E♭ of the Mesto must be resonant, though as quietly and gently stroked as you can manage. Hold still after the sound dies away. Bartók indicates 50 seconds of elapsed time for the entire opening statement, but I doubt that he would begrudge a second or so of atmospheric suspense. (In any event, his timings should be regarded as helpful guides, not mandates.)

The color of sound produced by your left hand during all this is crucial to the effect of the solo. Vibrato is needed, of course, but it must be used very judiciously: neither too fast nor too wide and wobbly, and always applied with control. The shading can be rather cool to start, rising and falling in intensity with the shape of the phrase. You may even choose to use open string for the D in m. 3, provided you   3 gradually drain the color from the several notes that precede, and simultaneously cut back on the speed of bow. The greatest heat of vibrato will rise toward and through bars 7–8. Don't cool the vibrato too quickly in the last five measures of the   7 solo. Even the piano tones of mm. 10–11 must retain some seething quality. Only   10 after the accented start of the A♭ in bar 13 should the timbre slope rapidly into   13 pallor.

Più mosso, pesante. The other three players will have been in a state of alert repose during the viola solo. Now, after just the right dramatic pause, the 1st violin will lead the attack on the forte opening of the fast section of the movement. No conscious downbeat signal is needed in m. 14; the ensemble will know from   14 rehearsal what tempo to expect, and can synchronize the entrance with the natural physical motion of the violinist's sweep of motion into the first, unison G.

I suggest that the quartet start the phrase upbow; this will result in a satisfying and effective upstroke on the D and a solid downbow on the C♯ in bar 17. Take a   17 fresh downbow for the A in m. 18; the melody in mm. 18–20 is a reflection of the   18 fortissimo statement in mm. 16–18, and the bowing should match. Your remaining strokes will then bring you to the appropriate downbow for the sustained chord that closes the statement.

Although there is no direct, thematic derivation from the viola solo, the shape of the unison phrase in mm. 14–18 suggests a tightly compressed reflection of the   14 viola's voyage in mm. 1–7. The flaring, essentially upward sweep of the quartet in mm. 18–23 counters the dejected, downward course of the closing bars of the viola   18 solo. At the same time, the tones of the 1st violin line in bars 18–23 are an immediate, augmented preview of that instrument's statement of the Vivace theme.

Vivace. If you start the phrase upbow, the two dotted 8ths in bar 25 will be   25 played with the necessary lift and spunk, near the frog of the bow. So also for the bowing of the 2nd violin in mm. 26–27. The remaining entrances in mm. 27–28 can   27 be up or down, as the judgment of the players dictates. By means of any necessary and unobtrusive bow change, however, each player must be in an upstroke upon entering bar 30. This will make possible a suitably grotesque thrust toward the forte   30 8th-note on the second half of that measure. The glissando in the upper three parts must be as broad and emphatic as the tempo will permit, to lend intensity to the crescendo. As I see it, the descending glissando in the 1st violin is a snarling transformation of the falling interval that closed the viola solo, back at mm. 12–13.

31   The grace-note transition to the high D in bar 31 must explode with clarity in the 1st violin part. From the high point, the line descends in an inverted view of the Vivace theme. Then, from the sustained landing point, the line slides to an abrupt

35   break (catch your breath at the end of bar 35) before proceeding.

36   Play the passage from mm. 36 to 53 with a hint of acceleration. That approach is suggested by the way the four voices tumble against each other, and especially by

48   the fact that short thematic fragments compress the dialogue in mm. 48–52. You have to evoke the breathless excitement of these lines.

53   Mm. 53–59 represent a temporary plateau of steadiness, clipped off by another

60   crescendo-cum-glissando. From bar 60, take off as though in a fresh start, pushing ahead into and past bar 68. The obstinate rhythmic figures in the cello in bars 68–80 should urge a forward thrust. This must yield only reluctantly to the musical brakes that are applied by the augmented, *marcato* notes in the upper voices.

    The pullback delivers us to the second theme of the movement, in slower

81   tempo, at m. 81.[4] Bartók asks that the theme be played in piano, *ma con calore*. The "warmth" of the 1st violin's treatment of the melody will come not only from quality of sound, but from suitable emphasis given to the onbeat 8ths: the second half of mm. 81–82, the downbeats of bars 83–84. By emphasis, I mean a gentle pressure and subtle extension of the length of the note in question, not any overt accent.

85   The 2nd violin's *grazioso* response, mm. 85–89, should wind its way sensitively through the line. Don't let the 6/8 rhythms take on any suggestion of naïve

89   singsong. The viola's turn in the spotlight, mm. 89–92, involves some convoluted crossing of strings. Look for fingerings and extensions that will make for the smoothest possible playing of the line. Supple inflection will help the music and the performer. The melody should not sound gnarled or agitated.

99   Both violins will lead the move toward the very lively tempo of mm. 99 ff. Once there, the pace is set and maintained by the alternating accents in the two inner voices. The ensemble is caught up in a wild game of musical leapfrog until it

109, 113   bursts into the clarion blare of bars 109–10 and 113–14. From the heights of the sustained E♭ and C, catch your breath for the abrupt drops to the piano figures that follow.

117   The respite is only illusory, for the race resumes, faster than ever, in m. 117. These athletic games cannot be led by any one player. All four are responsible for

126   the safety of the group. Slow practice of a passage such as mm. 126 ff. will make the terrain familiar, so that (in this instance) upper and lower duos can coordinate as they pass the musical strands back and forth.

    The tempo slows, and the texture of the part writing opens out as the

137   exposition section of the movement comes to a close (mm. 137–57). Let the violist make the most of the duple rhythms of bars 141–42, a moment of contrast against the prevailing, second-theme rhythm in these lines. The octave sigh of the two

153   violins in m. 153 must have an aura of nostalgia and yearning, further intensified by the exhalation on the sustained C and the very delicate responses of the low

155   voices (mm. 155–56).

157   Hold still at the end of m. 157; after the fevered activity that has preceded, the listener should be kept in suspense, all but convinced that the movement has ended. It is then up to the 2nd violin to lead the ferocious attack on the *pesante* and

158   fermata of mm. 158–59.

    This is the start of the development, and Bartók leaves no doubt that the focus will be on the principal theme of the Vivace. The subject is stated in augmentation: the first three notes bring us to the fermata in bar 159; the full statement ends on the fermata of m. 165. This is marked for a long hold; let it blaze with heat. The chord in question here—it contains C♯–D–E♭–F–G–B♭—is so pungent that it shakes with resonance. Give it all you've got, and let the ear of the listener soak it up.   159   165

There is a slightly longer stretch of measures before the next fermata (m. 179).   179   168
Upper and lower duos collide with each other at the start of bar 168. The violins bounce upward, away from this melodic impact. They then pull away from each other in the glissandi of bar 170, as though in aftershock. The smear in the 1st violin   170
must be slow and steady enough to occupy the full span of the dotted quarter; the 2nd violin's slide, though shorter, should also be well smeared, and loud enough to match the strength of the upper voice.

Immediately after, the pizzicati in the violins need to be heard, even though only in mezzo forte. And the chord in bar 179, again held "long," demands   179
fortissimo strength, even though not so marked. The sound here is a bit less crunchy than at the preceding hold (this chord offers only F-G-A-B), but you still want everyone to enjoy it.

Play the ostinato pattern woven by the two outer voices in mm. 180–94 clearly,   180
but in background to the duet of the inner parts. That duo is set in dynamic blocks, and the volume levels must contrast distinctly. Both duos are involved in quiet pattern work in mm. 191–93. The 2nd violin darts out of this, only to suspend for a   191
time on its F♯. This offers a window for the start of a new, pizzicato background figure in the viola (mm. 194 ff.); and against this the 2nd violin triggers a new   194
episode in the development.

This passage extends only from m. 197 to 222, but seems longer, for all four   197
instruments take turns at spinning a long, flaring line derived from the theme. You will need slow practice here, both individually and together, to work out fingerings and balances. It is very important that these intricate lines be played cleanly. And, at speed, there is no time for doubt or hesitation; your fingers must be able to play the patterns by reflex action. Only then can you concentrate on shaping the dynamic rise and fall of the line.

The time signatures here are mixed: 2/4 for the viola and cello in two different areas, against the continued 6/8 of the violins. This makes good sense. The duple signature is a convenience for the notation of the four-8th-note rhythms of the low voices.

The triumphant outcry of the 1st violin in bar 226 is the watershed of energy in   226
the development. Notice the crescendo mark under the cello response in the second half of this measure. You need a bit of time to make this swell happen in the space of the four-note grace that leads to the second beat of the bar. Take the time, for the grace has to sound melodic enough to show its derivation from the cello arpeggiations in the preceding four measures. Spreading the grace notes also lends extra weight to the force of the measure, before the downward plunge in bars 227–30.   227

The duple rhythms of 1st violin and cello in bar 230 need the sharpness and   230
impact of the snare drummer's rim shot. And the glissandi in the inner voices in the bars immediately following should be played with solid finger-pressure and slow bow stroke. The slide should move viscously through the indicated beat, filling the allotted time span with consistent gradation of pitch. In mm. 237–45 of the 1st   237
violin part, play the 16th-note figures accurately and audibly; the rhythms should

not suggest a mere continuation of the long trill that has preceded.

267   Note that the end of the development (like its opening) is signalled by fermatas. These, however, must be played not only extremely quietly, but with very cool sound. The cello after the first hold, and the 2nd violin after the next, should each give the go-ahead with a clear signal on the first couple of beats in the part, to assure that the given tempo is firmly established.

287   To my ear, the actual start of the recapitulation (mm. 287 ff.) is colored by the 2nd violin's apparent determination to continue the development. Though the other three voices are sounding the principal theme, the 2nd's downward chromatic scale injects a sense of unrest. This feeling is taken up by all four instruments in the

297 racing music of mm. 297 ff. It is only with the arrival of the second theme at bar 312 that a more restful sensation is created.

332   This gives way again to steeplechase running at bar 332. In these measures, viola and 2nd violin, respectively, should mark the accented pulse on the first and second beats of the bar to whip up the excitement. At the start of mm. 345 and 350, there should be a definite break in sound after the downward rush of 8th-notes, to mark the shock of the sudden piano.

    It is up to the 2nd violin to signal a new tempo and mood by playing the

354 second half of bar 354 in suitably contemplative manner. The 8th-note streamers in
355 mm. 355 ff. grow into a continuous line as they pass from voice to voice. Don't play these figures as though they are simply rhythmic repetitions. Listen to each other so

359 that the four bars, 355–58, build the melody to a peak, while mm. 359–62 allow some of the energy to drain away.

363   In the coda, mm. 363 ff., the left-hand pizzicati of the 2nd violin must be strong enough to add a definite layer of sound to the plucked chords that are being spelled

371 out by the viola and cello. The grace notes in the 1st violin part in bar 371, again, should not be played too tightly; they must sound melodic enough to counterbalance the 8th-note figures that grow out of the sustained tone. Further, the duple-meter rhythm in m. 373 needs broad and smooth emphasis to make the transfer to the tempo and spirit of the closing measures of the movement.

387   The final Lento (mm. 387 ff.) is controlled by the 2nd violin. There has been the constantly slowing ascent of the 1st violin to the sustained high A. The 2nd must choose the dramatically correct moment and the pacing of its move from the

388 sustained G down to the cadence notes of mm. 388–89. I have heard it suggested that the notes be played in a one-fingered slide. Such a glissando approach may have its merits, but I feel that the violinist will have more flexible control of the figure if it is fingered in scalewise fashion.

    This is the time to note that each of the first three movements of the quartet ends quietly, no matter what storms have been traversed en route. Hold tuning to an absolute minimum, so that the return to the predominant, Mesto thread of the work can be as smooth as possible.

II   *Mesto.* Except for the closing Mesto movement, Bartók's metronome marking for the three earlier, introductory Mestos is 96 to the 8th-note. The changes are in detail and part writing, not in speed. In the second Mesto, the cello restates the viola's original theme, transposed down a fourth, but otherwise verbatim, except

3 for two details: a duple rhythm in the first half of bar 3 and an inserted measure-
10 and-a-half (see mm. 10–11). The addition is a transposed repetition of the slurred figure immediately preceding. It helps carry the cello smoothly to its lowest register.

Throughout the Mesto, the 1st violin parallels the cello, not in exact imitation, but in free commentary on that melody. Both inner voices double the violin at the two lower octaves, in tremolo. Keep the shake as quiet and as rapid as possible, to add only the most unobtrusive shimmer to the violin line. The upper-voice chorus is muted, but don't rely on that restraint alone to temper the sound of the group. This Mesto is the cellist's solo, which is to be complemented, never covered, by the ribbon of sound the other three instruments provide. The cello's closing descent is countered by the rise in the accompanying voices, so that the musical texture seems to open and evaporate.

In the silence that follows, the 2nd violin has a short statement to make: a kind of mirror image of, a last commentary on, the figures the cello has been playing since m. 8; at the same time, it is a preview of the march theme that lies ahead. Use cool sound and the lightest of bow strokes, and play on the D-string. This moment in the piece has a pensive, suspended, isolated feeling about it. Convey this sense, before the ensuing raucousness breaks loose. And get the mute off quickly and quietly; be ready for the onslaught.

Marcia. Bartók asks for "resolute, strongly marked" playing here. To this, I think, should be added adjectives like swaggering, aggressive, vicious. This is a march to end all marches. It ridicules the marchers, while at the same time decrying the brutal purpose behind the regimentation.

Play so that you bring out the mordant quality of this music. The snapped figure must always start downbow, near the tip of the stick, and very much on the string. Make the swells noticeable, and place them where written. They help underscore the staggered entrances of the parts, so that the voices bump and grate against one another. Where the three upper parts trill together (as on the fourth beat of bar 24), the effect must be a snarl, ripping into the resolving downbeat.

Mm. 25 ff. are vitriolic in their caricature of the paraders. The rhythms lurch and stagger drunkenly. Note that short figures starting on an offbeat 16th are marked with a swell and a dot over the receiving 8th-note. The crescendo must be apparent; pull the dotted note brusquely off the string, with no hint of lightness. Those 16th couplets that start on the beat should fall abruptly away, as indicated by the dynamic mark. Practice the passage slowly. Work for synchronization, close matching of bowing style and dynamic gradation, and clearly differentiated placement of the on- and offbeat insets.

Listen to the cellist in mm. 32–33; you may have to allow for some stretching of tempo here as the cello works to evoke the quiet harmonics in the part. The *cantabile* marked in bar 33 applies not only there, but to the slurred figures that appear in the writing up to bar 42. The detached figures, on the other hand, must be played as sharply and gruffly as ever. In the animato measures, let the music sweep forward relentlessly until it runs into the stop at the end of bar 42.

The *risoluto* and *marcatissimo* instructions for the passage of mm. 42–49 again need informed translation. Play here as though depicting heavy boots that stamp and grind their way through the sound. The upper-voice trills and the cello's descending line in bar 48 move with crushing force toward the hard-bitten chord on the downbeat of m. 49. The cellist's immediate, high-pitched response to that impact kicks off a return to the lurching figures; these are now hard and flat, without their former, stumbling dynamics. A specially grotesque touch is the cellist's fall onto the sforzando, offbeat C♯s in bar 53; these notes should be played as gruffly as the instrument will permit.

16

8

24

25

32

42

48

53

58   Similar intensity of sound applies to the entire passage of mm. 58–73. The 2nd violin glissandi, climbing high on the G-string, have a wiry force that should be exploited by the player. Turn up the voltage with vibrato, play the rhythms incisively, slide relentlessly in the glissandi, and be aggressive on the swells.

    To reduce the stretching the violist has to do, it may help to play the two-

67 voiced lines in bars 67–68 in fourth position, on the C- and G-strings. Immediately afterward, of course, half-position on the middle strings will prove necessary. The

71 two violins, with their peg-legged rhythm in m. 71, set the tone for the ensemble's stumbling disappearance into the distance. Violins and cello finish this scene with

76 their gasping pressure on the syncope figures in mm. 76–77.

80   The cello returns from the vanishing point with the rubato of mm. 80–82 to open the middle section of the movement. You are completely alone here, so make the most of the composer's instruction: gradually, rhapsodically breathe heat into the succession of A♭s. You are in free control of tempo up to the Animato downbeat

83 of bar 83. Your glissando to the harmonic A can be long and sensuous; your fortissimo A♭, at once languorous and tigerlike.

    Though Bartók doesn't say so, the viola's back-and-forth sweep of pizzicato

84 chords in mm. 84–93 demands rubato treatment. The chords are always played against a sustained background (a held note in the cello, tremolo counterpart in the violins). Also, the composed rhythms incorporate acceleration. It is up to the player to move freely, so that the resolving chord (marked with an explosive wedge) fires the cello into each new declamation.

94   I think rubato is again the order of the day for the cello glissandi in mm. 94–97. There is no way that these yawning smears can be confined in strict metronomics. The accompanying voices will simply have to listen carefully to what the cellist is

99 doing. In the next passage (mm. 99–114), on the other hand, it is the 1st violin's turn to reign freely. Treading high on the tightrope of the G-string, the player needs time to maneuver. In any case, the change of meters in successive measures enforces irregularity.

115   The shape of the *Meno mosso* (bars 115–21) is clear from the writing: a moderate
118 but clear acceleration to m. 118, then descent in tempo, loudness, and register to
122 the return section of the March, mm. 122 ff. Note, by the way, that the viola in
120 mm. 120–21 takes on the introductory role first played by the 2nd violin, back at mm. 16–17. Underneath the viola, the cello spells out an augmented version of the
115 ostinato figure it has been playing since bar 115.

    In the return, all hands will be preoccupied with harmonics, double stops, octaves, or what have you. Don't let these concerns make you neglect the clarity of the snapped rhythms. Avoid rounding off the figures into triplet form. Keep in mind that, though the bow may be holding to the string for the *marcato* stroke, the left hand must stay rather loose, and without excessive finger pressure. Only thus can you manage the many quick shifts in these measures.

    I leave it to the violist to decide whether to take advantage of Bartók's offer of an "easier," single-stop line in place of the written octaves; and to the 1st violin,

126 whether to switch to the proffered, stopped-tone notes in mm. 126–27. I think the 2nd violin should also be free to choose whether to stay on the two lower strings all

124 the way into bar 124. Certainly the player ought to take advantage of Bartók's
125 marking in m. 125 and move to the higher strings on the fourth beat of that bar.

    In the remainder of the return, you will find events similar to those in the first part of the movement, with some exchange of roles between the voices of the ensemble. The closing section has the violins shoot to higher level (mm. 177–79) than in the earlier, corresponding measures.

177

A last archway of snapped rhythms (bars 181–84) brings us to the final measures, where the troops stagger their way toward the double bar. Be careful to place and emphasize the accents as marked in the lower voices in bars 185–86. The violins' octaves in mm. 187 ff. are given a wistful tone by the wide spacing between the lower strand and the harmonic upper thread. There is something indescribably desolate about this combination of sounds, a feeling that belies any jauntiness or swagger in the rhythm.

185

At the very last, the 2nd violin should see that the left-hand pizzicato B♯ sound strongly enough to balance the chords in the lower voices. You will have to use the little finger of your left hand to play these notes, for your third finger will be holding the G♯. Some experimentation with arm and hand position will be needed so that you can exert enough force with the fourth finger.

Mesto. Bartók manages to wring yet more anguish out of his sad melody in this third manifestation. In part, this intensification comes from the quiet lament in the voices that accompany the 1st violin solo. It derives, too, from the extensions the composer builds into the line: first, the painful, overlapping climb of the two violins—joined by the viola—in bars 7–13, and then the correspondingly long decline of mm. 14–18.

III

13
14

I have always sensed inexpressible bleakness in the 2nd violin line in the last three bars of this Mesto section. The tone should be absolutely cold; and some slowdown should prevail as you inch yourself through the chromatics toward the final, barren E♮.

Burletta. Moderato. Though Bartók calls this movement a "little joke," it is scarcely a laughing matter. The mirth is like that of a grinning death's-head: sardonic, bitter, chilling. You may enjoy it, but it will hurt.

Take the instruction, "at the frog," literally: use short, hard strokes, as close to the foot of the bow as possible, and very close to the bridge. You need the full resistance of the hair and the string to evoke the necessary force of sound. You may want to start m. 21 on an upstroke, so that you have the full weight of the downbow on the accented, offbeat 8th-notes of the measure. The downbow notes of bar 22 should be played as though marked with wedges: rifle shots of tone. Attack the syncope B in m. 23 with a downbow; the note needs electric intensity.

21

22

In mm. 24 and 25, the 2nd violin has to reflect the force of the opening, but now without the strength of numbers. Here you can test your force of willpower. (The same for the 1st violin in bar 27). Both violins will have to practice the intonation of mm. 26, 28, and 29, so that the quarter-tone separation in the unison can be maintained throughout the figure, including the glissando. You want that hot, cutting resonance that the deliberate mistuning provides. The 1st violin glissandi in these measures should exude vulgarity, while the two low voices compound the insult by means of the strut in their rhythms.

24

27
26

The violins' 8th-notes in mm. 33–34 sound right if all played upbow. Use a very short stroke, staying as much as possible in one spot of the bow, so that each note has a kind of dry, clucking effect. You may also decide to use this bowing also for the series of short notes in the measures that follow. In any case, arrange your bowing so that every quarter-note is taken downbow, the better to achieve the emphasis called for by the line marked over the note. Also, make sure that the dynamic contrasts and gradations stand out as marked. The acceleration in mm. 42

33

42

ff. rides on the continuous chain of short glissandi, so these must be assertively played, and always with thrust toward the second, clipped note of the couplet.

The rhythmic groupings in these measures override the bar lines, for the overlapping succession of twos and threes keeps the ear guessing. It is only when **45** all four voices line up for the fortissimo short-long at the end of bar 45 that metric order is restored. This is only illusory, however. Starting in the very next measure, the low voices spell out a 3/8 pattern, while the 2nd violin—soon joined by the 1st—insists quietly on jazzy, irregularly divided 4/4 rhythms. These proceedings have a Stravinskian air about them, and never more so than when they resolve into **59** the massed drumbeats of mm. 59–60. The repeated, hammered downstrokes on these notes contribute to the effect.

61 In the Tempo I section (mm. 61–69), the short, accented, or wedge-marked notes can best be taken on a short upstroke, cut incisively into the string to start, then briskly lifted, with intense vibrato to match. Arrange to play downbow on each lined note, whether 8th or quarter, to achieve the proper weight and pressure.

67 The disconsolate sigh of the viola in mm. 67–68 seems reminiscent of the ending of the viola solo that began the quartet. In function, it is like the lone, 2nd violin line that raised the curtain on the Burletta. Now, however, we are being introduced to a forlorn interlude. Locked as it is within the rough movement that surrounds it, this episode makes us feel not only melancholy, but marooned.

The melody of the Andantino is sober enough; but in addition, the metric frame keeps changing. Moreover, the slowly oscillating background figure, cast in rhythmic groups that deliberately blur the metric outlines, helps create a sense of being adrift, insecure. These measures are tricky to play. There is a temptation to emphasize the metric beats, so that the individual voice can hold its place against the counter-rhythms in the neighboring part. To do so, however, hardens the texture of the music, something obviously counter to the composer's intent. Again, slow practice is needed so that the rhythmic frictions can be learned and made second nature.

78 The relationship between parts is more straightforward from m. 78, though the emotional demands on the players remain high. In bars 80–81, the rise and fall in the 2nd violin part should be played as though in full awareness that the attempt to pull out of the bleak musical terrain is futile. The same holds true, over larger **82** spans, for the 1st violin line in mm. 82 ff. and 88 ff. One of the more oppressive **93** events occurs in mm. 93–94 in the inner voices, where those parts are made to give up the smooth 3/8 rhythms and stumble along, instead, in 8th-note couplets.

97 At the start of bar 97, it is up to the 2nd violin to gauge the 1st violin's progress toward the downbeat and to lead the lower voices into a precisely placed, snapped pizzicato. Raise the scroll of the instrument slowly to telegraph your reading of the solo violin's voyage. Then signal the attack on the downbeat. If you do your job right, it will look as though you are choreographing a (not-too-genteel) sneeze. The footnote for this downbeat is not informative enough, at least in the English and French translations. What Bartók asks for is a snapped pizzicato; that is, hook the tip of the index finger under the string, lift the string straight up (the tension of the string will tell you how much is enough), then let it snap against the fingerboard. The result is a strongly percussive sound, through which the indicated pitch emerges. The same procedure holds true for the snapped downbeat of 1st violin **101** and cello in bar 101.

98 The 1st violin will lead the fresh attack on the forte of m. 98. Avoid any rolling of the pizzicato chords, even in the case of the triple stops. The effect must be as close as possible to a single, solidly struck cluster of tones. In the slurred, pizzicato 16th-note couplets of bars 99 and 101, pull the string as vigorously as you dare. The left-hand finger that plays the first 16th should be lifted athletically from the string; then vibrate the second note intensely. Only thus can you hope to make the second note audible. 99

Vibrato is an essential tool, again, in playing the *espressivo* figures in the violin parts in bars 102 and 104. Lingering a bit on the second, loudest, warmest note of the group will also help the effect. In playing the slurred, pizzicato glissandi in mm. 103 ff., start the slide immediately after plucking the first note in the figure; otherwise nothing will be heard except the initial pitch. Be sure to press down firmly on the string with the sliding finger. In ordinary slides, you want to hide most or all of the voyage between the starting and ending tones. Therefore you use light finger pressure during the slide, to facilitate the shift. Here, on the other hand, you want the pitch gradation of the glissando to be heard; hence, the increased finger pressure. 102 103

Note the dynamics, accents, and wedge marks in the *Un poco più mosso* of mm. 110 ff. Follow them explicitly, so that the pizzicato sound will have shape and texture. In the bowed interjections, I think you will find that the printed bowing does not work too well. Instead, take the 16th-note triplet as a downbow ricochet stroke, with the following 8th (in some cases, two 8th-notes) on an upstroke. Give full value to the 8th-rests in mm. 117 and 118, so that the rhythmic groups don't telescope into each other. 110 117

On the other hand, once you get to the second half of bar 119, let the overlapping voices roll forward. Catch the breath suddenly for the drop to piano on the second 8th of m. 122, then think firmly of the 8th-note pulse as you slow down through the rest of the bar. Wait a tiny bit at the end of the measure before making a fresh start on the next downbeat. 119 122

In view of the militant connotations with which Bartók is dealing, it is appropriate that mm. 123–26 sound like something out of Stravinsky's *L'Histoire du soldat*. Even if there is no real connection, remember the Stravinsky piece as you rehearse this passage. Set up a steady, jaunty swagger, and stick with it until the acceleration sweeps you forward from bar 131 to the vanished sound at the end of m. 134. 123 134

One of the strongest performance tests in this movement is the jarring alternation between the forlorn meditations of bar 135 and mm. 138–39 and the crushing retorts of mm. 136–37 and 140–41. Exploit the contrasts to the hilt. It seems as though the pleading that starts in the 1st violin in bar 142 will be allowed to continue, but it too is cut off by the razor-edged glissando shriek of the three upper voices at the end of m. 144. By all means, take that glissando upbow, so that you can sweep the stroke off the string in full force. The 1st violin's E (downbeat of bar 145) can only be a harmonic, in order to cap the slide with a piercing, open resonance. 135 140 144 145

As in the earlier passage at m. 61, punch out the accented 8ths of bars 145 ff. on upstrokes, the lined notes, on downbows. From the third quarter of bar 147 (which will be most conveniently taken downbow), the violins can take the bowing as it comes. 147

The 2nd violin's G-string glissando at the end of m. 150 must be a very broad, brazen guffaw, while at the same time falling rapidly away to a piano. The same idea, spelled out in a different way, is found in the extreme contrast of the 150

152

sforzando, stopped-and-open E and the piano, low-register chord at the bar line of mm. 152–53. After this, only the last, pizzicato chord remains to be played with a transparent, tinkling resonance.

IV

Mesto. Now we arrive at the desperate, last, and fullest flowering of the sad theme. The Vivace, the Marcia, the Burletta, have become interludes on the way to this grim leave-taking. To play this brief finale is a test of the ensemble's skill in tone painting. But it is a far bigger test of the musicians' emotional stamina. The vista this music reveals is so unutterably cheerless and withered that it takes all the players' emotional stamina to explore it to the last degree. This is as true of the hundredth performance as of the first.

There are contrasts in this movement, but even the occasional turbulence brings its own chilling effect, making the quiet, thematic frame seem warmer by comparison. The first twelve measures of the Mesto, marked *espressivo*, are an expansion on the first half of the theme. The solo is most clearly heard in the 1st violin, though fragments of it surface in the accompanying meditations of the other three voices. The cello is the strongest counterbalance to the top line; between them, the outer voices stretch the musical space—and the tension—until it breaks on the

13

widely spaced C minor chord in bar 13.

This downbeat must be sustained with some heat. Out of it, the ripple of notes in cello and viola washes away loudness and warmth and delivers us as well to a slightly slower tempo. The outer voices continue alone, *senza calore*. Take this instruction literally: keep the left hand inert, hold the bow speed to a minimum; work for the coldest sound you can evoke. The viola entrance in bar 16 restores some flow of life, but the ensemble tone should remain cold until the crescendo of

18

mm. 18 ff. calls forth a very moderate warming. From the mezzo forte in bar 21, the sound should immediately drop back toward pale inaudibility.

22

The 8th-rest in m. 22 is a dramatic break. Hold still for a long instant before charging into the fast pace of the next scene. The terrain becomes rugged; the voices lunge up and down in register, the volume lurches from loud to soft. The dynamic range in mm. 22–30 extends only from forte to piano, but you should make the most of the contrast.

30
35

From bar 30 to 39, you are back in a subdued and wintry view of the theme. The projection (*in rilievo*) of the inner voices in mm. 35–36 must be gauged within the frame of the piano dynamic that prevails in this episode. In the *Più andante* that follows, the tempo is quickened, but the statement of the theme is augmented. The net result is that the melody seems to be caught in a time warp. The eerie sensation is underscored by the sustained chord of the lower voices that fills each bar. From the very slow pace of these chords emerges a frozen tempo, quite in keeping with the exceedingly quiet and cold sound called for by the composer. Your very breathing should be slow and shallow during these measures.

46

Mm. 46–54 revisit the theme of the first movement's Vivace, but slowed down, seen now through the moonlit haze of this Mesto. The second theme of the opening

55

movement is summoned up in bars 55–62, but with the instruction, *lontano*, to assure a far-off, scarcely recalled view of the tune. This is especially the responsibility of the inner voices, in mm. 55–58. It's the kind of playing that must be felt, more than rehearsed.

63

The music of mm. 63–71 summons up the phrase first heard at mm. 31 ff., back at the opening Vivace. In fact, the force of that original statement is even exceeded here, in mm. 67–69. This, however, is to set us up for the absolute despondency that will follow. 67

First violin and viola climb painfully up the Mesto theme in bars 72–75. Their dead march is set against the cold background of the chromatic scale—in parallel sevenths!—offered by the 2nd violin and cello. The tremolo of the violin adds an icy touch. The bow must be well over the fingerboard, and the stroke as rapid and small as you can manage. (I am in the habit of resting my right wrist against my knee when playing these measures, to assure that the bowing will be confined to the hand, with no involvement of arm motion.) 72

The four 32nds played by the 2nd violin and the viola, respectively, in mm. 75 and 76 are despondent whispers added to the cadential figure of the moment. The two clusters must be played cleanly and melodically; their notes differ, and the change must be clear to the listener. At the same time, the second grouplet responds to the first, so both have to be given an inflection that implies dialogue. Above all, each of these figures must shudder with apprehension, for each one is followed by the starkest, most forsaken sound in the entire quartet. 75

The ensemble chords at the end of mm. 75 and 76 are marked pianissimo, tremolo, and *sul ponticello*. Rest the bow very lightly on the string, the hair actually grazing the bridge itself. Shake the bow in an infinitely small and rapid oscillation. If skeletons could have goose flesh, their shivers might produce the kind of sound you are after. 75

The chordal shudders, however, are only commentaries on the essential business of these measures: the mounting of the cadential figures toward the last, protesting shriek—the fortissimo chord at the end of bar 80. This chord, like the two loud ones that precede it in the *Più andante,* drains away in volume. Each of the three should begin with intense vibrato, shading into cool tone along with the diminuendo. The first two are answered by low chords, which are to be played coldly indeed. 80

The ending of the fortissimo chord is controlled by the placement of the 2nd violin pizzicato. Be sure that the level of the chord has diminished enough to allow the plucked note to be heard. To help synchronize the pizzicato G♮ in bar 81 with the G♯ that starts the viola solo, the 2nd violin should give a discreet signal of agreement. The remaining pizzicato notes of that line, however, can be placed only with alert attention to the motion of the viola melody.

Bartók provides a specific tempo for the last six measures of the piece. My bet, though, is that the players will not be conscious of tempo when they get to the five dotted-quarter chords in bars 83–85. The violins will echo the low voices as though lost in a timeless landscape. 83

My experience, too, is that the last, harmonic chord of the violins is begun not so much as a result of the cello's G♯ on the downbeat of bar 85, but as something of a last, fresh start. The violin chord has a neutral transparency. The cello's pizzicato version of the theme wears an enigmatic major coloration. Out of the combination emerges a guarded hint of optimism. It seems that Bartók could not, after all, bear to close the work entirely without hope. And it must be recognized that the end of the first movement, in the same key and with somewhat the same color of sound, already foreshadows this ambivalent outlook. 85

SATURDAY EVENING, AUGUST 14, 1954
at 8:30

THE FINE ARTS QUARTET
LEONARD SORKIN, *First Violin*
ABRAHAM LOFT, *Second Violin*
IRVING ILMER, *Viola*
GEORGE SOPKIN, *Cello*
and
RUGGIERO RICCI, *Violin*
PAUL TORTELIER, *Cello*
JACOB LATEINER, *Piano*

Piano Trio in C Minor, Opus 101................*Brahms*
    Allegro energico
    Presto non assai
    Andante grazioso
    Allegro molto

Quartet in A Minor, Opus 132................*Beethoven*
    Assai sostenuto-Allegro
    Allegro, ma non tanto
    Molto adagio
    Alla marcia, assai vivace

INTERMISSION

Quintet for Piano and Strings,
    Opus 57................*Shostakovich*
    Prelude: Lento
    Fugue: Adagio
    Scherzo: Allegretto
    Intermezzo: Lento
    Allegretto

★ ★ ★

MR. UNINSKY uses the STEINWAY piano.

CHAPTER TWENTY-NINE

❧ Shostakovich ❧
Piano Quintet, Op. 57

I am puzzled by this work, to such extent that I have gone to some lengths to impose an extra-musical interpretation on it. On the face of it, this music is not thorny, certainly not inaccessible to player or listener. Despite its brash moments, though, there is an obscuring, private quality about the piece that makes it considerably more challenging to perform than might first appear. To me, the work seems to convey a secret and desperate protest, uttered in a time and place when an open outcry would have been perilous.

It is difficult to understand the workings of the political mind, especially as it applies to the arts. A little background information: Shostakovich's opera, *Lady Macbeth of Mzensk,* premièred in Leningrad in January of 1934. It was acclaimed in Russia, had many performances there over the next two years, and was also presented in other European countries and—in concert version—in America. In 1936, apparently at the direct instigation of Stalin himself, the opera was abruptly and officially condemned in Russia for its ostensible betrayal of the ideals of Soviet art. Beginning with his Fifth Symphony, late in 1937, Shostakovich was restored to his former prominence and favor, the sanctification made fully evident by the award in 1940 of the Stalin Prize to—the Piano Quintet.[1]

All of which proves, it would seem, that those in control had ears but heard not. This quintet is conventional enough in sound to have left the sensibilities of the politicos, high and low, unruffled. I find it strange, though, that what I sense to be the basic pessimism of the work aroused no dark suspicions among the censors of taste and civic virtue. Perhaps, if they detected it at all, they thought that Shostakovich's balefulness concerned only the actions of forces in contemporary Europe from outside Russia, with no regard for anything that had taken place

---

SCORE: Dmitri Shostakovich. 1964. *Piano Quintet in G minor, Op. 57.* Hamburg: Sikorski. Piano score No. 2275.

Left: Page from the program for concerts given by The Fine Arts Quartet and guest artists, the Ravinia Festival, August 1954.

within the homeland itself. Perhaps so. From my player's-eye view, though, I think they missed the point.

The ensemble working on the quintet may, of course, feel that I am spinning an untenable hypothesis about the external significance of the music. If the players end, nonetheless, by giving the work the intensity it demands, then I shall be content. The extremes of melancholy and excitement in this music can have great impact. I know this to be true, for I have been moved by the piece, both when performing it myself and when listening to other ensembles in concert.

I   *Prelude: Lento—Poco più mosso.* The opening, for piano solo, bears the marking, *pesante.* The instruction should be tempered with a bit of lyricism, for it is all too easy to hack away at these measures, breaking the Lento down into a fragmented, turgid, eight-to-the-bar succession of notes. In fact, the piano line moves expansively through eight bars, pausing on notes of longer value, then pushing off into active, 16th-note rhythms. You will note also that a held note in one staff is always countered by moving notes in the other, so that the sense of continuity is maintained throughout. The same holds true within the string group (with the cello leading) from number *1*, and between strings and piano through the rest of the introduction. Maintain an overall perspective; this beginning can be sober and forceful without sounding coarse.

3   Words don't always tell the whole story in music. At number *3*, the verbal indication of speed is *Poco più mosso*; the metronome marking, however, shows that each 3/8 bar here has the duration of one beat of the opening's 4/4 Lento. That is rather more than a *poco* increase in speed. The light-fingered bass line in the piano, coupled with the twirling motion in the treble, is further incentive to an easy, swinging pace.

7   The 1st violin line leading into, and especially after, number *7* is set exceedingly high before it makes its descent to more civilized levels. I take it for granted that the solo will be played with elegance and good intonation, but am concerned that the sound not be thin and whining. It is important that the other instruments play very softly here, so that there need not be any hint of forcing in the violin melody.

You will by now have noticed that, except for the grand pause before the *Poco più mosso*, there is no break in the sound anywhere in this Prelude. True, at number

12   *12*, when the Lento returns, there is an 8th-rest for all four strings, with the down beat stroke in the piano to be regarded possibly as a composed "silence." To my ears, the continuous flow of sound can feel a bit oppressive, and perhaps Shostakovich meant to create this sensation. In any event, the players should take advantage of breathing points and articulations in their lines to allow air and light to reach the listeners. They are going to need it, for the Lento, from *12* to the end of the Prelude, casts a veritable blanket of sound over the hall. Even as I play these measures I find myself threatened by the massive sonority, and welcome the double bar and the opportunity it promises for breathing easily once again.

II   *Fugue: Adagio.* The composer doesn't allow any time for such frivolity, though. From full-voiced fortissimo, he moves to a muted, pianissimo line for one violin, in a direct transition from one movement to the next—obviously, Shostakovich has calculated the shock value of his tactics.

In its own way, the Fugue is as dark and overcast in tone as the Prelude. At its start, the fugue subject has a few breaks, but then flows without interruption. It is in the nature of fugues, of course, to have the voices overlap each other as they make

their imitative entries. Also, at a few points Shostakovich thins the sound: from *22*
to *23*, the web of tones is carried only by the piano; from *24* to *25*, and for a few
measures at *26*, by the strings alone. As in the Prelude, though, we are again
covered by a continuous and constantly building aural fabric. The mutes are
removed en route and the dynamics mount, so that, by *28* and from then until *33*,
fortissimos rain down on us. Even then, the cello and viola cry out in forte
(instruments now muted once again) before falling back into the closing sections of
the fugue and the eventual descent to the final pianissimo.

As I indicated in my prefatory remarks, I think Shostakovich had his reasons
for writing so shrouded a pair of movements to open this quintet, or, indeed, for
returning to much the same tone for the fourth movement, the Intermezzo. Clearly,
the performance problems in these chapters are musical and emotional, as much as
technical. In the Fugue, the individual entries need *cantabile* playing, so that they
retain their identity as lines. Especially because of the muted sonority that prevails
in so much of the movement, flexible shaping of each voice is needed to keep the
parts from matting together into an impenetrable mass of tones. The danger of this
attaches as much to the quiet levels as to the louder points in the movement. The
lightness of the writing at *23* offers built-in relief, but the musical assault march
beginning soon thereafter will extend over four pages of score.

It is the marching that should concern the ensemble. You have to decide
whether to accept this aspect as essential to the movement, especially at the
climactic middle episode, or whether you think you can, or should, try to
counteract it by picking up the tempo as you get into numbers *28* and following. I
favor this tactic, though I don't really believe it masks the emotional lock step of the
music. In playing this fugue, I feel a fair degree of angst, both for myself and for the
composer.

Scherzo: Allegretto. Escape! Joy unconfined! Ebullience! Yet, wait a minute: in
fourteen pages of score there is again not a moment's peace. I find something
relentless and demonic about so extended and uninterrupted a spate of high jinks.
The composer stipulates *marcato* at the start of the movement and again at *55*. As I
see it, however, this playing attitude is appropriate to the entire Scherzo.
Everything is on the driving, hard-bitten edge of sound. Even the moment of
ostensible relaxation, starting at number *53 + 5*, is spiky, pushed, a devil's dance.

I can point to examples of what I find to be fairly grim humor throughout this
movement: the grinding counterpoint in the piano part between *47* and *48*; the
grunts in the string parts, from *50* through the first measures of *51*; the skeletal
rattling of the middle strings before *54*, and of the violins before *55*, then fully
orchestrated in the strings right up to *58*. True enough, there is some levity in the
music from *60* to *64*, but sterner tones then return, culminating in the rather brutal
and punching rhythms from *67* to the end. I can't help feeling that there is a
sardonic edge to Shostakovich's choice of title for this movement. If this is a joke (to
refer to the literal meaning of the term, *scherzo*), it seems a fairly bitter one. By
strange coincidence, this movement was written very close in time to that other,
even more melancholy joke, the Burletta movement of Bartok's Sixth Quartet.

A couple of technical hints: in measures such as *46 − 1*, the bow must be
recovered after the short downstroke on the first beat, so that the ensuing eighths
can begin with another downbow. In measures where three quarter-notes precede a
bar of 8th-note couplets (see, for example, *48 + 4*), the second and third quarters
must be linked in an upstroke, so that the 8th-notes can start downbow. The printed

22

24

26

28

23

III

45, 55

53+5

47
50
54 − 8

60
67

46 − 1

48+4

55	bowing should definitely be followed at number *55,* in order to preserve the
62	necessary percussive quality for the passage. At number *62,* the 1st violin will, I

think, find it easier to swing wholeheartedly with the hemiola couplets rather than try to adhere mentally to the 3/4 metric frame. The piano may also want to move with its own hemiola duples, even though they overlap those of the violin; in fact, it would seem that the composer deliberately exploits the friction of this overlapping, though he omits accents in the piano part.

63 – 7   In the four measures starting at *63 – 7,* the 1st violin and piano should play as though they are aware they are being pitted against one another. At the end of the movement, all hands should stress the time compression of the accented half bars in the 4/4 measures, as against the broader swing of the 3/4 bars.

IV   ***Intermezzo: Lento.*** After the wild hammering of the Scherzo, the shadowed tone of the Intermezzo seems almost a return to the temper of the Fugue movement. The tempo is even slower than in the earlier movement, but a sense of motion is assured by the quarter-note pulse in the bass line. Yet, as you will note from inspecting the score, that pulse never stops, except for two measures at

74   number *74,* when the strings seem to consult together before the theme—and the metric undercurrent—is allowed to return. The last six measures of the movement don't count in this regard, since they constitute a transition to the finale.

The insistence on the metric beat seems to me to be as ominous, in its way, as the hysteria of the Scherzo. Is it a mournful tolling, a dead march that Shostakovich

70   conjures up? I find it significant that the *espressivo* piano melody at number *70,* no mirthful ditty in its own right, is answered (number *71*) by a rather listless sigh in the 1st violin. No reassurance is forthcoming, either, from the mutterings of the

72 – 2   viola and cello, at *72 – 2.*

The return of theme leads, at last, to the tremendous outburst of the

75   *Appassionato* (number *75*). As I hear it, however, this is no release, but a massive cry, going nowhere but into the long, fatalistic descent to the movement's real ending (six measures before the double bar). I would suggest, moreover, that this conclusion of the Intermezzo is the true ending of the entire composition. The official Finale, with its predominantly easy, casual tone, seems not quite consistent with all that has come before. It has the flavor of an apology, of an effort to counteract the essential gloominess and depression that color the quintet as a whole.

V   ***Finale: Allegretto.*** It is for the piano to make the transition from the Intermezzo. The *attacca* makes literal sense here. At the end of the fourth movement, there is a measure of four quarter-notes; these should be played with enough improvisatory freedom that the upbeat, 8th-note couplet at the start of the finale can be folded in as a nebulous, "fifth" beat to join the quarters that precede.

81 – 1   The improvisatory tone should be preserved right up to *81 – 1.* The composer's mark of retard and of gradual return to tempo, spanning this opening, can only be realized by maintaining a sense of wandering, of search for focus, in these bars.

81   Though tempo is attained at number *81,* it would be untrue to the character of the music to play the ensuing phrases with great rigidity. There is a kind of fluid looseness and irregularity to these lines that must not be lost. Note, for example,

82   how the piano's succession of 4/4 measures, at number *82,* moves through a 3/4 bar to add a final, blurring touch to a melody that has already progressed with whimsical indecision. The string response is more regular, but a 3/4 measure (at

84 – 2   *84 – 2*) again ripples the waters.

It is not until *87* that a regular, metric frame really makes itself felt; and from *88*, the pulse has crystallized so far that a military drum beat has taken over the accompaniment role. From here the troops march boldly on, soon at an *alla breve* clip. It is noteworthy, though, that Shostakovich chooses to maintain this mood only for a time. He abandons it at its peak, moving (number *95*) back to the unsettled tone of the first part of the movement. From my experience with the work, I should warn that you may actually feel a bit unsettled, even disoriented, by the wavering of the line in the piano part, and by the rather random alternation of meters as the music unfolds.

    This calls to mind also the fact that, like each of the first four movements, this finale rolls from beginning almost to its end without a clear break point. It is only at *102* that the string chorus, with the 1st violin as soloist, makes a stand, in order to restore some of the anxious tone of the first, second and fourth movements, even with some suggestion of thematic reminiscence. Approaching number *104* and beyond, however, the music returns to its somewhat erratic course. The militant element, very quiet now, supplies the material for a long and rambling discourse by the violin, spanning no fewer than twenty-nine measures, some of them completely in solo. At last, the same theme serves the entire ensemble as, arrayed in deliberately shifting ranks, they make a cool and studiedly nonchalant exit: an enigmatic ending to an enigmatic work.

87

88

95

102

104

PROGRAMMA.

L. VAN BEETHOVEN   KWARTET in f, opus 95
(1770-1827)

                                Allegro con brio
                                Allegretto ma non troppo
                                Allegro assai vivace
                                Larghetto-allegro agitato

Benjamin BRITTEN   KWARTET nr. 2 in C, opus 36
(Geb. 1903)

                                Allegro calmo senza rigore
                                Vivace/Chaconna

PAUZE

W. A. MOZART   KWARTET in G (K.V. 387)
(1756-1791)

                                Allegro vivace assai
                                Menuetto/Andante cantabile
                                Molto allegro

CHAPTER THIRTY

❦ Britten ❦
Quartet No. 2 in C

At Columbia University in 1941, Benjamin Britten's first opera, *Paul Bunyan*, had its première, with the composer present. I was then a student at Columbia and served as concertmaster for the week-long run of the work. I never saw the composer again, but years later—after joining the Fine Arts Quartet—greatly enjoyed learning and performing Britten's Quartet No. 2.

Though the quartet has only three movements, it feels like a large work. This sense attaches especially to the finale, a set of variations on a ground bass. The year the quartet was written, 1945, was the 250th anniversary of the death of Henry Purcell, the great English composer. One of Purcell's distinctions was his masterful handling of the *basso ostinato*; it is by way of homage to Purcell that Britten chose to close his second quartet with an ostinato movement. Further, he titles the finale not with the continental term—*chaconne*—for such a work, but rather with an old English form of the word: *Chacony.*

I find the opening Allegro to be essentially lyric, though serious and reflective in tone. The second movement, Vivace, is a highly exciting experience for both player and listener; the frictions of its part writing challenge the ear. Coming after these two movements, the twenty-one variations and three cadenzas of the finale, short though they are individually, may add up to a large order for the audience. Over the years of concert presentation of this quartet, I sometimes found that the listeners seemed a bit too stunned to respond to the work as I would have hoped.[1]

Nonetheless, Britten's Second Quartet is a very impressive piece of chamber music by a major composer of our century.[2] I believe that time will only confirm the well-merited place this quartet holds in the concert repertoire. Moreover, the

---

SCORE: Benjamin Britten. 1946. *Quartet No. 2.* London: Boosey & Hawkes. Miniature score No. 89.

Left: Page from the program for the concert by The Fine Arts Quartet, the Bachzaal, Amsterdam, April 18, 1958.

ensemble studying this piece will find that it sharpens every aspect of their technical skills and their musical alertness.

I   *Allegro calmo senza rigore.* (I would prefer to translate the last two words of the movement title as meaning, "with freedom," rather than "without stiffness.") The rising interval of a tenth plays a primary thematic role in this movement. A tenth, presented in unison and octave for all four instruments, opens the quartet. The 2nd violin is given the contracted version of the interval, the third, in order to move smoothly into octave relationship with the 1st violin in the second half of

1   m. 1.

The thematic interval is presented elliptically, "calmly," with a decrescendo to the upper note, so that the ascent is veiled in the resonance of the initial tone. In the viola, the interval becomes a quiet, two-voiced pedal point, thus casting the veiled effect around the lines that move in the other voices. The sustained drone is taken

12, A   up by the 2nd violin in m. 12, and by the cello at *A*. In fact, the pedal point appears so often and in so many guises in the movement that it, too, must be given the status of a theme.

In playing the opening, be guided by the continuous hum of the drone. Its sound carries on through the rests in the other lines. Moreover, the notes on either side of the breaks in the first five bars are always E. In effect, then, the drone is

6   incorporated in the moving lines themselves. In mm. 6–9, the tones that bridge the silences are only a half-step or a minor third apart. All of this implies that the moving lines are to be played very smoothly, as though the rests themselves become part of the resonance.

The printed swell marks are quite narrow, implying that only the slightest of dynamic waves are to be imposed on the line. With the *poco crescendo* in m. 8 and

9   the compression of action in bars 9–10, the intensity can increase moderately, just
10   enough to bring you convincingly to the Cs in mm. 10–11, and to the fall off that ends the phrase.

12   The connection to the second phrase is seamless: in m. 12, G and its own rising tenth replaces the sustained C. Instead of a transposition of the opening, we now hear a new element—I'll call it phase 2—of that melody. The upward push at the close of this statement is longer and more decisive, extending over the seven bars

A − 6   starting at *A* − 6.

Once more, though, the surge of activity ends in an apparent surrender, the
A   sighing upward tenth at letter *A*. The interval is now based on the note, D. As at bar 12, the moving line here again extends and builds—phase 3—on the opening melodic thought. The three melodic elements presented in this first part of the movement all seem to me to be parts of a single theme. All three, however, are distinct and are so treated as the movement unfolds.

From the start of the movement, the moving lines have been presented by three voices, in unison and octave. There is a twofold rehearsal problem here. Several layers of sound have to be kept in tune not only with one another, but with a sustained pitch (in the fourth voice) that serves as a kind of tuning fork. Also, it is difficult for three players to stay synchronized while at the same time trying to shape their lines gracefully. Slow practice will help, of course. To maintain rhythmic alignment, an obvious answer is to follow the lead of the 1st violin. That works best, though, if ensemble rehearsal has already generated a clear idea of the desired melodic shape.

B − 10   Starting at *B* − 10, the drone spreads through all three lower parts; the resulting layering of tenths supplies the notes, G, B♭, D, F, A, C. This palette of tones also constructs the 1st violin's bridge (starting in *B – 7*), a span, however, that leads not to a second theme but to a new phase of the exposition, based on now-familiar melodic material. As the critic, Hans Keller, explains:

    B–7

> The first part of the exposition corresponds to the classical first subject, and the second part to the classical second subject. Nevertheless, the whole of the thematic material having already been stated at the outset, the second part of the exposition (including the bridge) also decidedly assumes *developmental* character...[3]

The violin's 8th-note line in the bridge passage hops back and forth across the strings of the instrument; I advise that the wedge marks be interpreted as a call for crisp, but not brittle or dry, sound. The bowing is actually a spiccato, to be played with limber wrist. Support the bow well in the hand, so that it does not fall awkwardly from string to string; and add enough vibrato to lend a hint of warmth to the tone. As you approach the *animato* of letter *B*, your reading of the wedge mark must change. The stroke gradually becomes shorter, more cutting, more aggressive.

As we have seen, the bridge is an arpeggiation of a drone. Now the rhythm and profile of the transition, in its turn, generates an *animato* melody that permeates all four voices. In so doing, the theme raises the drone element of the movement to prime importance: from *B* to *C*, everything is drone. Even though the lines enter and reenter individually, the 8th-notes of the several parts interlock and give the impression of a continuous texture of sound. This is true even before mm. *C – (4 to 2)*, where the motion in 8ths is constant in all four voices.

    B

    C–4

The part entries spark the fabric of this passage by stating an aggressive version of the upward tenth. Note that there is now a crescendo to the upper edge of the interval, with a grace note and double stop to add further weight to that side of the motive. Play the upstroke with verve; lift the double stop off the strings, with vibrato to support the accent. The overall dynamic is only forte, but the 8th-note pattern can generate a lot of sound when played by three or four voices. Be discreet and make sure that the motive of the tenth stands out in relief.

The 1st violin is given the motivic tenth in reverse, from top down, in m. *C – 5*. This is done deliberately, in preparation for similar motion that will appear in all three lower voices, a half measure before *C*. There, the downward leap leads to the lowest possible drone available to the instruments: the two bottom strings of each. The drone is sustained for a moment on the open strings, before entering a new guise.

    C–5

C to *D* (exploiting phase 1 of the theme) will take some diligent practice. In each instrument, a drone is sustained on one open string. At the same time, on the next string above, a moving line inches its way up toward the end of the fingerboard. The dynamic level throughout is pianissimo. Here, you want to adjust the angle of the bow so that dynamic balance within the double stop favors the upper string, not the lower. This will keep the resonance of the open string within bounds. Further, you have to maintain the clarity of the moving line, especially in the upper region of the string; and you must shape the upper line convincingly, all the while holding to the specified legato.

    C

In its quiet way, this passage is a tour de force. It suggests that a muted octet is at work, rather than a quartet. It's a danger spot in the movement, for the music can sound like a blurry mess if not very carefully played. Work toward giving it the transparent delicacy it must have. To this end, the left hand must feel relaxed and precise as it carries the melody upward. Position the arm so the hand is presented to the string without having to reach and stretch.

D   At *D* there are two marks: triple piano and *lusingando*. Of the various translations of the latter instruction that I have seen, "intimate" is perhaps the most appropriate here. For one thing, three voices have to offer quiet support to the solo;

E   that is carried in the 1st violin, and from *E* (at which point the whole texture is transposed and inverted), in the cello. Between the two solo passages, there are

E−3   several measures (*E* − 3) where all four parts move in the background vein.

The background is interesting because it is a kind of musing on an aspect of the principal theme. That melody is viewed here as though drawn in a chalk line that has then been smeared into a ribbon of color. Devote enough rehearsal time to comb through the interesting sounds that are generated by the relation between the

D   parts. From *D* to *E* + 9, 2nd violin and viola move in parallel seconds (major and minor); from *D* to *E*, viola and cello are in parallel fifths (perfect or diminished). Second violin and cello are, consequently, moving in parallel sixths. And the 1st violin, when it joins the background group, offers yet other interval relationships.

D to *F*   I suggest that you play from *D* to *F* slowly, in the various pairings of instruments. Assemble all three background lines, still slowly, until the notes fit comfortably. At that point, step up the tempo, observing the dynamics and the melodic inflection all the while, and finally add the solo lines.

F−4   The four bars before *F* are at forte level; they should still, however, be treated lyrically. Only the half measure leading into *F* warrants truly vigorous handling, to

F   unleash the music that follows. With the triplets in the first eleven bars of *F*, the 2nd violin assumes both the drone and leading function. The cross-string figures in that part can be played boldly, smoothly, and with some freedom.

The other three parts will orient themselves around the metric pulse of the drone. All four instruments, however, have to march to the drum of the phrase. The

F+4   target points are (counting *F* as m. 1): the downbeats of mm. 4 and 6; the third beat of m. 9; and the downbeat of m. 12. Shape your rubato to reflect these irregular divisions of the phrase. The source of these ardent declamations can be found back at letter *A*, in the first four measures of phase 3 of the principal theme.

The same area (*A* + 5 and 6), transposed and augmented, provides the melody

F+12   of mm. *F* + (12 to 15). Here the line is assigned to 1st violin alone, with the other three parts serving as drones. As with the sequence of events after *A*, the spiccato

G+1   8th-note element soon follows (*G* + 1). Assured bow control is even more important than before, for the pattern is now left completely exposed as it works its way down through the four voices in the quartet. Join the segments smoothly and make the style of bowing uniform, so that the line sounds continuous. That way, the shift of tone color from high violin register to the lowest cello range will show to full advantage.

H to *I*   From *H* (the start of the development) to *I*, the rising sweep of the thematic tenth is applied in a new way: a glissando to a harmonic. A sustained, four-part drone is established by the quartet; the glissandi are spaced randomly through the several lines of this chordal haze. Thus, flickers of bright sound emerge from a distant atmosphere. The glissandi alternate playfully between the outer voices in

I−7   mm. *I* − (7 to 5). Continuing the whimsy, the inner parts join for a simultaneous slide extending through an entire measure, the parallel lines moving at the interval of a major second (*I* − 1).

At *I*, the 1st violin monopolizes the glissando, incorporating it into a line that is written (though without any change in time signature) in 5/4. This makes for a constantly changing placement of the figure against the 4/4 meter in the lower voices. The repetition of figure in the violin makes that part the drone of the moment. Although the other three parts seem—in the early measures of *I*—to be involved in a pedal point C♯ of their own, the crisply pointed action in the inner parts carries the threesome into melodic action at bar *I* + 6.

Starting at *J* – 6, all four parts transit toward sterner thoughts. At *J*, and on to *K*, the drone has become a militant tattoo. From the glissando sevenths in the violin ostinato just concluded, Britten derives an active line of 8th-note couplets. This, in turn, blossoms into another *lusingando* passage that extends through the first four bars of *K*. More accurately, I should say that it goes on until *L*. There is, however, a brusque interlude, the *agitato* of *K* + (5 to 7). In those measures, the cello continues to focus on the seventh; the upper voices, though, revert to the thematic tenth, but present it in the form of a galvanic downward leap. You have to make a strong, abrupt shift in temperamental gear from the pianissimo of m. 4 to the "ferocity" of m. 5; and an equally swift change back into smoothness in m. 8.

The two inner parts trail away toward infinity at *L* – 1. They are cut off brutally by the cello entrance at *L*. The confrontation between upward seventh and downward tenth returns for some measures. By *L* + 5, however, everyone is dealing in tenths. We are witnessing an aggressive version of the theme, and a greatly tightened review of earlier events. This seems to combine development and recapitulation, though an actual return is signalled only with the trumpeting of C major at letter *M*.

The thematic treatment originally heard at m. *F* is brought back at *L* + 12, with some changes in detail, and worked up to yet higher intensity. Note that the rolling triplets (now assigned to the viola) progress to a lather of 16ths in the two bars before *M*. This helps deliver the ensemble to a veritable apotheosis of the movement's ideas.

The return is short and intense, its events extremely telescoped. In m. *M* + 1, the rising tenth erupts, with the second note of the interval transformed into a grand, upbow chord from all three upper voices. The cello is holding forth with the boldest of spiccato strokes, playing a line that recalls both the rolling triplets and the 8th-note figures first heard in the vicinity of *B*. Starting at *M* + 2, the 1st violin is grandly singing an augmentation of phase 2 of the theme. At the same time, the 2nd violin is declaiming the first part of the theme. And the viola loudly recites phase 3.

Four bars before *N*, the composer exhorts the 1st violin to play *con slancio* ("with outburst"). I doubt that you will need such urging. Rather, the whole ensemble must be careful not to let the excitement roughen the sound.

I think the movement's close is especially fine. Starting at *N*, an augmentation of the melody of *A* + 5 and 6 carries both the register and the tension down to a relaxed level. At *N* + 9 ff., a quotation from *A* + (9 to 12) guides us toward transparent 8th-note tracery. This had earlier formed a link to the development. Now it takes us into the coda.

The last twenty-three measures of the movement are devoted to the beatification of the tenth, in its original, C major setting. Three times, the interval pyramids through the four instruments, accumulating into a sustained, ethereal chord. Underneath, the cello strums four-string chords, not only duplicating the pitches of the upper voices (the G of the triad is never present), but also

I

I+6

J−6   *J* to *K*

K+5

L−1

L+5

M
L+12

M+1

M+2

N−4

N

N+9

incorporating a nostalgic recall of phase 3. Both in order to grab the notes and for evocative purposes, the cellist should take these chords freely.

The third time around, the violins space the sustained chord very widely indeed. The high E harmonic, the triple-piano level, the quiet resonance of the cello chords—all this is most effective. So is the last, hushed reminder of phase 3 in the lower voices as the violin harmonic fades away.

II   *Vivace.* For sheer technical difficulty, this is one of the most demanding ensemble movements I know. It's also a truly exhilarating performance experience. There is a bracing, clean sense about the rhythm and sound of the writing. At the double bar, you feel as though you've had a run through fresh, Alpine air, but are in such tip-top form that you don't even feel winded.

Britten's own instrument was the piano. He clearly knew a thing or two about string playing, though, judging from his perceptive choice of the accompaniment figure that runs through the end sections of the Vivace. The ricochet bowing of the

1   triplets, to and fro across the strings (see, for example, the inner voices in mm. 1 ff.), maintains itself almost gyroscopically, once you get it started. The composer helps you start it by providing the musical spark plug, the accented, up-and-down pair of 8ths at the beginning of the pattern. After that, let the built-in spring of the bow do the work; just have your hand apply the needed impulse at the start of each up- and downstroke to keep the motion going. And keep the stroke short; each triplet is played within a very small area of the bow. If you are doing things right, there will be no "creep" of the bow, no matter how many measures of the figure you have to play.

The score does not supply the downbeat accent for the inner voices at the start of the movement. Be sure to add it yourself; the first 8th-note of the measure must be strongly emphasized, with pianissimo following immediately after.

Look ahead to the closing measure of the movement; there the 1st violin offers a last, high, pianissimo flick of the up-down fragment, by way of leave-taking. The energizing molecule of rhythm has assumed thematic significance. It is important, then, to give it suitable prominence whenever it appears, whether alone or in "starter" role, and with due adjustment to fit the dynamic context of the moment. Always play the figure in the lower half of the bow, of course, both for proper impulse and also to be properly located in the stick if the ricochet pattern follows.

The rhythm of this movement suggests that you are playing a tarantella. Britten's irregular phrase lengths might confuse a dancer, but they add to the

1 to 12   ensemble fun. At the start of the Vivace, it takes five bars for the rhythmic motor to fire up. The first complete phrase, stated in the outer voices, occupies the next seven measures (grouped as 2 + 2 + 3).

There follows a two-bar idling of the motor. Then there is a second seven-measure phrase, now defined by the inner voices, balancing the downward thrust of the first phrase by pushing up to starting level. At this point, the five-bar introduction returns, along with the initial seven-bar phrase.

We seem to be in for a full, sectional repeat. But when the inner voices present the answering phrase in this second set, things follow a new track. Not only does the melodic line climb, but it adds two measures in the process, so that the phrase ends up with a total of nine bars.

You will have noticed that the phrase is always stated in unison by the given pair of instruments. This makes the melodic flares clearly audible. It also means that the unisons must be very accurate, both in tuning and timing; any discrepancy will be immediately noticeable. Moreover, as we will note in the next paragraphs, the second part of the Vivace colors its melody with seconds. All the more reason for the phrases in the first section to sound like a single line, colored but not shadowed by the doubling.

At *A*, we are in C minor, and in a new segment of the Vivace. Here, the introductions and interludes consist of explosive, ensemble chords, always to be played downbow. Once again, the phrases have varying length: five bars, starting in *A* + 3; four, starting in *A* + 10; and five again, starting in *B* − 9. Each phrase describes a low-slung arch, pointed up or down, and always with a fortissimo peak. The relationship between lines here is such that the melody is shot through with major and minor seconds. This creates a wonderfully tart and crunchy sound, great fun to hear.

At *B*, we are back to the initial phase of the Vivace, though it is now transplanted harmonically. The melodic statements are assigned first to the two lower voices, then—at *C*—to the violins. The violins head for the moon, or at least high C, in unison. Once there, they add a flourish to stake their claim to the territory. This not only makes for a fourteen-bar phrase, but also for some very thin ice for intonation. This is the kind of passage that not only takes slow practice in rehearsal, but a checkup before each concert.

A four-gun salute of ensemble chords in C major launches the 1st violin into a solo flight toward the middle section of the movement. (It is not so labelled, but should be thought of as the Trio of the Vivace.) The viola hangs in with a pedal point C until *D* − 2. It will be up to the cellist to bring the band back into action on the downbeat of *D*. The 1st violin could signal that beat, but is supposed to land there in triple piano, so the burden of leadership rests with the cello.

From many a performance of the work, I know that the rhythmic grouping of the 1st violin part in mm. *D* − (5 to 3) can be very confusing for the rest of the ensemble. Things sort themselves out in *D* − 3, but that leaves the three lower voices only a short time in which to reorient their thoughts and make their entrance. Not only that, but they have to carry the first three bars of *D* quite alone; thus, the rhythmic pattern they present must sound absolutely assured.

The key to all this rests in the hands of the 1st violin. The troublesome bars before *D* must be played quite steadily and without rushing. Write in some bowing marks to avoid confusion. Also, a discreet accent on the first 8th of each of the three bars will help make the line intelligible, both to soloist and hearers. I hate to add this touch of pedantry to the phrase, but anything that will help avoid messiness, both in the solo and the aftermath, is to be recommended.

The rhythmic background of the section from *D* to *H* is pretty straightforward: a galloping, triplet figure composed of a first 8th from the cello (later, the viola), completed by an answering couplet in two of the other voices. Through much of the section, the 1st violin plays a blues-y solo, in double stops, above this rhythm. The crooning phrases are played in 3/4 time, with a parenthesized time signature to reassure the soloist. If you imagine the way a duet of pensive jazz trumpeters would play the line, you won't go wrong.

Energetic, even spasmodic, outbursts break into the solo. The 1st violin plays these, and must change character—and even boost tempo slightly, with the aid of the ensemble—for these exclamations. These portions of the line are marked by a time signature (parenthetic again) of 2/4. The second outcry, starting at *E* + 2, is in 16ths, *brillante*. Once again, as in the transition to the trio, this solo passage of the

A

A+3, *A*+10, *B*−9

B

C

D−2

D−3

D to *H*

E+2

E+6	violin can be confusing. Hold steady in mm. *E* + (6 to 8).
F to *G*	There is yet another such passage, from *F* to *G*. This could be very troublesome, especially since it involves all three upper voices in the ensemble. Fortunately, the rhythmic groupings are not as tricky here.
	The transition back to the Vivace material takes the form of a very high-flying
H−12	violin duet. Give this passage (*H* − 12 ff.) some slow rehearsal, so that you won't sound like a pair of nightingales in distress.
	The return itself, at *H*, opens with the two violins and viola in a very quiet
H+2	pedal-point trio. The successive accents in the three parts (*H* + [2 to 4]) should barely ripple the surface of the triple piano; just tweak the bow very gently with the
H+6	fingers. So also, the staggered descents in the trio of instruments (*H* + [6 to 11]) should murmur, though very clearly.
I−15	The passage starting at *I* − 15, despite its extreme quietness, contains some of the thickest writing in the movement. Be patient enough to rehearse these measures, right up to *I*, slowly and repeatedly. Try to achieve transparency in those bars where all four voices move simultaneously through the triplets.
I	From I, as in the section starting at A, the paired voices move in lines that rub against each other in the close spacing of major and minor seconds. The alternating friction and resolution of interval depends on accurate synchronizing of the
K−10	melodic strands. In K − (10 to 4), the friction involves all four parts, and the tumult is increased by a crescendo to a fortissimo. Slow rehearsal is especially important here. The ensemble has to learn to stay on course until reaching the haven of the big
K−4	C major chords of K − (4 to 2).
	The movement begins as though in E♭ major, hints at a stronger allegiance to C minor at letter *A*, circles around F major in the trio, and finally ends by openly
K	avowing C minor. The entire coda, from *K* to the double bar, is devoted to a harmonic progress toward that admission. In the last thirteen bars, in fact, there is nothing but an affirmation of the C minor chord. Moreover, the coda is built entirely of the strong up-down fragment and the ricochet pattern, the same materials that made up the introductory measures of the movement. In its own intricate fashion, the Vivace is symmetrical.
III	***Chacony. Sostenuto.*** This finale is constructed of nine-measure sections, numbered *1* to *21*, and a somewhat longer concluding section, *22*. (Here the score labeling shifts from letters to numbers, and I make the same change in referring to measures in this part of my text.)
1, 20	Section *1* states the theme. I think that the last three sections, *20* to the end, are primarily reaffirmations of the theme, and should be regarded as a grand coda. That leaves the variations of sections *2* through *19*. After section *7* comes a cadenza for cello; for viola, after section *13*; and for 1st violin, after section *19*.
	Colin Mason describes the resulting three sets of variations as follows: "In the first group the variations are of harmonization, in the second of rhythm and texture, and in the third a counter-subject to the theme is developed."[4] There is, in fact,
4	rhythmic variation in sections *4*, *5*, and *6* of the first group, though it is applied to parts other than the theme-bearing voice. Overall, this first set of variations is quiet in its contemplation of the theme.
	In the second group, all voices—and the theme itself—are absorbed into heightened and sometimes turbulent activity. The theme surfaces through the
8	waves, however, in sections *8*, *10*, *11*, and *12*, and can be discerned within the
9	allover patterns of variations *9* and *13*.

Partly because of the calming influence of the counter-subject, the third set of variations returns to the temper of the opening group. In all three sets, however, the cadenza is launched with a burst of sound. The cadenza solos are bravura in their several ways, but all end by restoring quietness, if not always relaxation.

1. The theme is quite asymmetrical in its shape. The first four measures are alike and are linked in a rise to a fortissimo. Mm. 5–6 together constitute a hemiola, three-whole-note bar. The same can be said for bars 7–8, although the rhythmic tempo there is compressed, not broad. At m. 9, the theme cadences on a sustained C, in a quiet link to the first variation.

1
5
7
9

I don't think you should use much rubato in stating the theme. What with the swells and fallbacks in six of the measures, the large dynamic sweep, and the built-in tilt of the phrase outline, the melody has been preloaded with action. In fact, after this kind of opener, it comes as something of a surprise that the first variations are as quiet as they are.

In playing the theme, preserve the shortness of the 16th-note, as though you have in mind the characteristic rhythm of the French overture. Also, make clear distinction between lines and accent marks. Where a bracket appears over two successive notes (this holds true in the variations as well), play the two in one bow, but with very clear articulation of the short, second note. The separate strokes indicated in bars 4–6 will certainly induce a troublesome creep toward the frog unless you are careful to save your bow during the swells on the long note.

4

2. After playing a long sustained tone, hook the following 16th-note into the same bow stroke. The printed slurring in this variation does not provide for this, but you will run into some choked-sound situations unless you use your judgment about the bowing. Cello and viola will no doubt want to change bow unobtrusively in the long tones that stretch over four measures. Maintain the pianissimo, but work for freely flowing sound.

2

3. The statement of the theme in the 1st violin is slightly camouflaged by the inversion of some of the intervals in the melody. More of a change is provided by the chromatic harmonizations in the inner voices. The three upper lines are once again moving in simultaneous rhythm. See that the massed accents do not jar the pianissimo measures.

3

4. Play the dotted quarters in a gentle, *portato* stroke. There are three or more lines of sound against the 2nd violin solo in the quiet measures. Work for a balance that will permit the solo to lead the dynamic gradations without having to force. The 1st violin, viola, and cello should use very legato bowing in bars 5–8 of this variation, to contrast with the angularity of the thematic voice.

4

5. A slightly slower tempo may prove desirable in this variation. The bows should be drawn with the lightest pressure that will yield presentable sound, well up toward the fingerboard. In playing the inner parts, speed the stroke slightly on the way to the fourth and fifth beats of the measure, draw more slowly as you approach the suspension over the bar line. Don't overdo the effect; use it to let the line breathe suitably in the first four bars of the variation. The same process is applied in shorter compass in bars 5–6, and is adapted to the still shorter spans in m. 7. The idea is to have the suspensions dwindle, but not die. I think the variation should give the effect of trancelike musing. Note, by the way, that this is the first section in which there is no loud point. The only dynamic change is the moderate swell in bar 8, to accompany the lone accent mark in the melody. In the rest of the solo, lines have replaced accent marks.

5

5
7

8

6   **6.** The first few bars of this section continue the mood of the previous variation. Here the theme is concealed in the cello part; that voice also adopts and compresses the undulating motion formerly given to the inner lines. Go easy on the 16th-note that introduces each segment of the melody. Even in the forte measure, the note should be only moderately stressed, as much by stretching (not too much!) as by pressure.

7   **7.** If the tempo was slowed in section *5*, it has probably been restored in the course of *6*. The present variation returns to the completely synchronized rhythms of section *1*; the speed, too, should match that of the opening theme. The 2nd violin has the theme here, though the mood of the first half of the variation dictates that the solo should scarcely project over the surrounding voices. In the second four measures, however, the player should make the theme prevail. This is especially important in the eighth bar, where the 2nd violin is the only one trumpeting the B (against three C♯s!). It is from that note that the cello will at last snatch a short B as upbeat to the cadenza.

Cello   *Cello cadenza.* The notes leading to the fermata C take the place of the last measure of *7* (the only variation that otherwise would seem to have only eight bars). Be rather deliberate on your way up through the two octaves to the fermata. A slight speedup is in order in the descending couplets, but not too much; you will probably want to broaden out again on the rise to the E♭ fermata, and you should save a more obvious push for the accelerando that follows. Even then, see the retard coming, and gauge the tempo wave to stay short of seasick level. Like the preceding marks, the fermata sign for the F♯ is in parentheses, the composer's call for moderation. I shall let your artistic instincts guide you through the flamboyant remainder of the cadenza. Let me just suggest that there be no break after the fortissimo D♯; the rising chromatic run should seem to emerge directly from the sustained note.

8   **8.** Note that the tempo here is almost twice as fast as the starting speed of the movement. The indicated bowing is mandatory and (with the exception of the long notes, of course) should be performed at the tip of the bow, with the motion localized in the hand. Even the crescendo to the forte can be managed without leaving the tip area of the bow, by exerting suitable torque with the right hand.

9   **9.** The same bowing advice as in section *8* applies here. Since the rhythmic pattern is simultaneous in all voices, synchronization is important. Fortunately, a bit of rehearsal and a steady count will make togetherness all but automatic. But be alert as you play, should any minor adjustment be needed. For both sections *8* and *9*, vibrato on the dotted 8th-notes is needed for proper effect. Increasing the intensity of the vibrato will supplement bow pressure in achieving a convincing crescendo, especially in the great rise called for in section *9*. Note that the very last 16th has an accent; hook the note into the same stroke with the preceding dotted 8th.

10   **10.** Immediately after the downbeat 8th-note (which will still be in the fortissimo that ended section *9*), the viola should drop down enough in volume to allow for the 16th-note run's crescendo to the forte-piano. The alternating runs in the inner voices, as well as the cello part, are all cast in a forte framework. They serve as an active foil to the 1st violin's staccato outlining of the theme. The violin's

2   first declamation (at the bar line into m. 2) has an accent on each note. There seems no reason for the inconsistent marking of the later figures in the variation.

11   **11.** The *non vibrato* instruction is given only for the long notes in this section. In practice, I think it applies also to the short figures that flit through the several lines. Within the pianissimo dynamic, the clipped rhythms scarcely afford time for the coloration. More important is to link the rhythms in a continuous chain. The first and last notes of each accented group make up the theme statement here. If the stressed notes stand out against the murmuring line, the ear will be guided to the melodic thread.

12. Except for the last few notes in the 1st violin part, everything in the three upper parts would fit into a rendition by a trio of saxophones. Imagine that setting, and I think you will have a good idea of the style in which the inverted pyramids of sound in this variation should be played. In particular, relax the *portato* as you approach the end of each phrase, and suggest a trace of exhaustion as you trail away in the decrescendo. Regenerate the energy, and pump hard on the notes at the start of each statement. The cellist might also do well to think of the way a jazz pianist would play the bottom line.

13. The accented notes can sound twitchy in this variation. Make sure that you apply the *pesante* instruction to all notes, including those that are accented. Interpret the word to mean a sustained and legato stroke, not just a heavy one. Further, and without going so far as to make synchronization impossible, each player should treat the individual line with some melodic flexibility. The accented (thematic) groups will leaven the part writing. Even so, you should not let the listener get mired in a bog of pedantically measured triplets. In the last measure, either broaden, or push, into the start of the cadenza, depending on the way the violist will want to start that solo. It won't do simply to trot unknowingly into the double bar.

Viola cadenza. This bravura display is strategically plotted. Britten delivers you to the high-altitude takeoff point by the ascent in the final bar of *13*. And he gets you down to the low regions of the instrument in gradual stages. This leaves you reasonably free to concentrate on bringing out the combination of textures in the line: two-part; drone; and moving-part against drone. I think you can rest very briefly on the first low point, the mezzo-forte D♭, before traversing the broad arch to the final, sustained double stop. The indicated note equivalencies (8th = quarter = half) are designed to bring your reading down to symbols that are broad enough to match with those in the slow variation that follows. As for the 2nd violin's sustained, high C pedal point: come down quickly to the indicated piano, and then settle in, with a moderate vibrato. If you let the note hang there too prominently, people are going to start thinking of the old-time peanut vendor's steam whistle.

14. This is the 2nd violinist's cadenza. The viola has the theme, in augmented and tranquilized form. But the focal point of the variation rests on the violin's presentation of what Colin Mason calls the counter-subject to the theme. When I play this section, I feel that I am not opposing the theme so much as musing about it. Notice how closely the rhythmic pattern of the line reflects that of the theme itself: slurred pairs of quarters correspond to the long notes of the theme, while a quadruplet of 8ths coincides with the quarter-note that ends each segment of the theme. The 2nd violin and viola should take their own good time in this duet variation, bending the lines as they see fit. Let the outer voices adapt to what is going on above them (until the last few notes of the section, the 1st violin is in low duet with the cello).

15. As in section *12*, the composer again shows the relative importance of the parts through his dynamic markings. The theme, stated once more by the viola with

12

13

Viola

14

15

the harmonic reinforcement of the cello, is set at pianissimo. The ruminations above it—now carried in parallel thirds by the violin duet—are cast in a dolcissimo piano. I feel that the line symbol over the fifth note in the violin sextuplets is problematic. It is obviously intended to have that tone express a chordal link with the concurrent quarter-note in the lower voices. Unfortunately, the stress gives the sextuplet something of a limp and (because of triplet against quarter) shows its connection with the quarter-beat in the neighboring voice only if rather strongly overdone. The emphasis works best when it can establish some melodic continuity in its own right. As I hear it in performance, this happens in the oscillations of the violin parts in m. 7 and the first part of m. 8.

16. The three upper parts have a job to do here: to maintain true intonation, starting in very high register, in constant, parallel $^6_4$ chordal relationship; to synchronize a triple grace note, a half-note trill, and a two-note turn at the end; and to do this, measure after measure, while maintaining an exceedingly quiet dolcissimo, with miniature swells en route. Adding to the chores are the four beats (mm. 7 and 8) where the trio has to step gracefully from one trill to the next. This would seem to be a task suited only to the three Muses, provided they have drunk deep of Elysian waters. Nonetheless, you three mortal players will have to carry out the assignment.

The solo rests with the cello. There, the problem is to maintain a resonant, non-twangy sound in the pizzicato. Make a clear distinction between the chords that are to be solidly struck and those to be played arpeggiando. In the arpeggiated chords, try to time the strum across strings—and adjust the relative emphasis on the top or bottom note—to reflect the significance of the given chord in the shape of the melody. Rely on the upper-voice trio to allow room for your inflections.

17. This variation is, in a way, a second cadenza for the cello. The instruction, *senza rigore*, in the context of this cello melody, is little different from a call to play *ad libitum.* You need time to spread the range of the line through the languorous intervals of a seventh, ninth, and twelfth in the first three measures, and to stretch the rise of the upper edge of the melody against the drone G in mm. 7–8. You want to be able to accelerate through the sextuplet of bar 4 into bar 5, and to luxuriate your way through the descending sixths in mm. 5–7. The upper parts can easily accommodate you in this, for they are only sighing in admiration. Still, that the composer wants the theme statement to hold its own against the cello's meditations is evident in mm. 4–5 in the score. There he uses arrows to show that the theme line passes from 2nd violin to 1st, thence to the viola, before it returns to the violin at the end of bar 6.

18. The cello part in this variation is pizzicato. Since no special instruction is given in the score as to the way of playing the slurred pairs of quarter-notes, the performer will have to make a decision. If you choose to obey the slur literally, you will have to play the two notes on one string, plucking the first note of the pair and making a glissando to the second. Otherwise, play the pair on one or on adjacent strings, as seems most convenient, plucking the second note less strongly than the first, thus implying the slurred relationship between the two. My own vote is for the second alternative, for the glissando effect does not seem appropriate to the sound of the variation as a whole.

A series of repeated notes appears in m. 1; one or more repeated tones also follow many of the slurred couplets. All such notes should be played in a decrescendo, as though they are rhythmic excerpts from the fading resonance of the parent tone of that pitch.

The viola line should predominate, but mostly as though heard from a great distance. Coming as it does after the cello solo in variation *17*, the viola is in effect inspired by those prior ruminations. The viola line, however, is cast in rather high register, and will cut through too aggressively unless the bow merely floats on the string. Vibrato and swells must be exceedingly discreet, until the turbulence of the triplet hemiolas and dynamic outburst in mm. 7–8 break the trance.

7

19. Because the two parts are close together in register, the solo duet in this variation is that of the 2nd violin and viola. The 1st violin's octave doubling of the 2nd's line adds luster to the sound, but should not outweigh the lower melody. The viola line has a double function: it harmonizes the 2nd violin part and at the same time completes that part by continuing to move actively when the higher voice rests on a sustained note.

19

The cello carries the theme, but only equals, not outranks, the upper duet in importance. The cellist should interpret the *marcato* instruction judiciously. Instead of writing a continuous trill for that voice, the composer breaks it into quarter-beat segments, and wants the fractions to be audible. The effect is analogous to the cello's repeat-note pizzicati in variation *18*. Treat the repetitions as though they extend the initial resonance, with appropriate dynamic gradation.

Violin cadenza. Five *fermate* on a tremolo C–B, even with the melodic swirls that intervene, are enough to make a point; I would not linger too long on my way to the acceleration that leads at last to the peak on the high E♭. Also, as the accent marks imply, the expressive focus in the first phase of the cadenza should be on the moving segments of the line, not on the tremolos. The latter, obviously, constitute the drone line here.

Violin

Once you leap off the sforzando E♭, take a coloratura's swan dive through the triplets: use short, rather detached bowstrokes, highlighting the accented tones with glints of vibrato and pressure. Don't linger too long on the D♯ trill, and do make a legato connection into the start of the descending 32nd-note run.

The sound of the F♯s and G♯s against the G♮ trill in the closing phase of the cadenza has always grated on my ear in performance. It is asking a lot, I know, to call for some vibrato gravy on those tones, since the player's hand is busy with the first-finger oscillations to A♭ on the open G. Perhaps the answer is to balance the sound so that the upper line is not over-prominent until the F♮ settles in at the closing fermata.

20–22. I think the remainder of the finale should be regarded as one complex. In effect, the three sections comprise a closing cadenza for the ensemble, growing out of the two-part strand with which the 1st violin ends its solo cadenza. The single line of trill is replaced in section *20* by trills for the three upper voices; since they move in triadic parallel relationship throughout, the trio really constitute one trill that has been acoustically broadened. The trill is no mere drone, since it traces a linear arch of its own. There are, however, three of you playing, so take care not to submerge the cello's theme.

20–22

21. I don't think that the three-part tremolo in the lower voices will cover the forte chords in the 1st violin, but listen for the balance as the dynamic level rises. As for the violin chords, make them as melodic and legato as possible. Baste them with moderate vibrato, draw the bow slowly, especially on the quarter-notes, and minimize any rolling.

21

22. The 2nd violin gets the last turn at bat with the theme. You are surrounded by great, crashing chords from your three colleagues, who serve as the drone, now

22

raised to Gargantuan proportions. You are, therefore, entitled to feel that you must dig in to the violin and saw away for dear life. Don't yield to the temptation. There is enough daylight between the chords to let your line emerge. Just see to it that the other three voices start each swell low enough to correspond with your level. Bars 6 and 7 before the end will need some special attention, because the three rival lines are more continuous there. As for the last three chords, where each of the four players has a quadruple stop: temper the wedge mark. The sound will need enough length to end the quartet with triumphant resonance, not densely matted sound.

The key to a successful performance of this quartet, I believe, lies in the ensemble's delivery of this finale. As the musicographer Paul Hamburger has written, "Played well, this movement conjures up the impression, peculiar to great quartet writing, that the string quartet is a much richer and more variegated medium than the full orchestra."[5]

◌ Notes ◌

Introduction: Rehearsal and Performance
    1. Mozart, Leopold, *Treatise* 114.
    2. Donington *Interpretation*, 170
    3. Geiringer *Haydn*, 229.
    4. Dart, *Interpretation*, 34.

ONE   Haydn: Quartet in E flat, Op. 33, No. 2 ("The Joke")
    1. Haydn to Artaria, 18 October 1781, Landon, *Correspondence*, 32.
    2. Haydn to J. C. Lavater, 3 December 1781, *Correspondence*, 33. [Capital letters are Haydn's.]
    3. Larsen, *"Haydn,"* 339.
    4. Haydn to Prince Oettingen-Wallerstein, 3 December 1781, *Correspondence*, 33.
    5. Larsen, *"Haydn,"* 354.

TWO   Haydn: Trio in G, Hob. XV:25 ("Gypsy Rondo")
    1. Brown, *Keyboard*, 127, 54; Geiringer, *Haydn*, 110.
    2. Brown, (*Keyboard*, 377) calls this Andante a variation rondo in which "variation aspects spill over into the episodes." I feel the theme to be so dominant throughout that I am compelled to think of the movement as a set of variations.
    3. "Because the bass of the fortepiano doesn't project like a modern piano, the cello suddenly becomes more bass-like." —Comment in Larsen, et al., *Haydn Studies*, 269.
    4. Brown, *Keyboard*, 377. Note also Landon's comment (*England*, 433): "If we consider the character of the Finale, it may be that Haydn really did write all the rest of the Trio to precede it."
    5. Somfai, *Haydn/Bildern*, 60–61. Plate 95b shows "Hungarian gypsies playing in the courtyard of Esterháza castle." Plate 98 shows an enlarged detail of the same engraving, revealing the gypsy ensemble to consist of a violin, viola, cello, and cimbalom. The band marches merrily along in the midst of a large courtly promenade.
    6. Szabolczi, "Haydn, ungarische," 65.
    7. Landon, *England*, 434. See also Major, "Miszellen," where the Haydn melodies are superposed over the parallel melodies in question.
    8. Landon, *Supplement*, 44.

9. See works-list, section 3.Z, in: "Haydn," *New Grove*, vol. 8:393–400.

10. Eva Badura-Skoda, quoted in Larsen, et al., *Haydn Studies*, 268.

THREE   Haydn, Quartet in D minor, Op. 76, No. 2, Hob. III:76 ("Quinten")

1. Somfai, "The London Revision," 166–172.

2. Quoted by Landon, *Correspondence*, 164.

3. Somfai, "'Learned Style'," 325–349. Though I am not always convinced by what I consider Somfai's too rigorous application of authentic bowing style to the "Quinten" movement, his analysis of this Allegro instills respect for his insights into Haydn's ingenuity.

FOUR   Mozart: Quartet in G, K. 387[

1. See Leopold Mozart's letter to his daughter, 16 February 1785, in Anderson, *Letters, Mozart*, 886.

2. See footnote on p. 12 of the Bärenreiter score.

FIVE   Mozart: Piano Quartet in G minor, K. 478.

1. Deutsch, *Mozart*, 318.

2. Köchel Catalogue, 518, "Anmerkung."

3. Einstein, *Mozart*, 264.

4. *NMA, Kritischer Berichte, Serie VIII, Werkgruppe 22, Abteilung 1, 5–7, 16.*

SIX   Mozart: Viola Quintet in G minor, K. 516

1. Alfred Einstein (*Mozart*, 190) holds that Mozart's arrangement of the Serenade was carried out to speed production of a projected set of quintets, and that the transcription was "surely against his artistic conscience." I am inclined to agree.

2. Landon, *Mozart*, 193, 195–97. The writer cites the medical deductions of the physician, Peter J. Davies, based on contemporary descriptions of Mozart's outlook and behavior, to the effect that Mozart displayed the symptoms of a manic depressive. This hypothesis has already evoked an indignant rejection by Erich Leinsdorf (N.Y. Times Book Review, 25 February 1990, p. 9), but is sure to raise interesting speculations. For further ponderings on the emotional state of the composer, see Langegger, *Mozart*.

3. Einstein, *Mozart*, 191 f.: "What takes place here can be compared only with the scene in the Garden of Gethsemane."

4. The Eulenburg score gives the 1st violin two E♭s at the end of m. 36 in this Adagio; the Breitkopf score raises the ante by printing an E♭ on the next downbeat, as well! Both seem too exotic for my taste. The three E♮s of the Bärenreiter parts (after the *NMA* edition) have the sound I am accustomed to.

5. For a fascinating investigation of the documentary evidence of Mozart's concerns and changes of heart on this point, see Newman, "Mozart's G minor Quintet," 287–303. That essay also explores interesting ties between the writing of the quintet and the symphony (composed the following year).

SEVEN   Mozart: Clarinet Quintet in A, K. 581

1. Anderson, *Letters, Mozart* 638.

2. See Shackleton, "Clarinet," 440; Sadie, "Mozart," 720; Weston, "Stadler," 46

EIGHT   Mozart: Quartet in F, K. 590

1. Mozart to Michael Puchberg, 12 June 1790. Anderson, *Letters, Mozart*, 940.

2. Mozart to his Wife, 3 October 1790. Anderson, *Letters, Mozart*, 943.

3. Mozart to Michael Puchberg, 12 June 1790. Anderson, *Letters, Mozart*, 940.

TEN Beethoven: Quartet in G, Op. 18, No. 2 ("Compliment")
    1. *Cobbett's*, I, 106, 108.

ELEVEN Beethoven: Quartet in E flat. Op. 74 ("Harp")
    1. Bentley, *Shaw*, 84, 88.
    2. Anderson, *Letters, Beethoven*, I, 285, 294, 295–96.

TWELVE Schubert: Quintet in A, for piano, violin, viola, cello, and double-bass, D. 667 ("Die Forelle," "The Trout")
    1. Paumgartner, *Schubert*, 102.
    2. Westrup, "Chamber Music," 106.
    3. Mann, "Schubert," 146, 150, 152.
    4. Boyd, "Short Cuts," 20.
    5. Rosen, *Sonata Forms*, 287.

THIRTEEN Schubert: Quartet in D minor, D. 810 ("Death and the Maiden")
    1. Many German composers set to music the texts of the critic-editor-poet-translator Claudius (1740–1815), both in his own time and later. Schubert himself based twelve songs on poems of Claudius.
    2. Einstein, *Schubert*, 254.
    3. Einstein, *Schubert*, 254, 313.

FIFTEEN Mendelssohn: Quartet in D, Op. 44, No. 1
    1. Turner painted *Rain, Steam, and Speed* in 1844. Mendelssohn composed the D major quartet in the summer of 1838.
    2. To forestall any bewilderment on the part of those readers who think only of the very familiar Concerto in E minor, Op. 64, of 1844, I remind that there was an earlier concerto, in D minor (no opus number), dating from the year 1822.

SIXTEEN Schumann: Piano Quintet in E flat, Op. 44
    1. Tovey, *Chamber Music*, 151.
    2. Kohlhase, *Die Kammermusik Schumanns*, II:75, 77. It appears that Schumann at first meant to dedicate the work to the Archduchess of Sachsen-Weimar. Happily, domestic allegiance won out.

SEVENTEEN Brahms: Sextet No. 2 in G, Op. 36
    1. Letter to Breitkopf & Härtel, 16 Sept. 1865, quoted by Wilhelm Altmann in the Eulenburg score edition of the work.

EIGHTEEN Brahms: Quartet in C minor, Op. 51, No. 2
    1. Hill, "Brahms' opus 51," 123.

NINETEEN Tchaikovsky: Quartet in D, Op. 44
    1. Abraham, *Slavonic*, 111.
    2. Brown, *Tchaikovsky*, 217.
    3. Porter, "Russian Chamber Music," 412.

TWENTY Smetana: Quartet in E minor ("From My Life")
    1. Letter quoted in Rychnovsky, *Smetana*, 286.
    2. Large, *Smetana*, 318.
    3. Rychnovsky, 287.
    4. Rychnovsky, 286.

TWENTY-ONE   Fauré: Piano Quartet No. 1 in C minor, Op. 15
    1. Vuillermoz, *Fauré*, 6.

TWENTY-TWO   Dvořák: Piano Quintet in A, Op. 81 (B. 155)
    1. Robertson, *Dvořák*, 184.
    2. Clapham, "American Scene," 20.
    3. Nettl, "Furiant," 1152.

TWENTY-THREE   Dvořák: Quartet in F, Op. 96 ("American") (B. 179)
    1. Clapham, *Dvořák*, 124.
    2. Beveridge, "Primitivism," 25, 27.
    3. Clapham, "American Indian," 863–67.

TWENTY-FOUR   Debussy: Quartet in G minor, Op. 10
    1. Dotzauer, *Quatuor*.
    2. For further information, in a very interesting and extremely detailed survey of the professional chamber music concert scene in 19th-century Paris, see: Fauquet, *Les sociétés*.

TWENTY-FIVE   Hindemith: Quartet No. 3, Op. 22
    1. Hindemith, *Composer's World*, 123.

TWENTY-SIX   Crawford: String Quartet (1931)
    1. Nicholls, "Seeger," 421.
    2. Gaume, Seeger, 202.
    3. I am indebted for details about Ruth Crawford's life to Gaume, *Seeger*.
    4. Gaume, 204.
    5. Perle, "Atonality," 59.
    6. Perle, 60.
    7. See Perle, 59–60.

TWENTY-SEVEN   Bartók: String Quartet No. 5
    1. For a closely detailed and highly illuminating study of the work, see Beach, *Bartók*.
    2. Stevens, *Bartók*, 191.
    3. Beach, *Bartók*, various.
    4. See, for example, Downey, *Musique populaire*, 343.

TWENTY-EIGHT   Bartók: Quartet No. 6
    1. Babbitt, "Bartók," 384.
    2. See Suchoff, "Bartók's Sixth," and Vinton, "New Light."
    3. Suchoff, "Structure," 10.
    4. Downey (*Musique populaire*, 108) feels that this theme strongly resembles an inversion of a Magyar folk song cited by Bartók in his book, *Die Volksmusik der Rumänen von Maramures*, 1923. Downey adds, however, that "it is impossible to say categorically that Bartók was inspired by the Hungarians or Roumanians." It should be noted that Bartók himself stated that, though he took pride in having absorbed the "musical mother tongue of his native region, "in my own original works they [that is, peasant tunes] have never been used." (Excerpt from a Bartók lecture in 1941, quoted by Nelson, "Bartók's Synthetic Methods," 67.)

TWENTY-NINE   Shostakovich: Piano Quintet, Op. 57

    1. See: Schwarz, *Russia*, 119–132.

THIRTY   Britten: Quartet No. 2

    1. For a very clear description of the structure of the quartet, see Mitchell and Keller, *Britten*, 225–233. Another view of the work, especially as concerns the first movement, is found in Whittall, *Britten*, 107–111.

    2. Recognition of Britten's stature has not been easy. For a provocative view of this question, see Keller, "Resistances," 227–236. Also of interest is the same writer's article, "Britten and Mozart."

    3. Keller, in Mitchell and Keller, 227.

    4. *Cobbett's*, vol. 3, 95.

    5. Paul Hamburger, in Mitchell and Keller, 233.

❧ Bibliography ❧

Abraham, Gerald. 1968. *Slavonic and Romantic Music: Essays and Studies*. New York, St. Martin's Press.

Anderson, Emily, tr. and ed. 1961. *The Letters of Beethoven*. New York: St. Martin's Press. 2 vols.

_____ . 1966. *The Letters of Mozart and his Family*. 2nd ed. London: Macmillan. 3 vols.

Babbitt, Milton. 1949. The String Quartets of Bartók. *The Musical Quarterly* 35:377–385.

Baron, John H., ed. 1987. *Chamber Music: A Research and Information Guide*. New York, Garland Publishing.

Bartók, Béla. 1933. Hungarian Peasant Music. *The Musical Quarterly* 19:267–287.

Beach, Marcia. 1988. *Bartók's Fifth String Quartet: Studies in Genesis and Structure*. Ph. D. Dissertation, Eastman School of Music, University of Rochester. 3 vols.

Bentley, Eric, ed. 1955. *Shaw on Music: A Selection from the Music Criticism of Bernard Shaw*. Garden City: Doubleday Anchor Books.

Beveridge, David. 1977. Sophisticated primitivism: the significance of pentatonicism in Dvořák's American Quartet. *Current Musicology* 24:24–36.

Boyd, Malcolm. Schubert's Short Cuts. *Music Review* 29:12–21.

1973. *Benjamin Britten: A Complete Catalogue of his Published Works*. London: Boosey and Hawkes, Faber Music.

Brown, A Peter. 1986. *Joseph Haydn's Keyboard Music: Sources and Style*. Bloomington: Indiana University Press.

Brown, David. 1978. *Tchaikovsky: A Biographical and Critical Study. Vol. 1, The Early Years (1840–1874)*. London, Gollancz.

Burghauser, Jarmil, ed. 1960. *Antonín Dvořák: Thematisches Verzeichnis*. Leipzig: Breitkopf & Härtel.

Chissell, Joan. 1967. *Schumann*. London: Dent.

Clapham, John. 1966. Dvořák and the American Indian. *The Musical Times* 107:863–867.

_____ . 1979. *Dvořák*. New York: Norton.

_____ . 1981. Dvořák on the American Scene. *19th Century Music* 5:16–23.

Cobbett, Walter W., comp. and ed. 1963. *Cobbett's Cyclopedic Survey of Chamber Music*. 2nd ed. Suppl. mat. ed. Colin Mason. London: Oxford. 3 vols.

Dart, Thurston. 1963. *The Interpretation of Music*. New York: Harper Colophon Books.

Deutsch, Otto Erich. 1965. *Mozart: A Documentary Biography*. Tr. E. Blom, P. Branscombe, and Jeremy Noble. London: Black.

_____ , ed. 1978. *Franz Schubert: Thematisches Verzeichnis seiner Werke in chronologischer Folge*. Kassel: Bärenreiter.

Donington, Robert. 1965. *The Interpretation of Early Music*. New York: St. Martin's Press.

Dotzauer, Friedrich. n.d. *Quatuor, Op. 13, pour VIOLONCELLE, Deux Violons et Alto*. Leipzig: Breitkopf & Härtel.

Downey, John. 1964. *La musique populaire dans l'oeuvre de Béla Bartók*. Ph. D. Dissertation, the University of Paris.

Drabkin, William. 1988. Fingering in Haydn's String Quartets. *Early Music* 16:50–57.

Einstein, Alfred. 1945. *Mozart: His Character, His Work*. Tr. A. Mendel and N. Broder. London: Oxford.

_____. 1951. *Schubert: A Musical Portrait*. New York: Oxford.

Fauquet, Joël-Marie. 1986. *Les sociétés de musique de chambre à Paris de la Restauration à 1870*. Paris: Aux amateurs de livres.

Gaume, Matilda. 1986. *Ruth Crawford Seeger: Memoirs, Memories, Music*. Metuchen: Scarecrow Press.

Geiringer, Karl. 1946. *Haydn: A Creative Life in Music*. New York: Norton.

Hill, William G. 1952. Brahms' opus 51—a diptych. *Music Review* 33:110–124.

Hindemith, Paul. 1961. *A Composer's World: The Charles Eliot Norton Lectures, 1949–50*. Garden City: Anchor Books (Doubleday).

(1965). *Paul Hindemith: Werkverzeichnis*. Mainz: Schott.

Hoboken, Anthony van, ed. 1957. *Joseph Haydn. Thematisch-bibliographisches Werkverzeichnis*. Mainz: Schott. 3 vols.

Hofmann, Kurt, and Siegmar Keil, eds. 1982. *Robert Schumann: Thematisches Verzeichnis sämtlicher in Druck erschienenen musikalische Werke*. 5th exp. and rev. ed. Hamburg: Schuberth.

Hulme, Derek C., ed. 1982. *Dmitri Shostakovich: Catalogue, Bibliography and Discography*. Muir of Ord, Ross-shire: Kyle and Glen.

Keller, Hans. 1948. Britten and Mozart: a Challenge in the Form of Variations on an Unfamiliar Theme. *Music & Letters* 29:17–30.

_____. 1950. Resistances to Britten's Music: Their Psychology. *Music Survey* 2:227–236.

_____. 1956. The Chamber Music. In *The Mozart Companion*. Ed. H. C. Robbins Landon and Donald Mitchell. London: Oxford. 90–137.

Kerman, Joseph. 1967. *The Beethoven Quartets*. New York: Knopf.

Kinsky, Georg, and Hans Halm, eds. 1955. *Das Werk Beethovens: Thematisch-bibliographisches Verzeichnis seiner sämtlichen vollendeten Kompositionen*. Munich: Henle.

Köchel, Ludwig Ritter von. 1947. *Chronologisch-thematisches Verzeichnis sämtlicher Tonwerke Wolfgang Amadé Mozarts*. 7th ed. Ed. Franz Giegling, Alexander Weinmann, Gerd Sievers. Wiesbaden: Breitkopf & Härtel.

Kohlhase, Hans. 1979. *Die Kammermusik Robert Schumanns: Stilistische Untersuchungen*. Hamburg: Wagner.

Landon, H. C. Robbins. 1959. *The Collected Correspondence and London Notebooks of Joseph Haydn*. London: Barrie and Rockliff.

_____. 1961. *Supplement to: The Symphonies of Joseph Haydn*. New York: Macmillan.

_____. 1976. *Haydn in England: 1791–1795*. London: Thames and Hudson.

_____. 1989. *Mozart, The Golden Years, 1781–1791*. New York: Schirmer Books.

Lang, Paul H., ed. 1970. *The Creative World of Beethoven*. New York: Norton.

Langegger, Florian. 1978. *Mozart: Vater und Sohn*. Zurich: Atlantis.

Large, Brian. 1970. *Smetana*. London: Duckworth.

Larsen, Jens Peter. 1980. Haydn, (Franz) Joseph. *The New Grove Dictionary of Music and Musicians*. London: Macmillan. 8:328–407.

_____, H. Serwer, and J. Webster, eds. 1981. *Haydn Studies: Proceedings of the International Haydn Conference. Washington, D.C., 1975*. New York: Norton.

Lesure, François, ed. 1977. *Catalogue de l'oeuvre de Claude Debussy*. Geneva: Minkoff.

Lowinsky, Edward. 1956. On Mozart's Rhythm. *Musical Quarterly* 42:162–186.

Major, Erwin. 1929. Miszellen. *Zeitschrift für Musikwissenschaft* 11:601–604.

Mann, William. 1957. Franz Schubert (1797–1828). In *Chamber Music*. Ed. Alec Robertson. Harmondsworth, Middlesex: Penguin. 141–174.

McCorkle, Margit L., ed. 1984. *Johannes Brahms: Thematisch-bibliographisches Werkverzeichnis*. Munich: Henle.

1966. *Thematisches Verzeichnis der im Druck erschienenen Compositionen von Felix Mendelssohn Bartholdy*. 3rd ed. London: Baron.

Mitchell, Donald, and Hans Keller, eds. 1952. *Benjamin Britten: A Commentary on his works from a group of specialists.* Westport, Conn.: Greenwood Press.

Mozart, Leopold. 1951. *A Treatise on the Fundamental Principles of Violin Playing.* Editha Knocker, tr. 2nd ed. London: Oxford University Press.

Mozart, Wolfgang Amadeus. 1958. *Neue Ausgabe sämtlicher Werke*, Ed. E. F. Schmid, W. Plath, and W. Rehm. *Kritischer Berichte, Serie VIII, Kammermusik. Werkgruppe 22, Abteilung 1: Quartette und Quintette mit Klavier und mit Glasharmonika.* Kassel: Bärenreiter.

Nelson, Mark. 1987. Folk Music and the 'Free and Equal Treatment of the Twelve Tones': Aspects of Béla Bartók's Synthetic Methods. *College Music Symposium* 27:59–116.

Nettl, Paul. 1955. Furiant. *Die Musik in Geschichte und Gegenwart.* Kassel: Bärenreiter. 4:1152–1153.

Neumeyer, David. 1986. *The Music of Paul Hindemith.* New Haven: Yale University Press.

Newman, S. 1956. Mozart's G Minor Quintet, K. 516, and its Relationship to the G Minor Symphony, K. 550. *Music Review* 17:287–303.

Nicholls, David. 1983. Ruth Crawford Seeger: an introduction. *The Musical Times* 124:421–425.

Paumgartner, Bernhard. 1974. *Franz Schubert.* Zürich: Atlantis.

Perle, George. 1960. Atonality and the Twelve-note System in the United States. *The Score* 27:51–66.

———. 1977. The String Quartets of Béla Bartók. In *A Musical Offering—Essays in Honor of Martin Bernstein.* Ed. E. H. Clinkscale and Claire Brook. New York: Pendragon Press. 192–210.

Porter, Andrew. 1957. Russian Chamber Music (from 1800). In *Chamber Music.* Ed. Alec Robertson. Harmondsworth: Penguin Books. 410–421.

Radcliffe, Philip. 1967. *Mendelssohn.* London: Dent.

Robertson, Alec. 1962. *Dvořák.* New York: Collier.

Rosen, Charles. 1980. *Sonata Forms.* New York: Norton.

Rychnovsky, Ernst. 1924. *Smetana.* Stuttgart: Deutsche Verlags-Anstalt.

Sadie, Stanley. 1980. (Johann Chrysostom) Wolfgang Amadeus Mozart. *The New Grove Dictionary of Music and Musicians.* London: Macmillan. 12:680–752.

Schwarz, Boris. 1972. *Music and Musical Life in Soviet Russia, 1917–1970.* London: Barrie & Jenkins.

Shackleton, Nicholas. 1980. Clarinet. *The New Grove Dictionary of Music and Musicians.* London: Macmillan. 4:429–442.

Somfai, László. 1966. *Joseph Haydn: Sein Leben in zeitgenössischen Bildern.* Kassel: Bärenreiter. [Also available in English-language edition: 1969. *Joseph Haydn: His Life in Contemporary Pictures.* New York: Taplinger.]

———. 1973–74. The London Revision of Haydn's Instrumental Style. *Proceedings of the Royal Music Association* 100:159–174.

———. 1986. 'Learned Style' in Two Late String Quartet Movements of Haydn. *Studia Musicologica Academiae Scientiarum Hungaricae* 28:325–349.

Stevens, Halsey. 1953. *The Life and Music of Béla Bartók.* New York: Oxford.

Suchoff, Benjamin. 1967. Structure and Concept in Bartók's Sixth Quartet. *Tempo* 83: 2–11.

Szabolczi, Bence. 1959. Joseph Haydn und die ungarische Musik. *Beiträge zur Musikwissenschaft* 1:62–73.

Thayer, Alexander. 1970. *Thayer's Life of Beethoven.* Rev. and ed. Elliot Forbes. Princeton: Princeton University Press.

Tovey, Donald. 1944. *Essays in Musical Analysis: Chamber Music.* Ed. H. J. Foss. London: Oxford University Press.

Ujfalussy, Jozsef. 1972. *Béla Bartók.* Tr. Ruth Pataki. Boston: Crescendo.

Vinquist, Mary, and Neal Zaslaw, eds. 1971. *Performance Practice: A Bibliography.* New York: Norton.

Vinton, John. 1964. New Light on Bartók's Sixth Quartet. *Music Review* 25:224–238.

———. 1966. Bartók on his own Music. *Journal of the American Music Society* 19:232–243.

Vuillermoz, Émile. 1969. *Gabriel Fauré.* Tr. K. Schapin. Philadelphia: Chilton.

Werner, Eric. 1963. *Mendelssohn: A new image of the composer and his age.* Tr. Dika Newlin. London: Free Press of Glencoe.

Weston, Pamela. 1980. Stadler, Anton (Paul). *The New Grove Dictionary of Music and Musicians.* London: Macmillan. 18:46.

Westrup, Jack. 1947. The Chamber Music. In *The Music of Schubert.* Ed. Gerald Abraham. New York: Norton 88–100.

Whaples, Miriam K. 1968. On Structural Integration in Schubert's Instrumental Works. *Acta musicologica* 40:186–195.

Whittall, Arnold. 1990. *The Music of Britten and Tippett: Studies in themes and techniques.* 2nd ed. Cambridge: Cambridge University Press.

Winternitz, Emanuel. 1958. Gnagflow Trazom: Mozart's Script, Pastimes, Nonsense Letters. *Journal of the American Musicological Society* 11:200–216.

✑ About the Author ✑

Abram Loft was born in New York in 1922. He studied violin at music schools in New York, and with Herbert Dittler at Columbia University. He performed as a violist for ten years before returning to the violin in 1952. His studies at Columbia culminated in a doctorate in musicology. After eight years on the Columbia faculty, he left in 1954 to join the Fine Arts Quartet in Chicago. With that group, he concertized throughout the United States, Canada, western Europe, Israel, the Far East, Australia, and New Zealand.

He has made recordings of a major segment of the chamber music repertoire, as well as numerous broadcasts and telecasts, both in America and abroad. He performed for nineteen consecutive seasons in his quartet's concert series in Chicago. Loft was the author of scripts for three series of programs on the quartet repertoire for National Educational Television, and coauthor of scripts for two Encyclopedia Britannica films.

From 1963, the quartet members were tenured faculty at the University of Wisconsin—Milwaukee. In 1979, Loft resigned from the Fine Arts Quartet and from the University of Wisconsin to go to the Eastman School of Music of the University of Rochester as professor of chamber music and chair of the string department. The University of Rochester voted him its Edward Peck Curtis award for undergraduate teaching in 1984. He retired from ESM in 1986 with the rank of Professor Emeritus.

Articles and reviews by Loft have appeared in *Musical Quarterly*, Music Library Association *Notes*, and the *Journal of the American Musicological Society*. He is a contributor to the *New Grove Dictionary of American Music*, and author of *Musicians' Guild and Union* (dissertation, Columbia, 1950), and of *Violin and Keyboard: The Duo Repertoire* (1973, Grossman [Viking]; reprinted Amadeus Press, 1992). He has served on the editorial boards of both the AMS *Journal* and the College Music Society *Symposium*.

Abram Loft has judged various competitions and has lectured or coached at the Manhattan School of Music, Northwestern University, the Aspen School of Music, the Cleveland Institute of Music, the Southeastern Music Center, the

International String Workshop, and the Heidelberg Castle Festival. He lives in Rochester, where he writes on music as well as on his hobby, woodwork.

Recordings by Abram Loft, with the Fine Arts Quartet and guest artists (for Concert-Disc, Everest, Vox, Columbia, Decca, Pantheon, Gasparo, Turnabout, and Composers Recordings):

Samuel Adler: Quartet No. 6.
John Antes: Three string trios.
Milton Babbitt: Quartet No. 3.
Bach: *The Art of Fugue*.
Bartók: The six string quartets.
Beethoven: String quartet cycle.
Bloch: Piano Quintet No. 1; Quartet No. 5.
Brahms: The quartet cycle; Piano Quintet in F minor, Op. 34;
    Clarinet Quintet in B minor, Op. 115.
Ruth Crawford: String Quartet (1931).
Debussy: Quartet in G minor, Op. 10.
John Downey: Quartet No. 2.
Dvořák: Piano Quintet in A flat, Op. 81.
Haydn: Major portion of the complete quartet cycle.
Hindemith: Quartet No. 3, Op. 22; Octet.
Karel Husa: Quartet No. 2; Quartet No. 3.
Ben Johnston: Quartet No. 4.
Mendelssohn: Quartet in E flat, Op. 12; Quartet in D, Op. 44, No. 1; Quartet in
    E minor, Op. 44, No. 2; Octet, Op. 20; Four Quartet Movements, Op. 81.
Mozart: Quartet in D minor, K. 421; Quartet in E flat, K. 428; Quartet in C,
    K. 465; Quartet in D, K. 575; Quartet in B flat, K. 589; Quartet in F, K. 590;
    the viola quintet cycle; Clarinet Quintet in A, K. 581; Horn Quintet in
    E flat, K. 407.
Johann Peter: Six viola quintets.
Prokofieff: Quartet No. 2, Op. 92.
Ravel: Quartet in F.
Saint-Saëns: Septet in E flat, Op. 65.
Schoenberg: *Pierrot lunaire*, Op. 21.
Schubert: Quartet in A minor, D. 804; Quartet in D minor, D. 810;
    Octet in F, D. 803.
Seymour Shifrin: Quartet No. 4.
Shostakovich: Quartet No. 3 in F, Op. 73.
Charles Wuorinen: Quartet No. 1 (1971).